Love Across the Atlant

Love Across the Atlantic

US–UK Romance in Popular Culture

Edited by Barbara Jane Brickman, Deborah Jermyn
and Theodore Louis Trost

EDINBURGH
University Press

Edinburgh University Press is one of the leading university presses in the UK. We publish academic books and journals in our selected subject areas across the humanities and social sciences, combining cutting-edge scholarship with high editorial and production values to produce academic works of lasting importance. For more information visit our website: edinburghuniversitypress.com

Edinburgh University Press Ltd
The Tun – Holyrood Road
12 (2f) Jackson's Entry
Edinburgh EH8 8PJ

First published in hardback by Edinburgh University Press 2020

Typeset in 11/13 Monotype Ehrhardt by
IDSUK (DataConnection) Ltd, and
printed and bound by CPI Group (UK) Ltd,
Croydon, CR0 4YY

A CIP record for this book is available from the British Library

ISBN 978 1 4744 5207 6 (hardback)
ISBN 978 1 4744 5208 3 (paperback)
ISBN 978 1 4744 5209 0 (webready PDF)
ISBN 978 1 4744 5210 6 (epub)

Contents

Figures

Acknowledgements

The genesis of this book can be traced back to the 2014 conference of the International Association for the Study of Popular Romance (IASPR), 'Rethinking Love, Rereading the Romance', held at Aristotle University of Thessaloniki. Serendipitously, this provided an opportunity for two transatlantic scholars, from two institutions with a transatlantic partnership, to have their own 'meet-cute', bringing together Deborah Jermyn (from the University of Roehampton, London) and Catherine Roach (from the University of Alabama). That this meeting was facilitated in Greece – where, for nearly three thousand years, the terms *Eros*, *Philia* and *Agape* 'have been used in the West to triangulate the shifting concept called "romantic love" not just in philosophy and theology, but also in popular culture' (IASPR 2014) – speaks to the inevitably global dimensions both of US–UK collaboration and of interdisciplinary reflection on what constitutes 'romance'. Most importantly for the purposes of this collection, this meeting enabled us to start to ponder how our mutual interests in Romance Studies might provide a springboard to enrich our institutional partnership. Given our geographical locations, and the fact that one objective of such international university alliances is, in essence, to woo the other affiliate, a project on transatlantic romance seemed the perfect match.

So it was that in June 2017, twenty-two scholars working in diverse fields incorporating Cultural Studies, Film Studies, Literary Studies, TV Studies, Gender Studies and Religious Studies, and drawn from across the US, UK and continental Europe, gathered at the University of Roehampton for 'Love Across the Atlantic: An Interdisciplinary Conference on US–UK Romance', co-convened by Jermyn and Roach. What followed was a day rich in deliberation, the exchange of ideas and collaborative promise, as the multitude of possible ways into better understanding the infinite nuances and evocative instances of the 'special relationship' became apparent. A collection dedicated to chronicling some of the work undertaken that day was the obvious next step, and we are delighted that many of the illuminating papers given at the conference are gathered in this volume.

Our first thanks as co-editors, then, are due to the committee and delegates of the 2014 IASPR conference, most especially conference chair Betty Kaklamanidou, and to Catherine Roach, whose enthusiasm for further collaboration between the Universities of Roehampton and Alabama brought the three of us together. We are grateful to the International Offices of our respective institutions and to colleagues in our home departments for fostering and encouraging the partnership that has facilitated this project. At the University of Roehampton, additional thanks are especially due to the Southlands Methodist Trust, whose generous grant enabled Theodore Louis Trost to participate in the London conference.

In addition, at Edinburgh University Press we are indebted to Gillian Leslie, who wholeheartedly supported the idea for this collection from our earliest conversations; to Richard Strachan for his unfailingly attentive guidance throughout the writing and production process; and to our anonymous readers, whose instructive and positive feedback helped us shape some of the unruly and expansive territory of the special relationship into the more manageable contours of the final volume constituted here. Inevitably, we can only hope to have scratched the surface of a topic with such a long history and so many intense and, at times, contentions interconnections. And in this respect, we are grateful finally, too, to all our authors, who have written with insight, originality and energy through a historical juncture in which the 'special relationship' has taken on momentous new dimensions; their contributions together provide an invaluable account of some of the exemplary romantic texts, encounters and individuals that have paved the pathway here, and leave us with much to savour and contemplate as we ponder just what the next chapter of the US–UK 'love story' may be.

Barbara Jane Brickman would like to thank, first and foremost, the co-convenors of the 'Love Across the Atlantic' conference (and our first transatlantic match), Catherine Roach and Deborah Jermyn, who inspired me to become involved in this project and share an enlightening and invigorating scholarly adventure over the last few years. They both have become that priceless combination of both mentor and friend, a gift for which I will always be grateful. We Yanks were especially well looked after in Roehampton at the 2017 conference, so much heartfelt appreciation goes to the staff and our colleagues south of the Thames and, of course, to the College of Arts and Sciences at the University of Alabama for making my travel possible. On our side of the Atlantic, I have benefited enormously from the editorial expertise and dry humour of my co-editor and colleague at Alabama, Ted Trost, who always seems to take complications and unforeseen difficulties in droll stride. Lastly, although my own life's romance has only had to cross the 49th parallel, I could not have completed my work on this collection without the wisdom, patience and expert knowledge of royal family minutiae provided by my partner Lucy Curzon, a shameless Anglophile cleverly legitimated by a career as a British historian.

Deborah Jermyn wishes especially to thank colleagues from the Department of Media, Culture and Language, and the University of Roehampton. In particular, Anna Gough-Yates and Lourdes Melcion generously supported the 2017 conference and my 2018 visit to New College University of Alabama as a Residential Fellow, events that crucially enabled me to meet with US colleagues and develop the work for this collection, as well as our international partnership. It has been my pleasure to act as co-director of Roehampton's Centre for Research in Film and Audiovisual Cultures for some years, alongside Mike Witt, and I am tremendously grateful to him too for the encouragement he gave us to run the conference in the UK under the auspices of the Centre for Research in Film and Audiovisual Cultures. My fellowship at Alabama was an education and a privilege, and I am indebted to New College for the funding they provided, and all the US colleagues and students I met there: most particularly, Catherine Roach and my co-editors, Barbara and Ted – from Weybridge to Washington, I am immensely thankful to have had the opportunity to build our Anglo-American alliance. Finally, I dedicate my work for this book to Matt Wagner, from Ohio – the other half of my own 'special relationship' – and to all my US family, particularly Mary Ann, Joe and Joanie Wagner, for turning the theory into practice.

Theodore Louis Trost thanks the Capstone International Office under the direction of Dr Tricia Wise, the Dean of the College of Arts and Sciences, Robert Olin, and the departments of Religious Studies and New College – all at the University of Alabama – for research and travel support. In addition to welcome commentary from those assembled at the University of Roehampton conference, I want to express my gratitude for guidance from those assembled at the 2017 European Popular Culture Association conference in London, especially my co-panellist, Pekka Kolehmainen. It has been a great pleasure to work with Barbara Jane Brickman, who is a few steps down the hall, and Deborah Jermyn, who is seven days away, via Cunard; thank you both for your spirit of collaboration and your editorial insights (as applied, not least of all, to my own work). I am particularly grateful to my family: to our sons, Nathaniel and Benjamin, who sojourned with us in Europe during the summer of 2017; and to Catherine Roach, my partner in romance, whose insights and friendship have sustained me during the making of this book.

Barbara Jane Brickman, Deborah Jermyn and Theodore Louis Trost
London and Tuscaloosa
16 June 2019

Works Cited

IASPR (2014), 'Rethinking Love, Rereading the Romance (Greece, 2014)', The International Association for the Study of Popular Romance. Available at: <http://iaspr.org/conferences/previous-conferences/greece-2014/> (last accessed 10 June 2019).

The Contributors

Caroline Bainbridge is Professor of Culture and Psychoanalysis at the University of Roehampton in London. She is also Film Section Editor of the *International Journal of Psychoanalysis*. Her books include *The Cinema of Lars von Trier: Authenticity and Artifice* (2007) and *A Feminine Cinematics: Luce Irigaray, Women and Film* (2008), as well as a number of anthologies co-edited with Candida Yates. Together with Yates, she is the series editor of the 'Psychoanalysis and Popular Culture' book list published by Routledge/Karnac Books, and founder and director of the Media and the Inner World research network. She regularly writes and talks on psychoanalysis, gender, television, cinema and popular culture.

Jay Bamber is an independent scholar who holds an MA (with Distinction) in Film and Screen Cultures, and is completing a PhD examining the relationship between Disney and horror. In addition, he is a romantic novelist and the author of *Until There Was You* (2015), *The Restart Project* (2017) and *Welcome To Me* (2018). Jay is also a regular TV contributor at popmatters.com.

Barbara Jane Brickman is Associate Professor of Media and Gender Studies at the University of Alabama. Her work has appeared in *Camera Obscura*, *The Journal of Film and Video*, *Discourse* and *Journal of Popular Music Studies*. Since the publication of her first book, *New American Teenagers: The Lost Generation of Youth in 1970s Film* (2012), she has written a volume on the film *Grease* for the Cinema and Youth Cultures series (2018) and is currently working on a manuscript on lesbian camp in American popular culture. She is also the founder and director of the Druid City Girls Media Camp in Tuscaloosa, Alabama.

William Brown is a Senior Lecturer in Film at the University of Roehampton, London. Among his publications are *Moving People, Moving Images: Cinema and Trafficking in the New Europe* (with Dina Iordanova and Leshu Torchin, St Andrews Film Studies, 2010), *Supercinema: Film-Philosophy for the Digital Age* (2013) and *Non-Cinema: Global Digital Filmmaking and the Multitude* (2018). He has published numerous essays in journals and edited collections, and has directed various films, including *En Attendant Godard* (2009), *Circle/Line* (2016), *Letters to Ariadne* (2016) and *St Mary Magdalen's Home Movies* (2016).

Shelley Cobb is an Associate Professor of Film at the University of Southampton and the Principal Investigator for the Arts and Humanities Research Council-funded project 'Calling the Shots: Women and Contemporary Film Culture in the UK, 2000–2015'. Her main areas of research and teaching expertise are in women and film (both production and representation), gender and popular culture, celebrity studies and adaptation. Among her publications, she is the author of *Adaptation, Authorship and Contemporary Women Filmmakers* (2014).

Neil Ewen is Senior Lecturer and Programme Leader in Media and Communication at the University of Winchester, and co-convener of the Culture–Media–Text Research Centre. He is co-editor of *First Comes Love: Power Couples, Celebrity Kinship, and Cultural Politics* (2015), *Capitalism, Crime and Media in the 21st Century* (forthcoming), and journal special issues on the TV show *Friends* (*Television and New Media*, 2018) and populist celebrity politicians (*Celebrity Studies*, forthcoming). He is the Cultural Report section editor of *Celebrity Studies* journal.

Alice Guilluy is Course Leader of the BA (Hons) Filmmaking programme at the London Film Academy. Her research interests include audience studies and methodology, popular culture, film genre and media representation. She obtained her PhD from King's College London in 2017, which was funded by the Arts and Humanities Research Council and examined the reception of contemporary Hollywood romantic comedy in Britain, France and Germany.

Hannah Hamad is Senior Lecturer in Media and Communication at Cardiff University's School of Journalism, Media and Cultural Studies. She researches, teaches and supervises principally in the area of feminist media studies and the cultural politics of contemporary popular media, focusing in particular on feminist and postfeminist cultures of popular film and television. Among her publications, she is the author of *Postfeminism and Paternity in Contemporary US Film: Framing Fatherhood* (2013).

Deborah Jermyn is Reader in Film and Television at the University of Roehampton, where she is Co-Director of the Centre for Research in Film and Audiovisual Cultures. She is the author and editor of eleven books, and within these has published widely on romantic comedy, including as co-editor (with Stacey Abbott) of *Falling in Love Again: Romantic Comedy in Contemporary Cinema* (2009). Her most recent monograph is *Nancy Meyers* (2017), and she continues to write widely about both women directors, and ageing femininities in popular culture.

Veera Mäkelä is an independent scholar with a master's degree in English Philology from the University of Helsinki. Her one true love is the study of popular romance, but she is also known to conduct affairs with other aspects of popular culture and literature, with particular soft spots for literary adaptation, Jane Austen, revenge tragedies, and the fantasy novels of Scott Lynch.

Inmaculada Pérez-Casal specialised in English Studies at the Universidade de Santiago de Compostela (Spain) after graduating in English Language and Literature in 2013, and presented an MA dissertation on the contemporary American romance novel. Currently, she is working on her PhD thesis, in which she combines genre and gender studies applied to the development of the romance novel in English. Her research interests include feminism and gender studies, literature by women, as well as popular literature and cultural studies.

Karen Randell is Associate Professor in Film and Culture, and Deputy Dean of the School of Arts and Humanities at Nottingham Trent University. Her research interests are in trauma and war. Her publications include *The War Body on Screen* (2008), *Re-framing 9/11: Film, Popular Culture and 'The War on Terror'* (2010), *The Dark Side of Love: From Euro-Horror to American Cinema* (2011) and *The Cinema of Terry Gilliam: It's a Mad World* (2013).

Manuela Ruiz received her PhD in English in 2005 from the University of Zaragoza, where she is a Senior Lecturer in English. Since 2004, she has been a member of the university consolidated research team *Cinema, Culture and Society* (http://ccs.filmculture.net), exploring film genres in American and British cinema. She is currently participating in a research project entitled 'From the Transnational to the Cosmopolitan: A Methodology for Contemporary Cinema', which is funded by the Spanish Ministry of Education, Science and Technology. Her most recent book is *Hollywood Romantic Comedies of the Fifties: A Critical Study of a Film Genre* (2013).

Martha Shearer is Teaching Fellow in Film Studies at King's College London. She is the author of *New York City and the Hollywood Musical: Dancing in the Streets* (2016). Her work has also been published in *Screen* and *The Soundtrack*, and the edited collections *The City in American Cinema* (2019) and *The Oxford Handbook of Musical Theatre Adaptations* (2019).

Frances Smith is Lecturer in Film Studies at the University of Sussex. She is the author of *Rethinking the Teen Movie* (2017) and the co-editor (with Timothy Shary) of *Refocus: The Films of Amy Heckerling* (2016). Her monograph on Céline Sciamma's *Bande de Filles* is due for publication in 2019. Elsewhere, her work examines nostalgic stardom and the construction of British masculinity on screen.

Theodore Louis Trost is Professor in New College and Religious Studies at the University of Alabama. He has edited or co-edited several volumes on African and African American religions and authored a biography of twentieth-century ecumenist Douglas Horton. Recent publications include the article 'Theo-political Discourse and Rock 'n' Roll in the Reagan Era' in *Religion and Theology* (2018), and a chapter on the satire of Randy Newman in the *Routledge Companion to Popular Music and Humour* (2019).

Alexis Weedon holds the UNESCO chair in New Media Forms of the Book at the University of Bedfordshire. She is author of *Victorian Publishing: The Economics of Book Production for a Mass Market* (2003) and, with V. L. Barnett, *Elinor Glyn as Novelist, Moviemaker, Glamour Icon and Businesswoman* (2014), and has edited *History of the Book in the West* (5 vols, 2010). This work is a further development of her research on cross-media co-operation in the 1920s and 1930s (Arts and Humanities Research Council 112216).

Nathalie Weidhase is a Postdoctoral Researcher in Media, Culture and Communication at Bournemouth City University. Her PhD examined female dandyism in contemporary popular music. She has published on women in popular music and celebrity feminism in *Celebrity Studies* journal, as well as in the collection *Women, Celebrity and Cultures of Ageing: Freeze Frame* (2015).

INTRODUCTION

Still Crazy After All These Years? The 'Special Relationship' in Popular Culture

Barbara Jane Brickman, Deborah Jermyn and Theodore Louis Trost

In 1946, when Winston Churchill referred to the 'special relationship' between the US and the UK in his 'Sinews of Peace' address, he was referring to the strikingly close political, economic, diplomatic and military alliance between the two nations. Alongside and throughout the cultural history of this very pragmatic alliance, however, there have always existed US–UK 'special relationships' of another kind – love affairs carried out across the expanse of the Atlantic, as British and American peoples have flirted, courted and fallen in love, with one another but often too with the idea(l) of that other place across the ocean. US–UK love affairs have thus proven to be a mainstay of romantic narratives for generations, shared across literature, music, television, film and all the arts. At a critical historical juncture in the ongoing viability of the special relationship, this collection examines some of the history, contemporary manifestations and enduring appeal of this paradigm for a global and interdisciplinary audience. What are the economic and ideological factors that have fuelled this romantic framework? What have been its recurrent tropes across disciplinary, national and temporal boundaries? And how does the notion of 'love across the Atlantic' speak to collective fantasies of home, desire, escape and identity?

As is suggested by the volume's title, a key ambition – and challenge – for this book has been to situate the 'special relationship' across a range of media, while also wanting to capture something of both the rich history and the urgent timeliness of this paradigm. Hence, in what follows, this collection examines popular texts and discourses from the last hundred years, in the areas of film, television, literature, music, news, and politics, and how they together point to recurrent preoccupations found across representations of US–UK romance. Within this, a significant portion of the volume is devoted to film, which proved to be far and away the most popular focus in responses to our call for papers, suggesting that cinema is perhaps perceived as the medium to have represented the special relationship most ubiquitously and expressively during and since the twentieth century. Indeed, as we worked on the collection, in July 2018 it was fascinating to observe how the Working Title-produced romcom *Love Actually* (2003) began trending across social media in the run-up to Donald Trump visiting the UK; movie fans objecting to his excursion began animatedly sharing memes and clips of the cherished scene in which British Prime Minister (Hugh Grant) confronts the tawdry US President (Billy Bob Thornton) at a press conference by informing him, 'I love that word "relationship". It covers all manner of sins, doesn't it? . . . We may be a small country, but we're a great one too . . . A friend who bullies us is no longer a friend.' More than any newspaper summary that summer, this scene and the flurry of memes referencing it seemed to capture perfectly the enduring significance of the close tie between the two nations, while adroitly also dramatising the tensions that mark this political (and at times romantic) alliance.

The limitations of space, and the sheer volume of ways in which the 'special relationship' has been invoked and enacted, mean that this collection could not hope to cover such an expansive terrain in all its entirety; for example, it does not include chapters that consider romance within the earlier history of transatlantic commerce between nations, or between empire and colonies. At the same time, these and similar themes lurk inevitably in the background, even as identifications such as 'British' and 'American' are employed. More recent concerns that are not tackled by the authors collected here, one might note, range from the phenomenon of 'GI Brides' in the aftermath of World War II, to the changing legal and moral contexts of shifting immigration practices through the time period covered, to the discipline of postcolonial criticism, all of which might act as instructive further lenses to frame and understand the histories of US–UK romance in popular media. Readers here, then, will find that while the long history of Anglo-American relations includes such momentous themes as colonialism and revolution, the focus in these chapters falls largely upon the special relationship that pertains to the US and UK, particularly in the last century and primarily during the post-World War II era. Further, while having an eye to the past, the topics for this volume emerged particularly in the contemporary context of globalisation with its attendant concerns about such matters as immigration and national identity. Thus, it considers pressing questions for subjects impacted by globalisation, cosmopolitanism, transnational relations and neoliberal political and economic policies.

Love Across the Atlantic commences, then, in the 1920s with the richly illuminating figure of romance novelist Elinor Glyn, whose career and travels also provide the opportunity to glance backwards to the still hugely culturally evocative history of transatlantic voyaging embodied by the Titanic. The flip side of that powerful romantic narrative, of course, is that many people undertaking this journey from Europe across the Atlantic in the era of the Titanic did so entirely out of necessity, for economic survival rather than idealised desire; and here we would do well to remember the history of transnational arranged marriages conceived of entirely as pragmatic, and not romantic, agreements. These are, again, very often stories that go untold in the chapters collected here, forming a kind of inverse underbelly to a number of the narratives of love and sexual chemistry that follow. Furthermore, as numerous of our authors point to in their analyses, many of the chapters here underline how the transatlantic romances of popular media, like so much of pop culture romance generally, are overwhelmingly the love stories of white, heterosexual, cis-gendered, economically privileged protagonists. While reading, it is important to reflect, then, on the *missing* romances here, those love stories that have had, and continue to have, inequitable opportunities to flourish or to be told. Significantly though, the book closes in the present day in interrogating media representations of a relationship that would have been unimaginable even a generation ago: Prince Harry and Meghan Markle's early romance and the landmark 'alliance' formed therein between the British royal family and an American woman of colour.

In between these bookends, the volume's interdisciplinary terrain is managed by a comprehensive structure that organises the chapters within four key thematic areas: feminism, women and transatlantic romance; the global city, cosmopolitanism and transatlantic space; 'Britishness', 'Americanness' and identity; and political coupledom. While this organising principle provides boundaries within which conversations among thematically related texts can occur, these boundaries are permeable; much like the interdisciplinary milieu in which they have been constructed, they function to facilitate explorations across borders. For example, then, the question of racial identity that figures prominently in the volume's final chapter runs as a leitmotif throughout the book: from the discussion of 'whiteness' in the film *Bridget Jones's Baby* (2016) in Chapter 3, to the matter of race and gentrification in Chapter 5, to the indelibly white, fantasised milieu of Nancy Meyers's transatlantic lovers in Chapter 8, to the Beatles' tours of America during the civil rights era in Chapter 12; and to Winston Churchill's underlying racial – and racist – convictions in Chapter 13. And although, as noted, the vast majority of the romances considered in this collection (and, to be sure, in global mass media more generally) present a resolutely heteronormative ideal, the book's more contemporary examples importantly offer a thread through which to consider how intersecting, and often marginalised, identities expose tensions in, and challenges to, these transatlantic affairs.

'[Not] Just a Girl, Standing in Front of a Boy . . . ': Feminism, Women and Transatlantic Romance

In Part One, the collection opens with a focus on the woman at the heart of these predominantly heterosexual romances, and the challenges she often poses to convention or docile femininity, its subheading slyly inverting Julia Roberts's now iconic speech to bookseller William Thacker (Hugh Grant) in *Notting Hill* (1999), in which as superstar, Anna Scott, she implores him to see beyond her fame and recognise that in matters of the heart she is still, above all, 'just a girl'. Our opening chapters move from British romance novelist, filmmaker and business icon, Elinor Glyn, to more contemporary examples of feminism's (often contentious) interventions into the 'special relationships' that transatlantic movement enables. Together they interrogate how these romances cultivate particular constructions of the privileged women at their centre as 'feisty', adventuring or even angry, underlining how the emblematic figure of the 'modern woman' they focus on has long facilitated a richly instructive engagement with feminist debate. As Karen Randell and Alexis Weedon suggest, Glyn's œuvre, as well as her own frequent transatlantic travel, locates within the exchanges between the high-society circles of the US and UK a particular romantic ideal of the special relationship, which also reveals a significant shift in women's status in the early twentieth century. In particular, Glyn's novel *Six Days* (1923), with its combination of love and romance, transatlantic travel on the Cunard liner, secret military missions and political co-operation, offers a vision of the United States as a source of new opportunities for women, providing an important precursor to later representations of this ocean crossing, such as James Cameron's 1997 blockbuster film *Titanic*. Although she was not a declared feminist, Glyn's writings, and indeed her own life story, brought a 'new vocabulary to popular romantic fiction empowering women to express their own sexual needs and desires'. And in her representations of transatlantic romance, America at times came to represent a new world where 'early emancipation, popular acceptance of divorce and a woman's ability to own and spend her own money is intoxicatingly freeing'.

Possibly indicative of Glyn's lasting influence on romantic fiction, Veera Mäkelä's ensuing chapter examines a small surge of American heroines traversing the Atlantic to find love in the subgenre of 'Regency romance': Eloisa James's *My American Duchess* (2016) appeared around the same time as Maya Rodale's *Lady Bridget's Diary* (2016), the first in the latter's 'Keeping Up with the Cavendishes' series. The lively heroines of these novels have certainly charmed readers of romance, but in her chapter Mäkelä delves more deeply into why the Regency period might appeal and what we may learn from these American forays into it. She looks specifically at 'Keeping Up with the Cavendishes', begun in 2016, wherein wealthy young American sisters enter into and dramatically unsettle English high society of the Regency period. For Mäkelä, these invading American women come to represent a kind of revolution in the eighteenth century, in which a shaken English aristocracy is marked as vulnerable along gendered lines. Rodale's three recent novels in the series, beginning with *Lady Bridget's Diary*, all offer romance between the young American Cavendish sisters and a range of British suitors who represent the shifting social stratification of the period, dramatising the move from 'outside' Regency high society to a new kind of position 'inside'. In the end, the 'collision of transatlantic values' created by their womanly American invasion is resolved through romance and ultimately marriage but, in so doing, their love forces the Regency society 'to reshape itself to allow them their freedom', although, of course, with limitations, suggesting the establishment of a new society wedding the values of both cultures.

However, as Part One moves to recent film and television versions of these transatlantic romances, the optimism offered in the Cavendish sisters' 'happily ever after' seems in the distant past indeed. Released in the same year as Rodale's first romance in her Regency series (the eponymous heroine of which indicates more than a passing influence), the third instalment of the Bridget Jones films, *Bridget Jones's Baby* (2016), offers a significant American suitor for the beloved and befuddled Bridget, yet, according to William Brown, does so only to send our heroine back to her rightful British mate. There have been Anglo-American relationships in all three Bridget Jones films, such as Mark Darcy's involvement in the first in the series with the American lawyer Natasha (Embeth Davitz), with whom he moves to New York, and all of the films are also international co-productions involving British and American financing. But *Bridget Jones's Baby* foregrounds transatlantic romance most centrally for Bridget and, importantly for Brown, represents that relationship with the American Jack as 'filthy'. In so doing, Brown argues, the film uses her relationship with the brash US entrepreneur, who runs a dating app, to turn away from contemporary global change and back to the 'homely and familiar' safety of Mark Darcy. That is, the contemporary era of job insecurity and online hook-ups is characterised as American and desirable, but also impossible, as Bridget settles back down with Mark and helps her Conservative mother to win her local council election. While the latter's victory is supposedly based upon openness to racial, national or sexual others, the conservative turn away from Jack would suggest this as a fantasy of privilege in which a post-Brexit Britain really does want to keep its others at arm's length. Ultimately, Brown locates a sort of 'resentful attraction towards the US and the culture of techno-capital' – a transatlantic attraction the film must 'pretend to deny precisely because techno-capitalist culture demands the rejection of all other cultures in favour of white, conservative middle class (and in this case British) values'.

Likewise, in the final chapter in Part One, Caroline Bainbridge examines another remarkably popular female figure in recent global media – performer, writer, director and producer Sharon Horgan – whose troubled characterisations of transatlantic romance take a brutally comedic look at the discontented lives of (a certain exemplar of) contemporary women, painfully navigating the unsettling landscape of postfeminism. From *Pulling* (2006–9) via *Catastrophe* (2015–19) to *Divorce* (2016–), Horgan's work can be understood as unsentimentally tracing the warts-and-all life cycle of modern romance, in which 'difficult' women and hostile collisions take centre stage. Furthermore, while Horgan's career has been marked by her professional movement across both sides of the pond, so too has one of her most lauded series been centred on the tribulations of a transatlantic relationship, a backdrop that speaks to how contemporary producers must develop new series with an eye to international distribution. In *Catastrophe*, she co-stars with her US writing partner, comedian Rob Delaney, to develop what Bainbridge terms a characteristic Horgan 'woemance', a redolent space with which to give 'voice to the Anglo-American postfeminist experience' while enabling audiences to take pleasure in 'women's rage and discontent with neoliberal, white, middle class strictures'. In direct contradiction to the 'happily ever after' promised by Rodale's fiction or innumerable other transatlantic romances, Bainbridge finds Horgan offering instead an uncompromising picture of the psychological experience of transatlantic love in a postfeminist age.

Love Beyond Borders: The Global City, Cosmopolitanism and Transatlantic Space

In Part Two, we consider a number of examples, each taken from the worlds of film and television, to explore key issues for transatlantic romance in recent history and the contemporary moment, resulting, first, from increasingly globalised and gentrified urban spaces; second, from the fallout of neoliberal economic policies; and further, from the precarity, as well as the desires, of subjects living through these changes in both the US and the UK. Picking up on ideas offered in Brown's analysis of an age of 'techno-capital', this second section engages more closely with the lived experience of neoliberal economic conditions, where unleashed global markets and an emphasis on individual entrepreneurialism have a great impact on the characters (the fuller historical and political context for which will be forthcoming in Part Four). Together, the chapters in this section highlight the instability and fluidity of intimate relations in an increasingly interconnected, global and mobile existence, and the importance of place/space, non-normative identities and othering in this context.

Martha Shearer's opening chapter usefully crystallises numerous aspects of the themes of gentrification, intersectional identities, class and cultural legitimation in transatlantic TV romances, through her astute analysis of the series *Looking* (2014–16) and *You're the Worst* (2014–), particularly reflecting on how these shows 'take account of gentrification's class tensions as they intersect with issues of race and sexuality'. She finds that US–UK romance 'has been adapted to television in ways that speak to the importance of a transnational elite to gentrifying neighbourhoods', here played out in the cities in which they are set, these being San Francisco and Los Angeles respectively. Shearer points to how both shows depict Anglo-American white couples but also contrast their English characters with local working-class Latino men, perceptively arguing that while they construct their relationships differently – a white heterosexual Anglo-American couple with a Latino friend in *You're the Worst*, a gay love triangle in *Looking* – both shows use English characters to manage the class terms of their urban representation. While these English characters are, implicitly or otherwise, marked as working-class, their presence in these cities also suggests the idealised social and spatial mobility of a so-called 'creative class', with the English men in question working as a writer (*You're the Worst*) and in video-game design (*Looking*). Crucially, in *You're the Worst*, Shearer concludes, 'romance is an expression of class unity across national borders' in ways that enable protagonists 'to cast off their class origins', while *Looking* suggests, 'although perhaps not coherently or explicitly, [that] addressing the terms of intimacy in urban space is critical for queer publics and rejects what Solnit refers to as gentrification's "refusal to coexist"' (Solnit 2000: 121).

In some ways taking up the baton from Bainbridge's chapter at the close of Part One, we continue next with Frances Smith's illuminating and multifaceted account of *Catastrophe*, bringing further conceptual perspectives to bear on a text that is particularly richly expressive for the purposes of this collection. Smith's chapter provides an excellent counter-point to Bainbridge's, since, while, as outlined above, the latter considers the series primarily through the instructive lenses of psychoanalysis and multihyphenate creative Sharon Horgan's 'woemantic' œuvre, the former instead examines it in terms of its 'use of a globalised East London [to speak] to a transnational and upmarket aesthetic'. *Catastrophe*'s use of location constructs London as 'the quintessential global city', but impor-tantly, this is not a romantic vision of London recognisable to audiences from cinema's 'Curtisland', as the distinctively parochial vision of Eng-land propounded by writer and director Richard Curtis in films such as *Notting Hill* and *Love Actually* has come to be known. Instead, the edgier, though still palpably gentrified and aspirational setting here – specifically, London Fields in the 'formerly gritty' borough of Hackney – was selected in part for its marketability to American distribution. Smith finds that this choice of urban location is inherently entwined with the series' unide-alised, often fraught, representation of its transatlantic romance 'as a site of messiness'; together, these features mobilise 'discourses of authenticity, realism, and "quality" television itself', which elevate this 'romsitcom' above the deprecating reception so typical of romantic comedy. The trans-atlantic model of co-financing and distribution behind the series is one that combines traditional broadcasters with Streaming Video on Demand services – hence, in the US, *Catastrophe* went on to air on Amazon Prime. Fascinatingly, in terms of understanding the contemporary contours of both globalisation and the 'special relationship', then, Smith concludes that this compounding of setting, generic innovation and production model 'has allowed *Catastrophe* to court an elite audience, whose members *share more in common with their counterparts across the Atlantic*, than they might with many of their lower-class compatriots' (our emphasis).

Leaving television for film next, and in line with numerous other recent 'overseas' romantic film narratives concerned with transatlantic love stories, such as Nancy Meyers's *The Holiday* (2006), Manuela Ruiz analyses Drake Doremus's *Like Crazy* (2011) as a cultural text centrally signifying a cosmopolitan perspective. Her analysis examines how the film allows audiences to reflect on the positive effects of cross-cultural encounters, as well as on their most disquieting implications in an increasingly global society defined by new mobilities, cultural exchange, transnational experiences and a multiplicity of borderland spaces. Con-fronted with the challenges of a long-distance relationship and strict immigration regulations, *Like Crazy*'s central characters (British) Anna and (American) Jacob articulate the notion of 'love across the Atlantic' as a cosmopolitan endeavour that questions and destabilises how intimate culture is newly represented in contemporary cinema. Their affair may reflect a new cosmopolitanism, enabled by globalisation, which, for Ruiz, transforms relationships through a 'significant loosening of national identifications and a genuine and positive engagement with otherness and difference'. Yet, the film also suggests, through the couple's struggles to make their transatlantic connection work, that, in addition to the legal hurdles created by new immigration policies, there always exists a fragility and ambivalence within these cosmopolitan romances, marked by 'moments of empathy and bonding just as much as on personal struggles, occasional alliances and limited openness between the members of the couple'.

And it is to Meyers's *The Holiday* and her earlier film, *The Parent Trap* (1998), that Deborah Jermyn turns in detail in the final chapter of Part Two. As she observes, '[w]ith a cumulative box-office of over $1.3 billion to her name', and having earned the title 'the romcom queen', 'it is striking to note that two of Nancy Meyers's six films as a record-breaking director . . . have centred on transatlantic romances'. In her attention to the questions of space/place that run throughout Part Two, Jermyn's purpose is to move the analysis of romcom beyond issues of narrative and characterisation that have delimited so much scholarship on the genre. Instead, her chapter interrogates how these films' visual and spatial landscapes are central to the pleasures they afford, demonstrating the genre's part in mythologising the 'special relationship'. She points to how both films perpetuate particular fantasies of national difference, in which visions of traditional, 'old' England (affluent 'heritage' London in *The Parent Trap*; an idyllic Surrey village in *The Holiday*) sit alongside 'the upscale and verdant homes enabled by wealthy West Coast American entrepreneurialism, all of these marked by white privilege'. Drawing on close textual analysis, interdisciplinary perspectives pertaining to space, genre, film language, the cinematic city and film tourism, and visiting locations used by Meyers in both films, Jermyn concludes that, in each of them, Meyers attentively constructs 'a topography in which "mismatched" couples can make sense; in which the romcom's "magic space" (Deleyto 2009), and the aesthetics that help construct it, facilitate intimacy, optimism and revelation; and where the spectre of distance [need] not mean the demise of romance'. Moreover, within this, she posits, part of this '"magic" crucially lies precisely in their construction of Britain (and, more specifically, England) as the location of a certain (white) America(n)'s past – an embodiment of a mode of nostalgic "tradition" that the US cannot give them'.

Two Lovers Divided by a Common Language: 'Britishness', 'Americanness' and Identity

In keeping with some of the themes raised by Jermyn, Part Three affords the opportunity to examine more closely the substance of the twin national and cultural identities framing US–UK romance, as they are widely constructed, despite the evidently sweeping homogenisation that such simplistic characterising across diverse populations entails. The chapters contained here contrast the intertwined and conflicted notions of 'Americanness' and 'Britishness' as signs of classed, raced and gendered identities crossing the Atlantic and, at times, obstructing a mutually satisfying and successful relationship. If, as Jermyn suggests, the romantic comedy has generally suffered from a dearth of sustained critical interest compared to other genres, an important exception in this respect might be considered to be the body of romcoms made by the British production company Working Title, founded in 1984 and now owned by Universal Pictures. With their repeated trope of a somewhat hapless British chap and a powerhouse American woman forming a couple against the seeming odds, they have become something of a cultural touchstone for locating the unlikely attractions of modern transatlantic romance, as Jay Bamber's opening chapter traces – not least by initially pointing to how the Working Title films were called on by the UK media to frame the early romance of Prince Harry and Meghan Markle. Through close analysis of selected key titles, including *About Time* (2013), *Four Weddings and a Funeral* (1994) and *Notting Hill*, Bamber cogently contends that, in order for 'these duelling national identities' to reach romantic fulfilment, 'the films work to represent their American characters as attractive (to appeal to international audiences) but ultimately inauthentic without a British milieu and a British love interest to complement them'. Intriguingly, he argues that the films utilise the prestige hallmarks of British Heritage cinema to bring 'depth' to their British protagonists, which American characters might then hope to acquire themselves. In sum, Bamber situates Working Title's relationship with 'Americanness' as 'equivocal'; hence their association with 'low art' is *not* to say simply that the Americans do not bring anything to the table – indeed, Bamber suggests that they 'transfer on to their British partners some of the pleasures that make the films appealing to mass audiences: romantic spectacle, sexual sparks and aesthetic beauty'. Nevertheless, he concludes, in terms that will be portentous for Markle's future no doubt, that, by these films' end, 'The Americans have to sublimate their American qualities, including public success, in order to benefit from the authenticity of the British romantic identity; they have to quieten their public voice in order to have a more meaningful, personal voice.'

Our next chapter makes a noteworthy contribution too not merely to romantic comedy studies broadly but, particularly valuably for the purposes of this collection, to understanding how US film romance narratives can 'travel' among UK audiences, since Alice Guilluy is the first scholar in the field to produce an expansive study of the *transnational reception* of Hollywood romcom. Between 2013 and 2015, Guilluy interviewed audiences across Britain, France and Germany about their responses to the 2002 Andy Tennant film, *Sweet Home Alabama*. Starring Reece Witherspoon as a formerly simple Southern gal turned elite New York fashion designer who is wooed back by her first love when she returns to her small-town Alabama home, the film, as Guilluy observes, remains in the top twenty biggest-grossing romcoms of all time. Her chapter here focuses specifically on her UK audience's reception of the film, exploring how they expressed sensitivity to the film's perceived 'Americanness'. Interestingly, she finds that what most distinguished her British respondents from other European interviewees was their heightened engagement with and knowledge of issues pertaining to *sound* (accents, music, the pleasures of participatory mimicry), and in this respect it would seem that UK audiences' 'special relationship' with the film is, in fact, primarily located in, rather than undone by, a 'common language'. But in general, Guilluy reflects that British audiences' reading of the film was much closer to that of the German and French audiences than she had anticipated, and that 'all were marked by a strong critique of the conservatism and consumerism that participants saw as inherent to Hollywood cinema'. In contradistinction too from prevalent characterisations of romcom viewers as 'cultural dupes', she finds that there was a 'a widespread mistrust of US cultural hegemony and the American Dream, revealing the romcom to be an important and perhaps underestimated site of negotiation, in which audiences actively navigate the intersecting politics of class, gender and pleasure'; thus the special relationship between British film audiences and Hollywood romcom is revealed to be far from the uncomplicated love affair critics might too easily have presumed it to be.

Next, Inmaculada Pérez-Casal's chapter investigates the American infatuation with British culture, as depicted in the historical romance novels of author Lisa Kleypas. Pérez-Casal notes that the historical romance genre deploys an ideal of Englishness characterised by the rigidity of its class system, its well-defined gender roles and the decadent splendour of past colonial power. Against this background, Kleypas's novels advance certain defining characteristics of American identity or archetypal American traits, such as individualism, self-promotion, material success and industrial capitalism. Through the juxtaposition of competing yet complimentary cultural contexts, the novels achieve a twofold purpose: 'reinforcing the links between the US and the UK' – as love overcomes difference – 'and maintaining and perpetuating America's distinctive identity' to foster, thereby, the fantasy of American exceptionalism. In her conclusion, Pérez-Casal draws attention to the commercial context in which historical romance novels are produced, suggesting a connection between the virtues that the novels advance and the operative logic of the highly competitive market for historical romance novels.

Bringing Part Three to a close, in 'Imagine: The Beatles, John Lennon, and Love Across Borders', Theodore Louis Trost imagines the 'special relationship' between the US and the UK through the career of the British rock 'n' roll group, The Beatles, and the post-Beatles activities of founding member John Lennon. The chapter begins in Liverpool, a key site of commerce between the UK and the US – renowned both as the headquarters for the Cunard shipping lines and, in an earlier era, as the major port connecting the British Isles to the transatlantic slave trade. 'By virtue of their hometown, then', Trost notes, 'The Beatles were incorporated from the beginning into a special relationship that prevailed between England and America.' Perhaps as a consequence of their residence in this major port city, the Beatles are drawn to the rock 'n' roll music of American artists such as Chuck Berry and Buddy Holly. Wild enthusiasm for The Beatles in response to their recordings and their American tours subsides somewhat after John Lennon ventures some critical remarks about religion – widely regarded as a key element in American identity. After The Beatles decide not to return to America as a touring ensemble, they maintain their relationship with America through the love songs they continued to produce. Trost traces a development of The Beatles' love songs from the simple intimacies of 'just holding hands' to a world-embracing love with the power to challenge and change social structures. This romantic vision informs Lennon's later activities as both songwriter and political activist. Hence, in his song 'Imagine', Lennon envisions a world without countries, without borders and without religion. In terms of international politics, he focuses on the role of the US, whose military escapades in Vietnam threaten the prospect of world peace. But despite his critique of American ways, and in a desire suggestive of the push–pull tensions of the US–UK romance paradigm, Lennon also seeks to establish permanent residency in America: an effort that, as Trost shows, leads to a protracted immigration trial that ultimately altered US immigration policy and informs contemporary debates concerning the fate of immigrants in both the US and the UK.

Political Coupledom: Flirting with the
Special Relationship

Bringing the collection to an end, Part Four comprises chapters in which the 'special relationship' that prevails between the UK and the US is epitomised, summarised, symbolised or perhaps trivialised in the personal relationships that are fostered between the various political leaders and elites of the two nations. The first three chapters here all look at notable transatlantic political alliances since the mid-twentieth century and their role in shaping what is broadly understood on both sides of the Atlantic as the 'special relationship'; together, these chapters effectively trace an invaluable history of this evocative term in the period since the phrase first emerged, while provocatively demonstrating just how prevalently this paradigm has been evoked to foster a particularly *romantic imagination*.

Shelley Cobb's enlightening chapter opens this final section of the book, then, with a brief consideration of tropes emerging from the special relationship established by President Franklin D. Roosevelt and Prime Minister Winston Churchill, before reviewing some of the less celebrated interactions between post-World War II US and UK leaders. Significantly, she proposes that the most iconic representatives of the Anglo-American special relationship are President Ronald Reagan and Prime Minister Margaret Thatcher. Their 'closely aligned domestic policies to reduce the welfare state and increase the reach of laissez-faire free market capitalism during their concurrent terms in office established the neoliberal order of contemporary late capitalism' – a political and social landscape that, as noted, lurks in the background of many of this volume's chapters. Cobb suggestively analyses key media images of the Thatcher–Reagan relationship that serve distinct but related functions: mainstream media represent Reagan and Thatcher as political soulmates and a happy couple; meanwhile, satirical images of the two venture toward the lurid to suggest an extra-marital romance or even a sexual coupling. This latter attempt at critique, however, merely *reinforces* the power of their celebrity coupledom. Cobb brings her chapters to a close by comparing recent media images of President Trump and former Prime Minister Theresa May with prior representations of the Thatcher and Reagan relationship. Ultimately, she argues that all these images of celebrity coupledom 'deflect political critique and act as cover for destructive right-wing politics'. Thus, the relationship between May and Trump 'is not about love across the Atlantic' at all; rather, 'it is about [the exercise of] power'. This observation echoes the concerns that so animated Churchill's 'Sinews of Peace' speech at the beginning of the chapter. It also prepares the way for the book's next chapter and its consideration of yet another power couple.

As first posited by Churchill, the special relationship between the UK and the US was grounded in a military alliance. And indeed, during their terms in office, both Thatcher and Reagan pursued signature military engagements: Thatcher shipped troops to the Falkland Islands and Reagan armed Contra rebels in and around Nicaragua. But these were separate ventures. It was not until the aftermath of the 9/11 attacks in New York and Washington, DC, that the US and the UK reunited to pursue military action together in Afghanistan and Iraq under the leadership of US President George W. Bush and UK Prime Minister Tony Blair. As Hannah Hamad's chapter compellingly traces, Blair underscored his commitment to Bush's 'coalition of the willing' with one short phrase that rose to discursive prominence in news media reportage after the release of the Chilcot report in 2016: 'I will be with you, whatever.' With this covenantal commitment and the queer inflections it evokes in mind, Hamad interrogates the transatlantic 'special relationship' between Tony Blair and George W. Bush through the absorbing lens of '*bromance*'. This discursive 'formation of mediated masculine intimacy attained considerable currency over the course of the 2000s', arguably peaking towards the end of the Blair–Bush era with the success in the UK and the US of a cluster of so-called 'bromantic comedy' films, typified by John Hamburg's *I Love You, Man* (2009). This chapter asks, then, 'what is at stake in mediating the political, economic and military alliance between these two Anglophone nations through the irreverence of this topical gender discourse of masculine intimacy'? Crucially, Hamad places the Blair–Bush relationship at the discursive intersection between romance and violence, shining a light on the real life-and-death stakes resulting from their seemingly affectionately companionate alliance.

While prior understandings of the 'special relationship' between the US and the UK included within their purview a commitment to significant co-operation and collaboration with other nations, recent developments in the US and the UK have activated a new isolationist position symbolised, for the US, in the image of a wall intended to be built along the border with Mexico and advanced, in the decision on the part of the UK, to disentangle itself from the European Union. Neil Ewen opens his shrewd discussion of the current iteration of the special relationship with reference to the Comedy Central satirical film short *Brexit: A Titanic Disaster* (2017). The film, which went on to go viral, draws on the history of the doomed maiden voyage of the Cunard Line's *Titanic* from Southampton to New York in 1912 to suggest disastrous parallels with Great Britain's impending departure from the European Union. But Ewen's larger impetus is to interrogate the media's fascination with a series of incidents during which President Trump was photographed in an awkwardly intimate gesture holding hands with Prime Minister Theresa May. Is there more to this relationship than 'just holding hands', as The Beatles might have enquired? Given its recurrence, could it 'legitimately be surmised [that it] was a strategic PR decision', as Ewen astutely puts it: an attempt to capitalise on the 'pseudo-romantic imagery and innuendo' used by the media to frame the special relationship, as their political predecessors (see Cobb and Hamad above) had done? The chapter moves on to consider another transatlantic bromance, as it were, between President Trump and Nigel Farage, who has gone on since their first 'flirtations' to become leader of the Brexit Party. In the end, Ewen powerfully calls into question the media coverage that persists in 'reducing politics to spectacle' and gauges the quality of the relationship between nations by focusing on the personal interactions of their political leaders.

Finally, closing the collection in the contemporary moment, Nathalie Weidhase's chapter reminds us that 'special relationships' have a long history, not just between US and UK politicians, but between the British royal family and elite US social circles. Writing about UK media coverage of the relationship between Prince Harry and American actor Meghan Markle in the months leading up to their 2018 wedding, Weidhase opens by reflecting that this landmark Anglo-American marriage was in fact preceded in 1936 by that of Edward VIII and Wallis Simpson. It is a marker of a certain kind of progress that, eighty years on, Markle's having been married before was no impediment to her marrying again into the inner circle of the royal family, whereas, for Simpson and Edward VIII, Simpson's status as a 'divorcée' necessitated his abdication. More significantly here, Markle is a biracial American (to adopt the terminology she herself uses to describe her heritage); hence Weidhase's chapter provides another crucial space in the collection to consider some of the ways in which questions of race (and in particular, within this, colonialism too) have informed the history of US–UK romances. Looking at UK news reporting of Harry and Markle's relationship in the period leading up to their marriage, Weidhase argues that the temporal specificities of the months in which the courtship played out meant it became 'a "special relationship" which [had] to carry the weight of even more consequence, emerging as it did in a period marked by the rise of nationalist politics in both the US and the UK'. Crucially, Weidhase argues, Markle's race and her entry into the royal family are instrumentalised in the media against a backdrop of anxiety about the retrogression of Brexit to facilitate the 'rebranding' of the British monarchy; the inclusion of a woman of colour – and a self-identified feminist at that – into this relentlessly white, reactionary institution is assumed to signify its modernisation, and to be a riposte to criticisms that the nation is reverting to insularity. However, as Weidhase's perceptive account of the news coverage adroitly charts, with its references to Markle's 'exotic DNA' and the like, the reporting simultaneously underlines how, ultimately, 'a conservative institution cannot cover up the ideological underpinnings of a deeply regressive politics, and instead only works to make visible the imperial nostalgia at the heart of Brexit'.

In 2016, when we began to plan the initial project that led to this collection (the 'Love Across the Atlantic' conference held at the University of Roehampton in 2017), we had no idea just how timely, imperative and fraught new considerations of the 'special relationship' would become by the time this book was complete. Donald Trump had yet to secure the Republican nomination, let alone appear a serious contender for the job of President of the United States (POTUS). The Brexit referendum date had yet to be announced, much less its internationally divisive and polarising repercussions felt. And Prince Harry and Meghan Markle had yet to be set up on a blind date. Yet at the time of signing off this manuscript, the British press was currently ruminating over whether Trump's imminent and controversial state visit to the UK should ever have been mooted, given the widely held conviction that, as UK Shadow Foreign Secretary Emily Thornberry put it, the President has 'systematically assaulted all the shared values that unite our two countries' (BBC 2019); and much interest has been devoted to the fact that Markle, now Duchess of Sussex, has, unlike other royals, declined to meet him. Perhaps most pressingly, there is serious concern that Trump may use the ongoing uncertainty prompted by Brexit to make trade deals that gravely undermine UK interests. All of this sits uneasily with the White House statement that the visit would 'reaffirm the steadfast and special relationship' held between the two nations (BBC 2019).

It has become an unquestionably turbulent moment to be (re)assessing US–UK romance. But the ubiquity with which this discourse has once more prevailed across the media in myriad ways in contemporary times is testimony to its enduring and evocative suggestiveness, as well as its shifting and dynamic contours, and the marker of a profound and difficult love affair that this collection seeks in a small way to capture.

Works Cited

BBC (2019), 'Donald Trump: Details of First State Visit to UK Revealed', 24 May. Available at: <https://www.bbc.co.uk/news/uk-48400765> (last accessed 8 June 2019).

Deleyto, C. (2009), *The Secret Life of Romantic Comedy*, Manchester: Manchester University Press.

Solnit, R. (2000), *Hollow City: The Siege of San Francisco and the Crisis of American Urbanism*, London and New York: Verso.

Part One

'[Not] Just a Girl, Standing in Front of a Boy . . .': Feminism, Women and Transatlantic Romance

CHAPTER 1

Atlantic Liners, It Girls and Old Europe in Elinor Glyn's Romantic Adventures

Karen Randell and Alexis Weedon

Elinor Glyn, the popular early twentieth-century British romantic novelist, filmmaker, glamour icon and businesswoman, was an expert and frequent traveller across the Atlantic. Born in 1864, by 1924 she had taken twelve voyages on the Cunard–White Star luxury liners and had sailed on six different ships, including the *Lusitania* and the *Olympic*. These much-anticipated voyages were full of excitement and promise for the many celebrities who crossed on them from the old world to the new, famously attracting the British Prime Minister Winston Churchill, the producer Walt Disney and the film stars Ginger Rogers and Rita Hayworth during the period from the 1920s to the 1960s. For Glyn in the earlier period, such sea-going harboured romance and mystery, indulgence and danger, as her sister had survived the sinking of that other Cunard liner, the *Titanic*, in 1912, and had to face the subsequent government inquiry into the aftermath of disaster. In this chapter, we propose a notion of the 'special relationship' between the US and the UK predicated on romantic love, where tragedy and politics provide the background. Most particularly, in what follows we construct a detailed and reflective account of the years in which transatlantic travel and movement between the high-society circles of the US and UK were most central in Glyn's story. Her unique life narrative and the acclaim she won as a romantic novelist enable us to position her as a fascinating and resonantly emblematic figure in the history of the 'special relationship' in this period, one in which enduring preoccupations found in this discourse – around class, romance, gender, freedom and travel – are potently crystallised.

More specifically, Glyn's novel *Six Days* (1923), with its sense that the US offered resonant new opportunities for women, provides a rich antecedent for later representations of the transatlantic crossing, such as James Cameron's 1997 blockbuster film *Titanic*. Drawing on Glyn's archives, memoir, magazine articles and contemporary newspaper reports of her trips, this chapter examines how the romantic ideal of transatlantic

travel and the 'special relationships' figured in Glyn's work and signalled a significant shift in women's status in the early twentieth century.
(For more on the use of the transatlantic liner as an evocative stage for
US–UK romance, see also Jermyn's chapter in this collection.) While
Glyn fell in love with the US and saw it as a place where women of all
classes had greater freedom, she could not give up the pomp and privilege of old Europe while royalty and the ruling elite held sway. For Glyn,
brought up in the traditions of European aristocracy, the privilege of class
came with social responsibility as the wives of landowners cared for the
tenants' welfare, and the distinctions of class were a reward system within
that authoritarian structure. Glyn, then, was fascinated and attracted by
the freedoms of American women – and men – and sought to reconcile
her understanding with her European notions of social responsibility
and purpose. This conflict is implicit in Elinor Glyn's own transatlantic
adventures and her popular depiction of them in her romance *Six Days*,
and remains apparent too in the ways in which James Cameron's *Titanic*
(which visually echoes Glyn's movie) underpins a modern critique of the
liners' segregation of classes. Moreover, as we reflect in the latter part of
this chapter, the staggering success of Cameron's film speaks to the enduring potency of the transatlantic liner as a privileged site in playing out fantasies of US–UK romance, a space that speaks resoundingly of adventure,
hope and possibility, even while starkly perpetuating class divisions.

Elinor Glyn was fascinated by America and enamoured of the opportunities it gave to white European migrants, irrespective of class. 'England
is a man's country, not a woman's,' she said in the magazine *Britannia
and Eve*; 'America is a woman's country. Woman is supremely powerful
there' (Glyn 1929: 142). Glyn was not an avowed feminist or suffragette
but her writings at this time brought new vocabulary to popular romantic
fiction, empowering women to express their own sexual needs and desires.
For Glyn, the transatlantic appeal rests in her perception of the ability of
women to move beyond the confines of the British class system and marriage, where men hold the financial power in both personal and business
relationships. America held not only the 'dream' of opportunity and prosperity but also the 'dream' of autonomy in love – a new world, where early
emancipation, popular acceptance of divorce and a woman's ability to own
and spend her own money are intoxicatingly freeing.

Falling in Love with America

In her memoir, Elinor Glyn recalled that her first trip to America in 1908
was 'a very big adventure . . . travelling about by myself, in the role of

"Elinor Glyn the famous authoress", instead of in the company of my husband' (Glyn 1936: 138). The previous year Glyn had had international success with her eighth novel, which, in the US, had become caught up in the heated debate on marriage laws. Her novel entitled *Three Weeks* (1907) was about an affair between a Balkan Queen and a young Englishman. The mix of royalty, old Europe, English aristocracy and Elinor's own personal beauty and history were an attractive combination for the newshounds who met her. As soon as Cunard's *Mauretania* docked in New York, she learned:

> that the most fantastic stories had been printed while we were yet at sea. I myself was the heroine of *Three Weeks*, it was said, and one paper even published a number of names (derived from the 'Peerage', I imagine) of probable 'Pauls'. This avalanche so confused me that I fear I had no sensible answers ready to the usual pertinent questions: 'What did I think of America? What were my views on American divorce? How long was I going to stay? What had I come for? Would I tell the struggles of my early life? How did I react to the change from obscurity to fame?' (Glyn 1936: 139)

Glyn vividly recalled how this avalanche of questions 'so confused me that I fear I had no sensible answers ready'. She soon learned that discriminating between truth and falsehood, sincerity and kindness, in this new culture was confusing. Then and later, the American press told stories, and she corrected them (Glyn 1936: 139).

She wrote of the excitement of being 'by herself' but she was not alone, as she was often accompanied by friends and admirers. On this occasion in 1908, she was with Consuelo, Duchess of Manchester, and they were invited to Mrs Vanderbilt's stately home at Hyde Park on the Hudson. Elinor was awe-struck by the house. As she admitted, she had a love of 'such things as fine buildings, splendid rooms, rich silks and blazing jewels, adorning handsome, soigné men and lovely, carefree women' (Glyn 1936: 339) – a love that had been fashioned in the upper classes of Europe, where privileged women had confidence in their right to sexual fulfilment and took charge, discretely, of their own affairs. She now met the equivalent class in the moneyed families of old New York. She took it all in at the Vanderbilt estate, as her grandson reported:

> A long flight of marble steps led from the drive to the front door, and on every third step was a footman in knee-breeches and with powdered hair drenched in the pouring rain. The guests were . . . led through a series of salons to a great drawing room where their hostess was waiting to receive them, magnificently gowned and wearing some fifty thousand pounds' worth of pearls and long white kid gloves. (A. Glyn 1955: 137)

Glyn was less enamoured by the conversation: quips went unanswered and there was little of the dalliance she had come to expect in English country houses. Later, when she went to California, she became an intimate of William Randolph Hearst and, 'upholding equally the need for joyous earthly love and its fulfilment', accompanied his mistress Marion Davies, who was reluctant to go into social gatherings where society might disapprove of her affair with Hearst, who was not divorced (Glyn 1936: 339). Welcomed into the Chief's home, she witnessed the 'pageantry and show' that Hearst's Castle, with its 165 rooms and 123 acres of gardens, had in abundance. America simply dazzled her and she wrote about it in her novels, magazines and letters.

The trip in 1908 was not the first time that Glyn had crossed the Atlantic. As a child of eight, she had returned from Canada to the Channel Island of Jersey, her birthplace, leaving the Ontario ranch, where she had grown up, with her widowed mother and grandmother to stay at Richelieu, a manor house on the island, with her stepfather. This early voyage had brought the family from a French–Canadian rural existence in the new world to a middle-class upbringing in the old. Underpinning this first transatlantic crossing were both economic necessity and marriage, two imperatives that linked this crossing with her many subsequent ones. In fact, when, in the new century, Glyn sailed from England to New York, she did so as the family breadwinner. Having married into the aristocracy, she found that her husband had given her an *entrée* into this privileged world – but at a price. While Clayton Glyn gambled away his fortune, Elinor took up her pen to pay the household bills and became her own businesswoman.

Old Europe and Divorce Law

Glyn's 1907 novel had hit on a controversial topic. She wrote later that 'Whether you were "for" or "against" *Three Weeks* was quite an important matter in the US' that spring (Glyn 1936: 163). The dispute that raged in public in America was about what were acceptable grounds for divorce. These differed from state to state and there was no uniform US divorce law, causing people to move across state lines to find their settlement (Riley 1991). The discussion was provoked by the government's second statistical study on divorce, which showed that in the previous twenty years divorces had increased by around 30 per cent every five years. Glyn's novel hinted at some of the causes: a violent marriage, an absence of children, drunkenness, civil unrest – leaving out only bigamy and desertion. Reviewing the play, by the 'talented authoress herself', that toured America in 1909–10, a Nebraska newspaper said,

No book ever written has aroused so much discussion pro and con on both sides of the Atlantic Ocean as this powerful story of the unfortunate Queen, who gave her life in payment for a great happiness and yet by the sacrifice lifted a nation out of despair and at the same time inspired a man with the noblest thoughts and ambitions. ('Glyn's "Three Weeks"' 1909)

The scandal and tragic romance no doubt added to the audience, who in turn fell in love with the 'scenes of old Europe', especially those of Venice.

Three Weeks is about romantic love and a passionate affair, and for Glyn such fairy-tale romance can transcend class differences. She defined that 'special something' in a person, which gave them a sexual allure and charisma, as 'it'. Anyone could have 'it'. In her œuvre, the wage-earning shop girl and the miner, as well as the moneyed and landed gentry, find love and have 'it'. 'It' was daring, self-confident, playful, a swagger just kept within social bounds by 'individual discipline'. In a move away from the fairy tale, Glyn argued in her magazine articles that 'it' could be self-taught and could enable social movement across class boundaries. Glyn, herself, had 'it' and found 'it' when invited by the miners she went west to visit at the Nevada gold camp. *The New York Times* reported, 'Mrs. Glyn went after new things' and in the 'biggest gaming place in the camp, she wagered $200 on faro', spent the night at 'Stingaree Gulch, the Tenderloin of Rawhide', where there were '600 women in the street'. She 'witnessed a shooting scrap between a drunken prospector and a drunken gambler' ('Elinor Glyn Plays' 1908). George Graham Rice, owner of the news bureau, later wrote that the incidents were a set-up. 'Of course, the "murder" of these two gamblers, during the progress of a card-game for sensationally high stakes and in the presence of the authoress of "Three Weeks," made fine front-page newspaper copy' (Rice 1913: 232). Glyn knew how to flirt with the publicity machine, yet she was genuinely touched by their hospitality of the miners: 'One man had ridden ninety miles across the desert to fetch some yellow daisies . . . Ninety miles, there and back, across the desert, just to fetch her some flowers' (A. Glyn 1955: 148–9). For her, adventure, speculation and wealth had made these miners handsome with hope and hard physical work. They had 'it': 'They seemed to her the embodiment of everything that was best in the New World' (A. Glyn 1955: 149). Europe, she said, did not have men like these and she set the climax of two of her novels in the Nevada gold fields. America liberated her from the taboos of class endemic in the old world: beauty, wealth and charisma were the currency of romance in the new (Figure 1.1).

Figure 1.1 Elinor Glyn and the Rawhide miners. Photograph from Anthony Glyn (1955), *Elinor Glyn, A Biography*, London: Hutchinson.

Social Aspiration in Transatlantic Travel

Not only did Europe not 'have men like these . . . made handsome from hope', but it also did not have the glamour and allure of Hollywood, its stars and the film industry where those who had 'it' abounded. Like the fun and desirous adventure with the Rawhide miners, Hollywood was a huge draw for Glyn, as it was for millions of film-goers in the UK during the 1910s and 1920s. Cinema magazines, such as *Picture Goer*, enabled the general public to fall in fascinated love with the on-screen stars and their off-screen lives, and another special transatlantic relationship was born: the transatlantic love affair with Hollywood. Its glamour was increased and brought nearer to UK audiences by transatlantic travel's connection to Hollywood. The Cunard–White Star Line was the shipping company of choice for Hollywood stars visiting Europe, and its opulent first-class accommodation and public rooms transferred the five-star appeal of sophisticated city hotels to sea travel.

If the *Titanic* was, in Cameron's movie, the 'ship of dreams', the *Olympic* was the ship of stars, bringing Charlie Chaplin, Mary Pickford, Douglas Fairbanks Junior and celebrity royals such as Prince Edward, the

Figure 1.2   *Titanic* (right) and *Olympic* (left) in the Thompson graving dock while the *Titanic* is under construction, 1912. Photograph by Robert John Welch (1859–1936) for Harland and Wolff. Wikimedia Commons, 'Olympic and Titanic'. Public domain.

Prince of Wales, to and from Europe and the US. For instance, on 21 July 1920, Cary Grant (then Archibald Leach) travelled to the US to start his Hollywood career on the *Olympic*, alongside Fairbanks and Pickford on the return journey of their honeymoon. For Glyn, the attraction of glamorous travel, the salons, the cabins and the bars was matched only by the magnetism of those travelling and, in particular, the wealthy American, who epitomised the land of opportunity that Glyn saw for both men and women. This fascination translated into a story for the short novel, *Six Days*, which was published first in the US in 1923. In this, the first six days of the narrative are set on a transatlantic crossing on the White Star liner, *Olympic*.

Setting the novel on a real liner enabled the history of this ship to add credence to the story of postwar tourism, as well as allowing Glyn's readership to live out the fantasy of transatlantic travel. *RMS Olympic* was the lead ship of the Cunard–White Star fleet from 1911 to 1935 (Figure 1.2). During World War I, it was used as a troop ship and earned the name 'Old Reliable'. It was designed and built by Harland and Woolf and contained, to quote the advertising, a Georgian smoking room, 'luxurious cabins with

private bathrooms' and 'luxurious dining rooms with an a La Carte restaurant'. There was also a 'veranda café with palm trees', a swimming
pool, Turkish bath and gymnasium, and in 1913 a Parisian café was added
(along with more lifeboats). The journey on these fast steamers in fact
took only four days during the early 1910s, the speed necessary to carry
fresh provisions from one side of the Atlantic to another and, of course,
most importantly the post. However, World War I marked a change in the
business of transatlantic travel. To limit the raft of immigration to the US
after the war, the US government required a literacy test for all immigrants and in 1924 national quotas were enforced. Therefore, to attract
more passengers and enhance revenue in the early 1920s, Cunard slowed
down the voyage to accommodate the increasing number of first-class and
then second-class travellers, who enjoyed the holiday experience of sailing
from one continent to another.

Elinor Glyn's love affair with the US and luxury holiday liner travel was
well defined by the time she published *Six Days*. Her novel and the film
adaptation of *Six Days* present a romance between the old and new worlds,
which starts in the setting of a luxury liner. It proved appealing across
cultures and was the most popular of her books in Spain, with translations
into Italian, Swedish and Dutch, as well as selling well in the US and UK
(Riba and Sanmartí 2018). When the film adaptation came out, British
newspapers called it the sensation of the season and urged cinema-goers
to book in advance as the tickets sold out fast ('Hastings Amusements'
1924). The story incorporates romance, American wealth, British upper-
class etiquette and postwar diplomatic intrigue (never fully developed), to
produce a story that concludes with a transatlantic romantic union. The
novel focuses on a young, rich, free American heiress, Laline Lester, who
is travelling with her aunt from New York to Europe on the *Olympic* for
her first tour. In her party is the suitor of choice for her aunt, the British
Captain Jack Lumley, who had served with the Guards during World War I.
Looming in the wings is American Major David Lamont, who was part
of the US expeditionary force and was attached to Captain Lumley's bat-
talion in 1918. Major Lamont is travelling on the ship to carry out a secret
(never identified) mission, sanctioned by the President himself. David and
Laline fall in love during the voyage, and after the six-day, at-sea romance
the love affair continues on dry land as the American couple travel across
the scarred landscape of Europe. Setting the novel in a transatlantic and
transient setting enables Glyn to play with structures of class. Not only
has Europe been at war, but class etiquette has broken down: the Major is
unexpectedly granted leave and so is like a gentleman of leisure, the chap-
eroning aunt is left behind, and the couple take their road trip alone. In

Figure 1.3   Grand staircase of the *Olympic*, 1911. Photograph by William H. Rau. Wikimedia Commons, 'Grand Staircase'. Public domain.

an obvious trope relating to the suffocation of class and society in Europe, they are saved from being (literally) buried alive in a collapsing military dugout and throw off convention to embrace their passionate love.

Six Days of Transatlantic Romance

The transatlantic journey becomes the symbolic embodiment of good will in the special relationship, or, in our terms, the romance necessary to keep the relationship alive when reality pulls it down. The voyage in *Six Days* is a transitional moment when the hero and heroine journey from the new world to the old, and from a position in one society to another. Laline is moving to an easy role as a wealthy tourist, while David is taking up a more demanding vocation as an undercover agent. In Glyn's genre romance, this is an interlude of uplifting but indulgent luxury, where there is nothing to occupy Laline and David except the ship and their reflections on their purpose in life. The romance uses the liner's rigid segregation of

passengers to put the two in a bubble and keep them separate from the
other classes on board, who are notably absent in Glyn's writing. As many
journeys do, the transatlantic sea crossing becomes a rite of passage for
Laline. On day one, the novel states:

> Laline was looking for something in life – she did not know what. All the men she
> had met she could rule. She danced with them, listened to their love declarations,
> realized that they were all the same and then troubled herself no more about them.
> She was accustomed to their devotion, which contained no thrill. (Glyn 1924: 11)

David Lamont, on the other hand, having served during the war, is more
experienced at life and is looking for a quiet passage across the Atlantic, so
that he can focus on his secret mission and prepare himself for what might
lie ahead. He:

> arrived at the dock early on the Wednesday and went on board the Olympic
> before the rush began, and he was smoking a quiet cigar on the top deck where
> no one noticed him, when, with all the paraphernalia of rich Americans leaving
> for Europe, Laline and her aunt and Jack Lumley, came across the gangway. (20)

Glyn effortlessly includes the excitement, glamour and excesses of transatlantic first-class travel within the narrative, creating a strong visual
image that was hugely attractive to the readers of romance. They vicari-
ously enjoyed such indulgences, in which upper-class customers travelled
between these two countries (Figure 1.3), the experience enhanced by the
frisson of knowledge of the *Titanic* disaster.

On day two, Laline is 'so glad that she had had this lovely trousseau of
steamer clothes. A change for every day of the six days, and each tweed,
or woolly costume, and great, enveloping fur-trimmed wrap was more
becoming than the last!' (25). We learn that, before dressing, she takes a
'lovely hot bath' (38), and on this morning she decides that:

> she would wear the mauve wool shot with grey, and she would tuck in a bunch of
> Parma Violets. Countless boxes of flowers reposed in the chilled chamber waiting
> to be brought out fresh for each day of the whole voyage. (25)

The flowers are representative of the conspicuous affluence of the upper
classes. Glyn's focus is entirely concerned with the upper decks of the
ship. True to its genre conventions, the romance centres around wealth
and status; any working-class characters appear only as maids, valets and
waiters, and have no storyline of their own. Yet it is impossible today to
read *Six Days* with no cultural class context. The reality is that at least

1,000 of the passengers on board would have been steerage passengers, whose bunks were placed in basic dorms or large bedrooms, and bathrooms consisted of one sink with pumped water and one shared toilet.

Drew Keeling's work on passenger travel on the Cunard–White Star line from 1908 to 1935 tells us that the ships were designed with a particular logic 'of using different vessel sections to accommodate tourist, migrants, and freight, [and that this] applied across all the major passage lines' (Keeling 2007). He states that 'shipping lines were in the business of maintaining frequent and regular schedules . . . as part of their government mail contracts and for their prestige-bringing luxury class tourists and business travellers, but that they found migrant traffic to be an indispensable element within a cluster of jointly provided transit services' (2008: 18; see also Keeling 2012: 234–8). Migrant travellers were an essential means of filling the large vessel spaces below the opulent upper decks.

The glamorous advertising for the ships rendered the steerage passengers absent, as they were in Glyn's novel (Figure 1.4). Cunard focused its appeal on the minority of wealthy passengers who travelled first class, which catered to the most desirable tourists, senior government officials and businessmen – and the characters in *Six Days* (Keeling 2008: 18). As Keeling points out, 'Being a transporter of large numbers of migrants was not a source of prestige or public relations in the way that carrying of famous wealthy celebrities aboard mammoth state-of-the-art liners with luxuriously appointed upper decks was' (2008: 14; 2012: 237). Of course, this image of luxury enables the promise of the 'American Dream' and its opportunities for wealth and prosperity to be sold to the emigrating passengers too. (For more consideration of the resonances of the American Dream among Europeans particularly, see also Guilluy in this collection.) Glyn's novel and her articles on the stars for the Hollywood periodical press were all part of this glamorisation. Newspapers reported on the celebrities, authors, stars and wealthy businessmen and their wives who were travelling on these liners – including the cabin numbers of celebrity authors like Elinor Glyn.

But it is important to remember that it is not the income from the first-class passengers that kept the White Star–Cunard line financially afloat; rather, it was the wave of immigration to the US from Europe at the turn of the century and beyond. Between 1860 and 1914, 14 million Europeans immigrated to the US, these numbers increasing from 753,000 a year in 1899 to 1,745,000,000 in 1914. This resulted in White Star–Cunard's revenue from immigrant fares alone increasing from $14.2 million in 1899 to $28.2 million in 1914 (Keeling 2012). Compare that revenue to the $10.4

Figure 1.4.   Cunard poster featuring cross-section of the *Aquitania*, 1921. Wikipedia, 'Aquitania Poster'. Public domain.

million taken in 1914 for first-class passengers and it is easy to understand that, without the migration and travel of working-class travellers, White Star–Cunard would not achieved economic success.

Although the line did not use lavish advertising to sell directly to their main source of income, they did advertise in newspapers and promote the good accommodation that was provided for steerage passengers as they waited to sail (see also Kraut 1994; Taylor 1971). For instance, Keeling notes that:

> In Liverpool by 1903, Cunard had a 'complex of houses' that could accommodate two thousand passengers awaiting departure in 'ten bed dorms', with good sanitation and food, provision of separate Jewish diet, and staffs of foreign origin who spoke the appropriate languages. (Keeling 2008: 15)

When the fact is considered that the average home in the UK and the US at this time did not have an inside lavatory, this is quite some provision. In 1909, a magazine article in the *New York Herald* advertised travelling as the 'aristocracy of steerage' on the *Lusitania* and *Mauretania* with an 'all-closed berth' for steerage passengers ('Aristocracy': 12). Liner companies were swift to accommodate economic and cultural change and to keep transatlantic travelling in the public eye.

Echoes of *Six Days* (1924) in *Titanic* (1997)

Embedded too in this landscape of promise and possibility was a sense of women's burgeoning desire for self-determination through the period. The notion that America had opportunities for women was a strong one for Glyn, and the female agency that she perceived in the 1910s and 1920s can be seen writ large in the poster for the film adaptation of her novel, entitled *6 Days* (1924), which shows a flapper on the prow of the ship like an erotic figurehead (Figure 1.5).

Glyn's story is set on the White Star–Cunard's *Olympic*, which was the sister ship of the *Titanic*. It had become even more popular to sail on the *Olympic* after *Titanic* sank, as travellers wanted to experience a morbid voyeurism, as well as the voyage of the fated ship. Glyn's novel foreshadows later films that fictionalise that tragic journey, and in particular it is impossible as a twenty-first-century reader to read her novel – or see this lobby poster – without imagining scenes from Cameron's *Titanic* (1997). Cameron's script incorporates evidence from research on Cunard's liners from the 1980s onwards and the film gained audiences from the interest generated by fights over salvage rights and the ongoing attempts at that time to raise parts of the ship, including the first-class cabins on C deck ('Titanic's Hull' 1998; 'Triumph for Titanic' 1996).

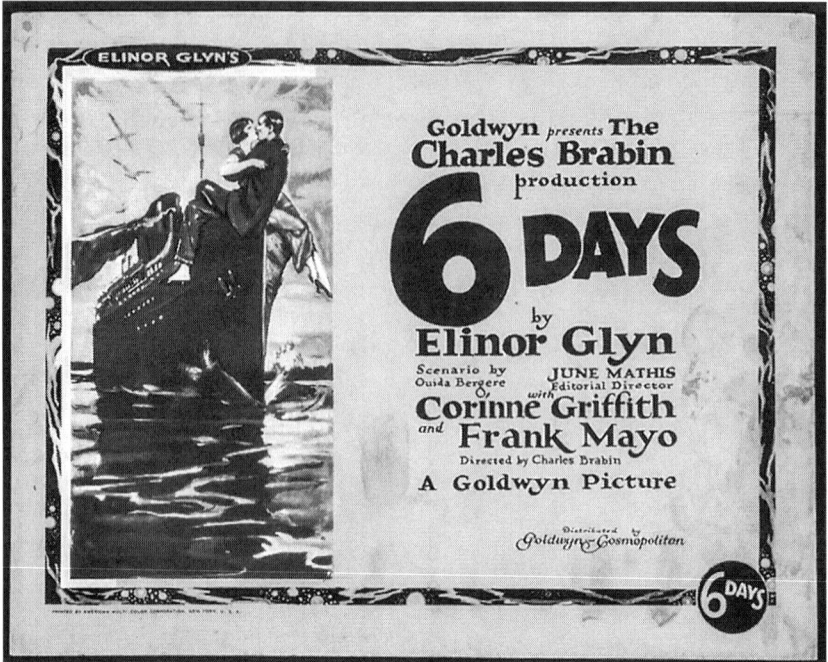

Figure 1.5   Lobby card for *6 Days*, Charles Brabin's film adaptation of Elinor Glyn's novel, showing its similarity to the movie poster for James Cameron's *Titanic* (1997). Reproduced by kind permission of Heritage/Heritage.com.

The movie's story has a rich American heroine, as in *Six Days*, but the hero, Jack, is booked into steerage. Although Glyn's novels increasingly propose the ability of romance to transcend class differences and argue for social mobility, Jack's cheeky assumption of social equality in the film would not have been possible for Glyn, who was no radical and whose genre novels feature well-to-do heroes and heroines with ambitions for romantic love, before wealth or advancement. When the central character of *Titanic*, Rose (Kate Winslet), her fiancé Cal (Billy Zane) and her mother (Frances Fisher) arrive at Southampton Docks with twelve suitcases and hatboxes, in their own separate chauffeured vehicle, it is easy to imagine that this is the wealthy 'paraphernalia' of Americans travelling in Europe that David Lamont, in *Six Days*, observes as he smokes his quiet cigar on the top deck. As Rose steps out of the car, she tips her hat and reveals her startled look at the enormity of the ship, and of course at the enormity of the life ahead of her as the bored wife of a rich American. Around her, porters rush for luggage and first-class passengers are ushered aboard via wooden gangplanks to rise to the higher decks, where they are met and greeted by liveried officers. The opulence of the first-class passengers, some arriving with large and small dogs, is in marked contrast to the steerage-class passengers, who are stopped by officials to check their papers, their teeth for cavities and their heads for lice.

This moment highlights the inequalities that will be apparent on board as the first-class passengers embark unencumbered by hygiene checks. In fact, the first-class passengers can take on their long-haired dogs with no checks whatsoever. Such an emphasis on class is built into the fabric and pathology of the ship (see Studlar 1994). The very structure of society outside the ship is designed into the architecture, so that when the ship goes down, those at the top are saved and those at the bottom perish. It is well recorded that of the 2,223 passengers on board *Titanic* only 329 were first-class; 199 of the latter were saved, including Elinor Glyn's sister Lucy, Lady Duff-Gordon, founder of the first global couture brand Lucile Ltd. Of the 1,517 lives lost, 85 per cent were second-class and steerage passengers, along with crew (Smith et al., 1912). Reading *Six Days*, we can be lured into a glamorous and safe world in which no one will perish because those that would be endangered do not exist at all within the narrative. For modern viewers, however, Cameron's film reveals the class structure of transatlantic travel and offers some insight into why millions of Europeans emigrated to America, a country that offered the hope of opportunity to increase wealth and prosperity that the class-based system of Europe did not.

Marriage, Migration and Money

If romance helped mask the economic drivers of transatlantic migration and travel, then it was a valuable tool. During World War II, wooing America was part of the British economic and military strategy. Winston Churchill said famously, of his daily letters to Roosevelt asking for arms and money, 'No lover ever studied every whim of his mistress as I did those of President Roosevelt' (Colville 1985: 624). Glyn too wooed her public on both sides of the Atlantic, gaining substantial economic rewards. She wrote article upon article for the editors of American magazines and the American press, who, unlike the British, gave her favourable notices. Glyn explored the linguistic and cultural differences between the UK and US, keeping her own lists of American slang and using her articles as an entertaining way of explaining their meaning before talkies brought American idioms into more common use in Britain. It was a lucrative approach and the magazines confirmed her success, saying that *Three Weeks* and

Six Days were 'money magic' and Glyn's profits were 'balance sheet facts' ('Advertorial' 1924: 326).

In large part due to the war, the economic situation was very different at the time of her early visit in 1908, on her second trip, and on her last return voyage in 1929. She was never unconscious of wealth, travelling on her own money and never like Rose or Laline, with the view of an inherited fortune. Famous Players–Lasky film corporation enticed her to New York in 1920 with the offer of $1,500 towards her and her maid's travelling expenses, an amount that allowed her to enjoy luxuries on board the liner. Within a month of her arrival, she received a further $1,500 on account for the cinematic rights to an original short story, a tidy income to spend in New York. If, then, she was keen to go further, the company would arrange a Pullman drawing-room car to take her to California ('Glyn Contract' 1920). Such a tempting offer was irresistible to Glyn, coming from the hardships of postwar Europe. When Keeling looks at travel across the Atlantic on the Cunard liners from 1885 to World War I, he notes the pattern of depression and growth, and concludes that 'the timing of moves to (and from) America was driven mostly by the economic factors in [the country]' (2008: 8). Glyn was no exception to this rule and travelled as a widow, with her own income from her writing and great expectations of Hollywood. The contract gave her female agency: economic independence, security and the freedom to choose her own companions.

Glyn was a businesswoman and was supportive of women in the workplace. For her, and for other writers, the rewards for Hearst's writers were great: 'Big money is paid for stories and scenarios to-day . . . a good bit bigger than is being paid in [shop girls'] salaries,' said Glyn (1922: 23). She admired American girls and their freedoms, and the comparison between American and British women made good copy. Glyn was paid $200 a week for two 600-word articles when she arrived. By July 1929, she was writing six a week. It was impossible for British magazines to match such sums as payment (Glyn Ltd 1924; Connolly 1929). However, German reparations and British World War I war debts were owed to America, and Britain borrowed heavily from New York in the 1920s. When the British withdrew investment from abroad, they abandoned the gold standard and monetary instability spread. In 1929, the effect of the turbulence led to the financial crash and Glyn's contracts dried up. She returned to Britain to make her own films.

For the millions who crossed the Atlantic, the journey was a new beginning; those who returned more often than not returned to gather family members to join them in their new lives. A return journey, then, was a hard one because, while the traveller had been away, the old world had moved on, as Glyn herself found. In Britain, she argued for a closer relationship with America, convinced that 'the hope of the world' lay in a 'more intimate knowledge of each other, a better acquaintance with each other, a better understanding of each other'. The best way to foster this, she believed, was through movies because they appealed to all classes (Glyn 1919).

Elinor Glyn used the trope of love and romance to explore many pertinent contemporary issues that affected women in the early twentieth century: divorce, motherhood, employment, marriage, relationships, and health and beauty. Her novel *Three Weeks* developed the debate about divorce, while *Six Days* glamorised transatlantic travel, igniting a romance between the old world and the new after the devastation of World War I. Her films and magazine articles were aimed at a widening reading and cinema-going public and her work gives us insight into the significant shift in woman's status in this period. Glyn was no social revolutionary or militant feminist, but her women readers were drawn to her romances and found in them a confident sexuality, a larger vocabulary to express their desire and an aspiration to self-determination. Such ideas were disseminated widely through Glyn's Hollywood successes, and she opened a space for debate about what it was to have 'it' and to own your sexuality and independence in a man's world. As this chapter has attested, more than a hundred years on from Glyn first visiting America, her story and recollections of her travels as a celebrated romantic novelist and transatlantic icon continue to stand out as a uniquely evocative memoir: the tale of a woman moving in aristocratic circles and energetically capitalising on the privileges newly afforded to her class and gender, and of the circumstances and desires that fuelled the 'special relationship' through the early part of the twentieth century.

Acknowledgements

This work was first presented as a keynote to the 'Love Across the Atlantic' conference at the University of Roehampton in 2016 and an earlier version was published as Randell and Weedon (2018). Alexis Weedon's work in this article is an outcome of the AHRC-funded project 'Cross-media Co-Operation Between British Novelists and Filmmakers in the 1920s and 1930s' (AR112216). References to archival material in this chapter are from the Elinor Glyn collection in the Reading University Archives. Our thanks to Mrs G. Chowdharay-Best for access to and permissions for the manuscript archive of Elinor Glyn and the staff at Reading University Archives.

Works Cited

'Advertorial' (1924), 'Advertorial for Glyn's *His Hour* and *Six Days*', in *The Moving Picture World*, 60, 4 October, p. 326. Available at: <archive.org/stream/movpicwor70movi#page/n325> (last accessed 26 April 2018).

'Aquitania Poster', Wikipedia. Available at: <en.wikipedia.org/wiki/File:Aquitaniaposter.PNG> (last accessed 25 May 2019).

'Aristocracy of Steerage' (1909), advertisement in *New York Herald*, 12 September, magazine section, p. 12.

Colville, J. (1985), *Fringes of Power: Downing Street Diaries 1939–1955*, London: Hodder and Stoughton.

Connolly, J. V. (1929), 'To Miss Gertie Aherns', 24 July, Papers of Elinor Glyn, University of Reading, RUA MS 4059, Box 5.

'Elinor Glyn Plays' (1908), 'Elinor Glyn Plays Faro', *The New York Times*, 29 May. Available at: <chroniclingamerica.loc.gov> (last accessed 12 March 2018).

Glyn, A. (1955), *Elinor Glyn*, London: Hutchinson.

Glyn, E. (1907), *Three Weeks*, London: Duckworth.

Glyn, E. (1919), 'English Relations with America: The Influence of Films', draft of her letter to *The Times*, Papers of Elinor Glyn, University of Reading, RUA MS4059, Box 13.

Glyn, E. (1922), *The Elinor Glyn System of Writing*, Auburn, NY: Authors' Press.

Glyn, E. (1924), *Six Days*, Philadelphia and London: J. B. Lippincott.

Glyn, E. (1929), 'The Advance of the English Girl', *Britannia and Eve*, 1:4, August, pp. 16–17, 142.

Glyn, E. (1936), *Romantic Adventure: Being the Autobiography of E. Glyn*, London: I. Nicholson and Watson.

'Glyn Contract' (1920), copy of Famous Players–Lasky contract with Elinor Glyn, 2 October, Papers of Elinor Glyn, University of Reading, RUA MS4059, Box 25.

Glyn Ltd. (1924), Agreement between King Features Syndicate Inc and Elinor Glyn Ltd., 28 May, Papers of Elinor Glyn, University of Reading, RUA MS 4059, Box 5.

'Glyn's 'Three Weeks'' (1909), 'Elinor Glyn's "Three Weeks"', *North Platte Semi-Weekly Tribune*, 14 May. Available at: <chroniclingamerica.loc.gov> (last accessed 12 March 2018).

'Grand Staircase of the Olympic', photograph by William H. Rau, Wikimedia Commons. Available at: <https://commons.wikimedia.org/wiki/File:Grand_Staircase_aboard_the_RMS_Olympic_(William_H._Rau_1911).jpg> (last accessed 25 May 2019).

'Hastings Amusements' (1924), 'Hastings Amusements', *Hastings and St Leonard's Observer*, 16 February, p. 7.

Keeling, D. (2007), 'Transport Capacity Management and Transatlantic Migration, 1900–1914', in A. J. Field, G. Clark and W. A. Sundstrom (eds), *Research in Economic History*, 25, Bingley, UK: Emerald Group, pp. 225–83.

Keeling, D. (2008), *Shipping Companies and Transatlantic Migration Costs Between Europe and the United States, 1900–1914*, European Business History Association Annual Conference, Bergen, Norway, working paper, 28 pages. Quoted with kind permission of the author. Available at: <www.ebha.org/ebha2008/papers/Keeling_ebha_2008.pdf> (last accessed 25 May 2019).

Keeling, D. (2012), *The Business of Transatlantic Migration between Europe and the United States, 1900–1914*, Zurich: Chronos.

Kraut, A. (1994), *Silent Travelers, Germs, Genes, and the Immigrant Menace*, Baltimore and London: Johns Hopkins University Press.

'Olympic and Titanic', photograph by Robert John Welch (1859–1936) for Harland and Wolff, Wikimedia Commons. Available at: <https://commons.wikimedia .org/wiki/File:Olympic_and_Titanic_crop.jpg> (last accessed 25 May 2019).

Randell, K., and A. Weedon (2018), 'Life and Legacy of Elinor Glyn', special issue of *Women: A Cultural Review*, 29:2, pp. 145–160.

Riba, C., and C. Sanmartí (2018), 'The Reception of Elinor Glyn's Work in Spain (1926–57)', *Women: A Cultural Review*, 29:2, pp. 188–215.

Rice, G. G. (1913), *My Adventures with Your Money*, Project Gutenberg. Available at: <www.gutenberg.org> (last accessed 12 March 2018).

Riley, G. (1991), *Divorce: An American Tradition*, Lincoln, NE: University of Nebraska Press.

6 Days, film, directed by C. Brabin. US: Goldwyn Pictures, 1924.

Smith, W. A., and I. Rayner (1912), '"Titanic" Disaster', Report of the Committee on Commerce, United States Senate. S. RES 283. Available at: <www.senate .gov/artandhistory/history/resources/pdf/TitanicReport.pdf> (last accessed 25 May 2019).

Studlar, G. (1994), 'Titanic/*Titanic*: Thoughts on Cinematic Presence and Monumental History', in T. Bergfelder and S. Street (eds), *The Titanic in Myth and Memory: Representations in Visual and Literary Culture*, London: I. B. Tauris, pp. 155–62.

Taylor, P. (1971), *The Distant Magnet*, London: Eyre and Spottiswoode.

Titanic, film, directed by J. Cameron. US: Paramount Pictures, 1997.

'Titanic's Hull' (1998), 'Titanic's Hull Is Hauled Up From the Deep', *Liverpool Echo*, 13 August, p. 32. Available at: <www.britishnewspaperarchive.co.uk/viewer/ bl/0000271/19980813/194/0032> (last accessed 19 November 2018).

'Triumph for Titanic' (1996), 'Triumph for Titanic Team', *Liverpool Echo*, 30 August, p. 10. Available at: <www.britishnewspaperarchive.co.uk/viewer/bl/ 0000271/19960830/063/0010> (last accessed 25 May 2019).

CHAPTER 2

'World Turned Upside Down': The Role of Revolutions in Maya Rodale's Regency-set Romances

Veera Mäkelä

A small surge of American heroines arose in the subgenre of Regency romance in 2016: Eloisa James's *My American Duchess* (2016) appeared around the same time as Maya Rodale's *Lady Bridget's Diary* (2016a), the first in her 'Keeping Up with the Cavendishes' series. The feisty heroines of these novels charm readers just as thoroughly as they do their heroes but their appearance also raises some intriguing questions: Why the Regency? Why not simply set the novels in America? Why heroines from America, specifically, as opposed to other British colonies? The answers to these questions simply may be that the Regency is an exceedingly popular setting and the authors of these novels are themselves American; therefore, it is logical that their heroines would share the authors' nationality and be placed in a familiar setting, one already recognised and loved by a wide readership.

I propose, however, that there is more to the matter, specifically in terms of the Regency setting. As Pamela Regis writes in connection with Georgette Heyer's historical romances,

> Regency details inform the heroine, the hero, and the core of the romance itself – the courtship. At the same time, however, heroine, hero, and courtship inform the setting. Heroine, hero, and their courtship throw the setting into high relief; characters and their actions comment on the setting. (Regis 2003: 127)

The nationalities of the heroines and the heroes are crucial, then; in this case, they lend a particular significance to the setting. The high society of the Regency period, in the form it is depicted in historical romance, is ordered by the aristocracy with strict rules of conduct. There are double standards everywhere: the rules are stricter for women than men, and the control the older women ostensibly have in the ballroom wavers under the influence of high-ranking men. This patriarchal set-up is upset by the entrance of Americans, who subscribe to a different ideology altogether.

American characters are best suited to making political statements in a Regency setting, as the collision of British and American differences forces a conflict. Recently independent of monarchy, their disregard for aristocracy and their inevitably different attitudes towards autonomy and rebellion not only make for amusing situations but also call the status quo into question.

The suitability of Americans particularly as heroines in the Regency setting boils down to revolution. Both the British and the Americans experienced revolution at the turn of the eighteenth century, the consequences of which were still fresh on their minds during the Regency period. The victorious Americans would find rebellion and revolutionary endeavours both beneficial and recommendable. The virtues advanced by the Declaration of Independence – 'life, liberty, and the pursuit of happiness' – read much like the ambitions of a romance novel heroine, among which affective individualism is perhaps chief (Regis 2003: 110). As the losing side of the war, the English were already politically unsettled when the French Revolution started. It was very different from the American Revolution: while the Americans rebelled against a far-away, essentially foreign monarchy, the French overthrew their own monarchy, a distressing prospect to another monarchy with close ties to France and one that had recently lost a war. The French Revolution was seen to stem from ungoverned passions and therefore led to a restriction of emotion, especially in men in England: the expression of emotion turned into rationality and stoicism. Michael Kramp notes in *Disciplining Love: Austen and the Modern Man* (2007) that in the wake of the French Revolution there was wide public debate over appropriate gender identities and that 'these discussions occurred during a time of economic and social transformation' (Kramp 2007: 17). The instability of the period caused the position of the aristocracy to waver as the middle classes began to rise. When class became an unstable marker of identity, gender gained more significance as a marker of identity (Kadish, summarised and quoted in Kramp 2007: 18).

The instability of rank and wealth and the shift in gender performance left English masculinity in a vulnerable state. The Cavendish sisters of Maya Rodale's 'Keeping Up with the Cavendishes' series, upon which this chapter concentrates, enter into English high society in 1823,[1] during this period of flux and shifting norms. The clash between their behaviour and the newly reserved English conduct shakes the social sphere to its core. This chapter will examine how the insecurity of Regency society reacts to invading Americans in Rodale's novels *Lady Bridget's Diary* (2016a), *Chasing Lady Amelia* (2016b), and *Lady Claire Is All That* (2017). Three aspects of this society will be considered: the characters who form 'the inside' of the Regency bubble that the sisters attempt to enter; the characters on 'the outside', who attempt entrance into Regency society; and the process that eventually results in admission to the inside. In order to breach the social bubble and live within it with a degree of acceptance, the outsiders must have inside support and face a gatekeeper at the entrance of society. The result of this collision of transatlantic values and, in the end, love is a new society as per Regis: at the end of a romance novel, there may be the accidental element of 'wedding, dance, or fete', promised if not shown, signalling how

> [s]ociety has reconstituted itself around the new couple(s) and the community comes together to celebrate this. For the heroine, this society represents a place to exercise her newly acquired freedom from ritual death and the barrier, however compromised that freedom might be by the very society she joins with in celebration. (Regis 2003: 38)

As all three Cavendish sisters marry, the Regency society they enter into is forced to reshape itself to allow them their freedom, although, as Regis is careful to point out, this freedom may not be all-encompassing.

The Inside

What constitutes 'the inside' for the purposes of this discussion are individuals – or, in one case, a smaller society – of aristocratic rank or connections who are accepted within the *ton*[2] without question. This group of wealthy social notables includes men and women alike, although, in the case of these novels, most of the truly influential figures are men. Being a member of the *ton*, or 'the Upper Ten Thousand' (Kloester 2005: 3), does not automatically make a character one of the insiders. The insiders are *haute ton*, the social *crème de la crème* of the *ton*, those born into the highest social ranks and wealth and who are unquestioning adherents to its rules, at least until an outsider questions said rules. The insiders can be divided into helpers and gatekeepers. Since the Cavendishes, with their foreign socio-political notions, depend upon the latter for approval, the gatekeepers are of particular importance to this chapter.

First and foremost among insiders is the hero of Rodale's first book, Colin Fitzwilliam Wright, Lord Darcy. Rodale makes his social status crystal clear from the beginning: the 'dark, disapproving Darcy' is 'the embodiment of the aristocracy' (Rodale 2016a: 51) and 'as a wealthy, respected, powerful peer of the realm, he was quite fond of civilization just as it was' (8). He embodies Kramp's description of what 'the post-Revolutionary English nation needs': a stable man 'who will not permit love to interrupt

[his] involvement in hegemonic social structures' (2007: 15). However, in a romance novel the hero must, of course, fall in love, as well as to his knees, thus acknowledging the heroine's power over him (Krentz 1992: 5). Darcy's eventual approval of, and love for, Bridget allows her to enter the Regency society. As Darcy's lady, no one would dare offend her or her family. Meanwhile, as a fairly young man, Darcy represents the younger generation of the aristocracy: his role as a gatekeeper and eventual rule-bender, therefore, serves to mark the formation of a new and better society.

There is also a representative of the older, fading generation of the aristocracy: Baron Wrotham, the uncle of the hero, Alistair, in the second novel, *Chasing Lady Amelia*. Wrotham determinedly denies his nephew acceptance at every turn and therefore, symbolically, excludes him from society. He is bitter over the death of his son and heir, and thus the focus is placed on preserving bloodlines: Wrotham's son was of entirely English parentage, whereas Alistair is half Indian. The barony is also impoverished, and therefore Wrotham plots to marry Alistair to one of the wealthy Americans, regardless of whatever feelings might exist on either side, all in order to secure his estate. This monetary ambition naturally speaks against the shared values of the heroine and hero for life, liberty and the pursuit of happiness. It also marks Wrotham as old-fashioned: he sees women as property rather than in control of said property.

Kin to Wrotham is Lady Wych Cross – also referred to as 'Lady Witchcraft' – in *Lady Bridget's Diary*. She is the Lady Catherine de Burgh figure of the novel and shares Wrotham's views of women and marriage exactly. During a dinner party, she and Bridget argue over whether marriage should be based on love or social and monetary advantage. Lady Wych Cross summarises her generation's view on matrimony in this way:

> Marriage is not about happiness, girl. It is for the purpose of accumulating wealth, prestige, and passing it to the next generation. It's utterly foolish to enter a marriage without considering such things. Happiness has little to do with it. Love, even less. (Rodale 2016a: 252–3)

Lady Wych Cross is one of the dragons of the *ton*, as the strict lady gate-keepers are called in the genre. Bred into her is the worldview of the men who grapple to retain their rule over society during an unsettled time. Women may be worth no less than men, but even if one believes in the relative equality of women, to show it would be unfeminine and rock the status quo, possibly with terrible consequences. In holding these tradition-bound notions, she perpetuates the patriarchal point of view and therefore is afforded control over other women on the inside of the bubble.

There is another bubble within the larger Regency bubble, and that is the Royal Society. In *Lady Claire Is All That*, the third Cavendish sister wants to breach not only the social bubble but the scientific one as well. The Royal Society actively resists Claire. While attending her first lecture, she and her chaperone are asked to take their seats at the back, where the visibility is poor. Claire is subsequently ignored during the question-and-answer session that follows until she receives inside help from not one but two men. The Royal Society differs from high society as gatekeeper in two ways. First, while the ballrooms are filled with women who retain the power to make or break individuals, the Royal Society consists exclusively of men. Second, entrance into high society can be granted by individuals, as opposed to the collective of the Royal Society. A young lady wishing to be included in the most respectable balls needs only to please one influential woman, whereas Claire first encounters opposition upon entering the hall from one faceless man and then, as she receives male support, from a cluster of them (Rodale 2017: 81).

These insiders form the sphere that the Cavendishes wish to enter. Its values are dictated by Wrotham and Lady Wych Cross's generation and are upheld – initially – by Darcy: strict decorum is to be maintained; things must be done as they always have been; and love is mere nonsense, a concern only of the most feeble-minded women. The Royal Society is also built on these notions; as evidenced by Claire's outright rejection by its body of male members, the Society considers reason an exclusively male capacity. Emotion is delegated to 'the weaker sex'. Lord Fox, the hero of *Lady Claire Is All That*, tells Claire on their first meeting to 'take care not to overtax [her] lady brainbox by trying to understand the rules of [*vingt-et-un*]' (38). Reason, he insists, is best left to more capable male brains. What he does not know at this point is that Claire is a mathematician and fully capable of deducing the rules of blackjack by watching the game. Because Claire is a woman, Fox, as a member of the inside, automatically assumes she must be driven by emotions and be incapable of logical thinking. His patronising way of speaking to her indicates that he expects her to conform to the requirements the *ton* places on young women at least superficially, and, should she fail, risk remaining outside the coveted sphere of social acceptance.

The Outside

By definition, the outsiders in these novels are primarily those *not* born to the aristocracy or even within the circle of high society. For our purposes, there are four main outsiders: the three Cavendish sisters and Alistair, the hero of *Chasing Lady Amelia*. They are all considered barely acceptable in genteel society and stand, most certainly, outside of its innermost circle.

Claire, Bridget and Amelia are American-born and therefore beneath high society's notice despite their wealth – although their brother's inherited ducal rank renders society unable to dismiss them entirely. Moreover, despite their father's British nationality and title, he chose to leave the idle aristocratic world in favour of making his own way as a horse farmer, thus deliberately excluding himself from the inside and thereby subscribing to an American work ethic and instilling the value of family, as opposed to class, into his daughters.

Alistair's situation differs slightly from that of the Cavendish sisters. As a baron's nephew, he has been born into the aristocratic class; but despite his position in society, Alistair's mother was Indian and his father did not himself hold a title.[3] When he becomes Wrotham's heir after the death of his cousin, law and convention leave the *ton* no choice but to accept him as future baron. This acceptance is hardly less reluctant than the acceptance granted to the Cavendishes: because he is heir to an impoverished title and is of mixed heritage, Alistair is aware that he is 'no one's definition of a catch' (Rodale 2016b: 53). His uncle pointedly disregards family in favour of social acceptability. Upon meeting Amelia, Alistair reflects how '[f]rom a young age he'd been made aware that he was different and didn't quite fit in' (Rodale 2016b: 82) despite his best efforts. Interestingly, gender does not help him: even though, as a man of future rank, his position on the inside should be secure, in the Regency society of romance novels race is a consideration above social rank and gender. Alistair's heritage means that he is just as ostracised as the Cavendish sisters, and therefore his relationship with Amelia is a union of two outsiders. This combination ought to exclude them from the possibility of their entering the inside as a couple, as Alistair himself realises towards the end of the novel (Rodale 2016b: 314). Under the old society he seeks to please, personified by Wrotham, he must either forsake Amelia or cease to wish for inclusion to the inside.

Amelia's attitude towards being an outsider is the opposite of Alistair's: while Alistair has spent his life trying to fit in, Amelia rebels against all advice she is given and does not care what society thinks of her. She takes pride in her nationality – she knows America to be 'a beautiful country full of forthright, spirited people' (13) – and refuses to adhere to the British code of conduct she finds limiting. Thus the novel connects Amelia with the theme of rebellion and reminds the reader of the American revolt against English rule and, subsequently, the American Revolution: the American heroine rebels against the social code imposed on her by a foreign society that seeks to curb her autonomy. Rodale is explicit about Amelia's dislike for the rules pressed upon her. While attending a ball in beautiful but uncomfortable shoes, she recalls how 'at home in America, she wore comfortable boots or nothing at all' (28) and decides to remove

the offending footwear, despite upper-class ballroom etiquette. A reader
familiar with shoes as a metaphor for the restrictions society places on
women in historical romance will already know what Rodale underlines
next: 'The removal of shoes wasn't merely a matter of comfort. It was
rebellion' (29). Amelia is openly rebelling and making society uncomfortable; at this point, however, she is outnumbered and, for a time, constrained by society's norms.

All heroines of Regency romance break the rules of society: as Kay
Mussell notes, '[s]ome heroines flout convention more than others, but
all are in danger of ostracism for inappropriate behaviour' (Mussell 1984:
56). Likewise, Penelope Williamson notes, in her essay 'By Honor Bound:
The Heroine as Hero', that '[i]n historical novels, the heroine is often portrayed as a woman out of step with the repressive society into which she
is born' (Williamson 1992: 128). While Amelia flaunts the rules of society openly, adhering to the ninth commandment of heroine conduct presented by Tan and Wendell – '[i]f in a historical, thou shalt desire to escape
from the domestic sphere' (Tan and Wendell 2009: 37) – middle sister
Bridget initially tries her very best to act according to the rules and yearns
for the domestic sphere. Bridget is the only sister who works very hard to
achieve acceptance and the one who most appreciates the guidance of their
aunt through marriage, Dowager Duchess Josephine. However, Bridget
is not without resistance: where Amelia sneers at high society at large,
Bridget quite literally turns her nose up at Darcy (Rodale 2016a: 85). This
has ultimately the same effect as Amelia's rebellion, for, as we have seen,
Darcy represents the whole younger generation of the aristocracy and, at
this early point in the novel, he still subscribes to the ideas of his elders
concerning how things ought to be. In the end, the rules of English society
sit with Bridget about as well as they do with Amelia:

> She was American born and bred, raised by a father who fled the life in the haute
> ton and married for love. She would never reorganize the priorities she'd been
> raised with. And if that meant she never quite fit in with all the fancy English
> people? So be it. (274)

Ultimately, Bridget would rather stay on the outside than compromise her
goals of love and happiness for access to the inside. Fortunately, an insider
falls in love with her, and the above extract turns out to mirror a statement about Darcy that appeared just two pages earlier: 'His battle wasn't
between lust for her and what everyone in the haute ton thought, it was
between everything he'd been raised to believe and to value and his love.
For her' (272). While not the dragon Bridget must face to enter society,
Darcy's approval as primary gatekeeper is not insignificant.

As seen in the previous section, the eldest sister, Claire, is doubly an outsider and, moreover, her wish to be insider in two spheres seems impossible, at least as long as her sisters remain unmarried: to breach the scientific sphere would render her unfeminine in the eyes of society and therefore disqualify her from ever being a part of it, which in turn would diminish her younger sisters' prospects of entrance. It is unfortunately the more scandalous circle Claire most wishes to join, and despite her best efforts, she is frustrated as she is 'too smart to simper on the sidelines of ballrooms' (Rodale 2017: 36). However, when it becomes clear that Claire, too, must make more of an effort after Amelia's scandalous disappearance for a day, she performs the part faultlessly, down to simpering helplessness (302). Here, an important bridge between the sisters is built: dressing Claire up to the nines for a ball, aided by Fox's fashionable sister, Lady Francesca, Rodale particularly mentions 'the uncomfortable shoes she wore' that prevent her from moving, followed by the addition '(but they sparkled!)' (301). This naturally reminds the reader of Amelia's early rebellion and, subsequently, the theme of revolutions. Revolution entails rebellion and conflict, and before the outsiders can infiltrate the inside, they must find their confidence and face some dragons.

The Dragons; or, Facing the Gatekeepers

In order to break into the upper sphere of society, at least one member of each romantic pair must face a gatekeeper of society. In all three novels, these are significant moments of character development: Bridget finally decides not to cater to anyone's will but her own and Darcy finally acknowledges her as she is; Alistair, likewise, decides it is time to stop trying to jump through impossible hoops; and Claire finds her scientific voice and confidence assisted by Fox, whose perception of what belonging to society means for women shifts considerably. All these encounters arise in opposition to older individuals or institutions and, therefore, against old values.

Claire, as we have seen above, faces the male body of the Royal Society. Insider help is crucial to her here: Fox is appalled at the request that she and Miss Green sit at the back because '[t]he ladies don't need to see' (Rodale 2017: 82, whereas Claire takes it as a matter of course:

'It is no trouble', Claire said. 'We shall sit in the back'.
'But–'
'We are lucky to even be here', she said softly. 'At least, I am'.
Because she was a woman – that was the real issue. (82)

Apart from Fox's realisation of gender inequality, the scene also contains another connection to the American Revolution here, the slyest in the series by far: Fox notes that Claire does not care where she sits as long as she is 'in the room where it happened' (Rodale 2017: 83). This is a reference to the internationally popular musical *Hamilton* (2016), about the Founding Fathers, written by Lin-Manuel Miranda: Aaron Burr sings a song titled 'The Room Where It Happens' and thus Rodale connects Claire to the patient, slow rebellion Burr represents in the musical. With Fox's help, and the approval of Royal Society insider, the Duke of Ashbrooke, to whom Fox has previously introduced her, Claire gains confidence and, at the end of the novel, after seeing her sisters married, publishes a scientific paper under her full name (Rodale 2017: 325). Society's acceptance comes to mean little when she pursues her happiness in the world of mathematics, with the support of Fox, a society darling. The Royal Society, while initially formidable, is no match for transatlantic cooperation.

The gatekeeper in *Chasing Lady Amelia* and the barrier between Amelia and Alistair is Wrotham, a much more formidable opponent to Alistair than the Royal Society is to Claire; moreover, Alistair faces his uncle alone. Calling out Wrotham's reasons for imposing impossible standards on him, he comes to the realisation that Wrotham cannot be swayed by any means in Alistair's possession. Fortunately, however, this does not matter much in the end: as stated above, Wrotham represents the old, dying-out order, whereas Darcy is the representative of the new, up and coming order of his own generation. After telling his friends of his encounter with his uncle, Alistair has the following interaction with Darcy:

> 'I am only *half* English', Alistair said. That other half Wrotham wouldn't let him forget – and he didn't want to forget it. But he didn't want the circumstances of his birth to be an impediment to love and acceptance.
> 'One's ancestry doesn't matter to people who matter', Darcy said softly.
> Coming from Darcy, that was something. (Rodale 2016b: 338)

Darcy's position as the epitome of new society outweighs Wrotham's influence, and with this support Alistair is accepted within the society of which he has so craved to be a part. This also removes the double outsider status of his and Amelia's union and makes the match feasible. Shortly after this, Darcy marries Bridget, thereby leaving society no choice but to accept Amelia as the sister-in-law of Lord Darcy.

Bridget, of course, gains Darcy's approval early on, but it is not until her encounter with the dragon that she can accept his favour. The dragon in question is Lady Wych Cross, and the final battle is waged during the same dinner at which the older lady explains her views on matrimony. For the first time in the novel, Bridget extends her opposition beyond Darcy:

'Perhaps some people do not wish for a lifetime of misery whilst accumulating wealth they will not even get to enjoy and titles that serve no purpose whatsoever other than to make a parade out of walking in to dinner', Bridget replied.

'Of course the Americans would say that', Lady Francesca said dismissively with her sharp little laugh that felt like it could cut glass.

'I may not know all your silly rules, but I do know who won the war', Bridget said, pointedly, with reddened cheeks. She'd had enough discussion of her prospects – or lack thereof. She'd had enough of being made to feel foolish for who she was: American, interested in love, impertinent.

'Excuse me', she said, and quit the table. (Rodale 2016b: 253)

Bridget's response to Lady Witchcraft ties her firmly to rebellion: money and rank mean nothing to her, an alarming notion in post-French Revolution England. That revolution had, after all, been founded on disregard for these very aspects of society and therefore dramatically overhauled the political core of a nation by rendering monarchy and social ranks meaningless. Moreover, Bridget knows 'who won the war', bringing up the American Revolution explicitly: she knows that rebellion, in the right cause, will prevail, and as an American she believes in it. She and her sisters are a threat to the already unstable Englishness, with their disregard of wealth and status, and in their refusal to adhere to the behaviour deemed suitable for young, genteel women. Lady Wych Cross is appalled; from this quarter, Bridget can expect no mercy or favour. Once again, however, Darcy has the final word, as 'the embodiment of aristocracy' (51), and as with Alistair, that word is favourable:

'I enjoyed your conversation at the table', he said, finally.

'Did you?'

'Enjoyed is perhaps not the right word. It was . . . *enlightening*', he admitted. It had made him see where he had gone wrong and it made him see how he could possibly, maybe make things go right. 'It was interesting. And admirable that you challenged old, tired, ingrained notions'. (255)

Both Bridget and Darcy have changed drastically from the beginning of the novel, and it is only this mutual change towards more or less the same goal that enables their 'special relationship'. Bridget and her values, it is to be noted, have rubbed off on Darcy, not the other way around.

Conclusion

Rebellion and revolution are themes that run through the Cavendish series and they are central to what these novels, and the romance genre more broadly, are about: changing society. In romance novels, the purpose is not to return matters to the status quo presented at the beginning of the novel but to reach a new and better situation. The courtship plot must lead to a new social order, more gender-equal than the one seen at the beginning of the novel, if only for the individual heroine of the work, as suggested by Regis's observation that the union of the heroine and hero leads to a new and better society (2003: 38).[4] Moreover, Jayashree Kamblé has recently argued that the romance aspect of the romance novel is 'no longer so much about the fantastic adventure-filled or sentimental story . . . but about regularly updated idealizations of various components (including the nature of the hero) of the imperfect world in which the love narrative is set' (Kamblé 2014: 14). In the case of Rodale's novels, the Americans act as a contrast to English society and subsequently test its old-fashioned values against new ones, pushing the world of the novel towards one that is more suited to modern tastes.

The French Revolution affected English society considerably and, likewise, the American Revolution shaped North America. The English male heroes of Regency romance are worried about the disturbance of the status quo from which their political power is derived – a point that is made clearly visible in the novels under discussion. As Lady Francesca observes to her brother in *Lady Claire Is All That*:

> [G]entlemen don't want to be confronted with a woman who is smarter than themselves because it makes them feel inadequate, which makes them question the validity of their position of authority in society. It calls to question the entire social order. (Rodale 2017: 161)

The intelligence of women that Francesca speaks of manifests itself in many ways – such as in questioning old values, a wish to explore the world and an interest in science. The old status quo – that is, English patriarchal high society – would consider these qualities exclusively male, and their bold exhibition in women is therefore highly marked.

This visibility, I suggest, is precisely the function of the American heroines. As outsiders to the Regency sphere, they are better prepared than their English counterparts to question its rules and traditions openly. English insider women do not question the restrictions set upon them explicitly: the Dowager Duchess and Lady Francesca live according to the rules they have grown up with, although, as intelligent women, they recognise the unfairness of their position (Rodale 2017: 77, 163). In the end, the Americans always have the option of returning to the US, whereas the English ladies are more vulnerable to the social consequences of openly flaunting the rules of the *ton*. Indeed, they have no escape, so they have adapted to these rules and learned to navigate the treacherous waters of double standards and whims of the powerful. Their experience is vital: without the help of Josephine and Francesca, the Cavendish sisters would have no hope of ever even getting their toes past the ballroom door. Insider help is certainly required and, as society changes, these insiders may also eventually benefit from it.

The main change happens in the heroes with the implication that, in time, the whole of society will be transformed for the better. As the men hold the power, it is crucial that they are made to see the heroines as their equals and learn something of their experience as the less powerful sex. Darcy comes to love Bridget and understand the pressures of perfection that society imposes on women. The same is true of Alistair, who learns the lesson that some people are beyond pleasing and, as Darcy tells him, 'one's ancestry doesn't matter to people who matter' (Rodale 2016b: 338). The pièce de résistance is Lord Fox, who not only comes to appreciate Claire as an intelligent individual but also realises the difficulties his sister faces in her attempt to keep on the good side of the dragons of the *ton*:

> 'Also, [Ashbrooke] is a man. He is allowed to display his intelligence. It's unbecoming in a woman'.
> This Francesca said with no small amount of bitterness. Even [Fox] noticed it. Even he took a second to consider that his fiercely smart sister might have to hide her intelligence behind a pretty smile, or simpering laugh, just so it wouldn't hurt the delicate sensibilities of some nitwit peer of the realm. (Rodale 2017: 162–3)

If the heroes can understand the worth of their heroines as individuals, and – as implied by Fox's epiphany – the worth of their own female relatives as well, then there is hope for a more gender-equal society. As Thurston observes, if readers demand the inclusion of 'autonomy, equality, cooperation, and compromise, as well as love and respect' as ingredients of an 'ideal male–female relationship', it is 'indicative of their aspiration' if not their reality (Thurston 1987: 111). It is a spark of optimism and hope.

This hope is best explained by the symbolic resonances these novels create. If the Regency is considered a symbol of patriarchal society and the Americans an allegory of the feminist movement, then it follows that if feminism infiltrates patriarchy and reaches its most powerful individuals, change is possible. This makes transatlantic romance a metaphor for the efforts for gender equality currently going on in Western society. The acts of rebellion the Cavendish sisters engage in are signals that something is amiss with the society they have entered: Bridget snubbing Darcy and turning down his first proposal are acts born out of a refusal to be treated as inferior; Amelia's removal of her shoes and escape from her room for

a day of freedom comment on the restrictions placed on women's movement; and Claire's unladylike success at blackjack and her participation in
academia are rebellions against the suffocation of female ambition. The
powerful members of society – Darcy, the Royal Society and, eventually,
Wrotham – are left with no choice but to recognise the issues, in the name
of love, of course.

As has been seen, the nationality of the heroines and both geographical
and temporal setting all function to create a very particular moral outcome
for the novels. Were the Cavendish sisters English, these novels would
be quite different. They would know the ins and outs of polite society,
and while they might question them, the threat of exclusion would loom
larger, as they do for the Dowager Duchess and Francesca. To set the
novels in America would likewise make for a very different set of novels,
for in them the English heroes would be the ones questioning – but having the coloniser question the mores of a former colony would produce
quite a different result. The time period is significant: the two countries
were out of the immediate turmoil of both revolutions by 1823 and far
enough removed from them for any of the principal characters to have
been involved in the unpleasantries. The Napoleonic Wars were likewise
over. This leaves a window of relative peace where the focus can settle on
society and amusement without the threat of violence in the background.

This peace leaves room for social revolution. The Cavendish sisters
and Alistair all rebel in one way or another during the course of their quest
to gain society's acceptance. What ties these four together is their foreignness: born to English fathers, their mothers are of other nationalities.
This mixed heritage, combined with the clash of ideologies between the
Cavendishes and English high society, bring Americanness and feminism
into close proximity. Life, liberty and the pursuit of happiness become
associated with women – the sisters' mother and themselves – and
opposed to the reigning status quo of male-dominated English society.
Thus the American heroines, combined with the English Regency setting,
make a particular socio-political statement. America is a newly independent nation and American women subscribe to feminist ideas concerning
the liberty of women. Additionally, two of these women bring Englishmen
to their knees, thus showing the men their understanding of the world
has been incomplete and helping them learn to respect women; the result
is a transatlantic partnership of equals. The symbolism of Amelia and
Alistair's relationship is not quite as clear, but a strong case can be made
for the notion of America as a melting pot in which half-Indian Alistair
can also enjoy freedom and find acceptance as the Cavendishes welcome
him into their family. As the Americans are accepted into the sphere of

English society, a new and better society is born, one in which women are allowed the same agency as men. Or nearly the same: for, as Regis observes, romance is not quite perfect because '[t]he law and society's institutions cannot be changed by the heroine, but she can obtain maximum freedom within them' (2003: 78). However, the close of *Lady Claire is All That* implies that this is merely the beginning; the novels leave the reader hope that, in time, the whole of society will be the better for another revolution.

Notes

1. Although the Regency period proper only lasted from February 1811 to January 1820, 'the term "Regency" is frequently used to describe the period of English history between 1780 and 1830, because the society and culture during these years were undeniably marked by the influence of the man who would become George IV' (Kloester 2005: 1).
2. The *ton* comes 'from the French phrase *le bon ton*, meaning "in the fashionable mode" and also known as Polite Society or the Upper Ten Thousand' (Kloester 2005: 3).
3. The system of titles and courtesy titles is complex and, at times, confusing. The siblings of members of the aristocracy do not necessarily hold titles. Alistair is referred to as 'Mr Finlay-Jones', which indicates that his father held no title, as otherwise Alistair would have inherited it at his father's death. However, his status as a baron's nephew and heir links him to the aristocratic class closely enough for him to be considered part of it. Likewise, while Darcy in *Lady Bridget's Diary* is an earl (Rodale 2016a: 130), his brother is merely 'Mr Wright' but is considered part of the aristocracy.
4. Here it would be useful to think of romance novel structure in comparison to that of traditional detective novels. According to John Cawelti, a detective novel starts with a status quo that is shaken and the end goal is to restore order; in other words, the detective novel seeks to return to the exact state of peace that reigned at its beginning (Cawelti 1979: 82). In romance novels, the goal is improvement: there is no return to the original status quo and the union of the heroine and hero leads to a completely new state, better than the previous one.

Works Cited

Cawelti, J. G. (1979), *Adventure, Mystery, and Romance*, Chicago: University of Chicago Press.

Hamilton: An American Musical, musical performance, written by L.-M. Miranda and directed by T. Kail. New York: Richard Rodgers Theatre, 21 April 2016.

Kadish, D. Y. (1991), *Politicizing Gender: Narrative Strategies in the Aftermath of the French Revolution*, New Brunswick, NJ: Rutgers University Press.

Kamblé, J. (2014), *Making Meaning in Popular Romance: An Epistemology*, New
    York: Palgrave.

Kloester, J. (2005), *Georgette Heyer's Regency World*, London: Arrow.

Kramp, M. (2007), *Disciplining Love: Austen and the Modern Man*, Columbus:
    Ohio State University Press.

Krentz, J. A. (1992), 'Introduction', in J. A. Krentz (ed.), *Dangerous Men and
    Adventurous Women: Romance Writers on the Appeal of the Romance*, Philadel-
    phia: University of Pennsylvania Press, pp. 1–9.

Mussell, K. (1984), *Fantasy and Reconciliation: Contemporary Formulas of Women's
    Romance Fiction*, Westport, CT: Greenwood Press.

Regis, P. (2003), *A Natural History of the Romance Novel*, Philadelphia: University
    of Pennsylvania Press.

Rodale, M. (2016a), *Lady Bridget's Diary*, New York: Avon.

Rodale, M. (2016b), *Chasing Lady Amelia*, New York: Avon.

Rodale, M. (2017), *Lady Claire Is All That*, New York: Avon.

Tan, C., and S. Wendell (2009), *Beyond Heaving Bosoms: The Smart Bitches'
    Guide to Romance Novels*, New York: Fireside.

Thurston, C. (1987), *The Romance Revolution: Erotic Novels for Women and the
    Quest for a New Sexual Identity*, Chicago: University of Illinois Press.

Williamson, P. (1992), 'By Honor Bound: The Heroine as Hero', in J. A. Krentz
    (ed.), *Dangerous Men and Adventurous Women: Romance Writers on the Appeal
    of the Romance*, Philadelphia: University of Pennsylvania Press, pp. 125–32.

CHAPTER 3

Bridget Jones's Special Relationship: No Filth, Please, We're Brexiteers

William Brown

Bridget Jones's Baby (2016) continues the account of the life of the eponymous diarist, as the film opens with Bridget (Renée Zellweger) turning forty-three, having aged only eleven years in the fifteen-year period since the franchise's first film, *Bridget Jones's Diary* (2001), in which Bridget was thirty-two. Single once again, Bridget none the less becomes pregnant after two one-night stands, one with American internet dating tycoon Jack Qwant (Patrick Dempsey) and another with childhood friend and old flame Mark Darcy (Colin Firth). Uncertain as to who the father is, Bridget allows both men to believe the child to be theirs, with both happy to prepare for parenting duties even after Bridget explains to both men her confusion over the father's identity at a meal at Gianni's, an Italian restaurant near Bridget's flat. A rivalry develops between Jack and Mark, with the former eventually losing out to the latter when Bridget grabs Mark's hand during the delivery of her child – a clear sign that he is the man for her rather than the result of pain-induced confusion. Although Jack is present at their wedding and clearly now a close friend, the film ends with Bridget marrying Mark, who also turns out to be the father of their son, William Jones-Darcy.

There have been Anglo-American relationships in all three of the *Bridget Jones* films. In the first film, for example, Mark is initially going out with American lawyer Natasha (Embeth Davitz), with whom he moves to New York, before returning to London to be with Bridget. In *Bridget Jones: The Edge of Reason* (2004), meanwhile, Mark is again associated with an American, Rebecca (Jacinda Barrett), who turns out to be obsessed with Bridget, as opposed to being her rival. What is more, Renée Zellweger, who plays Bridget, is of course an American actress playing a British woman – an idea to which I shall return – while all of the films are also international co-productions involving British and American funding. None the less, where, in the earlier films, Bridget had to choose between

Mark and playboy Daniel Cleaver (Hugh Grant) – who, in the third film, is supposedly dead after a plane crash, although a newspaper headline seen in the final moments suggests that he has been found alive (opening up the possibility for more sequels) – here she has to choose between British Mark and American Jack. This means that *Bridget Jones's Baby* foregrounds Anglo-American relationships more than the other films, since it is leading lady Bridget rather than love interest Mark who is torn between a Briton and an American.

While the *Bridget Jones* films have, of course, garnered scholarly attention as examples of adaptation (from Helen Fielding's source newspaper columns and then novels [Aragay and López 2005; Cobb 2008]), for their soundtracks (Rüll 2008), and in terms of how they fit into feminist/postfeminist discourse (or otherwise; see especially McRobbie 2003 and 2004), in this chapter I shall analyse the third film in terms of how it depicts Anglo-American (special) relationships. I shall argue that the film associates Americanness with both filth and technology, suggesting a seemingly contradictory relationship between technology and desire whereby British Bridget wants Jack as the technologised American other (even if he is also white and middle-class), but must suppress this desire in order to return to the homely and familiar Mark. In this way, the third film echoes the first two in figuring the US as a threat to Bridget's happiness, in that Jack stands between Bridget and Mark. However, it is here rendered in a particularly telling fashion through the visual and thematic associations between Jack and mud and between Jack and technology, specifically internet dating technology, which, I shall argue, brings into relief the contradictions between the promise of connection and the ongoing alienation and atomisation of contemporary neoliberal and digital society.

In other words, *Bridget Jones's Baby* suggests a sort of resentful attraction towards the US and the culture of techno-capital, but which it ultimately must pretend to deny – precisely because techno-capitalist culture demands the rejection of all other cultures in favour of white, conservative, middle-class (and in this case, British) values, in spite of some superficial attempts to demonstrate the contrary, as we shall see below. In this way, Bridget's rejection of Jack is in keeping with a nation that, in 2015, voted to leave the European Union and which, at the time of writing, seems shamelessly to be deporting citizens who came under invitation to the UK from the Caribbean as long ago as the 1950s but who now seem no longer to be welcome within the country's borders – a phenomenon referred to in the British press as the Windrush scandal (Grierson 2018).

Foreign Filth

We shall return to how *Bridget Jones's Baby* echoes the racial dimension of the Windrush scandal later, but for the time being let us recall that when, in 2015, disabled Canadian Margaret O'Brien was told to leave the UK after forty-four years living there, she said that she felt 'like dirt' (Gentleman 2018). This association between filth and the UK's others is also visible in *Bridget Jones's Baby*, although in a different, if telling, way. For, when Bridget and Jack first meet, it is at a music festival, where Bridget has gone with newsreader friend Miranda (Sarah Solemani). Miranda has told Bridget to 'shag' (sleep with) the first man she meets at the festival, not least because Bridget is feeling low after twice bumping into Mark in quick succession (including, for the first time, at Daniel Cleaver's funeral). Walking in high heels across a field in white jeans and jumper, Bridget inevitably falls into a large puddle of mud, out of which she is pulled by none other than Jack – for whom she immediately feels an attraction, as signalled by the exchange of looks between the two characters, emphasised through close-ups. In other words, there is immediately an erotic association created between Jack and filth: with Jack, Bridget can indeed hook up and have the sort of consequence-less sex that is supposedly redolent of the age of Tinder, a popular dating app namechecked on a couple of occasions by Miranda, who is an avid user.[1]

This initial association between Jack and filth can be contrasted with the association between Mark and children. For, while Bridget does, of course, also have a one-night stand with Mark, it is notably at the christening of the youngest child of old friend Jude (Shirley Henderson) that we see Mark look fondly at Bridget as she dances around to 'Gangnam Style' with a group of children. In other words, sex with Americans is for fun, while sex with British men is for the purposes of procreation.

The link between Jack and filth is maintained when he later turns up in London with the Wellington boot that Bridget left behind at the music festival. The return of the repressed boot would suggest that Bridget still wants to have sex for fun, but she represses this desire (as she does also via her famously oversized knickers), perhaps as a result of being middle-classed and British. The casting of Zellweger would suggest something similar: her American identity paradoxically allows her, as Bridget, to express an otherwise repressed British desire. The classed (and, as we shall see, raced) nature of this repression can be seen in the frank discussion that the make-up artist, Cathy (Joanna Scanlan), has about visiting sex clubs in Soho: the worker in the lesser role (who paradoxically improves people's appearance, at one point removing from Miranda her otherwise unruly and to-be-suppressed facial hair) is jolly and fat, but clearly not the sort of person with whom Bridget would hang out beyond the workplace, perhaps because Cathy cannot afford to go 'glamping' (glamorous camping) at a festival.[2]

That said, Bridget's repressed desire cannot but return at certain key moments, including at the music festival. In this way, while the film shows Bridget stumbling into Jack's yurt after going on an all-day drinking binge with Miranda (who ends up rolling around inside a zorb ball with popular musician Ed Sheeran), we might speculate that Bridget deliberately pursues Jack – but hides behind the double mask of her inebriation and her Britishness to claim that her entry into his yurt is a mistake. As a film, *Bridget Jones's Baby* itself wears a similar mask, since the film is disingenuous in suggesting that Bridget ends up with Jack only by accident, because their union has clearly been cued from their meeting and not least because Jack is played by recognisable heartthrob Patrick Dempsey, an actor perhaps best known for his role as Derek 'McDreamy' Shepherd in *Grey's Anatomy* (2005–), a television show that functions in the mould of *Ally McBeal* (1997–2002), in that, for all of its depictions of empowered, white and relatively wealthy femininity (as well as supposedly being 'colour-blind'), 'feminism has a spectral, shadowy, almost hated existence' (McRobbie 2003: 135) – a hatred for feminism that also applies to *Bridget Jones's Baby*, as we shall see. First, however, let us look at the role that technology plays in the film.

Tinder is the Night

Technology plays a key role in the *mise-en-scène* of *Bridget Jones's Baby*, not least because Jack is fabulously wealthy as a result of having made millions on his dating website, Qwantum Leap, which purportedly has brought together numerous couples through its supposedly infallible algorithm for matching together would-be partners. Indeed, according to the website, Jack and Bridget share a 97 per cent compatibility score, while Bridget and Mark are apparently only 8 per cent compatible, a statistic to which I shall return. For the time being, however, let us focus on how technology, especially the internet, functions as an outlet for otherwise repressed desire. Miranda's success in hooking up on Tinder would initially suggest this. More significant, though, is how Bridget types H into Google in front of a large audience at the London Media Show, supposedly in order to link to the real-time news broadcast offered by her company, Hard News. However, through predictive text (that is, based upon her past web searches), Google thinks that Bridget will be searching for how she can lose weight on her thighs, how she can get her boss fired and hot male pin-ups. That is: Bridget uses the internet to look not for love and connection, but for sex and violence, as her internet history suggests an emphasis on personal appearance, the destruction of other people's lives and the emphasis on the appearance of men.

While digital technology promises what Angela McRobbie might term 'liberalisation in regard to choice and diversity in domestic, sexual and kinship relations' (as an empowered woman, Bridget can have one-night stands and look up pictures of hot men on the internet), it also intensifies 'neo-conservative values in relation to gender, sexuality and family life', something that we see borne out in the film's narrative arc (McRobbie 2004: 255–6). However, if it seems that these two trends (liberalisation and neoconservatism) pull in opposite directions, I wish to suggest that in fact they both reinforce the conservative values of digital techno-capitalism, which involves a strong emphasis on what Rosalind Gill has identified as self-surveillance, monitoring and self-discipline, together with a focus on individualism, choice and empowerment (Gill 2007). This can be seen most clearly in the logic of the dating app, where a promised liberalisation of relationships (sexual or otherwise) is premised upon superficial appearances in photos. In order to be 'successful' on an app, one must become photogenic – to follow Susan Sontag's argument that the contemporary world is structured around preparing for photographs (Sontag 1979). In order to become photogenic, one must discipline one's body and appearance (hence the rise of gym culture – as seen when Bridget attends a spinning session on her birthday). This self-discipline in turn reinforces an emphasis on the self, the self-centred nature of which subverts the promise of liberal diversity and meaningful human relationships, precisely because self- as opposed to other-oriented.

It may be that Bridget consistently makes a scene by 'embarrassing herself' (that is, by losing control of situations – as per the scene at the London Media Show). But that this is funny (and that Bridget is embarrassed) only highlights the pressure on people always to be in control/photogenic. We may even contend that the consistent nature of her embarrassment signals that Bridget deliberately seeks attention by engineering embarrassing situations, a kind of double bluff that pretends to disavow and perhaps even to subvert self-centred and appearance-based neoliberal values, while in fact reinforcing them. With Bridget's use of digital technologies in mind, let us explore in greater depth the neoliberal nature of dating apps, since these also form a core focus of *Bridget Jones's Baby*, while also allowing us to clarify further some of the contradictions of the Anglo-American relationships that the film depicts.

Some dating apps, like Tinder, are obviously superficial in their emphasis on photographs and cursory bits of text (if any) in the bid to attract a potential partner. But even sites/apps that are more concertedly trying to help users find life, as opposed to sexual partners, buy into this logic of appearances and the self. This is not simply a case of the key role that profile pictures play. It also has to do with the fact that dating websites and apps reinforce the user's sense of self by asking them to think intensely about how they present themselves in both words and images, as well as in terms of how they would categorise themselves according to the various options that are given during the creation of a profile. In other words, the dating website encourages the user not to be a human being, but to become a salesperson, meaning that the dating website (as well as the app) has a capitalist logic at its very core, suggesting the ongoing economisation, if not the plain marketisation, of love in the contemporary age. That is, love has become (or remains) a market, which in turn means that it is a competition – as scholars like Wendy Brown (2015) and Eva Illouz (2007) have demonstrated in relation to the neoliberal and digital era in which we are living. While the ability of women to sell themselves might be regarded as an improvement upon the reduction of women to commodities in the era of arranged marriages, this perceived empowerment is still a means of interpellating women into the techno-capitalist logic of the contemporary era.

Furthermore, since love has now become a competition, the dating website paradoxically does not foster love, but in fact its opposite: a fear of missing out (or what is referred to commonly as FOMO), which involves a sense of not wanting to settle with anyone because one is always concerned that there may be a 'better' option just around the corner, with that better option here being defined by appearances far more than by anything like compatibility. No wonder, then, that apps like Tinder, which are, in principle, geared more towards hooking up, have followed and, in some senses, replaced the more traditional dating websites like eHarmony, upon which Qwantum Leap might seem to be based. For, in reinforcing singledom as opposed to union as a result of FOMO, dating websites and apps have at their core a logic of atomisation and separation (an emphasis on the self and not others), a logic of atomisation that can also be seen in the UK in the blatant xenophobia of Brexit and the Windrush scandal.

A Table for One

In her analysis of singledom, Kinneret Lahad argues that 'single women in different parts of the world are regularly typecast as desperate, hysterical, childish, irresponsible, or lazy' and that single women are 'disoriented, marginal subjects' (Lahad 2017: 45). In some senses, the *Bridget Jones* films go against this logic by seeking to empower Bridget as a single woman. However, as *Bridget Jones's Baby* culminates in both the birth of William and Bridget's wedding with Mark, the film would also seem to affirm Lahad's critique, since it is only via the temporal markers of childbirth and marriage that Bridget finally becomes a normalised subject, with the film thus fitting Diane Negra's schema of a society that endlessly celebrates weddings as a form of female fulfilment (Negra 2009).

Lahad suggests that, rather than single women simply seeking to get married, 'feminist resistance should pay attention to the ways in which temporality [or the need for women to be married and to have children by the time that they are, say, thirty-two – to take Bridget's age at the outset of the first film] is exercised to discipline and normalize the female body, punishing whoever cannot comply with these fixed rules' (Lahad 2017: 80). By offering the happy ending, *Bridget Jones's Baby* does not question or resist the temporal timeline prescribed for women by mainstream Western culture. Even if Bridget is now forty-three instead of thirty-two, the film still offers childbirth and marriage as the two temporal markers that validate her journey into normal, accepted womanhood, with the wedding here functioning as a fantasy occasion that disavows the likelihood, also explored by Lahad, that the longer a woman is single, the more likely she is to remain single, just as the longer one is on a dating website, the more one's chances of leaving that website diminish (Lahad 2017: 78). Certainly, the film does not question the expectation of happiness via heterosexual union, which Sara Ahmed has also critiqued as a means of disciplining women in late capitalist, postfeminist society (Ahmed 2010).

While Bridget's union with Mark might suggest that atomisation can be negated under techno-capital, in that, rather than remain single, Bridget does form a lasting bond with another human being, this is mitigated by the way in which Bridget rejects otherness in the form of foreigner Jack, instead returning (again) to her fellow Briton and childhood friend, Mark. That is, Bridget's union with Mark suggests a conservative regression back to the same, while the casting of Colin Firth might also suggest how the union is oddly problematic. For while Firth, of course, recalls his role as Mr Darcy in the BBC's adaptation of Jane Austen's *Pride and Prejudice* (1995) (the novel itself being a clear intertext with Helen Fielding's source material), his roles in films like *Mamma Mia!* (2008), *A Single Man* (2009) and *The King's Speech* (2010) all associate Firth with 'not quite being a (heterosexual) man', in that in the first two films his characters are or come out as being gay, while in the latter Firth plays a stuttering King George VI, who must overcome his speech impediment in order to become king (or at least a king fit for radio broadcast). In this way, Firth connotes a kind of sexually repressed or even asexual character, who will lead a relatively asexual life with Bridget, who herself has 'purged' her filthy desires with Jack, just as Mark has done the same in the first two films with Natasha and then Rebecca. In other words, theirs is likely to become a sexless and loveless marriage defined by an accidental parenthood that allows them to keep up appearances, while both unhappily repress their desire for other men.

The implied return of Daniel Cleaver also suggests that Bridget's happiness may not last. Indeed, Cleaver's funeral is attended by a gaggle of young, conventionally attractive (and typically foreign) women with whom he has had relationships, suggesting that his atomistic approach to relationships is, in fact, the true expression of love in the contemporary age, as we imagine him returning from the dead to jeopardise Bridget's otherwise happy marriage, since love cannot last in the face of competition and conquest. In other words, Bridget's wedding (and her baby) in some senses reaffirm the very opposite: the impossibility of happiness, especially through heterosexual union, at a time when everyone is encouraged to be alone (and to reject foreigners *à la* Brexit and the discarded Jack). Since one can neither be happy being alone, nor be happy being unhappy, Bridget's fantasy ending demonstrates the impossible position of supposedly empowered women under patriarchal neoliberalism. 'All by myself', mimes Bridget in sync with Jamie O'Neal. She may not want to be all by herself but solipsism/to be all by oneself (and to mime the words of others rather than to invent and to sing one's own song) is precisely the contemporary condition *par excellence*.

Qwantum Leap

As much can also be seen in the workings of Qwantum Leap, even though how and why Bridget has a compatibility score of 97 per cent with Jack and only 8 per cent with Mark remains unexplained. Indeed, these figures seem really to be a fabrication, since by virtue of having grown up together, Bridget and Mark clearly have more things in common than this score would suggest. That is, while Qwantum Leap claims to have a brilliant algorithm for predicting compatibility, it is in fact superficial – as reinforced by the superficiality of its creator, Jack, whose nationality would suggest that techno-capitalist values are American in provenance (more on this later). Indeed, after his one-night stand with Bridget, Jack turns up at her flat with Bridget's boot and other gifts so as to 'fast-forward' through their next few dates by talking about what hypothetically would have happened on them in order to get into 'a relationship' with Bridget, so that he can in turn legitimately act as the father of her child. Why Bridget does not throw out such a deluded man is not even broached within the film. But his description of their would-be dates also turns dates and dating themselves into superficial spectacles, or stories to be told, as opposed to experiences to be lived. In this way, we come to understand that dating apps, which by 2002 had already become the largest (legitimate) online paid content category (Illouz 2007: 76), are not about bringing people together, but about keeping them apart.

Indeed, how could internet dating sites not grow, except by virtue of the fact that more and more people are not in relationships? By this token, the dating site, with Tinder and hook-up sites like Blender as their logical extension, are techno-capitalist in their logic through their reinforcement of a sense of self, which in turn leads to a sense of solitude/solipsism, which in turn leads to the use of the site or app in a bid not to find a real relationship, but in order to find sex (in order to satisfy sexual desire) so as to continue being sovereign and alone. In some senses contrary to Lahad, then, singledom is not just an abject condition, whose members stand at the margins of mainstream society. Singledom is, in fact, the guiding logic of mainstream society: everyone is abjected or cast to the margins, made to feel alone and unhappy with their lot, in a bid precisely to control through fear one's behaviour, which becomes a relentless pursuit of a promised happiness that never arrives (except perhaps by consuming more – akin to what Gill (2008: 441–2) calls 'the makeover paradigm').

With dating websites, apps and Google functioning in the film as an expression of contemporary digital (and neoliberal capitalist and patriarchal) culture, the internet more generally can be understood as a chamber in which we allow our otherwise repressed desires to be expressed, rendered into data and thus commodified for the purposes of controlling those desires by never fulfilling them but by always leaving them unfulfilled (FOMO). In this way, it also involves the very economisation of desire, such that even that which is unconscious is turned into a market. Filth now no longer is an escape from the proper world of property (*propre* is the French term both for clean and for self); it, too, has been given an algorithm and has been brought under the control of techno-capital. If even our unconscious desires are thus working for capital, small wonder that we cannot think any more to change the world or to embrace collective resistance/collectivity as resistance to atomisation, as we do not just watch films that feature clichéd characters like the bubbly make-up lady, the sassy news reporter and the ne'er-do-well protagonist, but we also turn ourselves into those clichés as we begin to be defined and to define ourselves by our online profiles, which by definition are simplifications, perhaps even falsifications, of our embodied, flesh-world selves. If techno-capitalism induces solipsism and apathy, then this brings us to the role of politics in *Bridget Jones's Baby*, which, as we shall see, pays lip service to political engagement, but which ultimately gives expression to a burgeoning xenophobia.

Xenophobia

Bridget Jones's Baby presents to us a would-be critique of the neoliberalisation of the workplace as new boss Alice (Kate O'Flynn) arrives to turn Hard News from offering deep insight into contemporary global issues to running meme-like stories such as cats that look like Hitler. In principle, this coalescence with the attention economy involves an impoverishment of news (or what Alice refers to as 'olds'). But, in fact, the desire not to engage with politics characterises *Bridget Jones's Baby* as a whole, for while Bridget gets to speechify at Alice about her neoliberal values ('I'd rather be old fashioned and unemployed than be part of a show that celebrates the inane'), Bridget has done little to help another pregnant floor manager, whom we also hear was fired earlier in the film for being pregnant. What is more, the film features jokes about genocide, sexual torture and feminism, with the greatest challenge posed to news presenters not being how to report insightfully on the killing going on in a fictional place called Mirabundi (in an Africa where genocide 'just happens'), but correctly pronouncing the name of one of the generals from there (Nkoche). Meanwhile, barrister Mark says that he would 'prefer some good, old-fashioned genocide' to the case that he recently has been working on – as the counsel for a group of dissident foreign women clearly based on Pussy Riot, but here called Poonani (a name that also links foreignness to 'filthy' sex, as well as a 'filthy' feminism, as explored below).

Bridget is fired for mistaking the chauffeur (Chooye Bay) of Asian General Lu Tong (who stands charged with human rights abuses perpetrated by his government) for the General himself (Bruce Wang) – this after having allowed a group of men to bare their backsides on a live broadcast at the launch of the Hard News interactive website. And yet, given that both the bare backsides and the mistaken chauffeur are likely to attract rather than to put off viewers, not least because such 'errors' mean that the news constitutes its own news story, it makes no sense for Bridget to be fired – since she creates the kind of images that attract huge audiences. This value came to the fore recently in the widely viewed interruption by the children and wife of Professor Robert Kelly during a 2017 interview with the BBC: barely anyone recalls that Kelly was discussing the impeachment of Park Geun-hye; only the funny intrusion into the video of his children and then his wife are remembered (Johnston 2017). If Bridget is fired, then, it is because she embodies the supposedly 'inane' principles of Alice all too well. That is, in her total incapacity to engage with the clear human rights violations that are taking place around her, instead being completely absorbed with her love life, Bridget Jones – and by extension *Bridget Jones's Baby* – is not the antithesis of neoliberalism, but its perfect realisation.

Recalling McRobbie's analysis of *Bridget Jones's Diary*, it is also worth noting that feminism in particular becomes 'unbelievably annoying' as Shazzer (Sally Phillips) complains about how her arrival at Bridget's hospital bed after the birth of William was delayed as a result of a march related to Poonani. 'I mean, honestly, do we need any more rights?' asks Bridget's mother when she arrives, complaining about the same hold-up in traffic. However, where McRobbie suggests that feminism is spectral, shadowy and almost hated in the first film, fifteen years later it is present, 'filthy' (Poonani comes from a Jamaican creole slang term for vagina) and overtly hated for it.

We might argue that Bridget does get involved in the political campaign that her mother (Gemma Jones) is running to be part of her local parish council. She is clearly a Tory, given that her campaign colours are blue, and here we get to the conservative heart of the film. Bridget tells her mother that her campaign needs to be more inclusive and to include gays and immigrants and the like. With this in mind, her mother develops a more inclusive and ultimately successful campaign. What a wonderfully open film, we might think. And yet this is a film that is overtly middle-class and almost exclusively white. The owners of Gianni's are stereotypically Italian ('watsa da matter?'), while the only non-white character in the film is a man called Ariyaratna Sithamparanathan (Nick Mohammad), a name over which Bridget stumbles several times, before expressly excluding him from the lunch to which he thinks he has been invited. 'Bridget Jones is in labour,' the team at Hard News shout towards the film's climax. Clearly, they do not mean the political party.

Significantly, Ariyaratna is presented as a dullard to viewers as he tries to explain that he is a data manager – the other characters stopping him short from answering questions about his work, since inevitably he is boring. Paradoxically, then, information technology is denied to us as boring (even though Jack might well have something to discuss with Ariyaratna since they both work in the same sector), while through his ethnicity Ariyaratna functions as a reminder of the outsourced and exploitative labour upon which contemporary information technology industries rely. More than this, Ariyaratna seems to highlight the very whiteness of *Bridget Jones's Baby* and the very whiteness of its protagonist's world. With Bridget falling into the mud when dressed in white, sexual desire is associated with filth and the foreignness of Jack. Played by Patrick Dempsey, there is also a sense in which Jack carries with him the sort of postracial (interracial) relationships that characterise a supposedly colour-blind show like *Grey's Anatomy* (for more on this, see Warner 2015: 72 ff.). Poonani is a distasteful word to the majority of the characters in *Bridget Jones's Baby*, associated as it is with Jamaican history, dissident femi-nism and the foreignness of its members. No wonder, then, that Renée Zellweger is a by-word for whiteness in African American slang, for *Bridget Jones's Baby* would seem to reaffirm a white, middle-classed and conservative/xenophobic anti-feminism over alternative identities – and all in the name of a would-be progressive postfeminism (concerning how this latter is the preserve of whiteness, see Butler 2013).

Algorithmic Cinema

Of equal importance is how the film's characters do not want to know about algorithms – even though the latter do not so much find us partners as ver-ily play a key role in controlling our lives. To return to a point intimated earlier, algorithmic culture is thus 'othered' both as American (Jack) and as an unpronounceable and foreign name (Ariyaratna), about which the film's characters (and, by extension, its ideal audience?) wish to remain ignorant. And yet, as is made clear by the 2018 investigations into Ameri-can companies like Google and Facebook, as well as accusations regard-ing the rigging/influencing of election results by Russian hackers, data concerning internet users perhaps constitute the very stakes upon which our political and cultural futures depend – as those data are transformed into systems of control. Jack may be associated with filth but he also has the dirt on every Qwantum Leap user, such that he can, in principle, con-trol their very desires (arranging marriages for people). Bridget's rejection of Jack (and of the algorithm, which wanted to convince her of their 97 per cent compatibility) may signify a rejection of the American giants of data collection in favour of the parochial (white, middle-class Britishness). But, as discussed above, that ending rings false. Indeed, it suggests how conservative, white and middle-class British values were always already an algorithm, in the sense of being a tool for control, whereby the sup-pression of one's own desire (deliberately rejecting the supposedly better match) functions as a means for controlling society by relegating annoying feminists, boring foreigners and upstart Americans to the outside – even though they respectively stand for justice and give Mark a job, make a vital contribution to the UK's information technology sector, and are an object of desire.

If, in some senses, *Bridget Jones's Baby* is a critique of algorithmic culture, then there is perhaps some irony in that the film is itself a movie-by-algorithm that ticks so many boxes of the contemporary rom-com (stereotypical characters, moments of supposed mistaken identity, comedy by contact embarrassment, a final wedding and so on), while offering little in the way of depth or originality, even as it claims to cri-tique the superficial and inane nature of the contemporary world. Given the box-office success of the film (grossing just under US$212 million on a production budget of US$35 million), it would seem that audiences are entirely happy with the superficial, suggesting that movies always were precursors to algorithms as a means to influence and perhaps even to control society's desires. If the film's story tries to claim that the algo-rithms cannot work because they lack the human dimension, the success of the film itself would suggest that the algorithms work all too well.

Conclusion

To summarise the Anglo-American relationships developed in the film, the American dimensions of *Bridget Jones's Baby*, especially its stars, do not just suggest the techno-capitalist aspirations of this otherwise 'British' (or rather Anglo-American) film, as it seeks success in at least the British and American markets. They also allow the film to express an otherwise repressed reality. For as Bridget rejects Jack and gets together with Mark again, thereby reaffirming the distinctly white, middle-class British nature of their world, the American character of Jack allows space for filth and for the foreign to enter into the film's *mise-en-scène* – albeit that his is the acceptable white foreignness of techno-capital, with the film also enacting the suppression of different races and ethnicities, as mentioned.

In the era of Brexit as an expression of a capitalist desire not to touch or to be touched by anyone else, but rather to reduce the other and the self to merely a spectacle or an image, thus reinforcing one's sense of sover-eignty and self as separate from others (or what I am also calling atomisa-tion), the film helps to demonstrate the inescapability of filth, even as our unconscious desires become vented on the internet and then economised by the all-controlling algorithms of Google and other internet companies. If the links between the UK and the US constitute a historically 'spe-cial relationship', then the 'special relationship' that *Bridget Jones's Baby* depicts involves the rejection of the American other, but which really is the adoption of the exclusive and algorithmic ways of that American other, an 'adoption' that has at its own heart deeply conservative British values (white, middle-class values as a kind of pre-algorithm for control). This complex nexus of Anglo-American relationships is made clear by the presence of Zellweger as the American-other-as-British who lies at the heart of the film (and whose white appearance is heavily scrutinised, not least when undergoing perceived alterations of appearance, as happened in 2014 [Frost 2016]). For if Zellweger famously 'completes' Jerry Maguire in the film of that name (*Jerry Maguire* 1996), in some senses she also 'completes' the relationship between the US and the UK. The seeming rejection of the US, then, is really the adoption of American techno-capitalist values, since these have at their core the same solipsism as conservative British values. As Britain votes for Brexit and as the US votes for Donald J. Trump, in their respective bids for renewed sovereignty and separation (along national, class and racial lines), the US and the UK do indeed 'complete' each other in their respective solipsisms.

Notes

1. There are, of course, precursors to the British desire of Americans, most often represented as British men wanting American women. This can be seen in particular in the work of Richard Curtis, with *Four Weddings and a Funeral* (1994), *Notting Hill* (1999), *Love Actually* (2003) and *About Time* (2013) all involving British men in relationships with American women – with *Love Actually*'s Colin (Kris Marshall) in particular hoping to travel to the US in order to have a threesome with American women.
2. The association between Joanna Scanlan and perceived unattractiveness perhaps reaches its apogee in *Pin Cushion* (2017), where she plays a hunch-backed mother who eventually commits suicide after repeatedly being rejected from society as a result of her appearance.

Works Cited

Ahmed, S. (2010), *The Promise of Happiness*, Durham, NC: Duke University Press.

Aragay, M., and G. López (2005), 'Inf(l)ecting *Pride and Prejudice*: Dialogism, Intertextuality, and Adaptation', in M. Aragay (ed.), *Books in Motion: Adaptation, Intertextuality, Authorship*, Amsterdam: Rodopi, pp. 201–20.

Bridget Jones's Diary, film, directed by S. Maguire. UK and US: Working Title, 2001.

Bridget Jones: The Edge of Reason, film, directed by B. Kidron. UK and US: Working Title, 2004.

Bridget Jones's Baby, film, directed by S. Maguire. UK and US: Working Title, 2016.

Brown, W. (2015), *Undoing the Demos: Neoliberalism's Stealth Revolution*, New York: Zone.

Butler, J. (2013), 'For White Girls Only? Postfeminism and the Politics of Inclusion', *Feminist Formations*, 25:1, pp. 35–58.

Cobb, S. (2008), 'Adaptable Bridget: Generic Intertextuality and Postfeminism in *Bridget Jones's Diary*', in J. Boozer (ed.), *Authorship in Film Adaptation*, Austin: University of Texas Press, pp. 281–304.

Frost, C. (2016), 'Renee Zellweger Explains Altered Looks that Led to Mistaken Plastic Surgery Speculation in 2014', *Huffington Post*, 9 February. Available at: <https://www.huffingtonpost.co.uk/entry/renee-zellweger-bridget-jones-altered-looks_uk_57c9492fe4b09f5b5e35f486?guccounter=1> (last accessed 31 May 2018).

Gentleman, A. (2018), '"I Felt Like Dirt": Disabled Canadian Woman told to Leave UK After 44 Years', *The Guardian*, 24 April. Available at: <https://www.theguardian.com/uk-news/2018/apr/24/canadian-woman-told-to-leave-uk-margaret-obrien> (last accessed 28 April 2018).

Gill, R. (2007), 'Postfeminist Media Culture: Elements of a Sensibility', *Cultural Studies*, 10:2, pp. 147–66.

Gill, R. (2008), 'Culture and Subjectivity in Neoliberal and Postfeminist Times', *Subjectivity*, 25, pp. 432–45.

Grierson, J. (2018), 'Ministers Must Have Known of Removals Target, Says Former Immigration Chief', *The Guardian*, 27 April. Available at: <https://www.theguardian.com/politics/2018/apr/27/ministers-must-have-known-of-removals-targets-says-former-immigration-chief> (last accessed 28 April 2018).

Illouz, E. (2007), *Cold Intimacies: The Making of Emotional Capitalism*, Cambridge: Polity.

Jerry Maguire, film, directed by C. Crowe. US: TriStar, 1996.

Johnston, C. (2017), 'Prof Robert Kelly: "We were worried the BBC would never call us again"', *The Guardian*, 15 March. Available at: <https://www.theguardian.com/media/2017/mar/14/robert-kelly-children-interrupt-live-bbc-interview-south-korea> (last accessed 28 April 2018).

Lahad, K. (2017), *A Table for One: A Critical Reading of Singlehood, Gender and Time*, Manchester: Manchester University Press.

Love Actually, film, directed by R. Curtis. UK and US: Working Title, 2003.

McRobbie, A. (2003), 'Mothers and Fathers, Who Needs Them?', *Feminist Review*, 75:1, pp. 129–36.

McRobbie, A. (2004), 'Notes on Postfeminism and Popular Culture: Bridget Jones and the New Gender Regime', in A. Harris (ed.), *All About the Girl: Culture, Power, and Identity*, London: Routledge, pp. 3–14.

Negra, D. (2009), *What a Girl Wants? Fantasizing the Reclamation of Self in Postfeminism*, Abingdon: Routledge.

Pin Cushion, film, directed by D. Hayward. UK: BFI Film, 2017.

Pride and Prejudice, television series, directed by S. Langton. UK: BBC1, 1995.

Rüll, L. M. (2008), 'A Soundtrack for Our Lives: Chick-Flick Music', in S. Ferriss and M. Young (eds), *Chick Flicks: Contemporary Women at the Movies*, Abingdon: Routledge, pp. 79–91.

Sontag, S. (1979), *On Photography*, London: Penguin.

Warner, K. J. (2015), *The Cultural Politics of Colorblind TV Casting*, London: Routledge.

CHAPTER 4

Sharon Horgan, Postfeminism and the Transatlantic Psycho-politics of 'Woemantic' Comedy

Caroline Bainbridge

In her multiple roles as performer, writer, director, producer and show-runner, Sharon Horgan has become one of the most influential television comedy figures on both sides of the Atlantic in the 2010s.[1] Her success in breaking into the notoriously difficult US context as an Irish artist with a track record of writing for British television is striking, not least because of her markedly unapologetic, 'in-your-face' style. She is often revered as a 'queen of difficult women' (Wiseman 2016), and her work in shows such as *Pulling* (2006–9), *Catastrophe* (2015–) and *Divorce* (2016–) depicts what critics refer to as the 'brutal' (Blake 2016), 'bleak' (Wollaston 2016) existence of 'brittle' (Gray 2016) women who regularly 'f*** up' (Horgan, in Armstrong 2016). Horgan's comedies tackle complex and uncomfortable aspects of contemporary heterosexual womanhood that seemingly resonate for some women on both sides of the Atlantic in ways that I will link to the popular discursive 'postfeminist sensibility' (Gill 2007) that is highly evident across US/UK cultural contexts. The shows grapple with the postfeminist emphasis on heterosexual 'romance' as a key arbiter of selfhood, offering relief through humour from the paradoxical pressures of postfeminism while navigating the imperatives of relatedness at the same time. Looking primarily at *Catastrophe* and *Divorce*, this chapter interrogates the idea of 'romance', and its tropes that are so familiar in both the US and UK (and beyond), as symptomatic of the complex entanglement of heterosexual womanhood with postfeminist imperatives, with the aim of exploring how romantic television comedy can unravel the psychological knots associated with the postfeminist experience.

When commenting on her work, Horgan has remarked that it amounts to a kind of personal therapy (Wiseman 2016). She draws on her own lived experience of relationships as well as that of trusted friends, suggesting that comedy works here as a form of therapeutic engagement not only for the writer, but also, perhaps, for audiences at home on both sides of the Atlantic. Despite the fact that Horgan usually co-writes her series, in press coverage of the work, she is usually singled out as lead author, and this chapter follows this logic, taking Horgan as its focus. It explores her narrative emphasis on women's experience of heterosexual relationships in an era that has seen both a marked shift away from an obedient mode of neoliberal postfeminist romance in popular culture, and a widespread 'therapeutic' turn in ideology and lifestyle protocols across the transatlantic context. Television markets are becoming increasingly transnational and television drama is routinely now produced with this market in mind. The transatlantic market has a particularly visible impact, allowing stars to migrate from localised fame to international visibility at speed, and, thanks to streaming services, audiences can now easily access the wider body of work by their preferred performers. The popularity of Horgan's work with audiences in both the UK and the US can be understood in this context. Much of this dynamic is explicitly put on show in *Catastrophe*, for example, where the use of American stars such as Rob Delaney and Carrie Fisher heightens the appeal of the show for both US and international audiences more broadly.[2] This chapter argues that Horgan's focus on the conundrums of postfeminism invites reflection on the scope of television comedy to examine and acknowledge the psychological burden of postfeminism and the anger that it can engender for women on both sides of the pond. It draws on psychoanalysis to show how Horgan's seemingly cruel, 'woemantic' television comedy constitutes an outlet for the unconscious anger that runs under the surface of everyday female experience in the UK and US contexts, where the appetite for such humour is insistent.

As suggested above, one of the interesting things about Horgan's work is how it has travelled. *Pulling* and *Catastrophe* are British shows, initially broadcast in the UK on BBC3 and Channel 4, respectively, before being picked up for distribution in the US via Amazon; meanwhile, there have been three attempts to remake *Pulling* for a US audience, with the most recent iteration at NBC employing Horgan and co-writer Dennis Kelly as executive producers (Andreeva 2016). The US success of her work led to Horgan's collaboration with Sarah Jessica Parker on HBO's *Divorce*, which, to date, has aired two seasons domestically on HBO, and in the UK on Sky Atlantic. The critical reception of Horgan's work on each side of the Atlantic is notably uniform, and *Divorce* has been described as 'the final chapter in Horgan's trilogy of the wryly observed life cycle of a relationship' (Birnbaum 2016). This overt linking of Horgan's US series to its British antecedents reinforces the affinities between women's fields of experience on both sides of the Atlantic, using the tropes of romance to explore contemporary hetero-femininities. What is more, as a UK-born Irish artist working in the US as well as in the UK, Horgan provides an interesting point of condensation for the historical and cultural links between Britain, Ireland and the US, and her decision to work with an American co-writer (Delaney) has contributed to building the broader international visibility of *Catastrophe* in particular. Both Delaney and Horgan regularly refer to their transatlantic creative process, which involved both email and in-person collaborations in Los Angeles and London, providing Horgan with her first experience of the US production context and opening up pathways for the development of her work. Following the success of *Catastrophe*, she took up invitations to work with global US giants HBO and Amazon, and established the international visibility of her production house, Merman.

The consistency of tone in reviews of Horgan's work over a period of eleven years and across both sides of the Atlantic is striking. The 'bleak sitcom' (Blake 2016), *Pulling*, is characterised as 'a savagely unromantic . . . hardline approach to female friendship' (Blundell 2016), showing women who are 'messy, flawed, and allowed to behave like complete reprobates' (Blake 2016) and using 'scabrous, filthy comedy' (Ramaswamy 2016) to show us young women's 'desperate, sordid singledom' (Wollaston 2016) in ways that are 'biting but tender, like a well-hung steak' (Ramaswamy 2016). *Catastrophe* has been heralded as a story of what happens 'when marital bliss curdles' (de Souza 2016) on 'the rocky road to intimacy' (Enker 2016). Horgan and Delaney are praised for their 'relentless, caustic unflinching' (Wilson 2016), 'brutally honest' (Birnbaum 2016), 'acerbic, mean-spirited, genuinely hilarious' (Bevan 2016) 'rage/romance hybrid' (McNamara 2016), in which they show 'the horror of a marriage in progress' (Levin and Bianco 2016). Similarly, *Divorce* is praised for 'delivering a kick to the nuptials' (Raeside 2016) and 'shining an uncomfortably bright light on the nature of romantic love and how fleeting it is' (de Souza 2016). In a direct reference to US show *Sex and the City* (1998–2004), some critics note that *Divorce* is 'anti-Carrie' (Dominus 2016) – Parker having previously been best known for her role as 'sexual anthropologist' Carrie Bradshaw in this earlier HBO series – and insists on remaining 'heavy on the bitters' (Poniewozik 2016), so that it 'stays mired in the angry muck' (Willa 2016). Horgan's work, then, overturns any dream of the 'happily ever after' fairy-tale aftermath of the postfeminist wedding myth (which is, of course, also transatlantic), and the 'relentless celebration of the wedding in contemporary female genres' described by Diane Negra (2009: 81) in her discussion of the 'hypermatrimonial turn in popular culture'. Horgan's emphasis on the woeful mundanity of everyday lives punctures this broader neoliberal paradigm, where the emphases are on choice, perfection, the power of positivity, and the socio-cultural capital that accrues from coupledom. The transatlantic critical reception of Horgan's work shows how 'happily ever after' fantasies of conjugal life are shot through with complex emotional experience that runs the gamut from irritation, through anger, to violence, and that brings to the surface the often rather difficult lived reality of postfeminist mythologies of love, romance, marriage and domestic life. The underbelly of transatlantic tropes of romance (which I am coining as 'woemance') is foregrounded here, providing images that offer relief through recognition and the opportunity for laughter.

Dismantling Postfeminist Mythologies: Horgan as 'Unruly Woman'

Comedy as a source of relief is theorised by Sigmund Freud (1905) as having its origins in key aspects of human nature, such as relatedness and the drive to transgress social norms. It provides a means of expressing and exploring the bonds between individuals, and matters of social convention and conformity. For Freud, comedy provides relief from repressing unpalatable, antisocial or 'uncivilised' ideas. It dispels pent-up energy, allowing the expression of transgressive thoughts and feelings. Throughout Horgan's work, relationships are key, providing the context for 'the comic impetus' (Mills 2009: 49) of her narratives. Building on the familiar trope of 'the unruly woman' (Rowe 1995), Horgan's work puts 'difficult' female experience and feelings centre screen, avoiding the use of pedestrian gendered stereotypes once so predominantly associated with the television sitcom. In *Pulling*, *Catastrophe* and *Divorce* alike, the female protagonists frequently discuss their tiresome embodied and emotional experience, giving voice in unexpected ways to dimensions of women's lives that frequently go unspoken in the scene of transatlantic popular culture.

In *Catastrophe*, for example, Sharon regularly discusses with Rob her concerns about sex, desire and the (perceived) failures of her ageing body in ways that are self-deprecating (although far from melancholy in tone), but that also invite positive reassurance. In this way, her work inverts dominant expectations of how comedy operates in relation to scenes of oppression and repression. Challenging Platonic (360 BCE) and Aristotelian (350 BCE) notions of comedy as a form of 'abuse', in which pleasure is taken at the expense of a ridiculed minority, Horgan's approach has more in common with the Hobbesian (1651) account of humour, in which it becomes a strategy with which those without much access to power can begin to assert their dominance. As a subversive intervention, comedy affords an outlet for criticism of both powerful ideological forces and their internalisation. As Alessandra Lemma suggests, humour promises the possibility of regenerative transformation, suggesting that 'comedy's purpose is to upset established personal assumptions, beliefs or values, as well as external social order in the service of change and hopefully progress' (Lemma 2000: 35).

Horgan's comic strategies include writing women with a penchant for crudely and boldly enunciating sometimes shocking or distasteful opinions and thoughts. These moments reveal the importance of incongruity in the conventions of comedy, such that the apparent disparity between what is *expected* of women and what women *actually* say and do produces laughter. However, as Kathleen Rowe has made clear, 'the figure of the unruly woman contains much potential for feminist appropriation, for rethinking how women are constructed as gendered subjects in the language of spectacle and the visual' (Rowe 1995: 11). Horgan's work offers a rich opportunity for the interrogation of postfeminist mythologies of obedient neoliberal modes of femininity and romance. By naming unpalatable thoughts and feelings, Horgan's female protagonists open up spaces of relationality for those viewers who identify with the tribulations of key characters, albeit that much of the drama is focused on a narrowly middle-class and notably straight and white orbit of experience. Humour, then, begins to serve its transgressive purpose, enabling viewers on both sides of the Atlantic not only to understand 'its revolutionary potential as a deflator of the patriarchal order' (Rich 2004: 78), but also to see it as a tool with which to push back against the constraints of neoliberal postfeminism.

As a body of work, Horgan's comedies send up Anglo-American ideological formations of contemporary middle-class womanhood, heterosexual coupledom, mid-life experience, and the failures of shared neoliberal aspirational cultures in both Britain and the States. In *Divorce* (set on the affluent US East Coast), there is a seeming shift upwards in terms of the socio-economic capital of Horgan's main characters compared to those in her British series. While in *Pulling* and *Catastrophe* (set in the UK), we see the female protagonists working in everyday office jobs, a café and state schools, in *Divorce*, Parker plays Frances, an apparently wealthy soon-to-be-ex-wife who has the wherewithal to open her own private art gallery in the affluent county of Westchester in the state of New York (though this sits in some contrast to the recent fortunes of her husband, who is struggling to recover from a series of poor property investments). In *Catastrophe*, Sharon and Rob mix in wealthy circles but fall into an economically precarious situation when Rob loses his job while Sharon is still on maternity leave, a scenario that highlights the complexities of navigating transatlantic romance when one partner needs to migrate into unfamiliar ways of life to become culturally assimilated. Rob's apparent emasculation and his reversion to alcoholism as a form of psychological defence speak to debates about the 'crisis' of white masculinity and its association with postfeminist logics. Despite this, however, Sharon and Rob continue to live in an expensive house in a fashionable area of London, and even when they eventually consider 'downsizing', they seek a smaller house with all the taste markers associated with a particularly bourgeois aesthetic. Austerity politics appear to bite at the heels of Horgan's protagonists, who nevertheless cling on to the last vestiges of their meritocratic class privilege, despite Horgan's men struggling to hold down jobs, whether they are self-employed (Robert [Thomas Haden Church] in *Divorce*), unemployed (Rob in *Catastrophe*) or simply unemployable (in the case of Billy (Paul Kaye) in *Pulling*). In both *Divorce* and *Catastrophe*, economic privilege and cultural capital mask the pain of financial precarity, speaking to the paradoxical socio-economic context of transatlantic neoliberal postfeminism, with its differently gendered pressure points.

Significantly, however, and despite their mobilisation of 'urban affluence and privilege' (Negra and Tasker 2013: 351), neither *Divorce* nor *Catastrophe* leaves its female protagonist unemployed as a result of entry into or departure from married coupledom. Instead, both Frances and Sharon are depicted as economic anchors for their families, reflecting real-life statistical shifts in both the US and European contexts,[3] and they seek escape from the 'retreatist domestic bliss' of family life described by Negra and Tasker (2013: 352) in their important work on the postfeminist logic of the recessionary chick flick. At the same time, their hapless male partners are shown as failing to meet the needs of the family while suffering depression, jealousy and addiction, so that their images resound with the 'end of men crises' paradigm (Tirado Gilligan 2011), in which white, male losses are held up as the corollary of women's independence. In Horgan's work, such visions provide a comic foil against which to proffer images of women on both sides of the Atlantic succeeding (despite the constraints of economic precarity) in terms that evade or, at least, work around the recessionary tropes of postfeminist womanhood associated with 'stay-at-home motherhood' (Orgad and de Benedictis 2015). Nevertheless, neither of these shows grapples explicitly with issues of social inequality, poverty or struggle, and the white, middle-class assumptions about entitlement and privilege that they convey are insufficiently challenged by the comic strategies on show, despite the relief that these provide.

Nevertheless, television comedy and its recent turn toward female-led and female-devised humour open up space in which to play with the tropes of transatlantic postfeminist culture in order better to expose their workings. As I discuss below, a psychoanalytic approach to the dynamics of such comedy makes a contribution to developing the kind of analytical strategies discussed by Tasker and Negra (2007: 22) in their call for scholars to explore the 'figurations of female agency' at work in postfeminism. It also enables us to reflect on how the changing guises of transatlantic postfeminism require understanding in order to excavate potential spaces in which to restore a notion of cultural 'value' to feminist critique, and to move beyond the 'normalisation' of female 'pathologies' described by Angela McRobbie (2009) in her analysis of postfeminist disorders.

For newspaper critics, and for certain viewers, there are important parallels between Frances Dufresne in *Divorce* and Carrie Bradshaw in *Sex and the City*. In fact, one critic notes that

> it's hard to escape the feeling that Horgan is essentially daring the audience to compare the two shows. 'Look,' she seems to be saying. 'Forget the happy ever after fantasy *Sex and the City* sold you – this is reality, dissatisfaction in the suburbs and a life where every time your husband repeats a punchline rather than simply laughing, a little part of you shrivels and dies'. (Hughes 2016)

Writing in *The Guardian* – a left-wing, middle-class British newspaper with an increasing focus on US lifestyle coverage, once again pointing to the ever closer affinities of transatlantic cultures – Hughes suggests that the success of Horgan's work hangs on its shrugging off of any lingering tropes of what she calls the 'fizz and fun' associated with obedient postfeminist neoliberal femininities, striving instead to deal with the 'anticipointment' of lived experience once the illusions of 'having it all' have shattered (Hughes 2016).

This leads me to consider the changing shape of transatlantic postfeminist sensibilities during the eleven-year period in which Horgan's work has been broadcast. The perils and dangers of the postfeminist trap have been well articulated by many feminists, including McRobbie (2009), who describes the feminist project as now having to deal with the 'aftermath' of postfeminism, an assessment that signals the disastrous consequences of the early phases of the sensibility for conceptualising any ongoing need for feminism itself. More recently, Rosalind Gill (2016a) has argued that the consequences of postfeminism's sustained ascendancy have left feminists in a bewildered state. As she puts it, 'for every uplifting account of feminist activism, there is another of misogyny; for every feminist 'win', an out-pouring of hate, ranging from sexual harassment to death threats against those involved; for every instance of feminist solidarity, another of vicious trolling' (Gill 2016a: 613). For Gill, one of the upshots is that feminism now has a range of distinctive modes, including 'celebrity feminism', 'style feminism', 'therapeutic feminism' and 'hot feminism' – all of which she describes as 'not just feminism-lite but feminism-weightless, unencumbered by the need to have a position on anything' (Gill 2016a: 618). I agree with Gill's suggestion that 'post-feminist media culture should be an *object of analysis*, not a position or a perspective' (Gill 2016a: 621, emphasis in original) and, in my view, it is essential to pay attention to how postfeminism as an object operates at the *psychological* level, as well as working through everyday mediated exchanges and cultural experience.

Reading Comedy as a Psychological Object

Psychoanalysis understands objects as mentally internalised representations of others with whom we enjoy relationships in real-life environments. In object relations theory, patterns of relatedness (for example, in romantic coupledom) are shaped by the lived and fantasied experience of other people and the life situations that we encounter during childhood, but also as adults whose lives are always in process. A sense of selfhood is inflected by and expressive of object relations, and psychical life is determined by the unconscious defensive and creative uses that we make of mechanisms such as identification, internalisation and projection. Elsewhere, I argue that 'media objects have become imbricated with identity . . . shaping ideas of the self as an on-going project', showing how 'personal emotional and psychological experience is mirrored in characters that populate the screen worlds of consumption' (Bainbridge 2011: 35). Postfeminism and neoliberalism are now widely agreed to have an impact on ideas of selfhood (Gill and Scharff 2011; Türken 2015), suggesting that they ought also to be understood as significant psychological objects. With this in mind, I contend that the affective dimensions and emotional textures of transatlantic postfeminist logics are displayed and lampooned for viewers in Horgan's comedies.

These ideas are usefully condensed in Horgan's choice of title for *Catastrophe*, articulating the complex, conflicted and ambivalent relationship to neoliberal imperatives for white, middle-class, heterosexual women in the US and the UK in the postfeminist era. Horgan's work also neatly foregrounds how such women internalise the often impossible contradictions associated with postfeminism in her characterisation of Karen (Tanya Franks) in *Pulling*. In episode 5 of season 1, after a heavy night of drinking, she asks advice from fellow primary school teacher, Anna (Oriane Messina):

Karen: Anna, can I have a word?

Anna: Oh, I'm just finishing a story . . .

Karen: Children, do you want a story or money?

Children: Money!!!

(Karen throws coins to the back of the classroom for children to chase.)

Karen: Anna, am I, er, bad as a person? Well, you know I've given up drinking? Well, I was just sort of wondering, when I *am* drinking, am I really that bad?

Anna: Well, at the last PTA, you did try to get off with my husband . . .

Karen: Anna, how many times have I gotta apologise for that?

Anna: Once would be nice.

Karen: I'm sorry, Anna. Look, just tell me, am I bad when I'm drinking?

Anna: Karen, you're a catastrophe when you're drinking!

Karen: Right, so I should keep this up then, carry on . . .?

Anna: I would.

Karen: Okay. So, what am I supposed to do? I mean, I'm finding it a bit hard to know what to actually do. I mean, what do you do with yourself on a Friday night, say?

Anna: I dunno – watch DVDs and stuff?

Karen: Watch DVDs?

Anna: Yes.

Karen: Watch DVDs. That's great.

Karen's incessant binge-drinking is a way of forgetting the dreadful realities of trying to 'have it all' in line with the postfeminist fantasy of romance and being 'coupled up'. Bingeing on drugs, drink and sex allows Karen to express a refusal of these social 'norms' but it also requires her to turn her experience against herself, against her own body in damaging and ultimately unhappy ways. The irony here, of course, is that at the end of *Pulling*, it is Karen who gets married to the drug-addled Billy, as Horgan cocks a snook at the postfeminist logic of women's desperation to find 'the one'. The comic form allows the writers to invert the 'standard' experience of postfeminist pressure here, providing a comic space of relief from the psychological work it requires and creating critical distance from its ideological pull. The politics of this are fascinating, showing how comedy provides a transatlantic vehicle for the repoliticisation of an ideological formation that often provokes unconscious anger and self-loathing in women, or what Gill refers to as 'toxic insecurity' (Gill 2016b: 619). With its capacity to provide relief through recognition of shared (and largely unspoken) dimensions of experience, and also to subvert hegemonic assumptions about hetero-femininity, female-led comedy shapes a different kind of encounter with postfeminist imperatives around romance and relationships. In Horgan's work, postfeminism is exposed as being catastrophic for the psychological health of women on both sides of the Atlantic who are struggling to live within its bounds, despite its affective resonances with everyday pleasures and experience.

In making this argument, I am focusing on the connotations of postfeminism on the one hand, and those associated with the transatlantic critical reception of Horgan's comedy shows on the other. As we see in the work of Gill (2007; 2016a; 2016b) and McRobbie (2009), the negative experience of postfeminism is something akin to a disaster or trap that provokes anger and self-deprecation, leading me to conjecture that, in its role as a psychological object, postfeminism operates in conflicting and contradictory ways. It exerts influence, shaping a constant monitoring of the self, one's relationships and impulses to conform to widespread conventions of femininity and coupledom inscribed in the disciplined body, and dominant notions of 'beauty' and 'desirability'. Yet, postfeminism also becomes an object of resentment, prompting the discourses of rage discussed by McRobbie (2009) and revealing the emotional entanglement of ambivalence with structures of self-esteem and confidence. Postfeminism, in its guise as a psychological object, then, is experienced mentally as a catastrophe of sorts. In its demand that heterosexual women conform to impossible ideological formations of gender grounded in body size, beauty regimes, domestic responsibility, romantic love, workplace success, consumer culture and female friendship, postfeminism articulates hetero-femininity as a bottomless, claustrophobic pit in which anxious female subjects become mired in self-loathing.

I have written elsewhere (Bainbridge 2013) about the envious culture of attack that this provokes between women who work unconsciously to defend against such intolerable psychological experience by deploying defensive mechanisms such as projection. Horgan's female-led transatlantic television comedy provides space for recuperation from such destructive strategies. It provides room for women to hold off the imperative for attack, whether on the self or on others, and to witness at a distance a representation of their angry affective inscriptions in the ideological field. Comedy, then, provides an important way into examining fantasies of relatedness with other women at the psychological level, allowing a critical distance on feelings and selfhood to emerge.

In his psychoanalytic writing about thought, representation and catastrophe, Wilfrid Bion (1965: 8) follows the *Oxford English Dictionary* definition[4] and suggests that a catastrophe is

an event producing a subversion of the order or system of things; it is catastrophic in the sense that it is accompanied by feelings of disaster in the participants; it is catastrophic in the sense that it is sudden and violent in an almost physical way.

As Robert Hinshelwood notes,

> Bion elevated the experience of catastrophe to the most normal of all experiences. Every change requires the dissolution of the mind and a reformation into a new structure of thoughts and feelings. Thus a catastrophe must occur before a new idea is digested. (Hinshelwood 1997: 307)

These insights into the psychological experience of catastrophe help with understanding the emotional experience of trying to live with the consequences of postfeminism and its impossible demands, as well as the shift that is taking place in women's behaviour toward other women, where anger is often unconsciously directed through attacks on likeness. The catastrophic consequences of such behaviour arguably crystallise as strains of misogyny deepen and intensify, and the global media circulation of campaigns such as #metoo and of the political opinions of celebrity female role models such as Meryl Streep, Jennifer Lawrence and so on contribute to bringing to consciousness the catastrophic consequences of a persistent unquestioning engagement with the challenges of postfeminist ideology. Instead of being internalised and relentlessly attached to aspects of femininity, rage can be turned outward, as shown in the liveliness and insistence of such feminist campaigns, and in the rise of global women's protest movements and marches for equality – the catastrophe of postfeminism has become catalytic.

'Woemance' and the 'Rage Revolution'

The language of transatlantic journalistic reviews of Sharon Horgan's shows highlights the rage-laden emotional legacy of postfeminism, underscoring its psychological negativity for women, as discussed above. The 'savage', 'desperate', 'sordid', 'scabrous', 'caustic', 'brutal', 'biting', 'angry' tone of Horgan's comedy speaks volumes about the state of women's minds in this regard, highlighting the psychological violence of living in times when Milo Yiannopoulos's (2016) dismissal of feminism as a 'cancer' and the trope of the 'nasty woman' serve as barometric indicators of the cultural climate in both European and US contexts. That a channel for the psychological anger induced by such experience is necessary hardly needs to be pointed out. Horgan's success in making a much revered transatlantic career move during the Trump era is notable here.

In this regard, the extensive media commentary on the recent successes of a swathe of women comedians in both the UK and the US is also important. The politically astute, feminist tone of work produced by performing writers such as Amy Schumer, Tina Fey, Amy Poehler, Phoebe Waller-Bridge, Horgan and others has been seen as marking the rise of a newly 'angry' female voice in comedy, though, again, the whiteness of this field as it is often evoked is notable, and in this respect one must also recognise the rapidly rising stars of black women comic performer–writers such as Issa Rae and Michaela Coel. Writing in *The Guardian*, Eleanor Morgan has noted the sea-change taking place in the writing of female television characters, describing this as a 'rage revolution':

> Through the strength of the script and the actors playing them, these female characters regularly unleash rage, and it's not always righteous. Sometimes it's un-pretty and without clear reason. But this is what it's like for so many women, who live and breathe a lifetime of cumulative anger but feel they should keep a cork in it for fear of the seepage being seen as a character defect. That is why these women are so thrilling to watch. (Morgan 2016)

What McRobbie (2009) notes as the 'illegible rage' of women in post-feminism can be articulated and worked through, thanks to the generic mechanisms of comedy. While Amanda Lotz has argued that 'feminist discourse is predominantly found in the comedy genre because of narrative and generic qualities that both introduce and then contain potentially subversive content' (2001: 111), Horgan's rage and subversive humour overspill into the reception context, as seen in the reviews cited above. Comedy inflects the culture around it, enriching its political potency.

In Horgan's work, examples of anger are legion. In *Catastrophe*, for example, the very premise of the show's central relationship is founded on the mindlessness of a dominant 'hook-up', 'no strings attached' transatlantic sexual culture in which commitment, love and marriage are simply not on the table. Sharon and Rob's entanglement results in an unexpected baby, a deeply counter-generic marriage proposal and an ongoing narrative excavation of the messy underside of late-in-life ('geriatric') pregnancy, contemporary marriage and faltering sexual desire, the emotional and economic strains of metropolitan life, the sheer difficulty of mid-life feelings of helplessness and isolation, and the struggle to negotiate a transatlantic relationship with relatives scattered between the US, Ireland and the UK.

All of this is painfully put on show in this series. Within the first ten minutes of the first episode, Sharon meets Rob, an American who is in London on business for one week, subsequently discovers that she is pregnant, gets a diagnosis of pre-cancer and calls her best friend Fran 'a cunt'. Sharon catastrophises throughout, expecting everything to go wrong because it conceivably could, and she makes frequent wry, woeful jokes grounded in embodied experience and cultural attitudes. And yet her relationship with Rob pans out, albeit that it is often strained, turning the tenets of postfeminism (and the romcom) on their head. 'Having it all' is no longer equated with 'having a ball' here, and the stock romantic fantasy of happiness ensuing from marriage and love is exposed, as the sometimes tough emotional work involved in forging and sustaining committed relationships is depicted for viewers. Indeed, *Elle Magazine* explicitly hails the appeal of the show in terms that highlight this, explaining that Sharon and Rob 'are relationship goals even though they suck at their relationship' (Manson 2017).

If transatlantic postfeminism has produced this shift in the order of things, despite its neoliberal constraints, then following Bion's definition, *Catastrophe* is the perfect moniker for the show. In its deft sidestepping of the tropes of romantic comedy, such as the meet-cute and the fairy-tale wedding, we see the possibility of the dissolution of a postfeminist state of mind, and watch as the show recalibrates ideas of love and its associated woes in ways that feel more honest, lifelike and, indeed, feminist. (The show's feminism is expressly linked to its frank and frequent description of women's embodied experience of ageing, sexuality and mental health, and of the complex contradictions of femininity in the twenty-first century.) Sharon and Rob declare their love for one another only at the end of the final episode of season 2. And yet the show is celebrated for its depiction of the 'reality' of love and married life, such that, even in *America: The Jesuit Review*, one of the oldest US periodicals with a focus on Catholic faith and culture, Eloise Blondiau suggests that 'the beauty of marriage can show itself in those messy moments – no rose-tinted glasses required' (Blondiau 2017).

In *Divorce*, however, any hope vested in such imagery is once again overturned as we witness the ease with which it is possible to veer away from the mundanity of a humourless relationship through divorce. The show is candid in its exposé of the implicit misogyny at work around women in the US legal system, and its 'brutality' is often couched in the willingness of male lawyers, builders and soon-to-be-ex-husbands to vilify women. Frances is variously called a 'man-devouring bitch' and '*una vieja* [an old woman]' who is '*bien loca* [totally crazy]'; and her narcissistic ex-lover, Julian (Jemaine Clement), turns up at her gallery opening to tell her that he cyberstalks her every night, for which interest she should be thankful. The misogynist frame of experience is writ large, making uncomfortable viewing at times, and also giving licence to some critics to echo this misogyny in their reviews. In *The Daily Telegraph*, a British right-wing broadsheet, Benji Wilson (2016) remarks, 'Unfortunately, owing in large part to my distaste for her character in *Sex and the City* (the emotionally incontinent Carrie Bradshaw), Parker is a woman on whom I might wish a messy divorce', while, in *The Times*, Hugo Rifkind states,

> I'm already totally rooting for the husband . . . she also still looks a hell of a lot like Carrie Bradshaw in *Sex and the City*, and she was just one of the worst things that has ever existed . . . that show always seemed to – oh, God, is this going to sound bad? – bring out the raving misogynist in me. (Rifkind 2016)

The feminism of Horgan's work becomes more entrenched here, showing how contemporary women's battles with misogyny are certainly not purely internalised.

What women viewers' appetite for unbridled, 'in-your-face' honesty signals, I believe, is that a shift is taking place in the popular cultural ideological formation of gender politics. Bion argues that a catastrophe entails psychical development from a pre-catastrophic mental state to a post-catastrophic one. This shift can be measured by observing where violence lies and where it is enacted and expressed. In order to move to a post-catastrophic context, the violence of experience must be externalised so that it can be seen for what it is, rather than simply having to be deduced. In their display of unconscious anger, contemporary female-authored comedies externalise the psychological violence associated with postfeminist experience. The 'woemantic' comic form enables this because of its containing boundaries, and the licence it gives for laughter and relief as experience becomes recognised. Following Hinshelwood, then, I argue that shows such as Horgan's lead to a potential relinquishing of the postfeminist mind-set, and enable the reformation of alternative structures of thought and feeling around how to conceptualise femininity and, indeed, feminism. In this way, as Steven Groarke (2014: 34) has suggested, 'catastrophic reaction is a hopeful mode of psychic functioning' that opens up spaces for utopian longing for whatever has been violently savaged.

'Woemance', then, has its upsides, depicting experience in ways that resonate for female viewers on both sides of the Atlantic because they feel 'honest'. A key feature of the transatlantic relationship generated though Horgan's work is linked to the contexts of reception and consumption: viewers feel connected to Horgan (in the US) and to Parker (in the UK), thanks to their celebrity appeal and 'honest' depictions of femininity. For some feminist critics, claims to honesty simply perpetuate the cycles of postfeminism, as seen in discussions of Lena Dunham's *Girls* (2012–17) (Weitz 2016; Genz 2017). Here, strains of honesty are complicated by the structures of narcissistic self-fashioning that underpin the narrative as a whole. In Horgan's work, by contrast, and in the comic work of writers such as Fey and Schumer, honesty is contrived alongside unapologetic refusals of hegemonic expectations of what constitutes 'feminine' behaviour. As Gina Barreca notes in her discussion of Fey and Poehler, 'A woman making humor and creating comedy is a woman who is not going to apologise for wanting to be in control' (Barreca 2013: xxxiii). Appraising Fey's work on *30 Rock* (2006–13) as a form of camp that is grounded in the contradictions of postfeminism, Katrin Horn notes that the show usefully combines 'elements of critical distance and affective involvement to foster the audience's *detached attachment* to its central female characters' (Horn 2017: 111, my emphasis). Horgan's work cannot be assessed as camp; however, as this chapter has sought to show, by thinking about postfeminism as a psychological object and by focusing on its impact on the lived experience of romance and relatedness, it is possible to map the distance described by Horn at the level of fantasy.

This highlights the role of humour in manufacturing a move away from the kinds of narcissistic investment in the production of obedient selves in the neoliberal context, and from the popular cultural representations of neoliberal selfhood that dominate Anglo-American televisual fictions. Understanding the psychological dimension of the attachments of both viewers and critics to female characters enriches the critical and political scope of analysis, and enables discourses of relatedness to transcend the boundaries imposed on women through the discursive structures of postfeminism. Comedy such as that authored by Horgan walks a line between postfeminist experience and feminist interruptions of it by using everyday (and partially autobiographical) life experience to challenge assumptions about what it means to be a heterosexual woman in the contemporary contexts of middle-class America and Britain. Heather Brook argues that 'unorthodox, transgressive, or subversive ways of doing heterosexuality and being heterosexual' should be understood as 'heterodoxy' – a concept that 'cautions against understanding heterosexuality as always/already sexist, homophobic, and oppressive'. For Brook, heterodoxy 'aims not to recuperate or apologize for heterosexuality's sometimes brutal practices, but to seek out ways of theorizing change in the realm of the dominant' (Brook 2015: 250).

Horgan's comedy could be thought of as heterodoxical in this context, not least because of the critical distance that it manufactures on tropes of both heteronormative romance and postfeminist womanhood. Employing a psychoanalytic approach to thinking about how such comedy articulates spaces for relatedness and relationality between women deepens our understanding of the close imbrication of an entrenched postfeminist sensibility and a re-emergent logic of feminist critique, adding to the array of feminist critical methodologies. Humour, after all, has a socially binding role and 'its constructive effects are best observed in its function as a means of reconciliation: affirmation of common values; asking and giving support; bridging differences and reassurance' (Lemma 2000: 17). As E. B. White suggests, 'It is a catastrophe to be without a voice' (White 1970: 72). Horgan's body of comic work gives voice to the Anglo-American postfeminist experience of women who identify with her protagonists, as well as to those who take pleasure in viewing the depiction of women's rage and discontent with neoliberal, white, middle-class strictures. Horgan's heterodoxical style opens up space for diverse groups of women to find important psychological room for identification, relief and reflection. In some ways, then, 'woemance' should be understood as 'wo(e)man-ce', putting women and the feminine centre screen. There is little woeful in that.

Notes

1. During the course of writing this chapter, Amazon Studios announced a two-year collaboration with Merman, the production company established by Horgan with Clelia Mountford (Clarke 2018; Keady 2018). Remarking on the decision to work with Horgan, Amazon Studios' Head of Scripted Development, Sharon Tal Yguado, noted that Horgan's 'strong creative voice and storytelling sensibility have resonated with audiences globally' (Clarke 2018), signalling the extent to which Horgan has become the public face of success for her work, despite the fact that much of it is co-written. One could conjecture that Horgan's screen presence in *Pulling* and *Catastrophe* intensifies the sense of her as the author of both the fiction and the humour; but it is worth noting that she is also usually the agent of publicity for *Motherland* (2016–), on which she does not take an on-screen role, and other series on which she has worked with Graham Linehan or Dennis Kelly.
2. The production company Avalon states that *Catastrophe* has, to date, sold in nearly 150 countries worldwide, as well as being adapted as a scripted format in Canada, where the show was successfully remade for French language broadcaster Super Ecran (Avalon Television).
3. In 2015, IPPR, The Progressive Policy Think Tank, reported that that one-third of mothers in UK working families are breadwinners (Cory and Stirling 2015). According to *The Modern Families Index 2017*, more than 68 per cent of British families are dual-earner households (Working Families 2017: 7). In the US, 42 per cent of mothers are sole or primary breadwinners, with a further 22.4 per cent being part of a dual-earning household (Glynn 2016).
4. According to the *Oxford English Dictionary*, 'catastrophe' is defined as '1. An event causing great and usually sudden damage or suffering; a disaster. 1.1 Something very unfortunate or unsuccessful. 2. The denouement of a drama, especially a classical tragedy'.

Works Cited

Andreeva, N. (2016), '*Pulling* UK Comedy Gets NBC Remake from Molyneux Sisters and Sharon Horgan', *Deadline*, 4 November. Available at: <http://deadline.com/2016/11/pulling-uk-comedy-nbc-remake-molyneux-sisters-sharon-horgan-1201849062/> (last accessed 9 April 2018).

Aristotle (2000 [350 BCE]), *The Nicomachean Ethics*, Oxford: Oxford University Press.

Armstrong, K. (2016), 'Mum's the Word for Sharon and SJP: Horgan Tells How the Pair Bonded Over Being Working Mothers', *Daily Mirror*, Ireland edition, 11 October, p. 4.

Avalon Television, 'Catastrophe'. Available at: <http://distribution.avalontelevision.com/catastrophe/> (last accessed 20 May 2019).

Bainbridge, C. (2011), 'From "The Freud Squad" to "The Good Freud Guide": A Genealogy of Media Images of Psychoanalysis and Reflections on Their Role in the Public Imagination', *Free Associations: Psychoanalysis, Media, Culture, Groups*, 62, pp. 31–59. Available at: <http://freeassociations.org.uk/FA_New/OJS/index.php/fa/article/view/43> (last accessed 9 April 2018).

Bainbridge, C. (2013), 'The Spectacle of Envy and Femininity in the Press: A Psycho-cultural Perspective', in A. Mateos-Aparicio Martín-Albo and E. de Gregorio-Godeo (eds), *Culture and Power: Identity and Identification*, Newcastle: Cambridge Scholars Press, pp. 217–32.

Barreca, G. (2013), *They Used to Call Me Snow White . . . But I Drifted: Women's Strategic Use of Humor*, Hanover, NH: University of New England Press.

Bevan, N. (2016), 'The Dark Art of a Superb Sitcom', *Wales on Sunday*, *7 Days* magazine, p. 3.

Bion, W. (1965), *Transformations*, London: Tavistock.

Birnbaum, D. (2016), 'From *Catastrophe* to *Divorce*: Sharon Horgan Wryly Observes Relationships', *Variety*, 5 October. Available at: <http://variety.com/2016/tv/features/sharon-horgan-catastrophe-divorce-hbo-sarah-jessica-parker-1201877898/> (last accessed 15 March 2017).

Blake, M. (2016), 'On the Dark Side of Light: In *Catastrophe*, *Divorce*, Sharon Horgan Finds Humor in "Horrific Awfulness"', *Los Angeles Times*, 9 October. Available at: <http://www.latimes.com/entertainment/tv/la-ca-st-sharon-horgan-divorce-hbo-20161007-snap-story.html> (last accessed 22 March 2018).

Blondiau, E. (2017), 'While *Master of None* Looks for Love, *Catastrophe* Finds It', *America: The Jesuit Review*, 26 May. Available at: <https://www.americamagazine.org/arts-culture/2017/05/26/while-master-none-looks-love-catastrophe-finds-it> (last accessed 1 June 2017).

Blundell, G. (2016), 'Disasters of Romance and Other "Bad Stuff"', *The Australian*, 20 October, p. 17.

Brook, H. (2015), 'Bros Before Ho(mo)s: Hollywood Bromance and the Limits of Heterodoxy', *Men and Masculinities*, 18:2, pp. 249–66.

Catastrophe, TV series, created by R. Delaney and S. Horgan. UK and US: Avalon Television, 2015– .

Clarke, S. (2018), '*Catastrophe, Divorce* Co-creator Sharon Horgan Inks Overall Deal with Amazon', *Variety*, 16 January. Available at: <http://variety.com/2018/tv/news/catastrophe-sharon-horgan-amazon-studios-1202664979/> (last accessed 28 April 2018).

Cory, G., and A. Stirling (2015), 'Who's Breadwinning in Europe?', IPPR The Progressive Policy Think Tank. Available at: <https://www.ippr.org/publications/whos-breadwinning-in-europe> (last accessed 24 September 2018).

de Souza, A. (2016), 'HBO's *Divorce* Plumbs Marital Failure for Tragi-comic Laughs', *The Straits Times*, 19 October. Available at: <https://www.straitstimes.com/lifestyle/entertainment/engaging-slice-of-life> (last accessed 22 March 2018).

Divorce, TV series, created by S. Horgan. UK and US: HBO Entertainment, 2016–.

Dominus, S. (2016), 'Sarah Jessica Parker, Leaving Carrie Behind with HBO's *Divorce*', *New York Times*, 25 September. Available at: <https://www.nytimes.com/2016/09/25/arts/television/sarah-jessica-parker-leaving-carrie-behind-with-hbos-divorce.html> (last accessed 22 March 2018).

Enker, D. (2016), '*Catastrophe* Is Certainly No Disaster', *Canberra Times*, 2 October, Section C, p. 3.

Freud, S. (1905), *Jokes and Their Relation to the Unconscious. The Standard Edition of the Complete Psychological Works of Sigmund Freud, Volume VIII*, London: Hogarth Press, pp. 1–247.

Genz, S. (2017), '"I Have Work . . . I Am Busy . . . Trying To Become Who I Am": Neoliberal *Girls* and Recessionary Postfeminism', in M. Nash and I. Whelehan (eds), *Reading Lena Dunham's Girls*, Basingstoke: Palgrave Macmillan, pp. 17–30.

Gill, R. (2007), 'Postfeminist Media Culture: Elements of a Sensibility', *European Journal of Cultural Studies*, 10:2, pp. 147–66.

Gill, R. (2016a), 'Post-postfeminism?: New Feminist Visibilities in Postfeminist Times', *Feminist Media Studies*, 16:4, pp. 610–30.

Gill, R. (2016b), 'The Affective, Cultural, and Psychic Life of Postfeminism: A Postfeminist Sensibility 10 Years On', *European Journal of Cultural Studies*, 20:6, pp. 606–26.

Gill, R., and C. Scharff (eds) (2011), *New Femininities: Postfeminism, Neoliberalism, and Subjectivity*, Basingstoke: Palgrave Macmillan.

Glynn, S. J. (2016), 'Breadwinning Mothers Are Increasingly the US Norm', Center for American Progress, 19 December. Available at: <https://www.americanprogress.org/issues/women/reports/2016/12/19/295203/breadwinning-mothers-are-increasingly-the-u-s-norm/> (last accessed 24 September 2018).

Gray, E. (2016), 'Let Sarah Jessica Parker's HBO *Divorce* Lead You to *Insecure*', *The Philadelphia Inquirer*, 8 October. Available at: <http://www.philly.com/philly/columnists/ellen_gray/20161009_Let_Sarah_Jessica_Parker_s_HBO__Divorce__lead_you_to__Insecure_.html> ,(last accessed 22 March 2018).

Groarke, S. (2014), *Managed Lives: Psychoanalysis, Inner Security and the Social Order*, London: Routledge.

Hinshelwood, R. (1997), 'Catastrophe, Objects and Representation: Three Levels of Interpretation', *British Journal of Psychotherapy*, 13:3, pp. 307–17.

Hobbes, T. (1973 [1651]), *Leviathan*, London: Dent.

Horn, K. (2017), 'TV in/vs Postfeminism', in K. Horn, *Women, Camp, and Popular Culture: Serious Excess*, Basingstoke: Palgrave Macmillan, pp. 111–92.

Hughes, S. (2016), '*Divorce* Review: Sarah Jessica Parker Shines in Bleak and Bitter HBO Comeback', *The Guardian*, 6 October. Available at: <https://www.theguardian.com/film/2016/oct/01/sarah-jessica-parker-hbo-divorce-sex-and-the-city> (last accessed 15 March 2017).

Keady, M. (2018), 'The Great Television Writers Part 3: Sharon Horgan', *The Script Lab*, 26 April. Available at: <https://thescriptlab.com/features/screenwriting-101/8662-great-television-writers-part-3-sharon-horgan/#.WuLd2uAogS0.facebook> (last accessed 27 April 2018).

Lemma, A. (2000), *Humour on the Couch*, London: Whurr.

Levin, G., and R. Bianco (2016), 'Amazon Looks to "God", "Mad", and "Catastrophe"', *USA Today*, 12 January, *Life* section, p. 5.

Lotz, A. (2001), 'Postfeminist Television Criticism: Rehabilitating Critical Terms and Identifying Postfeminist Attributes', *Feminist Media Studies*, 1:1, pp. 105–21.

McNamara, M. (2016), 'The Culture of Anger: Being Mad Has Become All the Rage in TV Rom-coms', *Los Angeles Times*, 11 July, Sunday Calendar, p. 5.

McRobbie, A. (2009), *The Aftermath of Feminism: Gender, Culture and Social Change*, London: Sage.

Manson, M. (2017), '7 Reasons Rob and Sharon from *Catastrophe* are Relationship Goals Even Though They Suck at Their Relationship', *Elle Magazine*, 16 March. Available at: <https://www.elle.com/uk/life-and-culture/articles/a34683/7-reasons-rob-and-sharon-from-catastrophe-are-relationship-goals/> (last accessed 15 March 2017).

Mills, B. (2009), *The Sitcom*, Edinburgh: Edinburgh University Press.

Morgan, E. (2016), 'Rage Revolution: TV Needs Far More Seething, Devastating Women Like Fleabag', *The Guardian*, 29 August. Available at: <https://www.theguardian.com/tv-and-radio/2016/aug/29/fleabag-tv-needs-far-more-seething-devastating-women> (last accessed 15 March 2017).

Negra, D. (2009), *What a Girl Wants? Fantasizing the Reclamation of Self in Postfeminism*, London: Routledge.

Negra, D., and Y. Tasker (2013), 'Neoliberal Frames and Genres of Inequality: Recession-era Chick-flicks and Male-centred Corporate Melodrama', *European Journal of Cultural Studies*, 16:3, pp. 344–61.

Orgad, S., and S. de Benedictis (2015), 'The "Stay-at-Home" Mother, Postfeminism and Neoliberalism: Content Analysis of UK News Coverage', *European Journal of Communication*, 30:4, pp. 418–36.

Plato (2000 [360 BCE]), *Philebus*, Blacksburg: Virginia Tech.

Poniewozik, J. (2016), 'Goodbye, Mr Medium', *New York Times*, 7 October, p. C1.

Pulling, TV series, created by S. Horgan and D. Kelly. UK: BBC3, 2006–9.

Raeside, J. (2016), '*Divorce*: Sarah Jessica Parker's Comedy Is a Messy Breakup You Pray Never Ends', *The Guardian*, 11 October. Available at: <https://www.theguardian.com/tv-and-radio/2016/oct/11/divorce-sarah-jessica-parker-sharon-horgan> (last accessed 22 March 2018).

Ramaswamy, C. (2016), '*The Circuit* Review: *Pulling*'s Creators Take Aim at the Dinner Party', *The Guardian*, 26 August. Available at: <https://www.theguardian.com/tv-and-radio/2016/aug/26/the-circuit-review> (last accessed 22 March 2018).

Rich, B. R. (2004), *Chick Flicks: Theories and Memories of the Feminist Film Movement*, 2nd edn, Durham, NC: Duke University Press.

Rifkind, H. (2016), 'No Male Writer Could Skewer Women's Madnesses Like This: *Divorce* (Sky Atlantic); *National Treasure* (Channel 4); *The Missing* (BBC1)', *The Times*, 15 October. Available at: <https://www.thetimes.co.uk/article/no-male-writer-could-skewer-womens-madnesses-like-this-mb3zqwwsh> (last accessed 1 June 2017).

Rowe, K. (1995), *The Unruly Woman: Gender and the Genres of Laughter*, Austin: University of Texas Press.

Tasker, Y., and D. Negra (eds) (2007), 'Introduction: Feminist Politics and Post-feminist Culture', in *Interrogating Postfeminism: Gender and the Politics of Popular Culture*, Durham, NC: Duke University Press, pp. 1–26.

Tirado Gilligan, H. (2011), 'It's the End of Men. Again', *The Public Intellectual*, 27 June. Available at: <http://thepublicintellectual.org/2011/06/27/its-the-end-of-men-again/> (last accessed 22 March 2018).

Türken, S. (2015), 'Making Sense of Neoliberal Subjectivity: A Discourse Analysis of Media Language on Self-development', *Globalizations*, 13:1, pp. 32–46.

Weitz, R. (2016), 'Feminism, Postfeminism, and Young Women's Reactions to Lena Dunham's *Girls*', *Gender Issues*, 33:3, pp. 218–34.

White, E. B. (1970), *The Trumpet of the Swan*, London: HarperCollins.

Willa, P. (2016), 'The Brutal Romantic', *The New Yorker*, 92:11, p. 38.

Wilson, B. (2016), 'Screengrab: What Could Be Worse Than a Missing Child? Her Return', *The Daily Telegraph*, 15 October, Review section, p. 11.

Wiseman, E. (2016), 'Sharon Horgan: Queen of Difficult Women', *The Guardian*, 9 October. Available at: <https://www.theguardian.com/global/2016/oct/09/sharon-horgan-queen-of-difficult-women> (last accessed 15 March 2017).

Wollaston, S. (2016), '*Divorce* Review: Sharon Horgan's Drama is as Bleak as New York Winter', *The Guardian*, 11 October. Available at: <https://www.theguardian.com/tv-and-radio/2016/oct/11/divorce-review-sharon-horgan-sarah-jessica-parker> (last accessed 22 March 2018).

Working Families (2017), *The Modern Families Index 2017*. Available at: <https://www.workingfamilies.org.uk/wp-content/uploads/2017/01/Modern-Families-Index_Full-Report.pdf> (last accessed 24 September 2018).

Yiannopoulos, M. (2016), 'Feminism is Cancer'. Available at: <https://www.youtube.com/watch?v=YfLr4jJEHIQ&bpctr=1524139117> (last accessed 20 May 2019).

Part Two

Love Beyond Borders: The Global City, Cosmopolitanism and Transatlantic Space

'British People Are Awful': Gentrification, Queerness and Race in the US–UK Romances of *Looking* and *You're the Worst*

Martha Shearer

In his landmark 1996 book, *The New Urban Frontier*, Neil Smith argued that globalisation and the rise of neoliberalism had 'propelled gentrification from a comparatively marginal preoccupation in a certain niche of the real estate industry to the cutting edge of urban change' (Smith 1996: 8). Throughout his text, Smith makes repeated references to cinema, identifying what he calls 'an entire cinematic genre', including films such as *Crocodile Dundee* (1986) and *Bright Lights, Big City* (1988), dedicated to the 'urban frontier', tamed just like the 'Old West' (1996: 12). Smith valuably highlights not simply how culture mediates the impact of gentrification, but also the ways in which it may be constitutive of it, actively contributing to an enormously detrimental process. The frontier, however, is not the only means by which culture has engaged with gentrification. Stanley Corkin, amongst others, has highlighted connections between the revival of the romantic comedy in the late 1970s, even as its incompatibility with the modern (suburban) world was being confidently proclaimed, and New York's emerging gentrification in that period (Henderson 1978; Corkin 2011).

While Smith's examples are drawn from cinema, I would suggest that television is critical to contemporary cultural engagement with gentrification, not simply because of its significance as a mass medium, but also because television has been undergoing its own class transformation, what Michael Newman and Elana Levine call 'legitimation' (2012). Newman and Levine argue that while discourses of television's changing cultural value 'seem to be according respect to a medium that has long been denied it', such discourses do not dismantle but rather perpetuate 'prevailing structures of status' by '[moving] television up in the contemporary cultural hierarchy while leaving in place the distinctions of value and respectability that denigrated the medium in the first place' (3). While television has largely been understood as a suburban and domestic medium (Spigel 1992), recent scholarship has situated it as urban in terms of sites of exhibition, modes of spectatorship, and settings of its programming (McCarthy 2001; Kooijman 2009; Brunsdon 2018). This reading of the medium as urban might also reinforce parallels that have been drawn between legitimation and gentrification (Hassler-Forest 2014). However, such parallels have clear limits: gentrification entails material displacement, while legitimation is a more discursive process. Yet such parallels do raise questions of the extent to which such a connection is evident, explored or reinforced in programming itself. Helen Morgan Parmett has explored how what she calls 'site-specific television' contributes to gentrification through production processes and local tourism (Morgan Parmett 2016, 2018); my concern here, however, is to interrogate how these television shows themselves formally and ideologically engage with gentrification as a process.

I focus on two television shows that foreground US–UK romance in gentrifying American cities.[1] US–UK romance is a particularly illuminating subject matter in this context. An established romcom trope – evident especially in Working Title romantic comedies, but also in Hugh Grant's collaborations with director Marc Lawrence, *Two Weeks Notice* (2002), *Music and Lyrics* (2007), *Did You Hear About the Morgans?* (2009) and *The Rewrite* (2014) – US–UK romance has been adapted to television in ways that speak to the importance of a transnational elite to gentrifying neighbourhoods (Rofe 2003; Ley 2004). Furthermore, Christine Becker notes that the frequent casting of British actors in American prestige television has reinforced discourses of legitimation through their association with 'quality' and craft (Becker 2018). In *You're the Worst* (2014–19), Jimmy (Chris Geere), an abrasive British novelist, and Gretchen (Aya Cash), an American publicist and compulsive liar, enter into a relationship despite themselves in Los Angeles, and specifically the rapidly gentrifying neighbourhoods of Echo Park, Silver Lake, Los Feliz and Eagle Rock. *Looking* (2014–16) focuses on gay men in contemporary San Francisco and develops a love triangle between white, upper middle-class Patrick (Jonathan Groff), Latino, working-class Richie (Raúl Castillo), Patrick's boyfriend in the first season, and Kevin (Russell Tovey), Patrick's British boss at the tech company at which they work. In both shows, the British men work in creative professions (fiction, video games) in major global cities, indicative of the global mobility of labour, specifically of the 'creative class'. Indeed, one of the driving forces behind recent urban policy has been the idealised geographical (and transnational) mobility of that 'creative class', a term deployed by Richard Florida in tandem with his suggestion that cities ought to be redeveloped in that class's interests, in ways that have been critiqued as encouraging gentrification (Florida 2012; Peck 2005). Furthermore, gentrification foregrounds class in ways that conflict with hegemonic myths of American classlessness. In *You're the Worst* and *Looking*, UK–US romances rely on an association between British characters and a defined class system that enables both shows, in quite distinct ways, to take account of gentrification's class tensions as they intersect with issues of race and sexuality.

You're the Worst

Promotional images for *You're the Worst* show its main cast in bars, shot in grungy black-and-white photography, far from the brightly coloured gloss of numerous mainstream romantic comedies. Its promotion and reception presented it as something edgier and more 'real' than expected in a typical romcom, and fittingly, *You're the Worst* debuted on FX in 2014 before moving to sister channel FXX in its second season, due to that channel's pitch to a typically young, male demographic.[2] An article in *The Hollywood Reporter* on the show's third season renewal quoted FX President of Original Programming Nick Grad describing it as 'one of the most innovative' television comedies and its second season as 'honest', 'daring' and 'courageous' in its portrayal of depression; the article further suggests that FX Chief Executive Officer John Landgraf probably renewed the show off the back of its critical praise and that the move to FXX 'was designed to focus the show on FXX's younger-skewing 18–34 demographic' (Goldberg 2015). *You're the Worst* is repeatedly framed as innovative, edgy and authentic, marking out its distinction from many other television comedies and other kinds of romantic narrative.

That framing is fitting for a show that is particularly preoccupied with distinction. The development of Jimmy and Gretchen's relationship hinges on questions of taste. When Gretchen is choosing whether to go to the Tribeca Film Festival with a film director hook-up, for example, Jimmy bombards her with questions about whether she prefers Peter Gabriel's or Phil Collins's Genesis, metaphorical representations of him and the other man, respectively. The show is also preoccupied with literal questions of taste. Jimmy's roommate Edgar (Desmin Borges), an Iraq War vet and recovering junkie, lives with him for free in exchange for cooking. His cooking sequences are rapidly cut, rhythmic montages that are used not only to indicate Edgar's skills but also the show's own stylishness. By contrast, Gretchen's friend Lindsay's (Kether Donohue) frustrations with her marriage to bland finance nerd Paul (Allan McLeod) come to a head when he suggests they cook together using a fictionalised version of meal-kit service Blue Apron, culminating in another rapidly edited montage in which she stabs him in the side with a kitchen knife.

Given the show's preoccupation with taste, Jimmy's Britishness is both tonal – showrunner Stephen Falk describes the characters as 'the kind of people I liked watching on British sitcoms' (Wittmer 2017) – and a marker of vaguely subcultural taste. In the second season, when Gretchen is going through a depressive episode, Jimmy starts a flirtation with a local bar owner built on her recognition of his Halloween costume, from a (fictional) British comedy series. And Jimmy's second novel, which he writes during the third season, is comically loaded with British references: Take That, Glastonbury, even exact postcodes.

Although the character was not originally written as British (Zemler 2016), Jimmy's national difference marks out his distinction from his environment and his neighbours, augmenting the show's self-conscious contrast between its hipster main characters and suburban, domestic normativity, with people its characters variously refer to as 'white pro-creators', 'normal people' and 'sweater people'. *You're the Worst* also repeatedly suggests that its characters' sarcastic refusal of the normative may, in fact, mask their own emotional anxieties and desires for norma-tivity. At the end of season one, it is revealed that Jimmy had proposed to his previous girlfriend and been rejected; in the season two episode 'LCD Soundsystem', Gretchen becomes obsessed with an older hipster couple who live nearby and have a child and dog, coveting their concerns about their daughter's school interview, only to be disturbed to learn that they are not entirely happy. Jimmy and Gretchen's discomfort with their burgeoning relationship and the various clichéd milestones they go through (deciding to be exclusive, moving in together, a proposal and so on) indicates the tension between their normative desires and their pre-occupation with their own superficial difference. Indeed, Falk describes his characters as 'rather pretentious, narcissistic, provincial people, who are deeply afraid of being normal' (Travers 2016). Falk's use of 'provincial' here is notable, suggesting a class unity with those around them despite their preoccupations with their own sophistication and dif-ference, including national difference.

While early episodes show Jimmy and Gretchen's disdain for their sweater people neighbours, the show also maps its distinction between conformity and hipster edginess as a West/East Los Angeles divide. In the first season, Lindsay has moved west on marrying Paul, much to Gretchen's frustration. The show's hipsters, by contrast, are particularly associated with LA's East Side, with areas that are rapidly gentrifying off screen. Mark Greif closely associates the hipster with gentrification, referring specifically to Silver Lake, where Jimmy's home is located and identifying the emergence of the hipster out of the 'neobohemia' analysed in Richard Lloyd's 2006 study of Chicago's Wicker Park neighbour-hood (Greif 2010: 5–7; Lloyd 2006). Furthermore, in an interview with *IndieWire*, Aya Cash addresses the characters' abandonment of Sunday Funday – the group's brunch and ensuing drunken activities in the city, around which an episode in each of the first three seasons is based – after the season three episode in which it has become too popular, and does so by invoking parallels with gentrification:

> It makes me think about – and this is kind of a weird analogy – gentrification . . . The artists move in and create the culture of cool that raises the rents and then all the other people move in, and then the artists move out and do it again [somewhere else]. There's a weird tension around that because artists want to feel like they're authentically creating, and yet they're displacing people as well. It's a complicated issue. (Travers 2016)

What is gentrifying here is a social activity, but Cash also connects the milieu depicted in *You're the Worst* and this first wave of gentrification, which she frames critically. Yet she presents her ideas as a 'weird analogy', simultaneously acknowledging and disavowing the show's complicity in gentrification as a process.

You're the Worst's depiction of East LA is dependent on gentrification but also on the show's own displacements: of Silver Lake's gay communi-ties, of the Latino populations of its various settings. *You're the Worst*'s depiction of Edgar's post-traumatic stress disorder is notably sensitive, and in some ways stands as the equivalent of the emphasis on family systems in its examination of other characters' mental health problems (Gretchen's controlling mother; Jimmy's emotionally neglectful father; Lindsay's rivalry with her sister). Yet that also means that while the show is deeply preoccupied with the other character's relationships with their parents and how those relationships have shaped them, Edgar's family is absent, despite his being the only LA native of the four main characters. While Jimmy is geographically and emotionally displaced from his fam-ily in the UK, Edgar's background is simply never addressed. There is a running joke that he cannot speak Spanish.

The erasure of Edgar's familial and therefore ethnic background is closely tied to the show's geography. In season one, Edgar organises Sunday Funday, telling the group it will be the best yet because 'hipster shit is just poor Latino shit from 10 years ago', both highlighting and exploiting such an erasure. In a later episode, the group go on a scavenger hunt to find a notoriously elusive speakeasy, which leads them to the home of a Latino family; they then barge in, looking through all the rooms and cupboards before getting arrested, only to discover then that the toilet in their jail cell spins around, finally leading them to the speakeasy. The episode generates discomfort from how these hipsters disrupt the lives of working-class Latinos, who they regard as incidental props in their hunt for the hot new venue, yet the final joke is that this family was not real, that they actually were just tools to lead hipsters to a new bar. In this respect, the show has common ground with indie film romcoms such as *(500) Days of Summer* (2009) and *Her* (2013), which, Celestino Deleyto argues, foreground both coolness and whiteness, part of 'a long tradition of cinematic Los Angeles: the all-white city that summarily erases that which threatens its homogeneity' (Deleyto 2016: 89). Indeed, Deleyto describes *(500) Days of Summer* as 'an animated advertising prospectus for gentrification' (105).

While the show negates the presence of a local working class, it also presents LA as a place where class can be transcended, at least for its white characters. Gretchen goes to great lengths to avoid introducing Jimmy to her upper-class parents, for whom she puts on a show, playing tennis and visiting an art gallery. Her class background is a familial role that can be discarded in her everyday life. Jimmy, meanwhile, is depicted as having escaped his British, working-class roots, in line with utopian notions of the social and spatial mobility of the creative class. He tells Gretchen's parents that he is not from, as Gretchen has told them, the 'fancy part of London', but from the 'bad part of Manchester'. This insistence on Jimmy's working-class Mancunian background was not well received on the show's broadcast in the UK, particularly given the plummy accent of its Cambridge-born star. Numerous tweets complained that 'they need to sort out their English-ness references' and 'a guy from the rough part of Manchester wouldn't sound like Tom Hiddleston' (Leah 2016; Gray 2016). Particular opprobrium, from both UK and US viewers, was reserved for the season one episode where Jimmy's father sends him a jersey for the football team he supports, simply called 'Manchester' (Burtz 2014; Ivey 2014; Howard 2014). These audience reactions not only indicate how markers of local specificity resonate differently across transnational contexts but also suggest that *You're the Worst* was itself lagging behind its domestic audience's familiarity with British culture, enabled by, for example, US viewership of Premier League football (*BBC Sport* 2015). While Jimmy's middle-class presentation is unconvincing for viewers, in the show his working-class background up-ends the characters' assumptions about Britishness; Lindsay tells Gretchen that she thought British people were supposed to be 'fancy' but Jimmy's family are 'Alabama British people'.

Indeed, it is via class that Jimmy's Britishness becomes fundamental to the show's project. His disinterested father is presented as the root of his abrasiveness, and in the second season, his family come to visit and are portrayed as entirely grotesque: wildly racist, lazy, anti-intellectual, spending the entire visit watching a fictional equivalent of the Eurovision Song Contest. Lindsay's 'Alabama British people' line is a joke at the expense of her ignorance and snobbery, but her revulsion is also not something the show strongly contests. Visually, shots of the family all slumped around the television echo actual working-class Mancunian sitcom *The Royle Family* (1998–2012), yet without any of that programme's warmth, empathy or attention to local specificity; indeed, each of Jimmy's family members has a distinct regional accent. Instead, the family most resembles a cluster of so-called 'chav' stereotypes of the kind that, in a UK context, have been vehemently criticised, most visibly by the journalist Owen Jones, as fostering a denigration of the working class enabled by a neoliberal political consensus 'all about *escaping* the working class', in which social problems are not effects of flaws in capitalism but 'the consequences of personal behaviour, individual defects and even choice' (Jones 2016: 10).

The cluster of offensive stereotypes deployed in the depiction of Jimmy's family is used to build sympathy so that we understand his childhood emotional neglect. The show both celebrates hipsters and ironically implies that they are growing into the white, middle-class sweater people they loath; that perspective is set against the working classes, either absent, representationally displaced or actively reviled. Just as the show maintains a critical distance from its characters, inviting us to recognise what they cannot or will not see about themselves, it highlights its characters' role as gentrifiers (Edgar's 'poor Latino shit' comment) without a critical perspective on gentrification. US–UK romance here is an expression of class unity that is thoroughly dependent on gentrification, especially in its idealisation of a global creative class and in its wilful blindness.

Looking

Looking was created by Michael Lannan and based on his short *Lorimer* (2011) but was often framed as a collaboration with the British filmmaker Andrew Haigh, whose film *Weekend* (2011) had a successful US release. Haigh directed five episodes in each of its two seasons, writing or co-writing several, as well as directing and co-writing *Looking: The Movie* (2016), produced after the show's cancellation. Jack Cortvriend argues that the show's British character, Kevin, might be seen as 'an avatar for Haigh himself who has transgressed national borders to work' (Cortvriend 2018: 108). Indeed, Owen's (Andrew Law) response to his and Patrick's first encounter with

Kevin – 'British people are awful' – can be read as an in-joke at the expense
of the British creative personnel working on the show. Both Haigh and Kevin
are indicative of increasingly transnational conditions for the production and
reception of US television, evident in the frequent casting of British actors,
an increase in transnational adaptations (Beeden and de Bruin 2010: 5), and
the way digital technology 'liberates [television] from national schedules'
(Jacobs 2011: 511). Furthermore, Cortvriend notes that the stylistic tics evident in Haigh's feature films (distance, long takes, focus pulls) are also key
elements of *Looking*'s visual style, which has a 'consistent aesthetic framework' even in episodes directed by other notable filmmakers such as Jamie
Babbit and Joe Swanberg (Cortvriend 2018: 103). The show's transatlantic
style is also evident in its soundtrack, which consistently combines American
(such as Perfume Genius, John Grant, Hercules & Love Affair) and British
(such as Erasure, Pet Shop Boys, The 2 Bears) artists. *Looking*, then, was
transatlantic in both production and aesthetics, and compared with *You're
the Worst*, is far more attentive to the nuances of national difference and their
class implications.

A key intertext for *Looking* is another transatlantic show about gay life in
San Francisco, *Tales of the City* (1993–2001), which, Amy Villarejo argues,
used its 1970s setting in order to express utopian urban possibilities: 'a product of openly avowed nostalgia for pre-AIDS gay male sexual culture, it
nonetheless circulates . . . a dream of sexual and urban intimacy *untroubled
by antagonism, undivided by walls*' (Villarejo 2014: 134, emphasis in original).
Looking, however, is a far more anxious entity, self-consciously addressing
the contemporary state of gay urban culture. Contemporary San Francisco
is being aggressively gentrified in ways that threaten its ability to function as
a locus for queer publics. Lauren Berlant and Michael Warner have argued
that 'the heteronormative culture of intimacy leaves queer culture especially
dependent on ephemeral elaborations in urban space' (Berlant and Warner
1998: 562), and Warner has elsewhere lamented the erosion of the 'queer life
of the street' in 1990s New York due to zoning law, tourism and property
development (Warner 1999: 151). Manuel Castells, in 1983, described San
Francisco as an 'urban enigma' that had resisted the displacement occurring
elsewhere and retained its bohemian qualities:

> While transforming itself into one of the centres of the world's corporate establish-
> ment, it nevertheless houses expanding communities boasting alternative cultures,
> from the 1960s hippies to the 1970s gays. While the downtown area becomes more
> concentrated and more skyscrapers are built, old Victorian houses are renovated and
> street life is fostered. While the residential neighbourhoods are gentrified, its minor-
> ity population is maintained. While keeping its function as a port of entry for poor
> immigrants is continued, its ethnic ghettoes are hardly examples of dilapidation.
> (Castells 1983: 101)

This 'enigma' has in recent years become severely strained, especially with the impact of the tech industry based at nearby Silicon Valley. Rebecca Solnit has more recently argued that gentrification is 'driving out the poor and working class, including those who have chosen to give their lives over to unlucrative pursuits such as art, activism, social experimentation, social service', serving as a harbinger of the 'newest version of the American future' in which 'most of us will be poorer, a few will be richer, and everything will be faster, more homogeneous and more controlled or controllable' (Solnit 2000: 13–14).

The nostalgic 'happy gayness' that Villarejo identifies in *Tales of the City* is therefore inaccessible in *Looking* not only because of its post-AIDS crisis setting, but also because the threat of gentrification looms large throughout the series (Villarejo 2014: 140). Concerns with real estate, housing and property run throughout as a backdrop: Agustín (Frankie J. Alvarez) moves to Oakland both to live with his boyfriend and to seek cheaper rent; Agustín and Eddie (Daniel Franzese) work at a homeless shelter for trans youth; Dom (Murray Bartlett) spends much of the series attempting to find a viable space for his peri peri chicken restaurant; Doris's (Lauren Weedman) boyfriend Malik (Bashir Salahuddin) works in the mayor's office and mentions the level of concern about Google buses, a prominent site of anti-gentrification activism at the time of the show's production.[3] Maps of *Looking*'s locations available at real-estate blog *Curbed* show that key sites, especially in the second season, are the Castro and the Mission (Mericle 2014; Elsen 2015), the Castro as the city's gay district and the Mission a site of the city's Latino population, where Richie works. Both of these neighbourhoods have also recently been acutely affected by gentrification. Many of the Castro locations where *Looking* was filmed have since closed, and when maps of *Looking*'s filming locations are compared with those produced by the San Francisco-based Anti-Eviction Mapping Project, there is significant overlap, with the Castro and the Mission as two hotspots (Anti-Eviction Mapping Project).[4]

Like *You're the Worst*, *Looking* relies on a contrast between local Latino and British men, in this case as a love triangle. Reading the show in light of its gentrifying context, these two romantic options represent two forms of urbanism. Patrick and Richie's relationship is one initiated in public space, on the subway. Here Richie is first heard, off screen, speaking to Patrick, before moving to sit in front of him, leading to a forty-second take that starts with Patrick smiling, in contrast to his earlier tense responses to Richie's questions, and then continues with his indecision about whether to go to Richie's party or continue to his own. This use of long takes to express both social connection and uncertainty is indicative of the show's construction of urban space in general. Sean Sullivan argues that *Looking*'s long takes are marked by 'an interplay between people and environment that understands the negotiation of space as contingent, improvisatory', depicting San Francisco as 'a looping array of spaces with no particular beginnings or ends' (Sullivan 2017: 250). This is especially evident in the season one episode 'Looking for the Future' in which Patrick calls in sick and he and Richie wander around the city. The subway sequence, therefore, is indicative of the show's construction of urban space as uncertain, unstable, and reliant on an idea of public space as a site of cross-class and inter-racial encounter and unexpected social contact, spaces that function as hints of something utopian that gentrification's accelerated class stratification and displacement of working-class populations, and especially working-class people of colour, threaten to destroy.

Kevin, meanwhile, marked as working-class but in a senior position in a video-game company, represents the idealised social and spatial mobility of the 'creative class'. At the end of the second season, Patrick and Kevin move into a luxury condo, in a building depicted as both exclusive and overwhelmingly white. Looking out of the window, Kevin tells Patrick, 'I swear, when I was a kid I never thought in a million years I would live somewhere like this, above everyone,' foregrounding not only the physical height of the building but also what that means in class terms. Later, at a party for the building's residents, Patrick observes that everyone is white, which Kevin had not even noticed. Kevin's Britishness and tech industry job already identify him with the very forces that are producing the city's gentrification; the whiteness and social/spatial elevation of his new apartment replicates his identification with San Francisco's global city status and the tensions produced by the tech industry's impact on the city.

While *You're the Worst* is preoccupied with its characters' anxieties about their own normativity, *Looking* takes the palimpsest of the old queer city and the emergence of homonormativity as its subject. Defined by Lisa Duggan as 'a politics that does not contest dominant heteronormative assumptions and institutions, but upholds and sustains them, while promising the possibility of a demobilized gay constituency and a privatized, depoliticized gay culture anchored in domesticity and consumption' (Duggan 2004: 50), homonormativity has itself been linked to gentrification (Schulman 2012). The geographers David Bell and Jon Binnie argue that a 'powerful component' of Duggan's new homonormativity is the 'sexual restructuring of cities', whereby 'the presence of gay communities and spaces' – including neighbourhoods like Silver Lake and the Castro – has 'a central role in place promotion, as symbols of cosmopolitanism and creative appeal' (Bell and Binnie 2004: 1818), fuelling gentrification that ultimately threatens the continued existence of queer spaces. *Looking*'s relationship to homonormativity has been a prominent feature of its (academic) reception. Cortvriend and Cory Albertson describe *Looking* as homonormative, while, for Melanie Kohnen, it is one of several shows 'introducing queer relationships that feature people of color in central roles and challenging homonational and homonormative modes of representation' (Albertson 2014; Cortvriend 2018: 110; Kohnen 2016: 165). A desire for homonormativity is especially evident in the Patrick character, the least at ease with himself and his sexuality. Patrick is also, of the show's three leads (Patrick, Agustín, Dom), the one most representative of the new, gentrified San Francisco in his class background, tech job and normative aspirations. Yet Albertson and Cortvriend perhaps overstate the show's uncritical homonormativity: it maintains a critical perspective on Patrick, and its opening episode highly self-consciously contrasts its two San Franciscos, opening with a cruising sequence and ending in a gay marriage.

Patrick sees Kevin as a more appropriate match than Richie (professional success, working in the same industry), but the show makes it clear that this perception rests on the illegibility of Kevin's Britishness, and his class background in particular. Kevin's first appearance is at a party where Patrick is trying to figure out whether Kevin is gay or not; there are various scenes where Kevin explains British things: Take That, top trumps, rugby, a full English breakfast. Later episodes play up the sense that Patrick fundamentally cannot or will not read him, and one of the things that Patrick cannot seem to make sense of is Kevin's class background, continually reading Kevin as 'posher' than he is. When they go to a British-theme pub and Patrick asks Kevin if it is like a pub he would go to in England, Kevin replies, 'It's not shitty enough to be a Romford pub.' Patrick asks him of Romford, 'Is it like Wimbledon?', imagining 'rolling hills', much to Kevin's amusement. It is clear that the central problem in their relationship is a superficial understanding of each other, where Patrick reads Kevin in terms of clichés of Britishness that obscure his working-class specificity. The trigger for their break-up is Patrick's discovery, at the party in their luxury building, that Kevin is still on Grindr, which Patrick realises when he sees the screen name 'Romford', flagging up everything about his class and national background that remains, for Patrick, unknowable. The first season also foregrounds Patrick's discomfort with Richie's racial and class difference, such as his inaccurate claims to his friends that Richie is planning on opening his own business, and their relationship breaks down when Patrick is intensely anxious about the prospect of introducing Richie to his upper middle-class family.

Looking: The Movie's neat resolution of its love triangle has fuelled accounts of the show's homonormativity, but viewed through the lens of gentrification its conclusion is more nuanced and critical. A five-minute take at the movie's conclusion sees Richie and Patrick walking to the diner Orphan Andy's and discussing ways their plans for the future, where they each plan to live, are at odds. It is implied – through Patrick's suggestion and then, once they have joined their friends, Richie's slight head nod – that they will move to Texas together, but this is never explicit. Even at the resolution of its love plot, suggested through gesture, *Looking* remains resistant to easy categorisation. While Kevin's relationship with Patrick had enabled the show to foreground the city's class tensions, his romantic and geographical expulsion (he is returning to the UK) sidelines those tensions. By favouring Richie, however, the movie also valorises the kind of city that could produce such a relationship: a city that enables cross-class and interracial contact in public space.

In both shows, romance is depicted in terms of connection, shared intimacy, and a sense that this is television with greater emotional depth than other romantic comedies. Yet both these examples indicate divergent, complicated relationships between romance and gentrification that the use of US–UK romance foregrounds through associations between Britishness and a clearly marked class system. In *You're the Worst*, that romance is an expression of class unity across national borders in ways that enable both Jimmy and Gretchen to cast off their class origins, whereas *Looking*, although perhaps not coherently or explicitly, suggests that addressing the terms of intimacy in urban space is critical for queer publics and rejects what Solnit refers to as gentrification's 'refusal to coexist' (Solnit 2000: 121).

Notes

1. For an examination of London in this regard, see also Frances Smith and Caroline Bainbridge in this volume.
2. At the time of writing, the show's fourth season had not yet been made available for viewing in the UK either through broadcast or DVD. As such, my analysis is limited to the first three seasons and does not address either the fourth season or the yet-to-be-broadcast final fifth season.
3. Rebecca Solnit notes that 'Google bus' is shorthand for a number of corporate shuttles, using public bus stops and enabling high-paid tech workers to live in San Francisco and commute to Silicon Valley (Solnit 2014).
4. On gentrification and displacement in San Francisco, see also Tracy 2014; Moskowitz 2017: 123–60.

Works Cited

Albertson, C. (2014), '*Looking* – Who Are We Now?', *Contexts*, 13:4, pp. 54–6.

Anti-Eviction Mapping Project. Available at: <https://www.antievictionmap. com/?category=San+Francisco/> (last accessed 25 May 2019).

BBC Sport (2015), 'Premier League & NBC Agree New TV Rights Deal', 10 August. Available at: <https://www.bbc.co.uk/sport/football/33855590> (last accessed 12 June 2018).

Becker, C. (2018), 'Accent on Talent: The Valorization of British Actors on American Quality Television', in T. Cantrell and C. Hogg (eds), *Exploring Television Acting*, London: Bloomsbury, pp. 140–53.

Beeden, A., and J. de Bruin (2010), '*The Office*: Articulations of National Identity in Television Format Adaptation', *Television & New Media*, 11:3, pp. 3–19.

Bell, D., and J. Binnie (2004), 'Authenticating Queer Space: Citizenship, Urbanism and Governance', *Urban Studies*, 41:9, pp. 1807–20.

Berlant, L., and M. Warner (1998), 'Sex in Public', *Critical Inquiry*, 24:2, pp. 547–66.

Brunsdon, C. (2018), *Television Cities: Paris, London, Baltimore*, Durham, NC and London: Duke University Press.

Burtz, M. (2014), @mburtz81, Twitter Post, 9 September, 4:02 AM. Available at: <https://twitter.com/mburtz81/status/509174983030226944> (last accessed 24 April 2018).

Castells, M. (1983) *The City and the Grassroots: A Cross-Cultural Theory of Urban Social Movements*, London: Edward Arnold.

Corkin, S. (2011), *Starring New York: Filming the Grime and the Glamour of the Long 1970s*, Oxford and New York: Oxford University Press.

Cortvriend, J. (2018), 'Stylistic Convergences between British Film and American Television: Andrew Haigh's *Looking*', *Critical Studies in Television: The International Journal of Television Studies*, 13:1, pp. 96–112.

Deleyto, C. (2016), *From Tinseltown to Bordertown: Los Angeles on Film*, Detroit: Wayne State University Press.

Duggan, L. (2004), *The Twilight of Equality?: Neoliberalism, Cultural Politics, and the Attack on Democracy*, Boston: Beacon Press.

Elsen, T. (2015), 'Mapping HBO's "Looking" Season 2 Locations in San Francisco', *Curbed SF*, 23 March. Available at: <https://sf.curbed.com/maps/mapping-hbos-looking-season-2-locations-in-san-francisco> (last accessed 8 May 2018).

Florida, R. (2012), *The Rise of the Creative Class, Revisited*, New York: Basic Books.

Goldberg, L. (2015), 'FXX Renews "You're the Worst," Inks Creator Stephen Falk to Overall Deal', *The Hollywood Reporter*, 2 December. Available at: <https://www.hollywoodreporter.com/live-feed/fxx-renews-youre-worst-inks-845110> (last accessed 24 April 2018).

Gray, V. (2016), @vsjgray, Twitter Post, 15 September, 8:27 PM. Available at: <https://twitter.com/vsjgray/status/776502689333145600> (last accessed 24 April 2018).

Greif, Mark (2010), 'Positions', in M. Greif, K. Ross and D. Tortorici (eds), *What Was the Hipster? A Sociological Investigation*, New York: n+1 Foundation.

Hassler-Forest, D. (2014), '*Game of Thrones*: Quality Television and the Cultural Logic of Gentrification', *TV/Series*, 6, December, pp. 160–77.

Henderson, B. (1978), 'Romantic Comedy Today: Semi-Tough or Impossible?', *Film Quarterly*, 31:4, pp. 11–23.

Howard, B. (2014), @BenHowardOPT, Twitter Post, 12 September, 10:52 PM. Available at: <https://twitter.com/BenHowardOPT/status/5105464 42369245184> (last accessed 24 April 2018).

Ivey, B. (2014), @brandonivey, Twitter Post, 6 September, 2:14 AM. Available at: <https://twitter.com/brandonivey/status/508060697276592128> (last accessed 24 April 2018).

Jacobs, J. (2011), 'The Medium in Crisis: Caughie, Brunsdon and the Problem of US Television', *Screen*, 52:4, pp. 503–11.

Jones, O. (2016 [2011]), *Chavs: The Demonization of the Working Class*, London and New York: Verso.

Kohnen, M. E. S. (2016), *Queer Representation, Visibility, and Race in American Film and Television: Screening the Closet*, New York: Routledge.

Kooijman, J. (2009), 'Cruising the Channels: The Queerness of Zapping', in G. Davis and G. Needham (eds), *Queer TV: Theories, Histories, Politics*, New York and London: Routledge, pp.159–71.

Leah (2016), @leahphyllis, Twitter Post, 14 November, 9:28 PM. Available at: <https://twitter.com/leahphyllis/status/798276381377327105> (accessed 24 April 2018).

Ley, D. (2004), 'Transnational Spaces and Everyday Lives', *Transactions of the Institute of British Geographers*, 29:2, pp. 151–64.

Lloyd, R. (2006), *Neo-Bohemia: Art and Commerce in the Postindustrial City*, New York: Routledge.

Looking, TV series, created by M. Lannan. US: Fair Harbor Productions, 2014–16.

Looking: The Movie, film, directed by A. Haigh. US: Fair Harbor Productions, 2016.

McCarthy, A. (2001), *Ambient Television: Visual Culture and Public Space*, Durham, NC: Duke University Press.

Mericle, J. (2014), 'Mapping HBO's *Looking* Locations Across San Francisco', *Curbed SF*, 10 March. Available at: <https://sf.curbed.com/maps/mapping-hbos-looking-locations-across-san-francisco> (last accessed 8 May 2018).

Morgan Parmett, H. (2016), 'It's HBO: Passionate Engagement, TV Branding, and Tourism in the Postbroadcast Era', *Communication and Critical/Cultural Studies*, 13:1, pp. 3–22.

Morgan Parmett, H. (2018), 'Site-Specific Television as Urban Renewal: Or, How Portland Became Portlandia', *International Journal of Cultural Studies*, 21:1, pp. 42–56.

Moskowitz, P. (2017), *How to Kill a City: Gentrification, Inequality, and the Fight for the Neighborhood*, New York: Nation Books.

Newman, M. Z., and E. Levine (2012), *Legitimating Television: Media Convergence and Cultural Status*, New York and London: Routledge.

Peck, J. (2005), 'Struggling with the Creative Class', *International Journal of Urban and Regional Research*, 29:4, pp. 740–70.

Rofe, M. W. (2003), '"*I Want to Be Global*": Theorising the Gentrifying Class as an Emergent Elite Global Community', *Urban Studies*, 40:12, pp. 2511–26.

Schulman, S. (2012), *The Gentrification of the Mind: Witness to a Lost Imagination*, Berkeley and London: University of California Press.

Smith, N. (1996), *The New Urban Frontier: Gentrification and the Revanchist City*, London: Routledge.

Solnit, R. (2000), *Hollow City: The Siege of San Francisco and the Crisis of American Urbanism*, London and New York: Verso.

Solnit, R. (2014), 'Diary', *London Review of Books*, 36:4, pp. 34–5.

Spigel, L. (1992), *Make Room for TV: Television and the Family Ideal in Postwar America*, Chicago and London: University of Chicago Press.

Sullivan, S. (2017), '*True Detective* (2014), *Looking* (2014), and the Televisual Long Take', in J. Gibbs and D. Pye (eds), *The Long Take: Critical Approaches*, London: Palgrave Macmillan, pp. 239–52.

Tales of the City, TV series, directed by A. Reid. US and UK: Working Title Films, 1993–2001.

The Royle Family, TV series, created by C. Aherne and C. Cash. UK: Granada Productions and ITV, 1998–2000; intermittently 2006–12.

Tracy, J. (2014), *Dispatches Against Displacement: Field Notes from San Francisco's Housing Wars*, Edinburgh and Baltimore: AK Press.

Travers, B. (2016), '"You're the Worst": Why Sunday Funday Had to End, According to Aya Cash, Kether Donohue and Stephen Falk', *IndieWire*, 5 October. Available at: <http://www.indiewire.com/2016/10/youre-the-worst-sunday-funday-aya-cash-sunday-funday-interview-1201733408/> (last accessed 24 April 2018).

Villarejo, A. (2014), *Ethereal Queer: Television, Historicity, Desire*, Durham, NC, and London: Duke University Press.

Warner, M. (1999), *The Trouble with Normal: Sex, Politics, and the Ethics of Queer Life*, Cambridge, MA: Harvard University Press.

Wittmer, C. (2017), 'We Talked to the Creator of "You're the Worst" about How to Make a Delightful Show about Terrible People', *Business Insider*, 7 September. Available at: <http://uk.businessinsider.com/youre-the-worst-creator-stephen-falk-interview-2017-9> (last accessed 24 April 2018).

You're the Worst, TV series, created by S. Falk. US: FX Networks, 2014–19.

Zemler, Emily (2016), 'One of the Meanest Guys on TV Is Played by One of the Nicest Actors in Hollywood', *Esquire*, 31 August. Available at: <https://www.esquire.com/entertainment/tv/a48218/chris-geere-youre-the-worst-interview/> (last accessed 8 May 2018).

CHAPTER 6

Catastrophe: Transatlantic Love in East London

Frances Smith

A pivotal scene occurs early on in the first series of *Catastrophe* (2015–). Rob (Rob Delaney) floats the idea that he and new partner Sharon (Sharon Horgan) should relocate from London to Boston in the US. The move is logical. As Rob observes, living in Boston is 'cheaper by probably about, 500%', and given that his employers are increasingly sceptical of his plans to create a European office, his career prospects in advertising appear to be more secure in Massachusetts than they are in Greater London. None the less, a cut to Sharon's disgusted facial expression reveals that she is appalled by the very idea. 'Once you graduate to a city like London or New York, you don't regress to Boston,' she explains. Dismissing Rob's concerns about his unemployment, Sharon affirms that the couple will 'sort it out here'. The audience thus understands that *Catastrophe*, its characters and its (anti-) romantic narrative can be located only in London, the quintessential global city.[1] This chapter examines how love across the Atlantic, as embodied by Sharon and Rob's budding relationship, is mediated through its London setting. As I demonstrate, romance is increasingly viewed as a pragmatic, rather than idealised, solution to precarity in contemporary culture. In *Catastrophe*, this is made manifest through both characters' – and especially Rob's – troubled relationship to their urban environs. Examining the show's mobilisation of discourses of authenticity, realism and 'quality' television itself, this chapter considers why the show is set in the areas around London Fields, in the borough of Hackney. In the context of increasingly transatlantic models of television distribution, I argue that the show's use of a globalised East London speaks to a transnational and upmarket aesthetic that is modelled on the types of urban locales made visible in *Catastrophe*.

Crossing the Atlantic, Crossing Genres

Catastrophe is the fruit of a relationship forged across the Atlantic between Sharon Horgan, a London-born Irishwoman who co-wrote the less popular (though much admired) *Pulling* (2006–9) and *Dead Boss* (2012), and

Rob Delaney, an American stand-up comedian dubbed 'the funniest person on Twitter' (Erickson 2012). The two co-writers also star in the show, playing 'Sharon' and 'Rob' respectively, who, upon meeting in a hotel bar, embark on a '6-night stand' that concludes when Rob returns to the US.[2] When Sharon unexpectedly finds herself pregnant – the 'catastrophe' of the show's title – Rob moves permanently to London and establishes a relationship with her. In this brief plot summary can be found not only the serendipity of the initial encounter that is central to the romantic comedy, but also the subsequent development of that attraction, which brings into play elements of the domestic family sitcom, even while the humour in the series is frequently darker than that typically associated with both romcom and sitcom. The tension between the happenstance and sexual spark of the pair's first meeting, and a quotidian aftermath that is founded in duty as much as it is in physical attraction, is reflected in the indeterminacy of the television romantic comedy, sometimes termed the 'romsitcom' in reference to the genre's hybridity (Haggerty 2015).

Both the romantic comedy and the sitcom possess low cultural capital, as a result of their associations with artificiality. Tamar Jeffers McDonald's study of the romantic comedy film begins with her observation that the genre is (erroneously) believed to provide uncomplicated, escapist pleasures in a form that should 'remain below one's notice' (Jeffers McDonald 2007: 7–8). In turn, the sitcom's conventionally proscenium staging, studio audience and theatrical performances of characters whose situation never alters from one episode to the next likewise gives rise to criticisms that the genre lacks realism (Mills 2009: 14). Both modes are also associated with the feminine. Elana Levine and Michael Z. Newman's work on the legitimation of television observes that the medium's recent acquisition of cultural capital has been concomitant with the masculinisation of the medium. The television set was first promoted to women as an aspirational household object, alongside other modern conveniences like refrigerators and washing machines (Levine and Newman 2012: 10). In contrast, the exemplars of the recent so-called 'golden age of television', such as *The Sopranos* (1999–2007), *The Wire* (2002–8), *Mad Men* (2007–15) or *Breaking Bad* (2008–13), all focus on troubled male protagonists.[3] It is therefore significant that *Catastrophe*, a sitcom/romcom hybrid, co-written by a man and a woman, escapes the designation of the feminine and, as I demonstrate, is instead positioned in the terms of quality television.

A principal means through which *Catastrophe* escapes the low cultural capital associated with the genres to which it ostensibly belongs is through its preoccupation with discourses of realism and authenticity. Suggestions of verisimilitude abound in the show. Further to naming the show's leads after themselves, Horgan and Delaney use their own personal histories in the narrative. Perhaps most obviously, the very premise of *Catastrophe* takes its cue from the story of how Horgan met her real-life husband, himself an American advertising executive, whom she married soon after becoming pregnant with their first child (Iqbal 2017). In turn, Rob Delaney's namesake is, like the comedian himself, a recovering alcoholic. It is partly as a result of these claims to realism that *Catastrophe* has been effusively praised for its authenticity and brutality, with Horgan in particular described as 'honest, messy and real' (Iqbal 2017) and a 'brutal romantic' (Paskin 2016). This strategic deployment of discourses of authenticity and honesty allows *Catastrophe* to escape the low cultural capital associated with its ostensible generic positioning. The challenges encountered in the show, such as the fractious discussion over where the couple might raise their child, constructs this transatlantic romance as an especially difficult one. Thus, romance is not idealised, but rather presented as a site of messiness, realism and therefore authenticity. As I demonstrate, too, East London has also come to be associated with discourses of the authentic.

Despite adopting certain codes of realism, *Catastrophe* nevertheless continues to embrace significant elements of the romantic comedy. London-set examples of the genre in which romantic partners hail from either side of the Atlantic are commonplace, as seen in *Notting Hill* (1999), *Last Chance Harvey* (2008) and, more recently, *Bridget Jones's Baby* (2016). Beyond the show's supposed authenticity and brutality, *Catastrophe* is also praised for the chemistry between, and likeability of, the two leads, bringing it squarely in line with conventional markers of excellence in the romantic comedy (Raeside 2015; Hu 2016). While Horgan and Delaney decided to omit declarations of love from the show, thereby distancing themselves from the romantic comedy, Sharon and Rob are noticeably 'sweet' and affectionate towards one another (Moylan 2015). In turn, being white, middle-class and heterosexual, Sharon and Rob are precisely the kinds of normative figures that overwhelmingly populate romantic comedy. Clearly, then, the terms under which *Catastrophe* is deemed an original text differ from most of its generic stablemates.

Many studies of the cinematic romantic comedy make it clear that urban settings have been central to the genre (see Jermyn 2008; Jeffers McDonald 2007). As Deborah Jermyn observes, 'a spectacular aerial view or bravura panning shot across the New York City skyline signals entry into romcom territory' (2008: 11). That is, the very fact of establishing the film's location in a glamourised, glossy Manhattan immediately reveals that text's generic belonging. Jermyn argues that New York's status as a global city is central to its function in the romantic comedy. For her, the city's embodiment of modernity, and of possibility, corresponds with the uniquely American mythos of the 'pursuit of happiness', and secures the audience's belief that anything – even meeting one's soulmate – might be possible in such an environment. In New York, these qualities combine in the city's historic ambition to welcome immigrants from around the world, and relatedly in its ethnically diverse population. The vertically oriented architecture, spectacularly showcased in precisely the types of opening sequences Jermyn describes, thus constitute an index of, and proxy for, Manhattan's highly populated landscape. In the New York-set romantic comedy, the city's modernity and cosmopolitanism enable the central romance.

In contrast, despite London's shared status as a global city in Saskia Sassen's influential typology, the metropolis idealised in romantic comedy films set there retreat from modernity. Instead, as Claire Mortimer observes, London-set romantic comedies portray the city as a 'prosperous, sophisticated, cosy world that has seen little development since the nineteenth century' (Mortimer 2010: 96). This is not to say that the London found in the romantic comedy is not spectacularised. The London of the transatlantic romantic comedy focuses principally on the areas immediately around the Houses of Parliament, in Westminster, and takes in a number of internationally recognisable landmarks, including the London Eye, Tower Bridge and, to a lesser extent, Buckingham Palace. For Annabelle Honess Roe, such a narrowly focused representation of the city demonstrates these films' attempt to reinforce particular ideals of Britishness that dodge the realities of the modern metropolis in favour of a distinctly twee, even village-like, city of red buses, black cabs and reliably white Christmases (Honess Roe 2008: 85). Rather than finding romantic promise in the city's modernity and cosmopolitanism, these films construct the long-standing, monumental landscape, and the construction of Britishness evoked therein, as an index of the durability of the romance being established on screen.

Transatlantic 'Quality' Audiences

Catastrophe does not offer up this time-honoured London aesthetic. Nor does it follow Hollywood, offering a glamorous, modern aesthetic using the soaring follies of the City of London. Instead, the show is set in and around London Fields, in Hackney, a formerly gritty, inner-city borough of East London (London Borough of Hackney 2018). But the show's setting is not parochial. As *Catastrophe*'s director, Ben Taylor, reveals, the area was chosen with one eye on the show's marketability to American distribution. In so doing, he aimed to portray 'a beautiful, exciting and aspirational version of London. Not a Richard Curtis Notting Hill but a more Brooklyn-style East End, a bit dirty and textured and cool' (Taylor, quoted in Jones 2016). There is much to unpack in Taylor's brief description of his ideal setting for the show. The invocation of a 'Richard Curtis Notting Hill', against which *Catastrophe* is to be distinguished, foregrounds the latter as a site of authenticity and 'cool' in comparison to its aesthetically pleasing, though chintzy, Working Title forebear.[4] Second, the director's stated ideal of a 'Brooklyn-style East End' speaks to a transatlantic connection between Manhattan's less ritzy neighbour and the areas of East London in which *Catastrophe* takes place. Such a connection speaks both to the recent construction of a 'quality' audience that transcends national boundaries, and to the rapid gentrification and associations with hipster culture that both areas possess. I argue that the show's East London setting, with its troubled construction of authenticity and rapid urban change, is inherently connected to its articulation of precarious transatlantic romance.

The construction of authenticity of *Catastrophe* is secured through aesthetic choices as well as the show's tone, and the hints of realism discussed in the previous section. The frequent use of handheld camera seems to tie the show to a documentary–realist aesthetic rather than the three-camera set-up more often associated with the sitcom (Mills 2009). Further to the supposed realism of the narrative itself, the bleak veneer that *Catastrophe* casts over the romance, and its subsequent development into a nuclear family, seems to contest dominant postfeminist discourses idealising these heterosexual norms. While Taylor implicitly constructs the romantic comedy as idealising heterosexual romance and, in turn, the setting in which it takes place, it is notable that the very title of the show positions these conventionally happy phenomena as a form of disaster. A self-conscious positioning as an authentic, and thus problematised, vision of the romance narrative permeates *Catastrophe*, an element to which I will return.

The connection that Taylor makes between Brooklyn and London's East End demonstrates that Hackney is presented as bearing a transnational connection. Certainly, as previously stated, despite *Catastrophe* first appearing on Channel 4, the showrunners maintain that it was always intended for transatlantic distribution (Jones 2016). Jorie Lagerwey and Taylor Nygaard's study of what they term 'Horrible White People shows' is instructive in this regard. Typically thirty minutes in length and focusing on domestic spaces and families, these shows portray self-identified liberal, white characters, whose comedic difficulties are, they argue, 'complicit in a rhetorical shift toward white suffering that has helped sustain structural

white supremacy and worked to support the rise of the political Right'
(Lagerwey and Nygaard 2017). Significant to this cycle of programming,
which includes *Catastrophe*, is a transatlantic model of co-financing and
distribution that, combining traditional broadcasters and Streaming Video
on Demand (SVOD) services, seeks out commonalities of race and class
among an elite audience of highly educated urban dwellers in both the US
and the UK. In *Catastrophe*, this transatlantic audience is even modelled
on Horgan and Delaney's respective national backgrounds. Such an association is played out in Horgan's subsequent project, *Divorce*, made in the
US for HBO (2016–). Lagerwey and Nygaard argue that these elite audiences on both sides of the Atlantic have more in common with each other
than they might with others possessing lower cultural capital from their
respective nations (2017). In this way, national specificity, once crucial to
the reception of television comedy, is eroded in an increasingly globalised
television market in which securing small audiences for 'prestige' shows
emerges as ever more significant.

There is ample evidence to support *Catastrophe* positioning itself
for an elite audience. In the UK, the show is broadcast on Channel 4,
a terrestrial, free-to-air network. Despite its widespread availability,
Hannah Andrews observes that, since the end of the 1990s, Channel 4
has increasingly focused on youth markets, satisfying its public service
mandate to target minority audiences, while also honing in on the 'top end
ABC1 demographic' (Andrews 2012: 573). In the US, *Catastrophe* airs on
Amazon Prime, a SVOD service, for which users must pay a premium.
Both media cultivate a reputation for aesthetic distinctiveness, fostering
their perception as possessing high cultural capital.

That Channel 4 is keen to signal *Catastrophe's* positioning amongst a
landscape of transatlantic quality television is apparent from the show's
sponsorship. When first aired in 2015, *Catastrophe* was billed as the 'new
comedy from Sharon Horgan' and accordingly received as a further example of her acerbic comedy found in BBC3 shows *Pulling* and *Dead Boss*
(Raeside 2015). At this point, the show was sponsored by Fosters, a brand
of lager whose promotional idents have accompanied comedy commissioned by Channel 4 since 2010.[5] However, by the time of the third series'
broadcast in 2017, the show was sponsored by luxury car brand Lexus,
and presented not as a comedy, but as a drama. While the tone of the
series had become considerably bleaker between the first and third series,
it seems significant that Lexus's media planners position their idents as
accompanying 'talked-about, award-winning, critically-acclaimed, high-
rating programmes such as *Homeland*, *Fargo*, *The Good Wife* and *The Mill*'
(Thinkbox 2016). Thus, the change of sponsorship moves *Catastrophe* out

of the arena of the mass-market, domestic sitcom, or feminised romantic comedy, and into a transnational model of quality television.

Taylor's description of a 'Brooklyn-style East End' speaks to the connections between these spaces, as well as their inhabitants. Perhaps most obviously, these are areas outside the immediate economic and cultural centres, embodied by Manhattan and Westminster, respectively. What is more, both Brooklyn and East London have seen rapid and accelerating gentrification within the last ten to fifteen years. Studying this process in London through the lens of changing retail spaces, Phil Hubbard observes that the British capital has followed New York and other cities in the US in pursuing 'arts-led gentrification' (Hubbard 2017: 208). In this process, hard-up artists are attracted to an area for its low rents (and, frequently, large, disused industrial spaces). After some time has passed, that area starts to become known for its artist population, attracting first visitors, then those who wish to relocate to that area. Eventually, the extent and capital of these incomers push the prices of that area to such a level that even the now-successful artists can no longer afford the spaces they once occupied, and are displaced to another part of town, where the cycle seems doomed to repeat itself.[6]

On the other side of the Atlantic, Sharon Zukin's study of gentrification in New York City finds a certain irony in this process. As she observes, a significant factor making these areas attractive is their supposed authenticity, which here is connected to the bohemian mores of the artists and to the independent boutiques, restaurants and bars that surround them (Zukin 2009: 3–4). However, when others are attracted to that same area, these are precisely the features that are frequently displaced. This arts-led gentrification and its associated displacements and ill-fated quests for authenticity bring together Brooklyn and Hackney. Like these areas, *Catastrophe* derives its cultural capital from its supposed construction of authenticity and realism, tapping into precisely the same discourses impelling urban change.

A Hostile Environment?

In *Catastrophe*, Hackney is an area that the show's inhabitants have actively chosen. Although Horgan was, in fact, raised in the borough, it is implied through references to Sharon's parents and her oldest friend, still living in Ireland, that she and her brother, Fergal (Jonathan Forbes), have moved to London as adults. Strikingly, aside from the young children at Sharon's school, none of the show's principal characters is a native Londoner. While the latest census data states that 48.6 per cent of Hackney's population reported themselves as Black or Minority Ethic (BME), such an ethnic

TRANSATLANTIC LOVE IN EAST LONDON

profile is barely visible in *Catastrophe* (London Borough of Hackney 2018). Rob, of course, is American, and his move to the city occurs in the show itself. His American friend, Dave (Daniel Lapaine), has lived in the city only slightly longer than Rob. Scottish couple Fran (Ashley Jensen) and Chris (Mark Bonnar), and Fergal's Spanish wife, Mallandra (Marta Barrio), complete the ensemble. In this, we are perhaps closer to Jermyn's ideal of the modern, cosmopolitan city that provides fertile ground for romance to bloom than we are used to seeing of London in the romantic comedy. For all of these white, middle-class characters, London has been a conscious choice, providing an embodiment of not only the transnational quality audience with whom the show identifies, but also the incoming gentrifiers in East London.

Sharon and Rob are presented as incomers to the urban space they inhabit; their presence is paradoxically said to connote authenticity. Of the two, Rob is more obviously positioned as an outsider. As an American, he stands out among the show's characters, the majority of whom derive from other parts of the UK, or from EU nations who – at the time of writing, at least – are freely permitted to settle in London.[7] As a consequence, Rob is acutely conscious of his contingency, particularly when losing his job puts him at risk of losing his visa. His precarity is made clear through the show's use of urban space. In the first series' second episode, Rob ventures along the nearby Regent's Canal. As he walks along the towpath gazing at his surroundings, a cyclist yells, 'Get out of the way! Fucking idiot!', knocking him off balance. Undeterred, Rob next heads to Broadway Market, a short high street and occasional grocery market, which joins the canal to the southern tip of London Fields. Here, Rob goes into a café and, viewed from outside the window, he is seen knocking his head on a low-hanging lamp, before he takes his drink outside. Even this otherwise agreeable spot, in which Rob briefly smiles to himself, is marred by the presence of a bulldog, which proceeds to defecate in front of him. The dog's similarly gruff owner is unapologetic, grunting a confrontational 'What are you looking at?', after which he walks away, leaving the faeces immediately by Rob's table. Taken together, these instances give the impression that Rob's presence here is unwelcome, and undercut any romantic sensibilities that might have been fostered for this American for his new life in London.

These sequences make plain the extent to which, as an American, Rob is out of place in London's public spaces. A recurring theme is his physical size, described in *The Guardian* as '6ft 3in and broad with it – a huge petrol tank of a man' (Hattenstone 2017). Sharon finds his presence in her small flat stifling, while his body is not easily accommodated by the café he goes to. By series three, Rob's body has replaced Sharon's maternal body as a comedic site of excess. After yet another failed interview in advertising, he decides to sign up to a 'big and tall' modelling agency, who, seeming not to find him sufficiently big or tall, swiftly reject him. His dimensions mark him as out of place and tap into stereotypes of the large, coarse American, whose presence cannot be accommodated. Yet he is not of sufficient size to capitalise on being 'big and tall'. Instead, he simply does not fit, underlining the sense of out-of-place-ness inherent in the couple's unconventional transcontinental union.

These examples of Rob's precarity and bodily excess are played for comedy, which connects his body with the changing urban landscape around him. As Hubbard points out, ironic humour has been a central hallmark of retail gentrification in the UK and elsewhere. In both acknowledging and disavowing the displacement that occurs through gentrification, Hubbard claims that these moments of irony are a type of 'symbolic violence' (2017: 209). He cites 'the Asian Women's Advisory Centre' on Mare Street in Hackney, which was replaced by a 'burger and craft beer joint' dubbed 'The Advisory', while retaining the original signage. Further such attempts at comedy are apparent in 'The Job Centre' in Deptford, a bar that usurped an establishment of the same name, which served to locate employment opportunities for the unskilled. In both cases, organisations designed to assist the vulnerable and marginalised have been displaced in favour of middle-class spaces of conspicuous consumption knowingly retaining their original hallmarks. The new bars' comedic names not only work to domesticate and nullify such displacement, but also serve to anchor those establishments as somehow authentic to that part of London.

It would be a mistake to argue that the hostility that Rob briefly encounters is connected to his status as an immigrant.[8] *Catastrophe* is replete with cosmopolitan characters who have chosen to settle in London. None the less, Rob's position as an American does make him more contingent than the others. Sharon's Irish accent signals her as not originally 'from there', even while it is accompanied by white, middle-class privilege. For Sharon, the streets function as spaces where her anxieties might return. An unexpected encounter with ex-boyfriend Owen (Sam Spruell) prompts her to question whether she is still attractive, to ponder the doctoral thesis that she did not complete, and to compare herself negatively with the woman for whom Owen left her, who is now a successful author of young adult fiction. These anxieties, though, are private to her, in contrast to the very public hostility that Rob experiences. Both characters experience the streets of London as challenging when they are alone. The question, then, is how romance is presented as a solution to the characters' precarity.

Romantic Pragmatism

Lauren Berlant's study of what she terms 'cruel optimism' includes the following description of a scene from Mary Gaitskill's novel, *Two Girls Fat and Thin* (1991): 'a contingent being tries, aversively and indirectly, to induce through an improvised relation to a semi-stranger, an attachment that might become a solidarity that could produce more and better traction in the world' (Berlant 2011: 162). Such an account could well be applied to *Catastrophe*, in which a brief sexual encounter is transformed into the supposedly stable structures of marriage and the nuclear family. Berlant describes 'cruel optimism' as the situation 'when something you desire is an obstacle to your flourishing' (2). It is, she argues, the defining affective dimension of the late twentieth and early twenty-first centuries, wherein pursuit of 'the good life' is inevitably doomed to fail, owing to systemic precarity. While this term continues to describe the parlous economic situation of those on the very bottom of the social scale (see Savage et al. 2013), Berlant argues that precarity has progressed beyond the economic, such that it permeates the affective environment (2011: 192). What is more, the condition of precarity now subsumes those who might be regarded as privileged, such as Sharon and Rob.

Berlant's work chimes with the arguments put forward by Lagerwey and Nygaard, who argue that 'Horrible White People shows' emphasise the plight of the well-off, who must come to terms with 'their loss of access to markers of middle–class status' (2017). *Catastrophe* is no exception, as Sharon and Rob are depicted as both economically and affectively precarious. While an unexpected child puts pressure on both characters' finances, Rob's status as an American places the couple under additional strain and provides a clear pragmatic – rather than romantic – rationale for the pair to marry. It is because of his precarity that Rob disavows his scruples when he finds employment with an unethical pharmaceutical firm. It should, of course, be acknowledged that the couple nevertheless remain financially comfortable. Despite Sharon's frequent jokes about her 'teacher money', she nevertheless finds herself promoted to the position of Deputy Head following the death of one of her colleagues. Precarity is discussed in economic terms but perceived principally in affective ones.

Sharon and Rob's marriage is presented as a practical solution to their unplanned child. Despite the chemistry between the characters, then, romance and marriage are not idealised in the show. Questioning Sharon's decision to marry Rob, Melissa (Sarah Niles) reminds her that 'it's not 1934', with the implication that there no longer exists a societal, moral or financial imperative to marry the father of her baby. In response,

Sharon veers between the apocalyptic and the practical, arguing that she wants someone to 'plough a path through a nuclear winter', for her and the baby, and, more prosaically, that she appreciates his offer of domestic help. Marriage, then, is not idealised here in romantic terms but is referred to strategically, as a way of becoming less precarious.

The cityscapes portrayed in the series provide a considerable lens through which romance is not regarded as a 'happy object', to use Sara Ahmed's term (2010), but as a practical response to precarity. Whereas scenes of the characters alone in London are fraught, often taking place in grey, gloomy conditions, those in which the two characters are together take advantage of soft autumnal lighting and textures. Notably, these shots use limited depth of field such that the viewer focuses only on the characters, rather than on the landscape they travel through. Such a conception of romance is distinct from many cinematic examples of the romantic comedy, where the city provides an environment where romance might thrive. In contrast, *Catastrophe* shows London as a space in which the characters have only the most fragile of connections to one another. Marriage thus provides a legal means of anchoring themselves to the landscape that conspires to reject them.

Considering romance as a pragmatic, rather than idealised, phenomenon puts *Catastrophe* on the opposing side of postfeminist discourses in which heterosexual desirability – and its attendant realisation in a romantic relationship – is paramount (Negra 2009: 6). Here, I draw from Ros Gill's influential work in which postfeminism is figured as a 'sensibility' that characterises much of the contemporary media landscape (2007: 148). As Gill makes clear, regarding postfeminism as a sensibility has the advantage of making postfeminism itself the object of analysis, rather than an epistemological lens through which to view something else. In turn, Gill draws from Angela McRobbie's oft-cited claim that postfeminism 'takes feminism into account' (McRobbie 2004: 255) and is attentive to the ways in which postfeminism remains tangled up with feminism. Indeed, Gill reaffirms that the postfeminist sensibility both embraces key tenets of feminism as taken for granted, while also repudiating the need for continuing feminist activism. It is precisely such a doubled gaze – both within and outside the romantic comedy and the sitcom – that is in evidence within *Catastrophe*, and apparent in the use of landscape. The relationship could have occurred only in London, but the city also engenders the characters' economic and affective precarity.

In conclusion, *Catastrophe*'s setting, predominantly in and around London Fields in Hackney, serves a number of purposes that have an impact on the show's articulation of love across the Atlantic. In the first place, the show's aspirational yet 'authentic' setting, alongside its positioning on Channel 4 and Amazon Prime, has allowed *Catastrophe* to court an elite audience, whose members share more in common with their counterparts across the Atlantic than they might with many of their lower-class compatriots. Considering *Catastrophe* as an example of 'quality' television connects the show to its desirable East London landscape. Romance is thus displaced from its idealised position. While there is no question that the affection between the characters is genuine, romance is shown to be a means of finding security in a contingent space.

The differences between film and television should be noted in this regard. In *Catastrophe*, the wedding provides a fitting conclusion to the first series. However, it is by no means the end of the couple's story. In this, television romantic comedy provides a striking contrast to its cinematic counterpart, which conventionally offers a clear narrative denouement for the central couple. In portraying romance that goes beyond this initial high point of attraction and its subsequent development into a lasting partnership through marriage, the televisual romantic comedy provides greater scope for portraying the inherent instability and indeterminacy of the relationship on screen. In *Catastrophe*, such indeterminacy is particularly acute, given the couple's transcontinental union. As the UK–US 'special relationship' curdles under the current administrations' protectionist and populist tendencies, television's focus on middle-class precarity demonstrates that romance is a strategic defence, rather than an aspiration.

Notes

1. My use of the term 'global city' defers to Saskia Sassen's influential study, which deems London and New York to be global cities *par excellence* by virtue of their economic, political and cultural clout (Sassen 1991).
2. For clarity, I will refer to the pair as 'Horgan' and 'Delaney' in reference to the actors/writers, and 'Sharon' and 'Rob' when talking about the characters they play in *Catastrophe*.
3. The male showrunners, too, have acquired a reputation for talent and skill on a par with that of a cinematic auteur. See Martin (2014).
4. It should be noted that the construction of Notting Hill in Curtis's film as overwhelmingly white and middle-class, and the concomitant eradication of the area's ethnic diversity, were deemed problematic at the time of the film's release, given the area's strong associations with the history of immigration. See Orr (1999) and Jay Bamber's chapter in this volume.
5. Fosters has since been replaced by another beer manufacturer, Coors Light.
6. See Martha Shearer's chapter in this volume for a more in-depth look at gentrification and its impact on the romantic comedy.

7. Between the time of the show's broadcast in 2015 and the time of writing in 2018, the UK narrowly voted to leave the European Union. It is not currently known to what extent freedom of movement and labour will continue.
8. None the less, the UK's European Union referendum of 22 June 2016, and the election of Donald Trump to the Presidency of the United States in November that same year, were regarded as a victory for populist fears over immigration. In the UK, an unprecedented increase of 23 per cent in hate crimes against immigrants was reported in the 11 months following the vote (Bulman 2017).

Works Cited

Ahmed, S. (2010), *The Promise of Happiness*, Durham, NC: Duke University Press.

Andrews, H. (2012), '"This is FilmFour – Not Some Cheesy Pseudo-Hollywood Thing!": The Opening Night Simulcast of FilmFour on Channel 4', *Journal of British Cinema and Television*, 9:4, pp. 569–87.

Berlant, L. (2011), *Cruel Optimism*, Durham, NC: Duke University Press.

Breaking Bad, TV series, created by V. Gilligan. US: Sony Pictures Television, 2008–13.

Bridget Jones's Baby, film, directed by Sharon Maguire. UK and US: Universal Pictures, 2016.

Bulman, M. (2017), 'Brexit Vote Sees Highest Spike in Religious and Racial Hate Crimes Ever Recorded', *The Independent*, 7 July. Available at: <https://www.independent.co.uk/news/uk/home-news/racist-hate-crimes-surge-to-record-high-after-brexit-vote-new-figures-reveal-a7829551.html> (last accessed 26 May 2019).

Catastrophe, TV series, created by R. Delaney and S. Horgan. UK and US: Avalon Television, 2015–.

Dead Boss, TV series, created by S. Horgan and H. Walsh. UK: BBC, 2012.

Divorce, TV series, created by S. Horgan. UK and US: HBO Entertainment, 2016–.

Erickson, C. (2012), 'Rob Delaney: First Person to win "Funniest Person on Twitter"', *Mashable*, 7 May. Available at: <https://mashable.com/2012/05/07/rob-delaney-funniest-twitter/#J.kUzwuK2gqK> (last accessed 26 May 2019).

Gaitskill, M. (1991), *Two Girls Fat and Thin*, London: Simon and Schuster.

Gill, R. (2007), 'Postfeminist Media Culture: Elements of a Sensibility', *European Journal of Cultural Studies*, 10:2, pp. 147–66.

Haggerty, M. (2015), '*Catastrophe* Is the RomCom We've Been Waiting For', *New York* magazine, *Vulture*, 1 July. Available at: <https://www.vulture.com/2015/07/catastrophe-is-the-romcom-weve-been-waiting-for.html> (last accessed 26 May 2019).

Hattenstone, S. (2017), 'Rob Delaney Interview: "If I'm Not Feeling Funny About Something, Then That's Fine"', *The Guardian*, 25 February. Available at: <https://www.theguardian.com/stage/2017/feb/25/rob-delaney-catastrophe-twitter-feeling-funny> (last accessed 26 May 2019).

Honess Roe, A. (2008), 'A Special Relationship? The Coupling of Britain and America in Working Title's Romantic Comedies', in S. Abbott and D. Jermyn (eds), *Falling in Love Again: Romantic Comedy in Contemporary Cinema*, London and New York: I. B. Tauris, pp. 79–91.

Hu, J. (2016), '*Catastrophe* Season Two: Is There Life After the Rom-Com?' *New Republic*, 7 April. Available at: <https://newrepublic.com/article/132468/catastrophe-season-two-life-rom-com> (last accessed 25 May 2019).

Hubbard, P. (2017), *The Battle for the High Street: Retail Gentrification, Class and Disgust*, Basingstoke: Palgrave Macmillan.

Iqbal, N. (2017), 'Funny, Messy and Real: Why Sharon Horgan Is the Most Watchable Woman on TV', *The Guardian*, 7 March. Available at: <https://www.theguardian.com/tv-and-radio/2017/mar/07/funny-messy-real-sharon-horgan-most-watchable-woman-on-tv-catastrophe-divorce-rob-delaney> (last accessed 26 May 2019).

Jeffers McDonald, T. (2007), *Romantic Comedy: Boy Meets Girl Meets Genre*, New York: Wallflower.

Jermyn, D. (2008), 'I Love New York: The Rom-Com's Love Affair with New York City', in S. Abbott and D. Jermyn (eds), *Falling in Love Again: Romantic Comedy in Contemporary Cinema*, London and New York: I. B. Tauris, pp. 9–24.

Jones, A. (2016), 'How *Catastrophe* Revolutionized the Rom-Com', *Heatstreet*, 8 June. Available at: <https://heatst.com/world/how-catastrophe-revolutionized-the-rom-com/> (last accessed 4 July 2017). [site no longer operational]

Lagerwey, J., and T. Nygaard (2017), '*Catastrophe* and Transatlantic Horrible White People', Paper given at the National Cultures of Television Comedy Symposium, 16–17 November. University of Notre Dame in London: London, UK.

Last Chance Harvey, film, directed by J. Hopkins. UK and US: Overture Films, 2008.

Levine, E., and M. Z. Newman (2011), *Legitimating Television: Media Convergence and Cultural Status*, London: Routledge.

London Borough of Hackney (2018), *A Profile of Hackney: Its People and Place*, 29 January. Available at: <https://www.hackney.gov.uk/population?> (last accessed 25 May 2019).

McRobbie, A. (2004), 'Post-feminism and Popular Culture', *Feminist Media Studies*, 4:3, pp. 255–64.

Mad Men, TV series, created by M. Weiner. US: Warner Brothers, 2007–15.

Martin, B. (2014), *Difficult Men: Behind the Scenes of a Creative Revolution: From the Sopranos and the Wire to Mad Men and Breaking Bad*, London: Penguin.

Mills, B. (2009), *The Sitcom*, Edinburgh: Edinburgh University Press.

Mortimer, C. (2010), *Romantic Comedy*, London: Routledge.

Moylan, Brian (2015), '*Catastrophe*: The Romantic Comedy That Banned the Words "I Love You"', *The Guardian*, 22 June. Available at: <https://www.theguardian.com/tv-and-radio/2015/jun/22/catastrophe-rob-delaney-sharon-horgan-amazon-prime> (last accessed 26 May 2019).

Negra, D. (2009), *What a Girl Wants? Fantasizing the Reclamation of the Self in Postfeminism*, London: Routledge.

Notting Hill, film, directed by R. Michell. UK and US: Working Title Pictures, 1999.

Orr, D. (1999), 'It's Notting Hill But Not as I Know It', *The Independent*, 20 May. Available at: <https://www.independent.co.uk/arts-entertainment/its-notting-hill-but-not-as-i-know-it-1094619.html> (last accessed 26 May 2019).

Paskin, W. (2016), 'The Brutal Romantic', *The New Yorker*, 25 April. Available at: <http://newyorker.com/magazine/2016/04/25/sharon-horgan-the-brutal-romantic-behind-catastrophe> (last accessed 26 May 2019)

Pulling, TV series, created by S. Horgan and D. Kelly. UK: BBC3, 2006–9.

Raeside, J. (2015), '*Catastrophe* Review: Depraved, Sweet, and Very Very Funny', *The Guardian*, 20 January. Available at: <https://www.theguardian.com/tv-and-radio/2015/jan/20/catastrophe-review-sharon-horgan-rob-delaney-channel-4> (last accessed 26 May 2019).

Sassen, S. (1991), *The Global City*, Princeton: Princeton University Press.

Savage, M., F. Devine, N. Cunningham, M. Taylor, Y. Li, J. Hjelbrekke, B. Le Roux, S. Friedman and A. Miles (2013), 'A New Model of Social Class? Findings from the BBC's Great British Class Survey', *Sociology*, 47:2, pp. 219–50.

The Sopranos, TV series, created by D. Chase. US: HBO Entertainment, 1999–2007.

The Wire, TV series, created by D. Simon. US: HBO Entertainment, 2002–8.

Thinkbox (2016), 'Lexus Changes Gear with Drama on 4', 10 May. Available at: <https://www.thinkbox.tv/Case-studies/Lexus> (last accessed 26 May 2019).

Zukin, S. (2009), *The Naked City: The Death and Life of Authentic Urban Spaces*, Oxford: Oxford University Press.

CHAPTER 7

On the Fragility of Love Across the Atlantic: Cosmopolitanism and Transatlantic Romance in Drake Doremus's *Like Crazy* (2011)

Manuela Ruiz

To understand the meaning of love today it is not enough to understand the meaning of love today. We must also understand how the self, frontiers, the world and love all interlock. (Beck and Beck-Gernsheim 2014: 183)

In the context of a post-9/11 world, where Western discourses and politics are often defined by an intolerance of cultural otherness and an emphasis on the power of borders, cosmopolitanism has been intensely discussed as a multilayered philosophical, moral and social perspective mainly concerned with such issues as transnational mobility, hospitality, multiculturalism and global justice. These dimensions and concerns suggest a broad definition of cosmopolitanism as 'a condition of openness to the world', which entails 'self and societal transformation in light of the encounter with the Other' (Delanty 2012: 336). From a primarily cultural perspective, cosmopolitanism emerges as a new kind of identity, as well as 'a new kind of everyday space–time experience and of human sociability', defined by a significant loosening of national identifications and a genuine and positive engagement with otherness and difference (Beck 2002: 30).

In an attempt to redefine the mostly theoretical dimension of the contemporary debate on cosmopolitanism within the social sciences, some recent critical trends have moved in the direction of material analyses of the concept by highlighting the ways in which cosmopolitanism is performed in people's everyday lives. In contrast to universal and abstract formulations of cosmopolitanism, a number of critics have called for particularised accounts of 'actually existing cosmopolitanism' (Robbins 1998): in other words, for definitions of cosmopolitanisms that are historically situated, geographically grounded and embedded in material everyday practices (Skrbiš and Woodward 2013; Nava 2007; Appiah 2006). In a similar vein, Ulrich Beck and Nathan Sznaider (2016) have also argued for a critical need to pay more systematic attention to the cosmopolitan condition of real people. Seen in this light, cosmopolitanism cannot just be interpreted as a cultural and political disposition but must also be viewed as a physical orientation to the world (Molz 2006), as an active engagement in opening up to the 'world of the other' and the 'allure of difference' (Nava 2007: 19).

My analysis of the representation of transatlantic love in contemporary cinema will draw precisely on a specific notion of cosmopolitanism as performative that sociologists Zlatko Skrbiš and Ian Woodward have defined in the following terms:

> cosmopolitanism consists of a range of performative components: from cosmopolitan scripts and actors, to particular objects, spaces and settings, to audiences able to feel and appreciate the cosmopolitan implications of universal events and other's performances, to visual, aural and other media objects, to iconic human and non-human representations of universal human traits or values which convey cosmopolitan values at their core. (2013: 27)

Scripts, actors, spaces and settings can, thus, also work in filmic narratives as markers of cosmopolitanism that contribute centrally to the articulation of intimate relations in a world of borders. In an era characterised by unprecedented connectedness, in which cultures are embedded in the global and the transnational, contemporary cinema has captured the notion of cosmopolitanism not as an abstract philosophical perspective, but rather as a complex reality entrenched in people's everyday interactions, practices and routines. In order to trace the intersections between cosmopolitan theory and issues of cinematic representations, I will focus on a millennial filmic text, Drake Doremus's *Like Crazy* (2011), a transatlantic love story in which the plurality of male and female choices and practices mirrors the performative and fluid nature of the cosmopolitan subject.

In the film, Anna (Felicity Jones), a British student who attends college in Los Angeles, meets Jacob (Anton Yelchin), one of her university classmates, and decides to ask him for a date. On their first encounter, there is an immediate connection between them and they embark on a life-changing romance. Anna's desire to spend time with Jacob leads her to violate the terms of her visa so that both can spend the summer holidays together, in spite of Anna's legal duty to return to London on the immigration regulations schedule. After going back home for a time, Anna tries to return to California because their romantic relationship has continued at a distance, but she is not allowed to enter the US. With Jacob waiting for her at the airport with a bouquet of flowers to welcome her back to Santa Monica, Anna, in a melodramatic moment of confusion and frustration, is detained by US immigration officers and is forced to fly back to Great Britain on account of legal complications over her visa.

While separated due to immigration policies on both sides of the Atlantic, Jacob and Anna have transient affairs, but they both get in touch again and resume their transatlantic romance. Love at a distance is hard for both of them, and after Jacob's unsuccessful attempt to live in London with Anna, she asks him to marry her so that they can live together as a couple and, in this way, solve her problems with the US and UK immigration authorities. After their marriage is celebrated in London, Jacob's inability to relocate definitively to Great Britain with Anna prompts them to break up once again, as Jacob decides to go back home instead of starting a life as a married couple in London. But they are not able to live apart and eventually Anna moves to the US, once her problems with immigration issues are definitively solved. The film ends with the final reunion of the transnational couple, starting with an airport scene in which Jacob welcomes Anna, again offering her a bunch of flowers as he tried to do the first time. Drawing attention to the impact of border-crossing experiences on their love story, Anna and Jacob's transatlantic romance finishes with an unconventional ending in which emotional barriers occupy centre stage. The characters share the domestic space of the bathroom, having a shower together, but just as they attempt to create a special moment of intimacy that helps to reunite them as a couple, they seem to show an awareness of certain emotional borders that are now separating them and that might threaten their romantic relationship in the near future. From beginning to end, *Like Crazy*'s plotline revolves around the unpredictable power of borders to transform cosmopolitan personal relations and to force people to reschedule their life plans in a globalised world. Anna and Jacob's transatlantic romance will be no exception.

Having a cosmopolitan identity is not the same for every person, nor is it the same for each person across various settings. With the term 'being cosmopolitan', we can refer, as Skrbiš and Woodward have put it, to 'a set of outlooks and practices, a dispositional repertoire, increasingly available – yet not guaranteed – to individuals for the purposes of dealing with cultural diversity, hybridity and otherness' (2013: 27). For the protagonists of *Like Crazy*, being cosmopolitan will amount to coping with the limitations imposed by the geopolitical borders established by the UK and US nation-states on both sides of the Atlantic, which, in turn, will result in a more subjective kind of barrier dividing them as a couple. I will argue that, in this film, romance and marriage constitute a cosmopolitan test for the leading couple, who will attempt to reconcile their own shared expectations and desires with each other's individual everyday realities as they change places across the Atlantic in the name of romantic love. Anna and Jacob, like most people driven into transnational relationships, feel compelled to deal with borders, visa regulations, financial pressures and social conventions that challenge their romantic relationship.

In this chapter, I devote attention to some of the ways in which romance in recent filmic texts in general, and in *Like Crazy* in particular, are imbued with cosmopolitan fantasies of love across (transatlantic) borders. Transnational romantic experience in today's global world is subordinated to the protagonists' willingness and readiness to use what Gerard Delanty has called the 'cosmopolitan imagination' (2006) within the sphere of intimacy, romance and marriage. Delanty's notion of cosmopolitan imagination not only involves the idea of self-transformation through meaningful encounters with the Other, but it also highlights a sense of our incompleteness. As the cosmopolitan imagination occurs 'when and wherever new relations between self, other and world develop in moments of openness' (Delanty 2006: 27), it can be said to play a key role in the conventional romantic comedy learning process, in which the members of the couple are primarily in search of their own identity as a prerequisite to commit as a couple. In *Like Crazy*'s romantic encounters across the Atlantic, the cinematic representation of those transformative experiences illustrates the dynamics of intimate affairs in a global world. By rescripting transatlantic romance in the twenty-first century as a shared performance of cosmopolitanism, *Like Crazy*, together with many other contemporary cultural texts about romantic love, invites audiences to meditate on the distribution of power between the sexes across borders.

The open-ended unconventional happy ending in *Like Crazy* highlights the difficulties in distributing space between the members of the couple in the context of transnational gender relations. Anna's dissatisfaction with her professional options, as a result of her final relocation in the US, looms large at the time of narrative closure. Can love across the Atlantic be possible only when the creation of the couple becomes part of a cosmopolitan agenda or is transatlantic romance a 'crazy' adventure, as the film's title anticipates, doomed to failure in the absence of a shared cosmopolitan outlook? The answer to this question lies in how the members of the romantic couple face the various challenges associated with their own border-crossing experiences. In *Like Crazy*, these challenges ultimately result in an ambivalent representation of cosmopolitan relations. But before moving on to cinematic textual analysis, further clarity on the relevance of cosmopolitan theory for film studies from a genre theory viewpoint seems necessary. Doremus's cosmopolitan love story, I will argue, can be considered as exemplary of an emerging trend in romantic comedy that places cosmopolitan issues at the heart of the narratives.

A Cosmopolitan Approach to Contemporary Cinema and Romance

As a methodological tool enabling film scholars to approach twenty-first-century cinema, cosmopolitanism has proved to be a culturally relevant framework for interpreting a series of cultural texts that are ultimately produced and consumed in a global context. Rather than speaking of a cosmopolitan cinema in terms of a new conceptual category, I intend to draw on the idea that cosmopolitanism permeates a wide range of filmic discourses today. As Celestino Deleyto explains, a cosmopolitan approach to film studies needs to focus on 'how everyday cosmopolitanism is turned into discourse – how visual texts may evolve a specific set of formal strategies to insert themselves within a global society in which cosmopolitanism has become a prestigious cultural asset' (2017: 97). Identifying the formal strategies through which film narratives engage with cosmopolitan concerns would be the first step in the direction of a cosmopolitan perspective on cinema. Among the potential 'performers of cosmopolitanism' in contemporary cinema (Deleyto 2017: 98), special attention should be paid to the relevance of borders and the meanings associated with cosmopolitan spaces, as well as to the transformations brought about by moments of openness to the other, given the current significant aesthetic, cultural and ideological resonance of these aspects in filmic representation.

The concept of cosmopolitan spaces immediately evokes the presence of a range of borders, such as those spaces associated with modern mobile life like airports or multicultural street markets. While it is true that cosmopolitan encounters occur routinely in any social context, cosmopolitan spaces, also labelled *cosmospaces*, are particularly conducive to constructing 'networks within which cosmopolitan engagements become possible' (Kendall et al. 2009: 154). In my discussion of transatlantic romance, a cosmopolitan space will be identified as 'a zone structured by particular spatial and social characteristics which afford cosmopolitan socialization' (Kendall et al. 2009: 154). At times, cosmospaces may particularly foster the development of cosmopolitan romantic attachments, as is the case with a multicultural classroom or an airport boarding area. As many scholars have noted (Cooper and Rumford 2011; Popescu 2012), borders lie at the centre of contemporary experience, not only in economic relations and geopolitical strategy but also in the sphere of private life, as reflected by the increasing numbers of world families and transnational couples (Beck and Beck-Gernsheim 2014). Romantic comedy, as a traditionally fluid and resilient genre, has engaged with social transformations associated with globalisation by integrating transnational intimate matters into its generic repertoire of narrative motifs. In fact, it is possible to identify a new cycle of transnational romances taking place in a variety of cosmospaces.

The connection between cosmopolitanism, connectivity and transnational love that defines the main plotline in *Like Crazy* has become a recurrent generic pattern in contemporary romantic comedy and it is possible to theorise a significant cosmopolitan turn in an emerging trend of romantic comedy that I have labelled *overseas romances*. Comprising Hollywood productions and European films, overseas romances offer cinematic cosmopolitan pictures of personal life and self-transformation in the global age. *Under the Tuscan Sun* (2003), *A Good Year* (2006), *The Holiday* (2006), *Vicky Christina Barcelona* (2008), *Eat Pray Love* (2011) and *Chinese Puzzle* (2013) can be classified as examples of an expanding cycle, which would also include titles such as *Notting Hill* (1999), *My Life in Ruins* (2009), *Before Sunset* (2004), *Two Days in Paris* (2007), *Leap Year* (2010), *P.S. I Love You* (2007) and *10,000 Kms* (2014), among others. (For more on *The Holiday*, see Deborah Jermyn's chapter in this collection.) Overseas romances explore transnational landscapes of intimacy, love, family life, parenthood and divorce by commenting on how everyday practices in the sphere of private life result in ethical choices, emotional experiences, affective bonds and interpersonal negotiations in the space of a globalised world.

In these narratives, various processes of cosmopolitan self-transformation, frequently codified as unexpected international quests for identity and happiness, are brought to the foreground and come into play in the development of romantic and comic plotlines. The utopian, transformative space of romantic comedy is defined in these comedies as a cosmopolitan territory in which gender identities, family patterns and romantic expectations must be interrogated and validated. Whether by focusing on the protagonists' attempts to create new homes in a foreign setting or on their determination to explore unfamiliar locations in order to find a place in the world, the overseas romances draw attention to the significant role played by cosmopolitan practices and by transnational spaces. In the case of *Like Crazy*, UK and US settings and transatlantic mobility also emerge as key themes in the genre's discourses on love, coupledom and family life. The film, however, does not seem to share the essentially optimistic view of transnational love depicted in most overseas romances and their underlying discourses concerning the transformative potential of romantic relations across borders.

In *Like Crazy*, the potentially enriching self-transformative power of cross-cultural relationships remains highly ambivalent for both members of the couple, thus setting the film apart from other examples of the cycle.

The dichotomy established between familiar and foreign social worlds as interrelated spheres for intimacy and romance acquires paramount importance in the romantic plots of these comedies, a duality in which unfamiliar spaces invariably become modern Shakespearean green worlds where the protagonists eventually manage to negotiate their terms of commitment in order to start over again (Thomas 2000; Deleyto 2009). In *Like Crazy*, however, the host community in which Anna is expected to integrate, after Jacob refuses to settle down in London, does not seem to offer a very promising scenario for the female protagonist in terms of career prospects. The film's final shots, in which Anna comments on the lack of interesting job offers for her in Los Angeles, compared to her recent promotion to magazine editor in London, hints already at a potential obstacle for Anna and Jacob's UK–US marriage.

When confronted with the dilemma of playing either host or guest roles at the various stages of their transatlantic romance and marriage, Anna and Jacob show a significantly different cosmopolitan disposition to adapt to each other's culture and home town. The development of Jacob's cosmopolitan sensibility is presented as an intermittent process that has a relevant impact on the couple's romantic experience. The film, then, establishes a difference between American and European cosmopolitan dispositions from the very beginning. Jacob acknowledges his attachment to his home town as a strategy to search for happiness and fulfilment, whereas Anna contradicts that idea by highlighting the relevance of detaching yourself from familiar environments and comfort zones in order to mature. 'I think it's important to go away for some time from where you've grown up part of your life,' Anna remarks, thus revealing more explicitly her disposition to cross boundaries and engage with difference.

Like Crazy: Cosmopolitan Romance Across Transatlantic Borders

Coded as a millennial transatlantic Romeo-and-Juliet love story, in which the main obstacle between the lovers is not the antagonism of their families but the rules imposed by immigration authorities, *Like Crazy* creates a poetic, ambivalent picture of transnational intimate matters by drawing attention to how border-crossing experiences can result in long-term, satisfying romantic attachments at the same time as the film demonstrates that borders also enhance the fragility of love in an interconnected world. Relying on a distinctively transatlantic cast, with Felicity Jones, born in Birmingham, playing the role of British student Anna Gardner, who travels to Los Angeles and meets Jacob, played by the American actor of

Russian origin Anton Yelchin, *Like Crazy* turns the protagonists' US–UK love affair into its central narrative motif and delineates the romance between Anna and Jacob as an interplay of presence and absence across the Atlantic that allows audiences to catch a glimpse of the fragility of desire and love in our contemporary, mobile world.

Like other transatlantic romantic couples in recent films, Anna and Jacob begin their relationship in a typical romantic comedy scenario, in which, as Deleyto has put it, 'acceptance of engaging with difference becomes the condition and origin of attraction' (2009: 173). Even though *Like Crazy* does not specifically highlight US–UK national difference beyond Jacob's interest in tasting the diverse British brands of whisky that Anna and her parents keep offering to him throughout the film, it becomes clear from the beginning that US–UK national difference will lie at the centre of their love story, not just as a source of attraction but also as the origin of romantic tension. To begin with, it is the couple's different national origins that actually set the narrative plot in motion when Anna decides to spend the summer holidays with Jacob, ignoring the expiry date of her student visa instead of going back to London. Anna's choice to stay in Los Angeles illegally is not just a sign of passionate romantic interest on her part that energises the couple's desire, but it is also a conscious decision to ignore national borders and their corresponding mobility regulations. Anna and Jacob's readiness to cross borders and their attempts to find a space in each other's worlds across the Atlantic, whatever the legal or emotional consequences might be, suggest ultimately that it is the transatlantic, cosmopolitan dimension of their love story that makes the film's discourse on romance more realistic and attractive for audiences.

Cross-border communication between the US–UK couple in *Like Crazy* oscillates between dialogue and silence, virtual proximity and virtual absence, dualities that help to define the notion of 'love across the Atlantic' visually in the light of issues of mobility, connectivity and cosmopolitan performance. In this respect, key moments in the unfolding of the film's romantic plot correspond precisely to decisions that Anna and Jacob make to get either electronically connected or disconnected from each other as an occasion for emotional release and self-expression within their own romantic protocols (Figure 7.1). It is through strategic connections and disconnections that the protagonists try to redefine their individual space, which often means an increase of dissatisfaction and tension as a distant romantic couple. As Jennie Molz has argued in her study of togetherness in a mobile world, 'the decision to live a mobile lifestyle, which includes using information and communication technologies to stay in touch while on the move and at a distance, is a function of the modern understanding of identity-as-choice' (2012: 158).

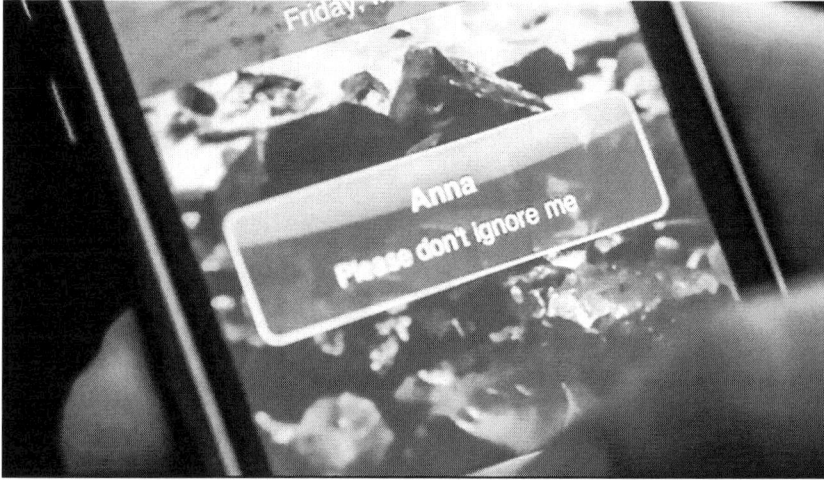

Figure 7.1   Mobile intimacies: (Dis)connections across the Atlantic. Scene from *Like Crazy* (2011).

When Anna and Jacob choose to privilege their respective daily cycles of work, sleep and socialising in London and LA, rather than working at finding moments to be virtually together with their mobile phones and laptops, they engage in an ambivalent cosmopolitan performance that vacillates between remaining open to the Other and restricting the scope of their private lives to the boundaries of their respective national borders. At this point in the film, both Anna and Jacob are presented as facing a dilemma directly related to the neoliberal concept of identity as the capacity to choose and decide, not just about what we consume, but also about our preferred patterns of intimacy.

Within the generic universe of romantic comedy, the redefinition of identity is a preliminary condition for the final achievement of romantic harmony and happiness. Conventionally, the members of the couple must undergo a 'learning process' entailing diverse moments of self-transformation that eventually allow the lovers to meet on common ground at the time of narrative closure (Neale 1992). In *Like Crazy*, Anna and Jacob's learning process, just like their romance and married life, is mainly defined by their transatlantic trips between LA and London, and the choices they make as part of such emotionally intense border-crossing experiences. Situating Anna and Jacob at a crossroads between London and LA, the film's discourse on transatlantic love is articulated around the resolution of a cosmopolitan dilemma that the couple is made to confront. Who will be the cultural host and guest in their future life together and how will this choice affect Anna and Jacob's story of transatlantic love? As the narrative progresses, this open-ended question posed by the film becomes increasingly central in the representation of Anna and Jacob's cosmopolitan relationship and continues to loom large at the time of narrative closure.

In the context of a society on the move, in which a growing number of transnational couples and world families are forced to deal with border-crossing as a routine in their daily lives (Elliot and Urry 2010; Chambers 2012), it is undeniable that borders play an increasingly important role in the definition of romantic protocols and domestic arrangements. As Sandro Mezzadra and Brett Neilson have noted, we are confronted nowadays with a multiplicity of symbolic, linguistic and cultural boundaries that are no longer articulated in fixed ways but, rather, 'overlap, connect and disconnect in often unpredictable ways' (2013: vii). Doremus's film presents borders as unstable lines that help to delineate the contemporary fluid and mobile landscapes of love, romance and family life in a cosmopolitan world, a territory in which (transatlantic) frontiers and, more specifically, the proliferation of border-crossing experiences today may well challenge individual pursuits of happiness.

The ambivalent meanings of borders in the context of transnational intimate relations, justified by their contradictory nature as porous meeting points fostering connectivity and as barriers reinforcing human separation and cultural detachment, are highlighted in *Like Crazy* through its plotline, as well as through *mise-en-scène*, cinematography and editing. Deviating times and spaces associated with Jacob's everyday life in Santa Monica and Anna's routines and lifestyle in London establish physical boundaries between them at the level of the plot. Two continents, two cities and different time zones turn their distant love into a challenging commitment for them. In this sense, the cinematic representation of Anna and Jacob's first date in LA draws attention to the ambivalent nature of cosmopolitanism, as a source of rewarding togetherness, but also of uncertainty in the encounter with the Other. Visually, the film hints at this tension through the display of a prominent, indefinite black obstacle on the screen, a disrupting line that divides the common romantic space the new couple wishes to create (Figure 7.2).

This visual metaphor of borders as both elements of romantic connectivity and anti-cosmopolitan barriers is further expanded through the images of the couple's first-date goodbye scene at the front door of Anna's college residence, when a conventional romantic kiss is replaced by a pretended touch of each other's hands across the door glass (Figure 7.3). Together but separate, the romantic couple is bound to be confronted with a multiplicity of inescapable borders that will gradually put their commitment to the test.

Figure 7.2 Bordering the space of transatlantic romance. Scene from *Like Crazy* (2011).

Figure 7.3 Love at a distance: redefining romantic protocols across borders. Scene from *Like Crazy* (2011).

Despite the protagonists' determination to pursue their transatlantic dream of romantic happiness, the proliferation of borders and border-crossing experiences in *Like Crazy* suggests that it will not be easy for Anna and Jacob to open to each other. High mobility and communication technology can obviously help them, as is the case with many other transnational couples, to create a common romantic ground, but gaps concerning time, space, professional satisfaction and other relevant issues in daily life routines and intimate matters are not easy to ignore and must ultimately be negotiated on the basis of a deeply felt connection to the transatlantic Other. It is by relying on cosmopolitan imagination that borders can ultimately be turned into meeting points in the sphere of intimate relations in the universe of romantic comedy, and, maybe, also in the social world.

The centrality of issues of fluidity, mobility and connectivity in distant intimate relations is also articulated in *Like Crazy* through cinematography and editing. For instance, when Anna returns to LA after she has exceeded her student visa expiry date, the unstable movement created by handheld camera highlights the dramatic tension of the protagonist's inability to cross the US border to meet her lover, who is striving to find a meeting point outside the airport detention centre that may allow the couple to reunite. Witnessing how Anna is informed about her illegal status in the country by US immigration officers becomes all the more frustrating when the handheld camera captures repeated images of Jacob wandering around the airport holding a romantic bunch of flowers for Anna that he will not be able to give her. The border between Anna and Jacob is visually identified with the geopolitical frontier represented by the detention office at the airport, a dividing line that is further highlighted through the absence of sound in the scenes in which they both unsuccessfully try to communicate with each other before Anna is deported to London. In sum, unsettling handheld camera movement makes us aware that Jacob will eventually have no chance to get in touch with Anna, in spite of his own opportunities for mobility within the space of Santa Monica airport.

Together with handheld camera movement, a recurrent editing strategy in the film's representation of borders and their impact on contemporary intimate relations is the use of montage. After Anna tells Jacob about her decision to ignore immigration regulations and stay for the summer so that they can be together, instead of going back to the UK on the due date, a montage scene made up of shots of the lovers hugging and sleeping in bed throughout the holidays punctuates the dissolution of borders from Anna and Jacob's viewpoint, visualising how neither space nor time represents an obstacle at this point in their newly established romantic relationship. Similarly, in a climactic scene at a British airport, after Anna and Jacob have married in London, borders are again metaphorically dismantled through the use of high-speed montage. The eye-catching contrast between the rapid movement of passengers randomly crossing the airport lounge and the static figure of Anna at the centre evokes the suffocating passage of the six months that, under the British law, must necessarily go by before applying for a marriage visa to travel to the US. *Fragile No. 4*, the title of the musical score accompanying this time-lapse scene, also seems to reinforce the point that, under the pressure of borders, Anna and Jacob's relationship is becoming increasingly fragmented and 'fragile'. *Like Crazy* thus capitalises on the ways in which temporal borders interact with subjective experiences and practices to create dissonances, interferences and interruptions that resonate well beyond the moment of border-crossing (Mezzadra and Neilson 2013: 133).

The Fragility of Liquid Transatlantic Love

From a purely sociological perspective, Anna and Jacob's love and marriage in *Like Crazy* might well be understood as an example of what Zygmunt Bauman has labelled 'liquid love' (2003). The film's discourse on the cultural conditions of romance in a globalised world echoes Bauman's conclusions on the evolution of contemporary intimate culture when he states that 'an unprecedented fluidity, fragility and in-built transience (the famed "flexibility") mark all sorts of social bonds', which, not long ago, 'combined into a durable, reliable framework inside which a web of human interactions could be securely interwoven' (Bauman 2003: 91). The fragility of 'liquid love' across the Atlantic in *Like Crazy* is ultimately encapsulated in the film's not-so-happy open ending when Anna decides to move back to LA in order to give her relationship with Jacob a second chance, now as part of a married couple with legal permission to live in the US. Unlike conventional happy endings presumed to be more typical of the genre, the closing scene of Anna and Jacob silently sharing intimate space in the shower, right after Anna's arrival to live in LA, poses the key question of whether their transatlantic relationship will continue happily now that they are no longer forced to cross borders to live together and that virtual connections can finally be replaced by non-virtual closeness.

The image of togetherness and intimacy with which the film concludes invites audiences to align with the utopian promise of happiness congenial to romantic comedy; however, the performances seem to go in the opposite direction. The characters' inexpressive and distant facial expressions, together with their restrained and passionless body language, can be read as signalling a mood of scepticism and uncertainty rather than one of confidence in a future happy ending (Figure 7.4). As the couple step into the

Figure 7.4 Liquid love in a world of borders: the fragility of transatlantic romance.
Scene from *Like Crazy* (2011).

shower, the extreme close-ups of their faces, framed together in a cheek-to-cheek intimate moment and followed by a brief romantic kiss, seem to highlight their shared desire to remain together after all they have been through, to make their transatlantic love story work. But an emotional divide is established between them by the editing through alternative individual close-ups showing special moments in Anna and Jacob's relationship when they first met, as they were perceived by each member of the couple. Flashing images of happy memories evoke their deep mutual affection across time and space borders but, at the same time, locate Anna and Jacob's romantic compatibility in an idyllic past with no continuity in the present time.

They are trying to remember only the 'better' while forgetting the 'worse', as conventional marriage vows demand. However, their distracted looks as they both gaze melancholically in opposite directions can easily be read as a hint of a rather elusive happy ending for the US–UK couple. The very final shot of Jacob, abandoned on his own by Anna in the shower as she leaves in silence, also comes to reinforce the idea that they may not be able to bridge the gap between them when living together as husband and wife, no matter how close they were before they had to deal with transatlantic border-crossing as an essential defining feature of their romance. They are not framed together at the film's end, right before the credit sequence, a separation highlighted by soundtrack music that seems to underscore the protagonists' shared mood of pessimistic uncertainty about their future life as a married couple. The touching slow rhythm of the melancholic *Opus 37* piano score, composed by Dustin O'Halloran, evokes, through its blend of music and silences, the sound of drops of water, or maybe tears, falling down in a moment of introspection. Oscillating between past happy memories and present anxieties about the future at the time of narrative closure, *Like Crazy* seems to conclude that love across transatlantic borders has certainly proven to be alluring and exciting but also 'liquid' and fragile.

In sum, the notion of 'love across the Atlantic', as represented in *Like Crazy*, defines overseas intimate relations as a cosmopolitan performance in which the desire to engage with the transatlantic Other must be reconciled with the conflicting demands of a global context where both borders and connectivity have come to play a significant role in our private lives. By defining the combination of romance and cross-cultural experience as a desirable but challenging recipe for happiness, Doremus's film acknowledges the impact of globalisation and cosmopolitanism on the dynamics of intimate life at the present time. The vicissitudes of Anna and Jacob's romance reveal an 'uneasy cosmopolitanism', which encompasses, as Jackie Stacey has argued, not only optimism about the outcome of cross-cultural encounters but also some sort of prejudice about the Other, which, in *Like Crazy*, prevents the protagonists from feeling completely at ease with their host culture (2015: 170). Anna and Jacob, like other real-life US–UK couples, accept the challenge to remain together across the Atlantic, even when they have mixed feelings about the consequences of their choice.

The global shift towards cultural hybridity that Timothy Brennan has identified as a defining feature of cosmopolitanism underlies the discourses on affective and erotic relationships articulated by *Like Crazy* and by other overseas romance films (1997: 2). In *Like Crazy*, I would conclude, transnational romance and intimacy are ultimately represented as an ambivalent cosmopolitan experience, alluring but fragile. Love across borders is said to be built on moments of empathy and bonding just as much as on personal struggles, occasional alliances and limited openness between the members of the couple. It is a self-transformation process in which the reward of *living happily ever after* may be possible but is never easily achieved in a cosmopolitan world.

Works Cited

Appiah, K. A. (2006), *Cosmopolitanism: Ethics in a World of Strangers*, New York: Norton.

Bauman, Z. (2003), *Liquid Love*, Malden, MA: Polity Press.

Beck, U. (2002), 'The Cosmopolitan Society and its Enemies', *Theory, Culture and Society*, 19:1–2, pp. 17–44.

Beck, U., and E. Beck-Gernsheim (2014), *Distant Love: Personal Life in the Global Age*, Cambridge: Polity Press.

Beck, U., and N. Sznaider (2016), 'Unpacking Cosmopolitanism for the Social Sciences: A Research Agenda', *British Journal of Sociology*, 57:1, pp. 1–23.

Brennan, T. (1997), *At Home in the World: Cosmopolitanism Now*, Cambridge, MA: Harvard University Press.

Chambers, D. (2012), *A Sociology of Family Life: Change and Diversity in Intimate Relations*, Cambridge and Boston: Polity Press.

Cooper, A., and C. Rumford (2011), 'Cosmopolitan Borders: Bordering as Connectivity', in M. Rovisco and M. Nowicka (eds), *The Ashgate Research Companion to Cosmopolitanism*, Farnham and Burlington: Ashgate, pp. 261–75.

Delanty, G. (2006), 'The Cosmopolitan Imagination: Critical Cosmopolitanism and Social Theory', *The British Journal of Sociology*, 57:1, pp. 25–47.

Delanty, G. (2012), 'A Cosmopolitan Approach to the Explanation of Social Change: Social Mechanisms, Processes, Modernity', *Sociological Review*, 60:2, pp. 333–54.

Deleyto, C. (2009), *The Secret Life of Romantic Comedy*, Manchester and New York: Manchester University Press.

Deleyto, C. (2017), 'Looking from the Border: A Cosmopolitan Approach to Contemporary Cinema', *Transnational Cinemas*, 8:2, pp. 95–112.

Elliot, A., and J. Urry (2010), *Mobile Lives*, London and New York: Routledge.

Kendall, G., I. Woodward and Z. Skrbiš (eds) (2009), *The Sociology of Cosmopolitanism: Globalization, Identity, Culture and Government*, New York and Basingstoke: Palgrave Macmillan.

Like Crazy, film, directed by D. Doremus. US: Paramount Vantage, 2011.

Mezzadra, S., and B. Neilson (2013), *Border as Method, or, the Multiplication of Labor*, Durham, NC: Duke University Press.

Molz, J. (2006), 'Cosmopolitan Bodies: Fit to Travel and Travelling to Fit', *Body and Society*, 12:3, pp. 1–21.

Molz, J. (2012), *Travel Connections: Tourism, Technology and Togetherness in a Mobile World*, London and New York: Routledge.

Nava, M. (2007), *Visceral Cosmopolitanism: Gender, Culture and the Normalisation of Difference*, Oxford and New York: Bloomsbury.

Neale, S. (1992), 'The Big Romance or Something Wild: Romantic Comedy Today', *Screen*, 33:3 (Autumn), pp. 284–99.

Popescu, G. (2012), *Bordering and Ordering the Twenty-First Century: Understanding Borders*, New York: Rowman and Littlefield.

Robbins, B. (1998), 'Actually Existing Cosmopolitanism', in B. Robbins and P. Cheah (eds), *Cosmopolitics: Thinking and Feeling Beyond the Nation*, Minneapolis: University of Minnesota Press, pp. 1–19.

Skrbiš, Z., and I. Woodward (2013), *Cosmopolitanism: Uses of the Idea*, London and New Delhi: Sage.

Stacey, J. (2015), 'The Uneasy Cosmopolitans of *Code Unknown*', in N. Glick Schiller and A. Irving (eds), *Whose Cosmopolitanism?: Critical Perspectives, Relationalities and Discontents*, New York: Berghahn, pp. 160–74.

Thomas, D. (2000), *Beyond Genre: Melodrama, Comedy and Romance in Hollywood*, Moffat, UK: Cameron and Hollis.

CHAPTER 8

The *Mise-en-scène* of Romance and Transatlantic Desire: Genre, Space and Place in Nancy Meyers's *The Parent Trap* and *The Holiday*

Deborah Jermyn

Over the course of an outstanding screenwriting, producing and directing career in Hollywood that is now approaching its fifth decade, Nancy Meyers has long been a name synonymous with romantic comedy. Through the 1980s and 1990s, she co-wrote and co-produced a number of star-studded romcoms, including *Baby Boom* (1987) and *I Love Trouble* (1994), continuing to work in the genre after moving to directing. With a cumulative box office of over $1.3 billion to her name, it is striking to note that two of Nancy Meyers's six films as a record-breaking director – *The Parent Trap* (1998) and *The Holiday* (2006) – have centred on transatlantic romances. Both films have also enjoyed a decidedly enduring visibility, their success marked not just by their box-office receipts on release but by the devoted fan followings that have fostered the films' afterlives since then, ardently attended to, for example, through Tumblr pages, event screenings and social media memes. While *The Parent Trap* is recalled particularly fondly as Lindsay Lohan's film debut, *The Holiday* has carved out a special place as a 'Christmas movie', widely (re)watched annually by fans in an affectionate seasonal ritual. But beyond the specificities of the particular allure each holds, the shared trope of the transatlantic love stories at their centres potently underlines the enduring and, indeed, highly commercial appeal of 'mismatched' US–UK couples to the romantic narratives of popular culture, as this whole collection vividly attests.

To date, the bulk of the scholarship around romantic comedy has tended to focus on matters of character, narrative and plot, often as a means to note the genre's predictability and political and intellectual bankruptcy. In this chapter, however, I want to address this inclination to overlook matters pertaining to aesthetics and place in the genre by examining how Meyers crafts the visual terrain of romance and transatlantic space in these films, and through this to reach a more thorough comprehension of the pleasures her films offer. The films' visual and spatial landscapes have been central to their success, demonstrating the genre's part in mythologising the 'special relationship'. They perpetuate particular fantasies of national difference, in which a vision of traditional, 'old' England sits alongside the upscale and verdant homes enabled by wealthy West Coast American entrepreneurialism, both of these marked by white privilege. What, then, might *The Parent Trap* and *The Holiday* tell us about certain pervasive constructions of US–UK romance as it is played out through cinematic spatialisation and, by extension, about the importance of scrutinising space and place in order to advance conceptu-alisations of both romcom and transatlantic romance in popular media?

To set the scene more fully first, both *The Parent Trap* and *The Holiday* entail love stories that bring Anglo-American couples together and cross-cut between the US (California) and the UK (London/Surrey). By the films' endings, all the transatlantic couples are pictured happily together, having evidently decided, however obliquely, that they will try to make these long-distance love affairs work. In the former, Annie Parker and Hallie James (both Lindsay Lohan) are eleven-year-old twins, separated as babies by their divorcing parents, Elizabeth (Natasha Richardson) and Nick (Dennis Quaid), who agreed on splitting up to take one daughter each to live with them in the UK and US, respectively. On serendipitously meeting at summer camp in Maine, the girls swap identities and trans-atlantic homes in a plot to reunite their parents, with Hallie travelling to Elizabeth's elegant central London townhouse while Annie goes to Nick's sprawling estate at his Napa Valley vineyard.[1] Some eight years after *The Parent Trap*, transatlantic love appears again in *The Holiday*. Meyers's third film brings together floundering London newspaper columnist Iris (Kate Winslet) and high-flying Los Angeles film executive Amanda (Cameron Diaz) when both find themselves with broken hearts as Christ-mas approaches, and they impulsively decide to trade homes for the holi-days through an internet house-swap site. On arriving at Rosehill Cottage, Iris's picturesque Surrey home, Amanda soon falls for Iris's charismatic brother Graham (Jude Law), while at Amanda's hi-tech gated mansion, Iris finds solace in both friendship with Amanda's retired screenwriter neighbour Arthur (Eli Wallach) and a burgeoning romance with film composer Miles (Jack Black).

In each film, the distinctiveness of these US versus UK homes and spaces is drawn evocatively to suggest both the differences between protagonists' lives, tastes and identities, and more broadly, the differ-ent experiential terrains of aspirational American versus British (and, particularly, quintessentially 'English') lifestyles. Where the UK offers the charms of traditional heritage-styled locations, the US, by contrast, offers capaciousness and modernity, both becoming 'benevolent, magical settings', as Manuela Ruiz Pardos puts it; in *The Holiday*, for example, this leads to an 'emphasis on the differences between Amanda's hectic lifestyle in sunny L.A. and her simple but gratifying routines in [small-town] Surrey' (2016: 145). Ruiz Pardos here echoes the illuminating work of Celestino Deleyto on 'the space of romantic comedy' as 'a magic space of transformation' (2009: 30–6), in which he traces the origins of the genre back to sixteenth-century Italian prose fiction and drama, and to Shakespeare's comedies. Deleyto insightfully highlights that dramatic tradition in which the movement of characters to a change of location prompts them to 'learn something about themselves that they did not previously know', where they might 'free themselves progressively of inhibitions' (2009: 31). In what follows, I demonstrate how the movement across transatlantic borders in both *The Holiday* and *The Parent Trap* enables exactly this kind of transformative evolution for the protagonists. In Deleyto's words, 'the comic space allows the spectator to glimpse a "better world"' (2009: 36), and in these films this 'better world' of personal and romantic discovery is inexorably interwoven with fantasies of US and UK national difference, all the while reinforcing fantasies of white privilege and affluence.

Over her career, Meyers's films have become synonymous with an identifiably lavish and upmarket approach to design as she attends to every opulent detail of her (unfailingly privileged, white) protagonists' homes, and despite her impressive track record of hit films, she has struggled to find very substantial recognition or appreciation among either film scholars or critics. A key element of reviewers' often dismissive accounts of her work has been precisely that this *mise-en-scène* of luxury is an empty distraction – a showy and seemingly irritating display of materialism that does not compensate for what remains highly generic and formulaic filmmaking. I want here to unravel this recurrent critique of her work and instead to examine how, in *The Parent Trap* and *The Holiday*, as in her other films, Meyers's use of place and *mise-en-scène* is absolutely central to the pleasures her films afford viewers and is intricately entwined with the assembly of character and narrative. Here, in these transatlantic love stories, Meyers lovingly crafts a *mise-en-scène* of romance, in which fantasies pertaining to ('old') British and ('modern') American homes, ways of life and landscapes can be embraced – savoured not only by transatlantic fans but by the global romcom audience. In *The Holiday*, for example, they may share in Iris's delight at seeing the pristine stacks of flashy tech and DVDs contained in film exec Amanda's LA 'media room'; later, this sequence is visually echoed in and evocatively relocated to the quaintness of old-time Surrey, when Amanda browses the copiously filled bookshelves in the library of publisher Graham's charming home. Importantly, too, both women find edification through their lifestyle swap and undergo the 'process of self-transformation' that Ruiz Pardos (2016) speaks of as fundamental to the millennium's wider trend of 'overseas romances'. Hence, earlier in the film, Amanda confesses that she buys and longs to read, but never finds time for, the endless novels others recommend, an opportunity her trip finally affords, while Iris finds new clarity on her own life by watching the women with 'gumption' in the classical Hollywood films she discovers through Arthur.

In tandem with the critical neglect of Meyers as a filmmaker, romantic comedy has struggled to win detailed scholarly and critical consideration. As a result, and unlike other genres, discussion of romcom has largely disregarded attentiveness to its use of *mise-en-scène*, space and place, or cinematography, as if it does not merit such scrutiny, being an entirely 'obvious' mode of filmmaking. Thus in what follows, I challenge this tradition while drawing on a breadth of interdisciplinary perspectives pertaining to space, genre, film language, the cinematic city and film tourism. In doing so, I am mindful of Charlotte Brunsdon's cautions regarding the seductiveness and limitations of work on 'the cinematic city' (2012) claiming interdisciplinary credentials, in an era in which declaring 'interdisciplinarity' has become a means for scholarship to assert a certain cachet. Within such work, first, the full nuances of each discipline cannot be equally marshalled,[2] and second (and most especially here), it is the specificity of the medium – *'of how meaning is made in film'* – that most particularly risks being pushed to the margins (Brunsdon 2012: 224, my emphasis). Thus, this chapter consciously places close textual analysis at its centre, so that amongst the interdisciplinary conceptual approaches informing it, attention to 'the expressive repertoires of filmmaking', as Brunsdon calls for, remains at its core (2012: 225). In sum, this chapter determines how, in these films, Meyers skilfully taps into collective fantasies of transatlantic love and national difference and identity to service the needs of the genre, while drawing on certain familiar cinematic travel tropes and continuing to finesse the distinctive style incurred in 'The Meyers Touch'.

The Space Between Us: Love Across the Atlantic

As inferred above, the tendency for romcom scholarship to sidestep close analysis of *mise-en-scène* and setting can be understood as a troubling lacuna in genre studies. But it becomes all the more a notable absence when located alongside 'the putative "spatial turn" in the humanities [since] the mid-1990s' (Hallam 2010: 277), in which attention to the terrain of space and place was reinvigorated. As a result of this movement, the study of space underwent a period of acute, interdisciplinary transformation, partly in response to burgeoning globalisation and that shift's attendant underscoring of the import of location. Hallam notes, then, how:

> a growing vanguard of researchers has been studying the relationship between film, space and place from disciplines that range from geography, urban studies, architecture and history, to literature, film, media and cultural studies. What motivates much of the work across this apparently disparate field is an interest in the ways in which the interdisciplinary study of moving images . . . provides renewed insights into our knowledge of the development of urban modernity and modern subjectivity. (Hallam 2010: 277–8)

The romcom, like all genres, must hit certain narrative 'beats' as it unfolds, here including the formulation of an obstacle blocking the formation of the nascent couple; and importantly, a commonplace generic motif in respect of how this plays out is that of locational distance or geographical separation. This is a recurrent narrative arc that continues to take on ever more potent resonance in the genre. First, for those of a certain socio-economic class in particular, globalisation has facilitated the greater likelihood of transcontinental and otherwise long-distance relationships; and second, recent times have seen an intensification of the policing and diminution of movement across national borders (see also Manuela Ruiz's chapter in this collection).

It is telling, then, that *The Parent Trap* should open with a sweeping shot of a rapid, rippling ocean, bringing the expanse of the Atlantic vividly to the fore at the film's outset. As the camera pans up from the water's surface, the bow of a liner appears, racing towards the viewer as camera and ship pass. Indeed, this opening capitalises on the cinematic history of what has been called the 'travelling shot' – that is, '[a shot] filmed from the perspective of a moving vehicle' (Edmond 2011: 131) – its fast, fluid trajectory underlining the vessel's colossal majesty while mining the travelling shot's visceral sense of movement and exhilaration (a theme I return to below). John Edmond argues, indeed, that 'the legacy of the travelling shot as an exciting cinematic attraction, and our own travelling experiences mean that we are perceptually primed to pay greater attention to a film's setting than normal' where they are used. Thus, he notes the prevalence of travelling shots utilised as *opening* shots, preambles that exploit 'the excitement and interest' such camerawork provokes (especially amongst 'otherwise static establishing shots'), to arresting effect (2011: 133). Here, as the camera continues to surge onwards, the shot reveals too that this is none other than the *Queen Elizabeth 2* – at one time the flagship vessel of the Cunard

Line – making the transatlantic Southampton to New York crossing. The ship's prominence at the very commencement of the film thus signals Meyers's marshalling of nostalgic notions of the old-time glamour, romance and indulgence with which transatlantic travel was once imbued[3] (bolstered by a jazz/swing soundtrack of Nat King Cole's 'L-O-V-E'), and, by extension, also points to the wealth and privilege of the protagonists. As the credits continue, a montage details a succession of abstract scenes glimpsing fireworks erupting, signatures on a wedding certificate and moonlight on the deck, until finally the couple are captured in a photo following their nuptials, radiant and seated in front of a lifebuoy bearing the ship's insignia, the picture becoming the cherished object that will later prove to the girls that they are twins. The use of location at the film's start in this romantic prelude is thus undoubtedly expressive, the Atlantic Ocean here evoking what Celestino Deleyto, as noted, calls the 'magic space' of romcom (2009). It facilitates the start of the love affair to begin with, while the relationship is also ceremoniously formalised and the twins subsequently conceived here, in this space between – quite literally, trans-Atlantic.

In keeping with the suggestiveness of this opening, both films are marked by a fantasy of free movement between the US and UK. This augments a sense of the nations' 'special relationship' in a manner that belies the actual conditions of such movement as being granted readily only to those with the 'right' passports and visas and sufficient economic privilege, here envisioned in an ocean voyage enjoyed only by wealthy white travellers. Indeed, the antithesis to this fantasy of free movement might be located in the history of slavery and slave ships, the vessels of an industry that made both the US and UK rich, and a past that is never made visible in films that are so insistently peopled only by white subjects. Such a reading chimes with Diane Negra's work on the 'tourist romances' of Hollywood in the 1990s, films that feature US women moving to Europe in a 'fantasy transcendence of US borders' (2001: 82), in which 'Europe has become an ideal staging ground for nostalgic fantasies of American whiteness' (90). In more recent times, debate around the raced and classed inequity of 'free movement' has been more vividly a part of the cultural agenda than at the time of either films' making, following the debacle of Brexit in Europe and the policies of the forty-fifth President of the United States. Thus, just as wealthy Londoner Annie James can freely elect to spend eight weeks in Camp Walden, so too can her mother and sister instantly travel to San Francisco to swap the girls back for return to their rightful homes, while in *The Holiday*, Iris and Amanda can arrange a transcontinental house swap within twenty-four hours. The romcom is not a genre to be overly consumed by the real-world practicalities of such logistical matters, still willing the possibility that love might transcend all. Here, the expanse of space and 'foreignness' between nations and the trials of managing these challenges across relationships is both explicitly foregrounded on occasion (for example, in earnest exchanges between couples trying to determine how a transatlantic relationship might work), but also somehow obscured, rendered opaque through economic privilege and within the more seismic emotional revelation of falling in love.

Towards the close of *The Parent Trap*, then, after Nick and Hallie have impulsively caught the Concorde to London to overtake Elizabeth and (the genuine) Annie on their journey home, Elizabeth does not simply swoon on unexpectedly finding Nick already there waiting for them. Rather, in a speech that verbalises the misgivings of the more pragmatically or cynically minded viewer, and recognises that both she and Nick have each established lives an ocean apart, she exclaims,

> I suppose you just expect me to go weak at the knees and fall into your arms and cry hysterically and say we'll just figure this whole thing out, a bi-continental relationship with our daughters being raised here and there and you and I just picking up where we left off and . . . growing old together . . . and . . . come on Nick, what do you expect, to live happily ever after?

Without hesitation, Nick replies, 'Yes, to all the above' and a lingering kiss seals the deal while the girls look on approvingly, such that here Meyers takes a side-swipe at simple resolutions and the romantic conventions of the genre, even while she delivers on them too. Elsewhere, as a sceptical Amanda prepares to travel back to LA in *The Holiday*, she resists a disconsolate Graham's efforts to persuade her to try a long-distance relationship, pointing out their fate will likely be to split up in six months, 'leaving two miserable people feeling totally mashed up and hurt'. By the end, love wins, as she extends her trip to spend New Year in Surrey with him, joined by Iris and Miles. The *option*, the fact of even having a choice to try being 'bi-continental', is never what is in doubt, then. Of relevance here, Charles W. J. Withers points to how dissemination of the terms 'time–space convergence' and 'time–space distanciation' has served to 'embrace [the] "collapse" of geographical space given technical advances (in travel time and in communications – consequences [of] "the information age" and "the network society")' (2009: 637). And yet, he goes on, pointing to the reductiveness of such an approach, 'There is, of course, much evidence to the contrary: that, in the face of "globalisation", questions of locality, sense of place and of identity in place matter now more than ever' (Withers 2009: 637–8). I want now to consider more closely how the films construct and savour such a position in aesthetic terms.

Trading (Transatlantic) Places

The films' allegiance to enduring presumptions about particular tropes of US and UK identities and experiential terrain, as outlined above, and the concomitant mutual attraction and fascination these hold for each nation is most vividly suggested in the films' reassuringly familiar visual topographies, where, for example, the grand history and architecture of 'old' London contrasts with the rolling space and golden light of California. Initially, in *The Parent Trap*, before the storyline of Elizabeth and Nick's renewed romance gets under way, some well-trodden and thus comfortably dependable ideas of national difference are set in place when Hallie and Annie first meet. Annie's sartorial code, for example, is strikingly formal, like that of a miniature adult, as she dresses in fitted suits with matching headbands and carries a vanity case, signalling ideas about British reserve and her upper-class, 'proper' pedigree. Though she is evidently equally privileged, Hallie, by contrast, is 'casual', with denim jackets and pierced ears that speak to a more relaxed deportment readily associated with popular notions of a Californian lifestyle. While Hallie's corner of the cabin is adorned with an array of pictures and postcards, from the Statue of Liberty and Audrey Hepburn to a Chicago Bulls ticket and the Polo Jeans logo, suggesting ideas of US commercialism and 'glamour', Annie stores her keepsakes in a box adorned with the Queen's portrait and her bedstead is decorated with an 'England' postcard and a toy double-decker red bus, suggesting the comforts (for some) of UK heritage and tradition.

But it is the detail of the protagonists' homes and surrounding landscapes that warrant the closest attention here. Hallie's imminent arrival in London is heralded by an aerial shot of Big Ben and the Houses of Parliament, an unambiguous signposting of what Brunsdon has called 'landmark London' (2007: 21), and one that is also linked directly to Hallie's vision (though not an actual point-of-view shot), since it is followed by a shot of her looking out of her aeroplane window. Hallie's keen gaze is therefore not only that of a child impatient finally to see the mother she has never known, but an avidly desiring *touristic* gaze. Having been collected by the family butler at the bustling airport – in what, interestingly if fleetingly, constitutes the most evidently multicultural sequence seen in any of Meyers's relentlessly white films – Hallie sets off on a drive across London to her interim Kensington home, in one of the capital's most exclusive boroughs, via a montage that constitutes another series of travelling shots and which exemplifies what Brunsdon calls the 'landmark montage' (2007: 22). Set to a lively soundtrack of The La's' 'There She Goes', the sequence moves between shots of iconic locations and of Hallie leaning out of the car window excitedly absorbing it all, as she passes Big Ben (again), Tower Bridge, the Royal Albert Hall, Harrods and the statue of Eros, amongst other sites, eventually pulling up outside her mother and grandfather's elegant home at '7 Pembroke Lane'.

Such a sequence feels far from original. To familiar eyes, it almost has the quality of stock footage or a promotional film. It would be entirely possible, in fact, to read these moments as ironic nods from Meyers, as self-conscious 'postcard' platitudes to please a touristic mind-set. But this is not to deny the affective role of the landmark montage in the film. As with those scholarly accounts that have argued that the travelling shot was part of the arsenal of techniques that made early cinema 'a cinema of attractions', to invoke Tom Gunning's landmark analysis (summarised in Edmond 2011), here the audience are invited to marvel alongside Hallie as she traverses these iconic London spaces. Indeed, there is a conceptual continuity here with the argument I have made elsewhere, that an integral but unacknowledged feature of 'The Meyers Touch' is how the director has recurrently built into her films a self-conscious awareness of the impact and spectacle of her '*mise-en-scène* of aspiration'. Her films repeatedly incorporate sequences in which characters stop to regard and appreciate the impressiveness – the wonder – of the spaces and scenery surrounding them (Jermyn 2017: 155–7), inviting the spectator to share this amazement with them. And while this is used consistently to show the protagonists' awe at the exquisiteness of the homes in Meyers's films, in the instances being examined here it is also tied up in an appreciative wonderment at being transported from the US to the UK, and vice versa. It is difficult to imagine what route to Kensington from any London airport would feasibly take in all these landmarks, but feasibility is not what is at stake here.

Hence, in *The Holiday*, one finds a parallel to *The Parent Trap*'s travelling shot of an awe-struck Hallie hanging out of the car taking in her surroundings, when it is matched by a sequence of Iris too doing just that as she travels excitedly to Amanda's home through sun-drenched LA. Her arrival in the US is heralded again by another magnificent sweeping shot across the ocean (here the Pacific) towards the land, waves breaking on a coastline overlooked by grand hilltop mansions; swooping closer to the beachside highway, the camera eventually comes to focus on a yellow cab driving along it. Iris is captured leaning out of the window beaming at what she sees, as travelling shots of the ocean, and palm trees, and a road sign for 'Sunset Boulevard' (more specifically establishing location) are interspersed with her closing her eyes and inhaling, before audibly exclaiming, 'This is amazing!' Also, as with Hallie, and in a structurally similar fashion to the sequence just described, Annie's imminent arrival at her father's home in Napa is anticipated by an aerial shot that here captures their car weaving through expanses of mountainous and lushly green vineyards. The action cuts to them talking in the car's interior, before Hallie gasps, 'Oh my God!' and leans forward, symbolically announcing the move to another travelling shot and a blurred glimpse of Nick's evidently splendid, sprawling Tuscan villa. Filmed at the real-life sixty-two-acre Staglin Family vineyard in Rutherford, the estate is seen from the perspective of the moving car, suggesting Annie's elated point of view.[4]

The space, sky and land of Napa are, in their contrasting fashion, every bit as arresting as the splendid historical architecture of London. Furthermore, the grandness of all these sequences is all the more acutely rendered because of their unambiguous alignment with a desiring (transatlantic) tourist gaze,[5] and the tenor of such scenes, with their delight in adventure and discovery, unquestionably anticipates and helps set the stage for romance. Indeed, in *The Holiday*, the atmospheric conditions of LA are, in themselves, suggestive of change, promise, movement; as Iris meets Miles for the first time, she comes out to speak to him in the fore-court of Amanda's mansion, and a gust of the warm wind outside blows something into her eye, prompting him to lean in to help her. 'Legend has it, when the Santa Anas blow, all bets are off, anything can happen,' he tells her, examining her eyelash (and paraphrasing writer Raymond Chandler), and the early frisson of something stirring between them is set from therein, in this strangely intimate moment.

It is important here to recognise that the production designer for *The Holiday*, Meyers regular Jon Hutman, has also collaborated with Meyers on *What Women Want* (2000), *Something's Gotta Give* (2003) and *It's Complicated* (2009), with the latter two films arguably containing the most revered interior designs of Meyers's œuvre. Furthermore, the cinematographer on *The Parent Trap* was Dean Cundey, who went on to act as Director of Photography on *The Holiday*. These collaborative relationships constitute creative alliances that remind one of how reductive it would be to propose an unquestioningly auteurist account of how 'The Meyers Touch' has come into being. While the homes of *The Holiday*, like those of *The Parent Trap*, unquestioningly speak of fantasies about US versus UK landscapes and space, they must speak too of individual character, and Meyers's fastidious attention to whether the smallest details of *mise-en-scène* are truthful to her characters is legendary. Of *The Holiday*, popular film blog locationshub comments,

Meyers purposely wanted to show the two locations as being polar opposite of each other. On the outside, Amanda's Los Angeles world is contemporary, green and lush. Iris's hometown is old, snow-covered, and dotted with bare trees. The inside

of their worlds are just as different. Iris's English cottage is small, cozy and warm
with lots of colors and mismatched furniture. Amanda's sprawling California house
is modern, sophisticated and sports a clean, neutral palette. (2013)

Of course, some of these differences are indicative of relative wealth,
as much as national distinctions (which is not to say that Iris's 'cosy'
Surrey cottage suggests anything other than that she is very comfortably
off indeed); for not only is space at more of a premium in much of the
UK than much of the US, the film is careful to emphasise that successful
businesswoman Amanda is, in her own words, earning 'big bucks'. Thus
on arriving at Amanda's home, a lengthy montage of the kind described
above shows Iris excitedly running from pool to room to room squeal-
ing with delight at what she finds, a sequence in which the exterior shots
were filmed in the affluent Californian city of San Marino at a mansion
designed by architect Wallace Neff (locationshub 2013).

While LA is romanticised in the narrative and dialogue as the historical and geographical nucleus of the golden age of cinema, it is notable
that, following Iris's arrival, the outside spaces and landscapes of LA are
not explored with further diverting establishing shots, or made somehow
characterful. The LA storyline moves largely between homes and other
interiors, as is entirely typical of Meyers's style, but this vision is arguably particularly apt here in evoking somewhere so famously characterised
as the epitome of anonymous urban sprawl, a place enduringly described
as a collection of suburbs 'in search of a city'. Furthermore, here this
approach is also one of the ways in which the film naturalises and embeds
its *whiteness*, constructing a landscape quite at odds with what Deleyto has
described at one level as 'a city characterized by staggering diversity' in
real life (2016: 2). He writes compellingly about the initial disconnect he
experienced on his first visit to LA, where he was struck by the breadth of
ethnicities there, the 'overwhelming numbers' of 'Mexicans, Latinos and
Latinas', which bore no relation to the white LA he thought he knew from
a lifetime of cinema (2016: 2), and *The Holiday* is entirely symptomatic of
what Deleyto describes. Furthermore, it is the particularities of *this* spa-
tiality, of LA anonymity, that facilitates one of the film's (self-reflexively
pronounced) 'meet-cutes', between Iris and elder next-door neighbour
Arthur. She introduces herself to him and drives him home after she spots
him lost and wandering on their street, where he tells her he got disoriented because he could not recognise anything any more, in a seeming
critique of the city's anonymous rebuilds.

Meanwhile, Amanda is initially at least rather nonplussed by, and out
of place in, Iris's 'cute' semi-rural cottage, with its unpaved path and too

small bathtub and tiny cupboard space; this is a 'quintessentially English' home (Cooper 2019), though of a very different kind to Elizabeth James's Central London townhouse, and a perplexed Amanda initially decides to fly home early. While the impeccable sense of order and control in Amanda's house thus speaks at one level to money (the security gates and intercom system, the electronically controlled blackout blinds, the bewildering array of devices in the media room), they work at the level of character to align too with her evidently controlling tendencies and her inability to 'switch off'. From a place of initial disconcertment, her burgeoning integration into Iris's comfortable but cluttered, rustic space, with its low ceilings and exposed beams, mismatched fixtures and fabrics, and trinkets on every surface in the style of a traditional homely cottage, is a measure of her character's narrative arc. Gradually relinquishing the anxious predisposition that has both enabled her success (professionally) and constrained her (romantically), she sleeps with Graham on meeting him, cancels her flight home to see him again instead at the village pub (a highly traditional and decidedly unglamorous 'local'), and is eventually welcomed into Graham's home by his young daughters, who tell her 'you look like my Barbie' and invite her to snuggle up in their play-den. As suggested by the contrasts between her flawless, opulent home and Iris's 'cosy' one, she learns to let 'disorder' in, and only then finds love. Indeed, again, the particularities of how space operates differently for her in the UK is, in a quite literal sense, what makes her relationship with Graham possible, as *this space* is what enables her to 'let love in'; they meet because she allows him into the house after he rolls up late at night, banging on the door and asking to use the bathroom (not realising that Iris is away). This is a 'meet-cute' that would have been impossible at her own security-conscious US home, where she lives, in a symbolically loaded even if geographically 'authentic' fashion, behind an iron gate and an intercom system.

On Tour with Nancy Meyers

Finally, if there is any doubt left as to the importance of space in these films, it is a telling facet of their lasting afterlives too that the locations of the ('real') transatlantic homes and settings of both *The Parent Trap* and *The Holiday* described above have come to constitute quietly celebrated fan-sites. They are revered among design bloggers, film location websites and Meyers fans, for example, not just through feature articles but through the process of making and commemorating a 'pilgrimage' of one's own to locations featured in the films. Indeed, in June 2016, when Lindsay

Lohan returned to the site of Annie's London home, actually located at 23 Egerton Terrace in Kensington, and shared a photo of herself on Instagram posing outside (Figure 8.1), with the comment 'a trip down memory lane', the post made international news. Scouring Instagram, Pinterest and YouTube, one finds numerous fans, many of them evidently American and overseas travellers, who have posted similar pictures and videos of their own outside the railings of the elegant townhouse, entirely chiming with Rebecca Williams's summation of the various and significant ways in which fans' 'affective ties to specific places' (2017: 98) are bolstered through such 'fan tourism'. In these acts of fan pilgrimage, Williams elaborates, fans are understood to enter into 'a liminal space which is outside of everyday life' (2017: 99) and to connect with others through 'communitas' (2017: 102), so that one might say these sites become a 'benevolent,

Figure 8.1   Annie's London home, 23 Egerton Terrace, in 2019, though 'it was number 7 in the movie', as Lyndsay Lohan observed on Instagram on returning for her 2016 pilgrimage there. Photo by Deborah Jermyn.

magical setting' for fans, to borrow Ruiz Pardos's phrase again (2016: 145). In this way, the simple act of taking the stroll from Knightsbridge tube station to Egerton Terrace and taking a photo outside number 23 can result in the rewarding sense of somehow entering into the world of a beloved text in an augmented fashion, a sensation perhaps made particularly acute here for overseas fans of these films in that these are, in a sense, films *about* (transatlantic) travel.

When 23 Egerton Terrace came up for sale in 2010, it was featured for a second time on 'hookedonhouses.net', a popular film fan website that lovingly details the design and locations of venerated movie homes. The feature analysed the appeal of Annie's house using interior and exterior stills from the film, alongside a link to the estate agent's website showing how 'the real interiors' look now (Sweeten 2010). This was a location evidently selected by Meyers for how it crystallises a certain idea of 'Englishness' (as with Rosehill Cottage), contrasting dramatically with the Staglin estate in Napa, and one that can be located by fans too, not as a pretend façade on a movie lot, but in a real London street. Yet with an asking price of £14 million at that time, it is evidently entirely removed from the lived experience of anyone but the UK's '1 per cent', such that it is both a real *and* imagined space. Having been built in the 1840s, with its elegant topiaries, Victorian-style wrought ironwork and balconets, the house is evidently one recognisable as aristocratically 'English' in design and style. But amusingly, and in keeping with my comments above about the hackneyed character of the film's 'landmark montage', more than one reviewer pointed facetiously to the *excess* of signifiers when the house is first pictured as evidence of the film's '[corny] vision of London' (Tookey 1998). It elicited a 'groan' from *Times* reviewer Geoff Brown (1998), cringing 'at the sight of that bicycling gent in a bowler hat, gliding through a litter-free London' who cycles past the classic luxury British Bentley sedan parked outside just as Hallie arrives, in a shot that seems like a moment frozen in time, another picture postcard just like Iris's snow-dusted cottage, both of them fantasies of 'old England'.

The UK scenes in *The Holiday* were shot largely in the Surrey Hills village of Shere, located in one of England's protected 'Areas of Outstanding Natural Beauty'. Today, one can visit the White Horse pub where Amanda agrees to meet Graham and friends for their first 'date', and enjoy a drink beneath a portrait of the pair framed to the left of the door as one enters, at the very spot where Graham is seated when he looks up and realises that Amanda did not go home to LA after all (Figure 8.2). With its 'quaint little cottages, medieval streets and waterside setting', it is no surprise that the village (population approximately 3,000) is consistently cited as one of the

Figure 8.2   The White Horse in Shere commemorates the seat where Graham
(Jude Law) realises Amanda (Cameron Diaz) did not go back to the US after all.
Photo by Deborah Jermyn.

most beautiful in the UK, a 'quintessentially English' and 'picture-perfect
village [that] looks like something from a story book' (Cooper 2019). For
a film that has been chided for its 'chocolate box' vision of an English
village, one of the most surprising aspects of visiting Shere for fans might
well be to discover it is not a set but *really does look like this*. And yet
Iris's beloved 'Rosehill Cottage', mounted photographs of which are available for sale in the village gift shop, was actually a simulacrum, a shell,
the façade of which was erected on a plot of land just outside the village.
Taking the track that runs behind the twelfth-century St James Church,
the distinctive spire of which can be spotted in exterior shots, one climbs
the path to find an empty field with a small sign bearing the legend, 'This
is the site of the cottage in the film "The Holiday"' (Figure 8.3) - such
that the spaces of *The Holiday* are inescapably, like *The Parent Trap* and all
uses of 'authentic' locations in film, both tangible and imaginary.

The perfect, fetishised English cottage in the 'real' village of the past
and tradition is thus revealed as a fiction, just like a cardboard Western

Figure 8.3 Visitors to Shere will find 'This is the site of the cottage in the film "The Holiday"'. Photo by Deborah Jermyn.

town on an LA lot, or any of the 'golden age' film scripts that Arthur wrote a half-century ago. While both films do make use of actual, locatable spaces, in each instance this space is but one, evidently highly rarefied, vision of how one slice of (high) society lives – and in this sense, too, these spaces are both real and not real, intertwining exclusive location and lavish set, as abstract to most of the inhabitants of the nations they 'represent' as they are to the transatlantic and international audiences they beguile. But there is no evidence to suggest that audiences do not understand this, or that through these sites Meyers somehow fails to keep faith with them, so frequently overt are the juxtapositions and the reuse of established tropes of 'national difference' she makes, as is the astonishing privilege of the milieu she captures. While, as noted, romcom scholarship has been largely negligent with regard to matters of place, this chapter has reminded us, as Elena Gorfinkel and John David Rhodes argue, that

> Identity is constructed in and through place, whether by our embrace of place, our inhabitation of a particular point in space, or by our rejection of and departure from a given place and our movement toward, adoption and inhabitation of, another. (2011: ix)

Through this chapter's consolidation of close textual analysis with a breadth of conceptual frameworks, it has also demonstrated how space and place here are part of the pleasurable topography of a Nancy Meyers film and of transatlantic romance. This is a topography in which 'mismatched' couples can make sense; in which the romcom's 'magic space' (Deleyto 2009), and the aesthetics that help construct it, facilitate intimacy, optimism and revelation; and where the spectre of distance – of modern love across the Atlantic – need not mean the demise of romance. At the same time, for American viewers particularly, it is possible to locate another aspect of the films' fantasy and 'magic' that lies precisely in their construction of Britain (and, more specifically, England) as the location of a certain (white) America(n)'s past – an embodiment of a mode of nostalgic 'tradition' that the US cannot give them. And in this respect, the pleasures of these films might be understood too as constituting evocative and enduring cinematic fantasies of whiteness.

Notes

1. Importantly, *The Parent Trap* is a remake of David Swift's much loved 1961 classic of the same name. But in Meyers's film the action moves from being located solely in the US to playing out across California and London, speaking suggestively to the ways in which such transatlantic settings have taken on increasing audience appeal and marketability, since the 1990s particularly.
2. For example, I am particularly aware here that the limitations of space (sic) prevent me from engaging earlier conceptualisations of place in Film Studies, which were particularly attentive to how 'movies take place' (Gorfinkel and Rhodes 2011: viii), in terms of both recording it, and being exhibited within it; for more on this theoretical history, see Gorfinkel and Rhodes (2011).
3. For more on the romance of old-time transatlantic liner travel, see Randell and Weedon in this volume.
4. Indeed, an intriguing point of comparative analysis here would be to examine these sequences alongside the revelatory estate shots of the UK's 'heritage film' tradition, but space again prohibits me from exploring this.
5. Significantly, in all the examples examined here, this desiring touristic gaze emanates from a female subject, and while the gendered dimensions of transatlantic travel are outside the scope of this chapter, Negra (2001) and Ruiz Pardos (2016) are absorbing in this respect.

Works Cited

Brown, G. (1998), review of *The Parent Trap*, *The Times*, 10 December, n.p.
Brunsdon, C. (2007), *London in Cinema: The Cinematic City Since 1945*, London: BFI.

Brunsdon, C. (2012), 'The Attractions of the Cinematic City', *Screen*, 3:1, September, pp. 209–27.

Cooper, H. (2019), '14 of Surrey's Prettiest Villages', *Surrey Life*, 31 January. Available at: <https://www.surreylife.co.uk/out-about/places/villages-in-surrey-14-of-the-prettiest-places-to-live-1-4348532> (last accessed 19 February 2019).

Deleyto, C. (2009), *The Secret Life of Romantic Comedy*, Manchester: Manchester University Press.

Deleyto, C. (2016), *From Tinseltown to Bordertown: Los Angeles on Film*, Detroit: Wayne State University.

Edmond, J. (2011), 'Moving Landscapes: Film, Vehicles and the Travelling Shot', *Studies in Australasian Cinema*, 5:2, pp. 131–42.

Gorfinkel, E., and J. D. Rhodes (2011), 'Introduction: The Matter of Places', in J. D. Rhodes and E. Gorfinkel (eds), *Taking Place: Location and the Moving Image*, Minneapolis: University of Minnesota Press, pp. vii–xxix.

Hallam, J. (2010), 'Film, Space and Place: Researching a City in Film', *New Review of Film and Television Studies*, 8:3, pp. 277–96.

It's Complicated, film, directed by N. Meyers. US: Universal Pictures, 2009.

Jermyn, D. (2017), *Nancy Meyers*, London and New York: Bloomsbury.

locationshub (2013), 'The Film Locations of Nancy Meyers' Romantic Comedy: The Holiday', 8 January. Available at: <http://www.locationshub.com/blog/2013/10/27/the-film-locations-of-nancy-meyers-romantic-comedy-the-holiday> (last accessed 17 February 2019).

Negra, D. (2001), 'Romance and/as Tourism: Heritage Whiteness and the (Inter)national Imaginary in the New Woman's Film', in M. Tinkcom and A. Villarejo (eds), *Keyframes: Popular Cinema and Cultural Studies*, London and New York: Routledge, pp. 82–97.

Notting Hill, film, directed by R. Curtis. UK: Working Title Films, 1999.

Ruiz Pardos, M. (2016), 'Cosmopolitan Space and Generic Boundaries in Hollywood Overseas Romances', in D. Walton and J. A. Suarez (eds), *Culture, Space, and Power: Blurred Lines*, New York and London: Lexington, pp. 139–50.

Something's Gotta Give, film, directed by N. Meyers. US: Columbia Pictures Corporation, 2003.

Sweeten, J. (2010), 'For Sale: The House from "The Parent Trap" Movie', *Hooked on Houses*, 30 May. Available at: <https://hookedonhouses.net/2010/05/30/for-sale-the-london-house-from-the-parent-trap-movie/> (last accessed 18 February 2019).

The Holiday, film, directed by N. Meyers. US: Columbia Pictures, 2006.

The Parent Trap, film, directed by D. Swift. US: Walt Disney, 1961.

The Parent Trap, film, directed by N. Meyers. US: Walt Disney, 1998.

Tookey, C. (1998), review of *The Parent Trap*, *The Daily Mail*, 11 December, p. 44.

What Women Want, film, directed by N. Meyers. US: Paramount Pictures, 2000.

Williams, R. (2017), 'Fan Tourism and Pilgrimage', in M. A. Click and S. Scott (eds), *The Routledge Companion to Media Fandom*, London and New York: Routledge, pp. 98–106.

Withers, Charles W. J. (2009), 'Place and the "Spatial Turn" in Geography and in History', *Journal of the History of Ideas*, 70:4, pp. 637–58.

Part Three

Two Lovers Divided by a Common Language: 'Britishness', 'Americanness' and Identity

'American, a Slut, and Out of Your League': Working Title's Equivocal Relationship with Americanness

Jay Bamber

On 27 November 2017, Clarence House announced that Prince Harry had proposed to American actor Meghan Markle and that they would marry in spring 2018. Their relationship had been officially acknowledged a year earlier on the back of what the Prince's Communication Secretary characterised as a 'wave of abuse and harassment' from online trolls and some media pundits (Communication Secretary 2016). By the time of the announcement, the impending royal wedding was being framed as blissfully romantic, with the Prince's declaration that he knew Markle was 'the one' the first time they met being circulated across social media (Reslen 2017). Still, it seemed that the media was divided on how to cover the union, partly undermining the pairing in reports marked by 'racial undertones . . . and . . . outright sexism' (Communication Secretary 2016) and partly swooning over the romantic appeal of what was seen as a highly unlikely and thus especially absorbing pairing (see also Weidhase in this volume).

Some journalists drew parallels between the couple's relationship and that of Edward VIII and Wallis Simpson (Rosenwald 2017), whilst others found a more apt comparison in the controversial liaison between Prince Andrew and American actor Koo Stark in the 1980s (Ridley 2017). Regardless of which historical lens journalists employed, the descriptor 'fairy-tale' was frequently adopted (Ellison 2017). Many commentators attempted to fit Meghan and Harry's courtship into what Sue Short sees as the quintessential fairy-tale narrative – that of 'the heroine who rises above misfortune and marries a prince . . . decisively putting an end to their woes by marrying Prince Charming' (Short 2014: 21). However, Short's use of the 'fairy-tale' descriptor demonstrates the limitations of this outdated framework: for example, by ignoring Markle's long-standing television work – most notably as Rachel Zane on *Suits* (2011–). Crucially, however, all this shuffling around the media's positioning of the courtship may help account for why other commentators reframed it by turning to a more contemporary, though perhaps equally fantastical, narrative – that of the British–American film production company Working Title romcom (Freeman 2017).

Since the 1990s, Working Title has been best known for producing a series of commercially successful films in which their signature formula has been to match a British male romantic lead with a dynamic American woman, seen in a run of titles from *Four Weddings and a Funeral* (1994) to *About Time* (2013) (see Honess Roe 2009). With Markle and Prince Harry's relationship forming a renewed real-world context for enthralment with the Working Title romcom, this chapter will employ close analysis of selected key titles – primarily *Four Weddings and a Funeral*, *Notting Hill* (1999) and *About Time* – to demonstrate how these films work to represent their American characters as attractive (to appeal to international audiences) but ultimately inauthentic without a British milieu and a British love interest to complement them. By demonstrating how these films engage with discourses around 'high' and 'low' art, I unpack Working Title's validation of the British romantic identity through an intertextual relationship with literature, thereby conferring the British with literature's greater cultural authenticity and esteem. Conversely, through discussion of how these films create particularly female narrative arcs, I argue too that they limit the agency of American identity by devaluing the concept of popular art, this despite being (highly successful, commercial) popular art themselves. In doing this, I examine the ways in which these films utilise the hallmarks of the Heritage genre to suggest a depth to their British protagonists that can be extended to American characters only when they adopt certain tropes of Heritage cinema. Finally, by analysing how these duelling national identities culminate in romantic fulfilment, this chapter will interrogate what Americans bring to the 'Anglo-American' union (Hochscherf and Leggott 2010: 9). I argue that while the identities of the British romantic protagonists are not radically altered by their love affairs with Americans, they do nevertheless become more expressive as a result of these US–UK alliances.

The Heritage Doesn't Belong to *Her*: Heritage Cinema and the Othered American

Although *Four Weddings and a Funeral* was not the first romantic comedy produced by Working Title or the first Richard Curtis romcom to find resonance in the coupling of an American and a Brit – an honour that went to *The Tall Guy* (1989) – it was the first to become a noted cultural and financial phenomena. Historically, the British film industry's most successful output in the North American market had been the Heritage film:

a genre that focuses on classics of English literature, is set in the past and features classically trained actors. Claire Monk stresses how important Heritage films such as *A Room with a View* (1985) were in establishing international recognition for the British film industry and how, as a result, their success somewhat limited the scope of what UK financiers were willing to invest in (Monk 2011: 10). Central to Monk's understanding of the Heritage genre are issues of 'quality' and 'cultural value' (Monk 2011: 145), which are provided by the films due to their literary source material and lovingly detailed aesthetics. *A Room with a View*, for example, is an E. M. Forster adaptation, as are the Heritage cinema classics *A Passage to India* (1984) and *Howards End* (1992). For the purposes of this chapter, what is most instructive about the Heritage genre is its connection to the notions of 'high art' and authenticity. As Jaimey Fisher points out, these concepts are essential to the financial viability of Heritage: 'literary linkages, after all, are a proven marketing technique for Heritage Cinema' (Fisher 2010: 187). It is within this context that I suggest that Working Title romcoms use aspects of Heritage cinema to appeal to international audiences, as well as to endorse the romantic viewpoint of those who align with the tropes and concerns of the Heritage genre.

Four Weddings and a Funeral charts the romance between Charles (Hugh Grant), an upper middle-class Brit, and Carrie (Andie McDowell), an American living in London, as they interact with each other at the four weddings and one funeral that make up the film's title. The film signals its preoccupation with national identity immediately; the first thing that the audience learns about Carrie is that she is American. After meeting briefly, Charles stares over at Carrie at a party and asks his friend Fiona (Kristin Scott Thomas) about her. Fiona tells Charles Carrie's name and quickly follows this by describing her as a 'slut' and 'quite out of [Charles's] league'. These descriptors are illustrative of the film's equivocal viewpoint partly because they are contradictory: they suggest that Carrie is too (sexually) available yet still (romantically) unobtainable, at least to someone like Charles.

The film also uses the location of this scene to 'Other' Carrie and validate the British viewpoint simultaneously. Although it is set largely in London, Carrie is introduced in a contemporary pastoral idyll. The audience first sees her in rural England, a setting closely aligned with the Heritage genre, which, in the view of Andrew Higson, reduces British history to the 'soft, pastoral landscape of Southern England, untainted by the modernity of urbanization' (Higson 2012: 608). Paul Dave argues that the relationship between the pastoral and Heritage is so close that there is almost no room for other rural narratives (Dave 2006: 6). By mimicking one of the pre-eminent settings of Heritage cinema – well characterised by the filming location of Dyrham Park in *Remains of the Day* (1993) – we can see how *Four Weddings and a Funeral* lends legitimacy to Charles and signals that his emotions are the ones that should be the audience's primary concern. This is Charles's literal and emotional domain. Yet Carrie is framed as a prize that Charles has no chance of winning; Carrie and her Americanness are thus denigrated moments before being valorised, a collision of sentiments that muddies easy interpretations of how the Working Title films view Americanness.

Indeed, *Four Weddings and a Funeral* signals its ambivalence to Americanness even before it lets its American character speak. In the shooting script for the film, Charles compliments Carrie on the hat she is wearing, as the stage directions read 'Carrie is American, Charles likes her' (Curtis 1996: 9). The fact that she is American is presented, then, as defining her – as if her national identity is a character trait in and of itself. The British characters are given the authorial voice partly because the story takes place in their milieu. They are offered the 'first say' because they can most easily fit in the classic, and therefore legitimate, world of Heritage cinema. Carrie is made Other by her location, her attire and her inability to speak for herself. The group of Brits watch the sole American from a distance – like the characters in the 'gossip novels' of Evelyn Waugh and Jane Austen (Schantz 2008: 18) – isolating Carrie from the group and signifying Americanness as something to be fascinated by, but also something that the British are, or should be, cautious of.

Here, the balancing act Working Title romcoms perform in relation to negotiating national identity starts to become evident. American characters have to be seen as attractive in order to appeal particularly to American audiences, and thus succeed at the box office, but the viewpoint must remain British to enjoy Heritage's legitimacy. The idea that *Four Weddings and a Funeral* was very much made with an American audience in mind is reinforced by that fact that it arrived at American cinemas before British ones and was advertised in Britain as 'America's No. 1 Smash Hit Comedy' (Murphy 2000: 85). Consequently, this put the film in the position of being produced in Britain, yet using its financial success in America as a way of encouraging British audiences to see it. This suggests that the British may hold narrative or cultural authority, but the Americans have the economic one – a long-standing extra-textual notion perpetuated again in the opposition that these films often present. In essence, here Americans are glamorous figures but the British can ultimately provide more substance; and while Americans offer the pleasures of the romantic comedy, the British provide the depth of 'high art'.

The American Can Be on the Poster, But She Can't Have the Voiceover

This tension for British characters between being attracted to, and yet wanting to remain at arm's length from, American qualities is explicit in the opening sequence of *Notting Hill*, a London-set romance charting the love affair between a British bookstore owner, William (Hugh Grant), and Anna (Julia Roberts), a Hollywood star. As with the character of Carrie in *Four Weddings and a Funeral*, Anna is not given the opportunity to introduce herself. The film begins with a montage of red carpet footage of Anna; Anna is a silent image, aspirational (like Carrie) and gazed upon (like Carrie). It is an appealing yet isolating introduction, suggesting success at the expense of her personal relationships. This is in opposition to how William is introduced moments later; he has many friends but little financial success, replicating the trope created with Charles in *Four Weddings and a Funeral*.

As with *Four Weddings and a Funeral*, the American protagonist is talked about before she talks, a distinction that is drawn into sharper relief by William's introduction. The images of Anna on the red carpet are followed by a voiceover from William in which he details where he lives. William, then, is all exposition, whilst Anna has next to none. The difference, and the narrative privilege, are clear; William tells the story, while Anna, as with Carrie, has her story told. Furthermore, by problematically erasing the cultural diversity that makes up real-world Notting Hill, creating what Paul Knox and Steven Pinch refer to as 'Curtisland' (Knox and Pinch 2010: 308), the film places William in a de facto pastoral idyll. William's description of Notting Hill as a 'small village in the middle of a city' reinforces the idea that *Notting Hill* is consciously deurbanising the area. In constructing Notting Hill in this fashion, William is provided with the legitimacy of the Heritage milieu, while also advancing the interpretation that his life is 'real' and therefore preferable to Anna's 'fake' Hollywood life.

This male voiceover device recurs in Curtis's romantic comedy/drama *About Time*, which tells the story of Tim (Domhnall Gleeson), a young time traveller, and examines how his unique abilities shape his romance with a young American, Mary (Rachel McAdams). As with Charles in *Notting Hill*, Tim's voice opens *About Time*, indicating his authorial control. His ability to go back in time and 'redo' key moments of his life furthers that control in ways that some critics found uncomfortable (for example, Toro 2013). Tim, then, has three separate 'meet-cutes' with Mary: in a restaurant, in a gallery and, finally, at a party. Each time he exploits the knowledge gained in their previous meetings to woo her, arguably making

Mary a bystander in her own romance. Again and again, Mary's 'decisions' are actually influenced by Tim's ability to travel through time.

This raises important questions about Mary's agency, questions that *Notting Hill* presents as concerns for Anna, too. As an actress, Anna delivers the words that are dictated to her by a screenwriter, in a fashion that is dictated to her by a director. Anna questions the viability of this lack of personal and professional agency. Taking William's advice, she eventually stars in a Heritage film to extend her viability both as a film star and, importantly, given the esteem the genre confers, as an *actor*, underlining again how Working Title reveres the Heritage genre.

In *Notting Hill*, Anna's defining feature before falling in love with William is her fame. The narrative provides little information about her childhood or her family and so she is rendered history-less. Instead, Anna's history is constituted out of a series of images, further bolstering discourses of Americans as shallow and defined by popular images. Her films are seen projected on screens (in the cinema screens of the opening montage and in William's trip to the cinema), and sordid photographs from her past threaten to derail her career. Whilst Working Title films provide the British characters with authenticity garnered through their ability with words, Americans are made attractive by their alignment with images. Still, when naked photographs of Anna are released, she expresses frustration that she is unable to address and explain the controversy; the images have rendered her silent. Images define Americans in these films; Carrie is associated with a magazine known for its obsession with beautiful, highly stylised images (she works for *Vogue*), while Anna has found success in an art form that is beloved because it makes beautiful images accessible to the masses in a reproducible fashion.

The audience, then, is denied knowledge of these American characters' lives before their arrival in Britain. This presents American identity by contrast as rootless, advancing the suggestions that Britishness is authentic, and that to be American is to search for the same level of authenticity – a search that is primarily conducted through a special (romantic) relationship with a British protagonist. On an early date with Tim, Mary says that she 'loves' the British supermodel Kate Moss and describes her as a 'normal, cheeky girl'. 'Normal' and 'cheeky' are part of the Working Title semantic field of Britishness and Mary elevates them above other artistic considerations. Moss's work appeals to Mary because, to her, it has a British authenticity that shines through the gloss of American consumerist media. On their first truly successful date (Tim's third time meeting Mary, Mary's first time [again] meeting Tim), Tim repeats Mary's reasoning for liking Kate Moss verbatim to her. She believes that they have the same viewpoint, but Tim is merely reciting the monologue that Mary delivered the last time they met.

Tim thus takes her words from her and uses them to gain a romantic advantage, a manipulation that the film does not criticise but which, as noted, proved troubling to some reviewers (for example, Gilby 2013). However, *About Time* is unwavering in its insistence that Tim's Britishness is more authentic than Mary's Americanness, refusing to frame Tim's activities as deceptions.

There are no consequences for Tim's lies and the film consciously frames Tim as fundamentally truthful. When Mary's parents arrive for a visit, Mary asks Tim to lie about their relationship, worried that her parents will disapprove. Mary proves to be an adroit liar, whilst Tim is unable to lie, slipping up and revealing the truth. The contradiction of Tim being able to lie to Mary but not her parents is not addressed by the film, but is an example of *About Time* signifying his 'honesty'. The suggestion seems to be that love, when validated by the actions of the British, is inherently authentic – Tim is not able to lie, so his romantic machinations are framed as truthful. It is easy to see here the implication that Tim's authenticity elevates Mary to the point where she can both recognise and replicate the legitimate British viewpoint – through transatlantic love, Mary is able to legitimise herself.

Whilst Tim is provided a closing narration in *About Time*, *Notting Hill* removes this device, ending instead on a montage sequence set to Elvis Costello's cover of the Aznavour and Kretzmer song, 'She' (Costello 1999). William is not provided with a closing narration, perhaps, to suggest new-found equality and unity between the protagonists (indeed, Anna's assertion that she plans to stay in Britain 'indefinitely' constitutes the final dialogue of the script). By repeating the song 'She', the film highlights Anna's transformation: the first time the song is employed Anna is on the red carpet; the last time, she is in the pastoral gardens of Notting Hill, ensconced in the milieu of Heritage cinema. Although the film does not allow Anna direct address to the audience, the repetition of this song, with its use of the female pronoun, signals to the audience that *Notting Hill* is about Anna and that her narrative is of primary importance. Through accepting authentic British love and turning her back on the American film industry, she is able to achieve authenticity and agency. Anna is provided with the opportunity to make choices about her life: to be married, to be a mother and to pursue more fulfilling (less American) film work.

He's Got the Brains, She's Got the Looks, Let's Make Lots of (Box Office) Money

In *Four Weddings and a Funeral*, Fiona's initial assessment of Carrie as someone who 'used to work for *Vogue*' aligns with a fear expressed by

Anna in a pivotal scene in *Notting Hill* – that she will become 'some sad, middle-aged woman who looks a bit like someone who was famous for a little while'. The past tense invoked in 'used to' and 'was' suggests a flimsiness to the female characters' existences (and to the nature of female stardom) that the films seem to 'rectify' through transatlantic love. Whilst Carrie, Mary and Anna are linked to pictures, Charles, Tim and William's intellectual and emotional weightiness are associated with books.

This calls to mind the British film industry's previous reliance on the Heritage genre and suggests a reticence on the part of the filmmakers to commit to the generic conventions of the American romcom without simultaneously citing British literary history. William's bookstore becomes a metaphorical and liminal space; it is ultimately transnational and (at least for Anna) transformative. The fact that it is a travel bookstore signals that, despite his comfort with Notting Hill, William is open to the idea of a 'foreign' love. William's livelihood depends on British travellers' desire to expand their horizons further than the British milieu, suggesting that William needs something to shift and disrupt what is presented as a romantically unfulfilling British identity.[1] Anna and William meet in the bookstore, but it is also the place in which she finally rejects the power of the images and of image-making that characterise her American identity. After a second-act break-up, Anna makes a last-ditch attempt to rectify their relationship. Her attempt is unsuccessful, partly because, as William says, 'there are just too many pictures' of Anna.

Surrounded by the books that are closely aligned with William, Anna makes her now iconic and much-quoted assertion that 'The fame thing isn't really real you know? And don't forget I'm . . . I'm also just a girl, standing in front of a boy, asking him to love her.' If the fact that Anna is shrugging off her identity is not clear, her romantic gesture is to give William a painting. She hands William an image, that thing which *Notting Hill* has aligned Anna with and in many ways the symbol of her national identity. In his dismissal of Anna's affections, William tells her, 'I live in Notting Hill . . . You live in Beverly Hills' – the land of the image-obsessed, once again suggesting a conflict between (British) authenticity and (American) artifice. The two motifs of these national identities are forced into conflict and Britishness emerges as the victor. Anna reveals the artificiality of her identity ('It's not really real'), hands over a signifier of her power (the image) and leaves broken-hearted, whilst William stays with his books and has his identity reinforced as authentic, if frustrating; he is still the fumbling Brit that began the film.

The final scene of *Notting Hill* reinforces the idea that William's lifestyle (and therefore Britishness) is somehow preferable. Anna and William are in the Notting Hill that the film has constructed as a place of authenticity and romance (despite the film's inauthentic representation of Notting Hill as only a white, privileged, 'enchanted, faux carnival London' [Spicer 2004: 82]). William, meanwhile, is pictured reading: a scene that underlines his more cerebral (British) status again. For this relationship to be truly successful, and for the film to have the much anticipated 'happy ending' that audiences probably expect, *Notting Hill* suggests that Anna must adopt the 'quirky, underachieving ways of the Brits' (Honess Roe 2009: 84) and radically rework her relationship to America and Hollywood. Instead of positioning British characters who are 'under-achieving' negatively, Working Title films reframe and elevate them by virtue of the fact that they lack the *over*-achieving (American) qualities that the films are most suspicious of: namely, new money, commercialism and pop culture.

In both *Four Weddings and a Funeral* and *Notting Hill*, the association between the British characters and literariness is also undercut and used to reinforce the dynamism of the British–American love connection. At the funeral that makes up part of *Four Weddings and a Funeral*'s title, Matthew (John Hannah) memorably recites W. H. Auden's poem 'Funeral Blues' (Auden 1940: 91) to the crowd who have gathered to mourn the death of his partner, Gareth (Simon Callow). This sequence is the most unabashedly emotional of the film, and it leads to Charles having a revelation, which the film later disproves – that the 'waiting for one true love stuff . . . gets you nowhere'. If Charles cannot have the grand love that Matthew and Gareth experienced, then he will be pragmatic and settle for comfortable. Kyle Stevens presents this moment of literary and emotional revelation as Charles's 'most self-reflexive look at love and marriage, cementing his belief that they need not go hand in hand' (Stevens 2009: 137). It leads to Charles declaring his authentic love for, but desire *not* to marry, Carrie. Hearing 'Funeral Blues', then, both reinforces Charles's realistic (read: British) identity and allows him to embrace a more radical notion of what romance might mean for him: namely, love without tradition.

American culture is invested with no such power; before Carrie's unsuccessful marriage, Charles begs her not to get hitched. His plea takes the form of the lyrics to 'I Think I Love You' (Partridge Family 1970), an American pop hit sung by one-time heart-throb David Cassidy. Once again, Americanness is presented as effusive but not authentic enough to provide true transformation. Even the title of the song speaks to American shallowness; the verb 'think' reveals a reticence in Charles's first declaration of love, which stands in contrast to his final declaration that, for the first time in his 'whole life', he is 'totally and utterly in love with another person'. Charles moves away from appealing, though depthless, American pop culture and settles on a deeper understanding of love and companionship.

Similarly, in *Notting Hill*, William's hope for a true love affair is temporarily dashed when William visits Anna on the set of a Henry James film adaptation. Literature enables Anna to expand her horizons and challenge her abilities, playing on a previously expressed fear that she 'can't really act', while it solidifies William's view of himself as a romantic oaf. His worldview is reconfirmed by the literature that he introduced Anna to. Yet both of these literary inspirations are signals to the audience that romantic reconciliations will happen. Significantly, W. H. Auden was born and educated in the UK before he became an American citizen, and Henry James (who moved permanently to England and gained citizenship) found his greatest critical and commercial successes in his explorations of the romantic travails and social differences between the British and their American counterparts. Richard Curtis has thus chosen what are, in many ways, transatlantic texts, to suggest that it is the blending of national identities that makes for a harmonious union.

An American Fail: Working Title and the Dismissal of American Identities

This harmonious union usually suggests that Americans are useful in expanding the British characters' emotional vocabulary, before they are required to capitulate to the British way of life. There is almost never a suggestion that the American characters have family or commitments that would make them want to move back to the US. Though it does not look at a US–UK romance (but rather US–Irish union), for the most damning portrayal of Americanness in the Working Title stable we can look to the national identity-obsessed *The Matchmaker* (1997). *The Matchmaker* finds comedic fuel from the culture clash between Marcy (Janeane Garofalo), an American political campaign manager, and the eccentric inhabitants of a rural Irish town. Marcy is tasked with finding the long-lost relatives of her Senator boss so that he can capture the 'Irish vote' and appear authentic to the Irish–American Boston electorate. Interestingly, *The Matchmaker* is an anomaly in the Working Title catalogue in that it has a female lead and suggests that whilst love is important (it is a romcom, after all), it is not as important as ethical/political transparency.

The Matchmaker quickly signals its belief in seeking positive transnational relations, as Marcy arrives into the Irish airport and is greeted with a mural of former US President John F. Kennedy, the most venerated of the Kennedy Irish–American political clan. Marcy believes in her cause and is idealistic about her Senator's intentions for America, often

WORKING TITLE'S RELATIONSHIP WITH AMERICANNESS 169

extolling his virtues. At the same time as unearthing the Senator's gene-alogy, she begins a romance with bartender Sean (David O'Hara), who has turned his back on a successful career as a journalist. It is through her romance with Sean that Marcy learns of the Senator's corruption, including his spotty voting record and disinterest in progressive politics. In a particularly illustrative sequence, Marcy even learns that the Senator has no Irish heritage and that his public persona is built on a lie about his national identity. This betrayal is presented as more heart-breaking to Marcy than any of the romantic mishaps she experiences with Sean; her belief in 'American values' is shaken and her identity disrupted in ways that force her to question her own complicity in fooling the electorate. Like Anna in *Notting Hill*, Marcy is forced to acknowledge that her career and ideals are 'not really real'. She was tasked with creating an image, and that image is shown to be false and harmful. Americanness here is not only self-serving but also isolating. When Marcy is in America, she is usually alone, a trope that Diane Negra sees as typical of these films, not-ing that 'the heroines are inevitably socially isolated – in *Four Weddings and a Funeral*, American Carrie is virtually always alone, as is Anna in *Notting Hill*' (Negra 2006: 91). This isolation expands on the idea that America is a place in which political authenticity and authentic emotional connections are almost impossible to come by.

Marcy's knowledge of Irishness and (somewhat subversively for Working Title) her uniquely American familiarity with image-making finally allow her to find romantic and political fulfilment. In order to scorn the visiting American Senator for treating the Irish as stereotypes, Marcy instructs the villagers to lean into stereotypical behaviour in obscene ways. She ruins the Senator's publicity campaign because she is 'able to author a scene that reflects her newfound knowledge of the distinction between authentic and fabricated community and legitimately reproach her employer' (Negra 2006: 179). Once again, Working Title uses the rom-com genre to interrogate debates around authenticity and image, and finds Americans lacking. Marcy finds career reinvention and romantic joy in turning her back on American fakeness and instead embracing the natural rhythms of rural Irish life, as exemplified by the emotional and romantic breakthroughs she experiences on the Irish cliffs (much like the characters who experience pastoral emotional exhilaration in Heritage cinema: for example, in *Pride and Prejudice* [2005]). Marcy is yet another example of an American who receives pastoral validation when denouncing parts of their American identity. Just as Anna gets the private gardens of Notting Hill, and Carrie a thunderbolt, Marcy is rewarded for her adoption of a different way of life by the environment around her.

Hollywood Handbook: What Working Title
Americans Teach Brits

However, it would be simplistic to suggest that these films are entirely critical of America, since to do so would be to risk isolating the lucrative American market. Andrew Spicer suggests that it is through the partnership of these two nationalities that the characters learn to understand themselves – 'the romance is a process of self-discovery through which both parties come to understand their own identities' (Spicer 2004: 78). American protagonists are desirable, even if flawed, and push the British characters to 'open up' in ways that they were not able to when they were exclusively in their British milieu. This speaks to one of the central narrative threads that allow Working Title films to function and encourage American audiences to engage with them, in that Americans, before they adopt the British way of life, provide excitement to the Anglo-American love match. In much the same way, elements of the (American) romantic comedy genre provide excitement to the accoutrements of the (British) Heritage one, arguably propelling the Working Title films to significantly more robust box-office takings.

Bradshaw and Dennis argue that these films remain mindful of American tastes and, indeed, somewhat glorify the American viewpoint. In fact, they go as far as to observe that 'Americans love this *Notting Hill* for it's a movie more about their needs than the reality of London's dynamic cultural diversity' (Bradshaw and Dennis 1999). Additionally, Andrew Wallace Chamings suggests that, by making the female characters American in these British (and Irish) settings, they become empowered in ways that American films do not allow: 'even the two romantic leads invert the typical gender roles of the genre' (Wallace Chamings 2014). A narrative in which an American woman is forced to denounce all of the markers of her national identity would feel exploitative to many audiences, so the American characters are shown as invaluable and instructive in the narratives as they allow the British characters to explore new emotions. These Working Title pictures represent transatlantic romance as a form of identity exchange (even if the lionised identity is the British one and its connection to heritage and history). Thus, American protagonists transfer on to their British partners some of the pleasures that make the films appealing to mass audiences: romantic spectacle, sexual sparks and aesthetic beauty.

The idea that Americans provide something necessary to Britain is bolstered by the way that the American characters are shown as financially independent (often to the point of being extremely wealthy) and in control of their sexuality. As Torben Grodal notes of *Four Weddings and a Funeral*, 'the negotiation of a possible bond of love is between two equals', which results in 'there [being] no sign of a male patriarchal gaze' (Grodal 2004: 111). The idea that *Four Weddings and a Funeral*, and Working Title films in general, avoid the male gaze is hard to match with the alignment of American characters with image culture, but Grodal's assertion points to the American characters' equal participation in the narrative (barring *About Time*). If Britishness is presented in these films as preferable to Americanness, the contributions that the American characters provide suggest that they are truly meaningful to the story. It is precisely because the American characters are different, yet not maligned, that they are able to reach their romantic denouements. As Nigel Mathers explains it, they offer 'the possibility of a synthesis of progressive and traditional tendencies and social outlooks' (Mathers 2006: 159).

This framework is to be found too in *Wimbledon* (2004), which tells the love story of a nearly retired UK tennis pro, Peter Colt (Paul Bettany), and a more successful upstart American player, Lizzie (Kirsten Dunst). In their first real interaction, Lizzie bets Peter that he will not be able to hit two targets in a row, something that he has been unsuccessful at just seconds earlier. With Lizzie by his side, Peter wins the bet. Lizzie's American presence re-establishes Peter's identity, while her ambition helps him rise up the rankings once again. Her Americanness has much to offer Peter, renewing his confidence and reinvigorating his tennis game, and in the process aligning her with other Working Title Americans who are useful to British characters, imbuing them with the ability to express their emotions and improve their confidence. Lizzie has many of the traits of her other American Working Title cohorts examined here: she is ambitious, image-conscious and isolated. But also like them, she works to open her British partner's worldview whilst reinforcing his British identity. Just as Anna gives up her Hollywood career and Marcy turns her back on politics, Lizzie loses her game and loses Wimbledon. But, the Working Title movies argue, this does not really matter as long as these American love interests help their British partners take a chance on love. The Americans have to sublimate their American qualities, including public success, in order to benefit from the authenticity of the British romantic identity; they have to quieten their public voice in order to have a more meaningful, personal voice.

Meghan Markle's abandonment of her acting career thus echoes this motif, familiar from Working Title's American romcom women, at the same time as it speaks to some of the concerns the British media evidenced when covering her nuptials. These included how Markle would assimilate to the British way of life (Ritschel 2018) and how she would represent the heritage and protocol of the royal family (Mills 2018). Much of this dialogue was predicated on the question of how Markle had to change: what she would need to learn and, more importantly, what American accoutrements she would have to unlearn. Meghan's Americanness (like that of the Working Title heroines) has allowed Prince Harry to expand his public persona, to redraw himself as the sort of man who would call his partner 'the one'. Now she is tasked with becoming as British as possible, whilst her Americanness is simultaneously framed as an identity that will help reinvigorate the royal family. Markle's similarities to the Working Title American heroine in all these ways are striking. But what is perhaps most arresting is how the media, like these films, discourage rumination on what is lost in playing down the American identity for the British one. The assimilating of Americanness *does* come with sacrifices on the part of the Working Title Americans; they have to move away from their families and often have to adopt less high-profile careers. By aligning the English romantic identity with Heritage cinema, Working Title films argue that that identity is essentially preferable. It is presented as largely a fixed identity that opens up by interacting with an American partner but does not *really* change. Like the fairy-tale narrative structure and discourses that have been used to position Markle and Prince Harry's relationship, and which are often invoked to describe the romcom genre (Tiffin 2007: 350), Working Title films are stories of transformation. But it is the burden of American females to be transformed: whether it be by stepping (further) into the spotlight and becoming a princess, or by shunning the spotlight in order to become 'just a girl, standing in front of a boy, asking him to love her'.

Note

1. This premise takes on new resonances at the time of writing, during the post-Brexit referendum debates. For more on this theme, see the chapter by William Brown in this volume.

Works Cited

A Passage to India, film, directed by D. Lean. UK: EMI Films, 1984.

A Room with a View, film, directed by J. Ivory. UK: Merchant Ivory Productions, 1985.

About Time, film, directed by R. Curtis. UK: Working Title, 2013.

Auden, W. H. (1940), 'Funeral Blues', in *Another Time*, London: Faber and Faber.

Bradshaw, P., and F. Dennis (1999), 'Is This Film Too Cute for Its Own Good?', *The Guardian*, 31 March. Available at: <https://www.theguardian.com/film/1999/mar/31/news> (last accessed 1 May 2018).

Communication Secretary to Prince Harry (2016), 'A Statement from the Communications Secretary to Prince Harry', *Royal UK*, 8 November. Available at: <https://www.royal.uk/statement-communications-secretary-prince-harry> (last accessed 2 May 2018).

Costello, E. (1999), 'She', from the album *Notting Hill*, London: Island Records.

Curtis, R. (1996), *Four Weddings and a Funeral: The Screenplay*, London: St Martin's Press.

Dave, P. (2006), *Visions of England: Class and Culture in Contemporary Cinema*, Oxford: Berg.

Ellison, J. (2017), 'Can Meghan Markle Rewrite the Royal Fairytale?', *Financial Times*, 6 December. Available at: <https://www.ft.com/content/d78a849c-d9e1–11e7-a039-c64b1c09b482> (last accessed 1 May 2018).

Fisher, J. (2010), 'German Historical Film as Production Trend: European Heritage Cinema and Melodrama in *The Lives of Others*', in J. Fisher and B. Prager (eds), *The Collapse of the Conventional: German Film and Its Politics at the Turn of the Twenty First Century*, Detroit: Wayne State University Press, pp. 186–216.

Four Weddings and a Funeral, film, directed by M. Newell. UK: Working Title, 1994.

Freeman, H. (2017), 'When Harry Met Meghan: It's Every Richard Curtis Movie Rolled into One', *The Guardian*, 9 December. Available at: <https://www.theguardian.com/uk-news/2017/dec/09/when-harry-met-meghan-richard-curtis-movie> (last accessed 10 April 2018).

Gilby, R. (2013), 'The Sexual Misdemeanour That Casts a Long Shadow over Richard Curtis's *About Time*', *New Statesman*, 29 August. Available at: <https://www.newstatesman.com/film/2013/08/sexual-misdemeanour-casts-long-shadow-over-richard-curtiss-about-time> (last accessed 8 September 2018).

Grodal, T. (2004), *Embodied Visions: Evolution, Emotion, Culture, and Film*, Oxford: Oxford University Press.

Higson, A. (2012), 'Re-presenting the National Past: Nostalgia and Pastiche in the Heritage Film', in B. Grant (ed.), *Film Genre Reader IV*, Austin: University of Texas Press, pp. 602–28.

Hochscherf, T., and J. Leggott (2010), 'Working Title Films: From Mid-Atlantic to the Heart of Europe?', *Film International*, 1 December, pp. 8–20.

Honess Roe, A. (2009), 'A "Special Relationship"? The Coupling of Britain and America in Working Title's Romantic Comedies', in S. Abbott and D. Jermyn (eds), *Falling In Love Again*, London: I. B Tauris, pp. 79–92.

Howards End, film, directed by J. Ivory. UK: Merchant Ivory Productions, 1992.

Knox, P., and S. Pinch (2010), *Urban Social Geography: An Introduction*, London: Routledge.

Mathers, N. (2006), *Tears of Laughter: Comedy-Drama in 1990s British Cinema*, Manchester: Manchester University Press.

Mills, S. (2018), 'Meghan Markle Has New Role to Master: British Royal Protocol', *Reuters*, 7 May. Available at: <https://www.reuters.com/article/us-britain-royals-protocol/meghan-markle-has-new-role-to-master-british-royal-protocol-idUSKBN1I800B> (last accessed 6 May 2018).

Monk, C. (2011), *Heritage Film Audiences*, Edinburgh: Edinburgh University Press.

Murphy, R. (2000), *British Cinema of the 90s*, London: BFI.

Negra, D. (2006), 'Romance and/as Tourism', in E. Ezra and T. Rowden (eds), *Transnational Cinema: The Film Reader*, London: Routledge, pp. 169–81.

Notting Hill, film, directed by R. Michell. UK: Working Title, 1999.

Partridge Family, The (1970), 'I Think I Love You', New York: Bell Records.

Pride and Prejudice, film, directed by J. Wright. UK: Focus Features, 2005.

Remains of the Day, film, directed by J. Ivory. UK: Merchant Ivory Productions, 1993.

Reslen, E. (2017), 'The Most Romantic Things Prince Harry Has Ever Said About Meghan Markle', *Good Housekeeping*, 28 November. Available at: <https://www.goodhousekeeping.com/life/entertainment/news/a47053/prince-harry-meghan-markle-quotes/> (last accessed 7 May 2018).

Ridley, J. (2017), 'This is the Meghan Markle of the '80s', *The New York Post*, 7 August. Available at: <https://nypost.com/2017/08/07/this-is-the-meghan-markle-of-the-80s/> (last accessed 28 April 2018).

Ritschel, C. (2018), '11 British phrases Meghan Markle Will Have to Learn Before the Royal Wedding', *The Independent*, 1 May. Available at: <https://www.independent.co.uk/royalwedding/meghan-markle-royal-wedding-british-phrases-learn-prince-harry-a8312571.html> (last accessed 2 May 2018).

Rosenwald, M. (2017), 'The Last Time a Royal Tried to Marry a Divorced American It Sparked a Crisis', *Independent*, 29 November. Available at: <https://www.independent.co.uk/news/uk/home-news/meghan-markle-prince-harry-engaged-royal-wedding-divorced-american-crisis-windsor-castle-king-wallis-a8081986.html> (last accessed 23 April 2018).

Schantz, N. (2008), *Gossip, Letters, Phones: The Scandal of Female Networks in Film and Literature*, Oxford: Oxford University Press.

Short, S. (2014), *Fairy Tale and Film: Old Tales with a New Spin*, London: Palgrave Macmillan.

Spicer, A. (2004), 'The Reluctance to Commit: Hugh Grant and the New British Romantic Comedy', in P. Powrie, A. Davies and B. Babbington (eds), *The Trouble with Men: Masculinities in European and Hollywood Cinema*, London: Wallflower Press, pp. 77–89.

Stevens, K. (2009), 'What a Difference a Gay Makes: Marriage in the 1990s Romantic Comedy', in S. Abbott and D. Jermyn (eds), *Falling in Love Again*, London: I. B. Tauris, pp. 132–46.

Suits, TV series, created by A. Korsch. US: USA Network, 2011–.

The Matchmaker, film, directed by M. Joffe. Ireland: Working Title, 1997.

The Tall Guy, film, directed by M. Smith. UK: Working Title, 1989.

Tiffin, J. (2007), 'Film and Video', in D. Haase (ed.), *The Greenwood Encyclopedia of Folktales Volumes 1–3*, London: Greenwood Press, pp. 342–50.

Toro, G. (2013), 'NYFF Review: Time Travel Rom-Com "About Time" Starring Rachel McAdams & Domnhall Gleeson', *Indiewire*, 23 September. Available at: <http://www.indiewire.com/2013/09/nyff-review-time-travel-rom-com-about-time-starring-rachel-mcadams-domnhall-gleeson-93369/> (last accessed 25 April 2018).

Wallace Chamings, A. (2014), 'The Subversive Awkwardness of *Four Weddings and a Funeral*', *The Atlantic*, 16 April. Available at: <https://www.theatlantic.com/entertainment/archive/2014/04/the-subversive-awkwardness-of-em-four-weddings-and-a-funeral-em/360703/> (last accessed 1 May 2018).

Wimbledon, film, directed by R. Loncraine. UK: Working Title, 2004.

CHAPTER 10

'It's the American Dream': British Audiences and the Contemporary Hollywood Romcom

Alice Guilluy

Within the fast-expanding field of romantic comedy (or 'romcom') studies, the analysis of the 'special relationship' between Britain and the US has mostly centred on Working Title productions of the nineties and early noughties, with a particular focus on films associated with the writer–director Richard Curtis, such as *Four Weddings and a Funeral* (1994), *Notting Hill* (1999) and *Love Actually* (2003). Annabel Honess Roe, for example, notes that by constructing Britishness in opposition to Americanness, Curtis's films offer a homogenised version of British national identity that 'neglect[s] the cultural and ethnic diversity of contemporary Britain' (Honess Roe 2009: 90). Andrew Higson attributes this restricted representation to the process of transnational film distribution, during which '"national cultures" are often reduced down to brand images' (Higson 2011: 93). This converges with the work of Richard Maltby, whose analysis of the reception of Hollywood films abroad emphasises the inevitable distortion of media messages when consumed by non-domestic audiences. He thus suggests that the version of America consumed by British audiences of Hollywood films is necessarily less complex than that of domestic audiences (Maltby and Stokes 2004: 2–3). Like Maltby's, my focus here is the distribution and consumption of film across the Atlantic and, more specifically, the reception of Hollywood cinema in Britain. Where this chapter differs from other contributions in this collection is in its methodology, as I approach the transatlantic romance between Britain and the US via audience studies. Drawing on original empirical audience data (see Guilluy 2017), I want to question the 'specialness' of this relationship by focusing on British audiences' responses to a genre closely associated with Hollywood: the romantic comedy.

The material upon which this chapter is drawn comes from a set of original interviews conducted with romcom viewers in Britain, France and Germany between 2013 and 2015. The respondents were recruited both online and through word of mouth, with a view to investigating the impact of national identity on cinematic consumption and taste. This chapter draws primarily on interviews with UK audiences, conducted in London, Manchester and Kent. The majority of the ninety participants were students and young professionals in their twenties to early thirties. Most were also white and educated to degree level, and two-thirds of participants identified as women. As this chapter will demonstrate, what mostly differentiated British participants from other European audience members was their greater familiarity with and more nuanced understanding of film's use of sound. In this respect, a real 'special relationship' between the UK and the US was visible – or, rather, audible. Overall, however, British audiences' reading of the film was much closer to that of other European participants than I had originally anticipated, since all were marked by a strong critique of the conservatism and consumerism that participants saw as inherent to Hollywood cinema. In these interviews, the 'special relationship' between Britain and the US was overshadowed by a widespread mistrust of US cultural hegemony and the American Dream, revealing the romcom to be an important and perhaps under-estimated site of negotiation, in which audiences actively navigate the intersecting politics of class, gender and pleasure.

Researching Contemporary Romcom Audiences

The interviews analysed in this chapter were conducted as part of a broader doctoral research project on the European reception of contemporary Hollywood romantic comedy. Interviews lasted just under three hours on average and were structured in two parts: the first was a participant-observation section in which the participants and I watched the film *Sweet Home Alabama* (2002). This was followed by a semi-structured discussion of the film in particular, and the romcom genre more broadly.[1] Since my research originally set out to compare the national reception of global Hollywood, *Sweet Home Alabama*'s 'obvious' Americanness – particularly its pointed references to American history and culture – made it an interesting and highly pertinent case study.

The film centres around Alabama-born Melanie (Reese Witherspoon), a rising star of the New York fashion scene, who gets engaged to Andrew (Patrick Dempsey), a politician and the son of New York's mayor, Kate Hennings (Candice Bergen). However, Melanie turns out to be still married to her childhood sweetheart Jake (Josh Lucas), whom she believes to be working in a tyre factory. The film follows Melanie as she returns to her native Alabama and reunites with the friends and family she left behind. At the end of the film, she leaves Andrew at the altar and gets back together with Jake, who has since secretly founded a high-end glassware company. The couple eventually move to New York together, where the film's closing montage indicates that they both go on to run successful businesses and start a family.

One of my research questions was, effectively, to see whether European audiences would 'get' the film, or whether some of its more nuanced references to US history and culture – for example, in relation to idea(l)s of 'the South' – would be lost in translation. The film's box-office results seemed to fit this hypothesis, as the film was much less successful in other parts of the world than in the US, where it remains in the top twenty biggest-grossing romcoms of all time (Box Office Mojo). There were also significant variations in the film's success between France (where it performed particularly poorly), Germany and the UK. I thus also set out to test whether these quantitative differences would be reflected in the qualitative interview data.

The interviews were conducted between 2013 and 2015, during a shift in the critical and popular discourse around the romantic comedy genre, which Martha Shearer has called the 'death of the rom-com narrative' (Shearer forthcoming). This followed the steep and much-commented-upon decline in romcom studio productions in the early 2010s (Nicholson 2014), at a time when actors previously associated with the genre were very publicly moving away from them. This context undoubtedly shaped participants' responses. Thus, a large number of my interviewees made comparisons between *Sweet Home Alabama*'s Josh Lucas and American actor Matthew McConaughey, whose 'McConaissance' was then making headlines (Syme 2014). At the same time, and with the exception of *The Mindy Project* (2012–17), the interviews took place before the genre's much-commented shift to television, and the development of critically acclaimed shows such as *Catastrophe* (2015–),[2] *Master of None* (2015–17) and *LOVE* (2016–18). Particularly significant for this chapter is also the political context for the interviews, all of which were undertaken before the Brexit referendum or the US presidential election of 2016. In retrospect, this cultural and political setting was certainly relevant to contextualising the interviewees' responses. Indeed, on rewatching the film today, it seems striking that only one participant compared *Sweet Home Alabama*'s blonde, trouser suit-wearing female Democrat politician to Hillary Clinton [Interview 31, London]. As the rest of this chapter will seek to demonstrate, however, what is striking about the interview results is how scathing British and other European participants' assessment of the American Dream was well before the 2016 presidential election.

Sweet Home Alabama: **The Politics of Sound and Music**

Participants across all three countries were unanimous in their description of *Sweet Home Alabama* as a 'very American' [Leo, Group 24, London] film. This sort of emphasis was frequent: indeed, when I asked participants to discuss the film's Americanness, I was often met with laughter and disbelief: 'Oh my god, [it's] *so American!*' stressed twenty-three-year-old Noel [Interview 29, London], whilst student Laura noted that the film 'can't get *more* American!' [Group 28, London]. In fact, this seemed so evident to my participants that they sometimes struggled to express what, exactly, made the film American. Nevertheless, most seemed to concur with graphic designer Tina that this was immediately recognisable: 'You *know* it's American,' she stressed [Interview 27, London].

One of the features identified by participants as '*so American*' was the film's use of sound, and most particularly its soundtrack. Thus, when I asked what characterises the romcom genre, Neil pointed to 'the *bouncy* music when the comedy part happens [. . .] just to let you know it's a comedy bit' [Group 31, London]; meanwhile, Betty highlighted the use of '*zippy* music' in montage sequences to 'put you in the *mood*' [Group 23, London]. A similar point was also made by participants in Group 28 (London) when I asked them why they felt the film was so American:

> Karen: Even in like – like the [with emphasis] *conventions* (they use), the *music* at the *beginning* and . . .
>
> [the group chuckles]
>
> Lola: Yeah . . . the music [chuckles]
>
> Karen [laughing]: And them *constantly* playing 'Sweet Home Alabama'.
>
> [Group 28, London]

The film's repetitive use of music, then, is seen by most participants as characteristically American. This fits into a broader trend amongst participants, which is to associate Hollywood cinema – and Americanness more broadly – with excess, both stylistically and ideologically. For example, almost all participants, whether in France, Germany or the UK, viewed the film as overly consumerist, and a number also criticised Reese Witherspoon's Melanie for being exaggeratedly feminine in her appearance – her blondeness, in particular, was singled out as artificial and stereotypical [Group 1, Berlin; Groups 18 and 21, France].

However, if the musical choices mark the film as clearly 'foreign' to these audiences, the pleasure they provoke also seems to stem partially from recognition and familiarity. This is exemplified by participants' reactions to *Sweet Home Alabama*'s village fair scene, in which the film's title song (Lynyrd Skynyrd 1974) is performed by a local band. Participants audibly and visibly demonstrated their familiarity with the scene: the song sometimes elicited laughter (Noel joked that it 'had to happen' [Interview 29, London]) or groans ('it makes me *sick*,' complained Arabella [Group 30, Manchester]). Several participants also danced along in their seats or tapped their foot along with the music:

[Felicity and Betty dance in their seats]

Felicity [smiling]: I don't care, I love this song!

[. . .] Betty: It *is* good! It's a complete classic! But still, there's a side to me that goes 'leave' once the title of the film's been said.

Felicity: Really?

Betty: Yeah! Like, clap and leave.

[Group 23, London]

Hence, the familiarity of the song could also be a source of pleasure for participants, which was displayed both orally and physically. At the same time, the pleasure in the song was 'hedged' (Billig 1989: 210), as the interviewees also used it to display a form of superiority to the film (as seen in Betty's comment about 'clap and leave').

Groups in the UK were more likely to engage with the film's score and sound, most likely because of the familiarity of the language. In addition to tapping and/or dancing along to the music, a number knew the song well enough to hum and sing along. Louis, a writer and film aficionado [Group 33, London], even told me during the interview that he'd been 'resisting from picking [his] guitar up and joining [in]!' At the same time, the reactions to 'Sweet Home Alabama' as an emblem for the South and, for many groups, American culture in general, seems to support Richard Maltby's previously cited argument about the distortion of cultural productions when consumed outside of their home country (Maltby and Stokes 2004: 2–3). Indeed, only one group, or rather only one participant, discussed the song's relation to American history and politics at length:

Neil: You know this song is a whole – it's just a . . . it's a like a *beef* between them and Neil Young? [pause] Cos Neil Young wrote a song called 'Southern Man'? Where he's talking about how people from Alabama just . . . like to crack whips.

Henry: Is it the guy who's in Roses though?

Neil: Huh?

Henry: [laughing] Is it a Guns 'N' Roses song?

Neil: This?

Nate: Yeah.

Neil: No Lynyrd Skynyrd they're called. They're from Alabama.

Henry: Okay.

Rose: Yeah but isn't – is this song (about) slavery?

Neil: [quoting along] 'A Southern Man don't need him . . . '

Rose [jumping in]: No . . .

Neil: No this song [pause] this song is about [pause] Alabama being a fucking great place to live.

Rose: No, this song is about slavery.

Neil: No, 'Southern Man' is about slavery.

[Group 31, London]

The confusion in this exchange is significant, with the participants in disagreement about the historical and political positioning of both Neil Young and Lynyrd Skynyrd. By contrast, all participants (regardless of their national identity) read the film as a clear glorification of the US Confederacy: all laughed and ridiculed the film's 'battlefield' sequence, in which Melanie's father engages in a historical re-enactment of a Civil War battle. Others were also very critical of the film's erasure of the South's historical racism, particularly the issue of slavery. This was best highlighted by PhD student Annie: 'they're *celebrating* the house of the plantation, with obviously [. . .] *none* of the political *history* that comes with the plantation. And they have black servants as well!' [Group 34, Kent]. And whilst participants were very critical of this erasure, very few seemed aware of how the song contributed to this dynamic. This is perhaps even more striking considering the high level of cultural capital across my sample, evident in participants' demonstrated knowledge of filmic conventions, as well as detailed knowledge of US history. Even in his own group, for example, Neil struggled to get his point across.

British groups also displayed a particular sensitivity to the film's sound(s) with regard to accents. This was a lot less frequent in the French and German groups because a large proportion of them (nearly all in the German cases and just over half in France) watched the film dubbed into their own language. Moreover, neither of the dubbed versions attempted to adapt the North/South accent difference to their national context; in both the French and the German versions, all actors speak with the same unaccented language. Hence, the cultural and social differences upon which much of the film's romance narrative relies are at least partially erased in the French and German versions. In France, meanwhile, the groups that did seem to display a sensitivity to the accents were Groups 16 and 17 [Paris], both of which included participants with particularly high cultural capital, as they had lived/studied in either Britain or America for extended periods of time. Thus, some of the class and historical issues bound up in regional accents were effectively lost in translation for French and German audiences, whilst a 'special' relationship was retained for British viewers in this respect. There were, however, limitations to this familiarity: as the above exchange illustrates, some of the political and historical nuances of US popular music were still lost on a number of UK viewers.

British participants' engagement with the film's Southern accents was generally playful. Indeed, some viewers who had already seen the film seemed to find substantial pleasure in quoting along with, or pre-empting, the actors' lines, in a similar manner to the fans watching *The Empire Strikes Back* (1980) in Will Brooker's study of the *Star Wars* franchise (Brooker 2002: 59). In each group, this tended to be the 'role' taken by one person in particular, often the group organiser and someone who had already seen the film several times, as was the case with Betty in Group 23 [London], Arabella in Group 30 [Manchester] and Annie in Group 34 [Kent]. This playfulness, however, again displayed participants' ambivalence towards the film and American – particularly Southern – culture. Indeed, quoting along was also a form of distinction, as the accents and tones of voice used were frequently mocked and exaggerated:

> *Jake and his friends are sitting on top of the town's water tower, and all are suggesting where they should go to next.*
> *Eldon: Come on, let's go to the Roadhouse.*
>> Annie [fake Southern accent, deep voice]: Roadhouse!
>> [group laughs]
> *Sheldon: Or should we drive up to Fairview and bowl a few frames?*
>> Annie [same voice]: Bowling!
>> Valerie: I think my favourite part actually of this is Annie saying things.
>> Annie [laughing]: Sorry! [the group laughs] That was like a *Family Guy* quote!
>> Lilly: Do you know you're doing it? [they laugh]
>> Annie: Yeah!
>> [Group 34, Kent]

The playfulness of the participants' response to American accents is evident in this extract, as Annie's imitation of the film becomes an accompaniment to the screen performance. The reference to *Family Guy* (Fox, 1999–), an animated television sitcom known for its crassness, suggests a form of value judgement alongside the evident pleasure of familiarity. For a number of participants, quoting dialogue was a clear source of collective enjoyment. With many British participants also noting the clear class divide created between the film's two locations – New York and Alabama – the act of quoting along also becomes a performance of social 'distinction' (Bourdieu 1979): a display of superiority to 'redneck' (namely, white, working-class, rural) American culture. This aligned with a general 'political' performance from participants in that, throughout the discussions, Americanness and Europeanness were constructed as political binaries, with Europe (or rather Britain, France or Germany, depending on the location of the interview) defined as socially liberal and America associated with capitalism and conservatism. Hence, through the act of exaggerated repetition, Americanness is simultaneously embraced and mocked. British audiences thus, to some extent, demonstrated a 'special relationship' to the film's use of sound and music, in that they were more attuned to the social and historical connotations associated with Southern accents, or the significance of country music to a degree. On the other hand, as we shall now see, UK audiences' readings of *Sweet Home Alabama*'s romance narrative is remarkably similar to that of other European groups.

The American Dream

In his history of the American Dream, Jim Cullen notes that the concept has played a central role in shaping the idea of the American nation, though its meaning has shifted significantly along the way. In its contemporary iteration, Cullen defines the Dream as the assumption that 'in the United States anything is possible if you want it badly enough' (2004: 17). Thus, the Dream has become strongly associated with class mobility and, as Karen Sternheimer notes, 'the deep-seated American belief that both hard work and luck can lead anyone to rise above their beginnings' (Sternheimer 2014: 10). The significant and long-standing gap between this universalist rhetoric and the real, stark inequalities of everyday life in the US has particularly come to the fore in recent political discourse. This was perhaps more prominent in the summer of 2017, with the Trump administration's termination of the Deferred Action for Childhood Arrival (DACA) programme, a move described in a number of progressive US publications and organisations as a 'threat to' or 'the end of the American Dream' (Blanc et al. 2017; Noguera 2017). By contrast, what is significant about my participants' assessment of the Dream – several years before the election of Donald Trump – is their emphasis on its inherent impossibility.

Though the precise term did not necessarily come up every time, a third of viewers – most of them British and German – strongly identified *Sweet Home Alabama*'s narrative of class mobility with Americanness. When asked to summarise the film, a number of participants highlighted the central couple's narrative of social mobility: 'It's like in that American way, it's American-dream-esque? [. . .] Like going away and making something of themselves. Like she had nothing, and she made out of nothing [sic], like hard work and all that crap,' explained charity worker Felicity [Group 23, London]. The parallel between the protagonists' trajectory is reinforced in the film, as the expression 'making something of oneself' bookends the film, where it is used to describe both Melanie and Jake. Thus, early on in the film, New York Mayor Kate commends the former 'for making something of herself'. Later, this is echoed in the final confrontation between Melanie and Jake: 'Why didn't you tell me you came to New York?' she asks. 'I needed to make something of myself,' he responds.

Broadly, participants were quite critical of the film's parallel between the two protagonists, which they read as presenting the happily-ever-after as a reward for social mobility. Hence when Melanie starts to get curious about the beautiful glass used at the street fair, Nate [Group 31, London] correctly guessed that this must be related to Jake, before noting: 'What's funny about that is that the subtext of that is: "Oh right you're *successful* now! *Okay*! Divorce is off!"' His girlfriend Rose, however, disagreed: 'Yeah but she's already successful on her own, and also she's marrying someone who she met (somewhere else) and is much richer than he is.' This was not a moral argument as such, however, as both Rose and Nate agreed that Melanie's love for Jake should not hinge on his financial success. Rather, their disagreement was based on whether the narrative supported or undermined this argument. Participants were thus clearly sensitive to the strong association between romantic and economic success. At the same time, this association is reinforced by the structural similarities between the romcom plot and the American Dream narrative.

The Romance Narrative

Catherine Roach defines the romance narrative, or romance story, as 'the story of love, as a noun, [which] reduces down in its essence to a verb. In its most condensed form the story is a command, a verbal imperative: "Love!"' (2016: 20). Roach breaks down the romance narrative, which she identifies as present in everything from romance novels to pop music and, crucially, romantic comedies, into nine key components:

1) It's hard to be alone, especially 2) in a man's world, but 3) romance helps as a religion of love, even though *it involves 4) hard work, and 5) risk* because it leads to 6) healing, 7) great sex, and 8) happiness, and it 9) levels the playing field for women. (Roach 2016: 21, my emphasis)

It is this individualised imperative to love, or rather this representation of the romantic happily-ever-after as the outcome of risk-taking and hard work, that parallels the self-determinism at the heart of the American Dream.

The argument can also be reversed: if the romance narrative is intrinsically self-deterministic, whereby happiness in love is based on individual hard work, the American Dream in current popular culture can also be described *as* a romance narrative. In June 2014, for example, the screenwriter, actress and 'queen of rom-com' (Rackham 2016) Mindy Kaling was invited to give a speech at the Harvard School of Law, which she finished thus:

I am an American of Indian origin whose parents were raised in India [. . .] They met in Africa, immigrated to America, and now I am the star and the creator of my own network television program. The continents travelled, the languages mastered, the standardised tests prepared for and taken over and over again, and the cultures navigated are amazing even to me. My family's dream, about a future unfettered by limitations imposed by *who* you know, and dependent only on *what* you know, was only possible in America. Their romance with this country is more romantic than *any* romantic comedy that I could ever write. And it's all because they believed, as I do, in the concept of the inherent fairness that is alive in America; and that here you could aspire and succeed, and my parents believed that their children could aspire and succeed to levels that could not have happened anywhere else in the world. (Kaling 2014)

A transgenerational narrative that posits America as the land of freedom and equality (made, importantly, in the pre-President Trump era), Kaling's speech is a rephrasing of the American Dream, or rather, a retelling of the Dream *as* a romantic comedy. Indeed, it is possible to map the contours of her speech using Catherine Roach's blueprint for the romance narrative. Kaling's narrative hints at an initial situation characterised by unfairness and inequality ('it's a hard world': elements one and two of Roach's model), which is transcended through 'amazing' hard work and risk (stages four and five) and near-religious 'belief' in America ('romance as religion', stage three), to achieve a state of true and fair equilibrium ('level playing field', stage nine).

Several cultural scholars have already noted the important role played by film in the propagation of the American Dream. Thus, for Jim Cullen, the Hollywood film industry of the 1920s came to embody the American Dream (2004: 173–7). Emmett Winn, meanwhile, points to the Cinderella narrative – a romcom staple – which he sees retold in *Working Girl* (1988), *Maid in Manhattan* (2002) or *Pretty Woman* (1990) as a gendered version of the American Dream (2007: 87–98). However, what is also striking is the similarity of the narrative structure between the American Dream and the contemporary romcom, which presents romance as an overcoming-the-odds narrative. To put it another way, both success and romance, it seems, favour the bold. And indeed, in the traditional romantic comedy, fortune and love tend to come together.

Out of all the interviews, a British group spent the most time inter-rogating the concept of the American Dream, which was framed within a discussion of class and ideology. Group 31 [London] returned to the notion of the Dream several times during the screening and discussion, including when I asked them to compare British and American romantic comedies. Rose was the first to respond; she reinforced the connection between national identity and class formation by noting that British rom-coms featured less successful characters then their American counter-parts. Citing *Notting Hill*, she noted the film's emphasis on the social difference between the multimillionaire actress played by Julia Roberts and Hugh Grant's shop owner, adding:

> Rose: and like, they all take the piss out of Hugh Grant's character for being a complete dork.
>
> Henry: Julia Roberts's character.
>
> Henry: But she still fell for him though! Again it's that . . .
>
> Martin [jumping in]: What about [in exaggerated cheerful tone]: 'You can do it!'
>
> [Rose laughs loudly]
>
> Henry: 'You got it guys!'
>
> Rose [laughing, same tone as Henry]: 'Keep going!'
>
> Henry: 'You can just be a *normal* book seller and fall in love (with a movie star!) It happens!'
>
> Rose [speaking at the same time]: 'And live in a *really* expensive house in Notting Hill.'
>
> Henry: [back to normal voice] It doesn't – it *never* happens.
>
> [Rose laughs]
>
> Nate: I mean it *does* happen, just, statistically, it's unlikely.
>
> Henry: It *doesn't* happen!
>
> [Group 31, London]

Of course, the group clearly notes the exaggerated class difference between the two protagonists: Hugh Grant's William may, for the purposes of the film, be economically inferior to American superstar Anna, but his '*really* expensive' Notting Hill property clearly distinguishes him from most of the British population.[3] Most importantly for Rose and Henry, the romance narrative and the American Dream are connected because they follow the same (empty) trajectory, falsely promising a happy ending that is (allegedly) available to everyone. Importantly, the group's statements take the form of a series of quotations, which establishes a firm distance from the message they see entrenched in the film. Moreover, their parody of *Notting Hill*'s message takes the form of imperative statements, which echo Roach's definition of the romance narrative as a command to 'Love!'

This connection between romantic union and economic success has long been central to the American Dream (Sternheimer 2014: 133), and in romantic comedy romance is almost always associated with economic success. Note how Group 31 associated the two: whilst Henry's focus was on the romance narrative, albeit one rendered difficult by class and national differences ('you can fall in love'), Rose's completion of his sentence focused solely on material comfort ('and live in a really nice house'). Significantly, in the context of this volume, Group 31's reading of the UK–US relationship presented in *Notting Hill* emphasises the difference between the two countries, rather than their closeness.

As noted, this particular group engaged in some depth with the concept of the American Dream. Henry brought this up very early on in the discussion, when I asked them to describe the film (the first question on my list):

> Henry: Can I say [. . .] that this film *again* is a classical Hollywood making . . . it gives *hope* to the everyman.
>
> [Rose chuckles]
>
> Nate: Oh!
>
> Neil: How does it give *hope* to the man?
>
> Alice: Yeah, what do you mean?
>
> Henry: No every person, sorry.
>
> Neil: Every person, yeah.
>
> [Group 31, London]

Henry is not the only participant to highlight the significant role that Hollywood cinema has played in disseminating the American Dream, though he articulates it the most clearly. To emphasise this strength of feeling against the Dream, it is worth reiterating the context of the interviews. A useful point of comparison here is another speech made by Mindy Kaling, this time at Dartmouth University in June 2018. Kaling is much more forceful than in 2014 in denouncing the limitations of the American

Dream, stating early on that, as a woman of colour, she is 'not someone who should have the life I have now'. Her tone is also more overtly political than in her Harvard speech, as she discusses the #MeToo movement and systemic racism, and pokes fun at Donald Trump. Yet the speech still associates success with self-determinism, and the belief in America discussed in her 2014 speech is replaced by a belief in oneself: 'Don't let anyone tell you that you can't do something. But especially not yourself. Go conquer the world. Just remember this: why not you?' she finishes (Kaling 2018). Whilst a high level of cynicism and criticism may be expected two years into the Trump presidency, it seems even more striking that my participants' comments were made during Barack Obama's second term in office. For British as well as other European viewers that I interviewed prior to 2016, the American Dream is already characterised by false promises.

Interestingly, Group 31's reading of *Notting Hill*'s American Dream narrative is focused on Hugh Grant's William, rather than Julia Roberts's Anna. This may be because most of the participants in this group were men, as most of the other groups discussed the romcom genre's focus on women's narratives of social mobility. In Manchester, for example, Arabella suggested that the chick flick genre prioritises women's self-empowerment and rewards them through romance:

> Arabella: There's always – the women are like generally trying to *better* themselves, or get to like an *end* point, and then the *man* falls back in line.
>
> Celia: Yeah . . .
>
> Arabella: So whatever their ambition was . . . the man can't align with it, and then they somehow come to a mutual understanding. And then you're like [high-pitched]: "Oooh! We can have it *all*!"
>
> [Group 30, Manchester]

Key to Arabella's comment is a reflection on how the romantic comedy positions the female viewer. Her joking reference to 'having it all' also taps into contemporary debates about the direction of the women's movement, particularly the much-debated notion of postfeminism (Winch 2012; Ruti 2016). Rosalind Gill has argued that postfeminism should be conceived as a 'sensibility' articulated (notably) in the media, and which 'constructs a suture between feminist and anti-feminist ideas . . . effected entirely through a grammar of individualism' (Gill 2007: 142, 162). This corresponds with comments by several participants, including Group 31, on the film's individualistic representation of the American Dream, particularly within Melanie's trajectory:

> Nate: It's definitely about the *woman's* journey, isn't it?
>
> Rose: Yeah.

Neil: (Her things to do.) These men are just pieces of furniture. [pauses] In her life essentially.

Henry: Natch.

Neil: I mean – she needs them to fulfil herself *emotionally*, but *they* have no bearing on their destiny.

Neil: Like *she's* in charge of her destiny.

[Group 31, London]

Much of the scholarly and popular criticism around the romcom has criticised the political void of the genre's contemporary cycle, particularly regarding the politics of race and class (see, for example, Ferriss and Young 2008; Abbott and Jermyn 2009). This issue was also picked up by numerous interview participants. Several groups, for instance, criticised *Sweet Home Alabama*'s 'token black characters' [Group 1, Berlin], the joking way in which the film handles issues of domestic violence [Group 23, London] and white supremacy [Group 31, London] or its symbolic annihilation of lesbian, gay, bisexual, transgender and queer (LGBTQ) and Jewish characters [Group 9, Berlin; Group 16, Paris; Groups 23 or 24, London]. Such comments echo Gill's definition of the postfeminist individual that 'has replaced almost entirely notions of the social or political, or any idea of the individual as subject to pressures, constraints or influence from outside themselves' (2007: 162–4). Once again here, participants across all three countries point to a disconnect between the film's falsely egalitarian 'happily-ever-after' and the superficial way in which it engages with the real forms of discriminations and inequalities in contemporary America.

On a narrative level, then, *Sweet Home Alabama* directly associated the romance story and the American Dream by 'rewarding' its upwardly mobile protagonists with romance. Additionally, however, I want to suggest that there is a deeper structural parallel between the American Dream and the contemporary romcom's iteration of the romance story, as it presents romantic fulfilment as the result of a self-determinism unimpeded by social or material realities, and indeed intersecting identities. At the same time, there was a strong sense across my interview participants – one most directly articulated by UK viewers – that the universalism of both the American Dream and the romance narrative's happily-ever-after rested on an empty promise. Both are framed as attractive false promises: allegedly available to everyone, but attainable for only the most privileged. For Henry [Group 31, London], for example, the American Dream was defined by its impossibility. *Sweet Home Alabama* 'gives *hope* to the everyman', he says, before explaining: 'I mean that in *reality* that's never gonna happen . . . And so it's like, you know, that American Dream.' Hence, the American Dream is not the achievement of upward mobility, but the false promise of mobility that is mediated through film, media and political discourse.

Conclusion: A (Somewhat) Special Relationship?

This chapter has sought to question the 'specialness' of the US–UK relationship, as played out in the transatlantic consumption of Hollywood romantic comedy by British audiences. In this respect, the 'special relationship' is no steadfast happily-ever-after romance. Rather, it is characterised by a combination of mistrust, the performance of moral superiority, and strong familiarity. Other researchers into the European reception of Hollywood films and stars have painted a similar complex, push–pull relationship between American cinema and its global audiences (for example, Stacey 1994; Meers 2004). The viewers I interviewed in the UK, as well as other European countries, also clearly distinguished between American cinema and their own national productions. However, this love/hate relationship with Hollywood (which is simultaneously foreign and familiar) feeds into their 'hedged' (Billig 1989) consumption of *Sweet Home Alabama* in particular, and the romcom genre more broadly. This ambivalence also characterises British audiences' 'special relationship' with Americanness as enshrined in the film's sound, which fluctuates between pleasurable familiarity and sceptical distinction.

British participants also engaged a little more directly with the concept of the American Dream: once again, a language issue may be at play here. Significantly, a number of German participants also used the English term in their discussion. Generally, however, British audiences were very similar to French and German audiences in their criticism of the shallowness and false promises of the American Dream, as well as *Sweet Home Alabama*'s superficial engagement with the realities of racism and inequality in contemporary America. Ironically, although British, French or German participants never referred to themselves as 'European' viewers, what united them and effectively defined their Europeanness was their rejection of the empty promise of the American Dream – or, to return to Roach's framework, a refusal to follow the injunction to 'Succeed!' (2016: 20). To quote Jill [Group 34, Kent]: 'We're just like *fed* these apple-pie versions of the American *Dream* and . . . I don't *buy it*! I've got kids, I've got a job, and I don't . . . I don't know, I can't relate to this . . . namby-pamby . . . patheticness, personally.' In some ways, this highly sceptical reading of the American Dream seems to me to highlight the relevance of the interviews, even a few years on: whilst one might imagine that a similar research protocol conducted after 2016 would have generated even stronger criticism of US politics and culture, the extent of viewers' mistrust of Hollywood cinema, as represented by *Sweet Home Alabama*, is striking.

Notes

1. The interviews were transcribed verbatim; for ease of reading I have removed here some of the stutters and pauses but have not rephrased any of the participants' comments. A few of the sentences quoted in what follows may therefore seem a little awkward.
2. For discussion of *Catastrophe*, see the chapters by Frances Smith and Caroline Bainbridge in this volume.
3. For more on the US–UK romance of *Notting Hill*, see the chapter by Jay Bamber in this volume.

Works Cited

Abbott, S., and D. Jermyn (eds) (2009), *Falling in Love Again: Romantic Comedy in Contemporary Cinema*, London and New York: I. B. Tauris.

Billig, M. (1989), 'The Argumentative Nature of Holding Strong Views: A Case Study', *European Journal of Social Psychology*, 19:3, pp. 203–23.

Blanc, I., C. Chavez, Teresa Alonso Leon and Blanca Rubio (2017), 'Donald Trump Is Threatening the American Dream', *Time*. Available at: <time.com/4934059/trump-daca-undocumented-state-representatives/> (last accessed 25 October 2018).

Bourdieu, P. (1979), *La Distinction: Critique sociale du jugement*, Paris: Les Éditions de Minuit.

Box Office Mojo, 'Sweet Home Alabama'. Available at: <boxofficemojo.com/movies/?id=sweethomealabama.htm> (last accessed 25 October 2018).

Brooker, W. (2002), *Using the Force: Creativity, Community and Star Wars Fans*, New York and London: Continuum.

Catastrophe, TV series, created by R. Delaney and S. Horgan. UK and US: Avalon Television, 2015–.

Cullen, J. (2004), *The American Dream: A Short History of an Idea that Shaped a Nation*, new edn, New York: Oxford University Press.

Family Guy, TV series, created by Seth MacFarlane. US: Fox, 1999–current.

Ferriss, S., and M. Young (eds) (2008), *Chick Flicks: Contemporary Women at the Movies*, New York: Routledge.

Gill, R. (2007), 'Postfeminist Media Culture: Elements of a Sensibility', *European Journal of Cultural Studies*, 10:2, pp. 147–66.

Guilluy, A. (2017), 'A Big Sugary Confection? The Reception of Contemporary Hollywood Romantic Comedy in Britain, France and Germany', unpublished PhD thesis, London: King's College.

Higson, A. (2011), *Film England: Culturally English Filmmaking Since the 1990s*, London and New York: I. B. Tauris.

Honess Roe, A. (2009), 'A "Special" Relationship? Americans in British Romantic Comedy', in S. Abbott and D. Jermyn (eds), *Falling in Love Again: Romantic Comedy in Contemporary Cinema*, London: I. B. Tauris, pp. 79–91.

Kaling, M. (2014), 'Mindy Kaling's Speech at Harvard Law School Class Day 2014'. Available at: <youtube.com/watch?v=a7_49EXuLoQ> (last accessed 25 May 2019).

Kaling, M. (2018), 'Dartmouth's 2018 Commencement Address by Mindy Kaling '01'. Available at: <youtube.com/watch?v=JgUDjixWB5I> (last accessed 25 May 2019).

LOVE, TV series, created by J. Apatow. US: Netflix, 2016–18.

Lynyrd Skynyrd (1974), 'Sweet Home Alabama', Universal City, CA: MCA Records.

Maid in Manhattan, film, directed by W. Wang. US: Columbia Pictures, 2002.

Maltby, R., and M. Stokes (2004), *Hollywood Abroad: Audiences and Cultural Exchange*, London: British Film Institute.

Master of None, TV series, created by A. Yang and A. Ansari. US: Netflix, 2015–17.

Meers, P. (2004), '"It's the Language of Film!": Young Film Audiences on Hollywood and Europe', in M. Stokes and R. Maltby (eds), *Hollywood Abroad: Audiences and Cultural Exchange*, London: BFI, pp. 158–75.

Nicholson, A. (2014), 'Who Killed the Romantic Comedy?', *LA Weekly*. Available at: <laweekly.com/news/who-killed-the-romantic-comedy-4464884> (last accessed 18 October 2019).

Noguera, P. (2017), 'DACA and the American Dream', *The Huffington Post*, 10 September. Available at: <huffingtonpost.com/entry/daca-and-the-american-dream_us_59b4108fe4b0bef3378ce092> (last accessed 25 October 2018).

Notting Hill, film, directed by R. Mitchell. UK: Universal Pictures, 1999.

Pretty Woman, film, directed by G. Marshall. US: Touchstone Pictures, 1990.

Rackham, C. (2016), 'Mindy Kaling Has Written All of Us a List of Her Favorite Rom-Coms', *BuzzFeed*, 6 January. Available at: <Buzzfeed.com/caseyrackham/mindy-kaling-knows-rom-coms> (last accessed 25 May 2019).

Roach, C. M. (2016), *Happily Ever After: The Romance Story in Popular Culture*, Bloomington: Indiana University Press.

Ruti, M. (2016), *Feminist Film Theory and Pretty Woman*, New York: Bloomsbury Academic.

Shearer, M. (forthcoming, 2019), 'Frances Doesn't Live Here Anymore: Gender, Crisis and the Creative City in *Frances Ha and The Giant Mechanical Man*', in J. Andersson and L. Webb (eds), *The City in American Cinema: Postindustrialism, Urban Cultures and Gentrification*, London and New York: I. B. Tauris.

Stacey, J. (1994), *Star Gazing: Hollywood Cinema and Female Spectatorship*, New York: Routledge.

Sternheimer, K. (2014), *Celebrity Culture and the American Dream: Stardom and Social Mobility*, 2nd edn, New York: Routledge.

Sweet Home Alabama, film, directed by A. Tennant. US: Touchstone Pictures, 2002.

Syme, R. (2014), 'The McConaissance', *The New Yorker*, 16 January. Available at: <newyorker.com/culture/culture-desk/the-mcconaissance> (last accessed 25 May 2019).

The Mindy Project, TV series, created by M. Kaling. US: Fox Television, 2012–17.

Winch, A. (2012), 'We Can Have It All', *Feminist Media Studies*, 12:1, pp. 69–82.

Winn, E. J. (2007), *American Dream and Contemporary Hollywood Cinema*, London: Continuum.

Working Girl, film, directed by M. Nichols. US: 20th Century Fox, 1988.

CHAPTER 11

Business-like Lords and Gentlemanly Businessmen: The Romance Hero in Lisa Kleypas's *Wallflowers* Series

Inmaculada Pérez-Casal

The outstanding success of various popular culture manifestations, ranging from the blockbuster film *Notting Hill* (1999) to the recent media coverage of Prince Harry's wedding to the American actress Meghan Markle, reveals that romance plots play an important role in the (re)presentation of British and American relationships. These narratives display the idiosyncrasies of each of these countries at the same time as they suggest that love is enough to overcome disparities. Nevertheless, fictional attempts at a harmonious representation of affective coupling are frequently jeopardised by the singularities of the countries involved, whose cultural, ideological or economic differences emerge and compromise the relationship between the protagonists.

As in films and magazines, American mass-market romance fiction revels in this fascination with transatlantic relationships. The subgenre of historical romance, in particular, confirms the American attraction to all things British, and the genre's most notable examples perennially evoke the history, landscape and cultural mannerisms of England specifically. This chapter investigates this peculiar infatuation with English culture and settings, and suggests that it is rooted in a continuing desire to project a distinctive American identity. Most historical romance novels deploy an ideal of Englishness based on the rigidity of its class system, its well-defined gender roles and the decadent splendour of past colonial power. In this study, I argue that the romance genre perpetuates and advances the values that our collective imaginary associates mostly with the US, thus playing an important part in the configuration and projection of the American identity.

Lisa Kleypas's *Wallflowers* series is exceptionally suitable for the study of national identity in popular romance fiction. In these novels, the male protagonists are a most interesting blend of aristocratic Englishness and American capitalist entrepreneurship. More specifically, the heroes in the *Wallflowers* series are represented either as business-like lords or as gentlemanly businessmen. This results in an imaginative combination of Americanness, epitomised by the ideology of the self-made man, and the grandeur of patrician Englishness, mainly represented in the landed gentry. The following pages analyse Kleypas's (re)creation of a very specific image of the UK and of the US, through the study of the writer's casting of English and American identities.

Identity Politics in Historical Romance Fiction

Historical romance is one of the most popular subgenres within mainstream mass-market romance fiction. Kristin Ramsdell relates its success to

> our basic fascination with life in past times and to our not-so-latent yearning to escape, if only for a moment, to a time when life was simpler, better defined (especially regarding roles and rules), infinitely more exciting, and much more romantic . . . Like memory, Historical Romances filter out the unpleasant, mundane, uncomfortable realities of everyday life and leave only the desirable, exciting, and romantic elements. (Ramsdell 2012: 191)

Ramsdell subscribes to the view of many popular romance literature scholars, who have long believed that escapism is the key to the genre's appeal for (women) readers.[1] Thus, the 'history' part in historical romance fiction would be a rather subjective, even depoliticised, (re)creation of real events. However, Ramsdell fails to explain the prevalence of certain locations or time periods in the genre, as is the case with nineteenth-century England in historical romance.[2]

Critics such as Jerome De Groot have recently drawn a more complex picture of historical fiction, pointing at the ways in which it helps us to '"understand" past moments' (De Groot 2016: 2) and reflect upon contemporary conceptualisations of 'memory, ethics, history, and identity' (14). On the latter point, Tim Edensor has stated that 'the nation remains the paramount space within which identity is located. At cognitive, affective and habitual levels, the national space provides a common-sense context for situating identity' (Edensor 2002: 65). Taking this into account, and in accordance with De Groot's hypothesis that historical fiction provides various 'modes of knowing the past' as well as an opportunity to reflect on the present (De Groot 2016: 3), I would argue that historical popular romance asserts the readers' cultural and national identity via the fictionalised retelling of specific past events and lifestyles. Similarly, the romance critic Jayashree Kamblé has proclaimed that historical fiction 'is not just a fantasy of the past; it serves to observe one's own time historically' (Kamblé 2014: 42). My contention, therefore, is that beneath an apparently innocuous choice of nineteenth-century English settings, there lies a clear affirmation of American identity and values, based on principles such as individualism, hard work and material success, all linked to industrial capitalism. Thus, historical romance novels provide escape as well as a defence of certain national values, and serve to regain and even to foster a reflection on historical relationships between America and the UK.

The romance critic Laura Vivanco has even argued that romance novels can be read as political fiction in its broadest sense. After discussing more than forty romance titles, Vivanco concludes that mainstream romance fiction largely celebrates the distinctive characteristics of the US, asserting that

> implicitly, and sometimes explicitly, US romance novels express political 'truths' that the majority of Americans have held to be self-evident: that 'Family values are the most valuable American values' (Nachbar and Lause [1992]: 95), that the US is a land of opportunity (particularly for those willing to work hard) and that it has a special responsibility to spread freedom and democracy internationally. (Vivanco 2016: 142)

Pamela Regis, too, has detected an 'Americanization' [sic] of the genre since the late 1970s, motivated by the success of Janet Dailey's novels (Regis 2003: 155–6). Even so, a brief glance at the romance fiction market shows that the lure of Englishness remains strong. The most popular writers of historical romance, Lisa Kleypas included, often choose to set their novels on the other side of the Atlantic.

The *Wallflowers* series perpetuates a specific model of Englishness based on aristocratic wealth and power, large manor houses and elegant manners, all of which are taken as representative of the early 1800s. This description matches Christine Berberich's assertion that the 'mythical, pastoral England is [the] one that is still celebrated today', where the pre-industrial English South has come to represent quintessential Englishness in our collective imaginary (Berberich 2015: 159–61). As Tim Edensor also specifies, the rural setting 'frequently encapsulates the *genius loci* of the nation, the place from which we have sprung, where our essential national spirit resides' (Edensor 2002: 40). The central *locus* in the *Wallflowers* series is Stony Cross Park, a fictional estate located in Hampshire. As will be evident in the analysis of the novels, this place typifies the best of England; it is the perfect example of old, aristocratic grandeur that Kleypas takes great delight in representing.

This allegedly idyllic image, however, is not entirely free of contradictions and tensions. Kleypas's portrayal of mythical Englishness is obscured by the presence of business-like lords, and threatened by the gentlemanly businessmen who populate her books. In her *Guide*, Ramsdell claims that the focus of Victorian Period Romances [sic] is frequently placed on 'the gradual shift in power from the landed gentry and nobility to the industrial magnates and the moneyed middle-class' (Ramsdell 2012: 209). The *nouveaux riches* in the *Wallflowers* series are either born in the US, or embody the American values of individualism and free-market economy. Their penchant for industrial progress jeopardises the mythical image of England described by Berberich and Edensor, much in the same way that Maya Rodale's *Cavendishes* threaten the Regency society following Veera Mäkelä's reading (see Mäkelä in this volume). Consequently, in Kleypas's novels the aristocrats are forced to find alternative ways to survive, and these invariably entail the adoption of a typically American individualist, capitalist mentality. In other words, they become business-like lords. In practice, this transformation exalts the principles associated with the US, reinforcing the readers' American cultural values and national identity. Kleypas's portrayal of the US and the values that define the country has much in common with Vivanco's description, but also with the ideology of American exceptionalism, conceptualised by the British commentator Godfrey Hodgson as 'the idea that the United States is not just the richest and most powerful of the world's more than two hundred states but is also politically and morally exceptional' when compared to other nations (Hodgson 2009: 10).

The novels under consideration negotiate a tension between sameness and difference as they explore America's perceived individuality in relation to the United Kingdom, represented here by England. The UK has featured in the collective American imaginary since at least Washington Irving and Ralph Waldo Emerson, as the mother country against which America and the Americans have developed an identity of their own. As Tim Edensor notes, 'identity is conceivable through identifying difference, but, again, this is an ongoing process of identification rather than the reified continuation of absolute antipathy, even if it involves the same others continuously being distinguished from the self' (Edensor 2002: 24–5). Kleypas takes her readers to a historical period during which the American national identity was still developing in relation to political and (capitalist) economic factors. She portrays the relentless decline of the English economic system, based on feudal land tenure practices, and highlights the American capitalist value system. As the *Wallflowers* series depicts the transformation of heroes into gentlemanly businessmen, and especially into business-like lords, these novels reveal the significance of transatlantic relationships in the configuration of American national identity.

Case Study: The *Wallflowers* Series

The *Wallflowers* series is made up of four main books: *Secrets of a Summer Night* (2004b), *It Happened One Autumn* (2005), *Devil in Winter* (2006a) and *Scandal in Spring* (2006b). The female protagonists are all 'wallflowers', or young women forced to wait for a marriage proposal from a man, preferably one belonging to the English aristocracy. Two of these heroines, Lillian and Daisy Bowman, are heirs to the fortune of a wealthy American entrepreneur from the soap industry. As for the remaining two, Annabelle and Evie, both have respectable origins and partake in English upper-class society. Eventually, Lillian and Evie secure blue-blood husbands with business interests, whereas Annabelle and Daisy marry men who, despite their great economic success, are still regarded as commoners. In addition to these four books, *Again the Magic* (2004a) and *A Wallflower Christmas* (2008) are generally considered a part of the series because they are linked by characters and themes. These two instalments include heroines belonging to the English aristocracy and heroes who are capitalist businessmen.

Despite the fact that two of the heroines in the *Wallflowers* series are American-born, the heroes are the primary characters who transmit the core values of America. The following pages discuss the ways in which the male protagonists, classified as either gentlemanly businessmen or business-like lords, are made to represent the American principles of individualism and industrial capitalism, among others.

Gentlemanly Businessmen: Praising America

As the series' prequel, *Again the Magic* largely sets the tone for the whole series. The hero in this novel is a self-made man, John McKenna, a successful champion of industrialisation who returns to his native Hampshire after spending some years in the US. As a boy, McKenna had been employed at Stony Cross Park and had an affair with the Earl's daughter. The first line of the novel already introduces the underlying conflict: 'A stable boy wasn't supposed to speak to an earl's daughter, much less climb up to her bedroom window' (Kleypas 2004a: 6). By the end of Chapter 3, Lady Aline dismisses him because he is not a 'gentleman' – that is, a nobleman – and therefore marriage is out of question (32). Readers are informed that Aline abandoned McKenna out of fear of her father's retaliation, although the hero is never told about the real reasons behind their break-up. Consequently, McKenna resolves to overcome class differences. It is only after he has accumulated enough wealth that he returns to England to take revenge upon the heroine and, by extension, upon the whole aristocratic system. With this purpose in mind, McKenna invests money in the railway system that will radically transform both the English landscape and its society.

In this novel, America and England are largely represented as opposites. McKenna improves his economic circumstances on the other side of the Atlantic, implying that England, with its rigid class system, excludes people with aspirations. *A priori*, this projects a glorified vision of an American value system that offers equal opportunities for anyone. Unsurprisingly, McKenna's role model is John Jacob Astor (73), historically one of the most prominent exponents of American glamour and wealth. The idea that anyone may prosper through effort and hard work continues to be closely associated with Americanness, and McKenna represents the ethos of the American Dream in its purest form. He truly regards America as 'an opportunist's paradise' (52) and places the responsibility for self-improvement exclusively upon the individual: '[In America] you can make a lot of money if you're willing to do what it takes' (74–5). Certainly, the rags-to-riches story popularised by Horatio Alger has become one of the founding myths of the US, and it is inseparable from the patterns of immigration that have marked the country's history.

According to Hodgson, tales of economic prosperity based on individual effort have largely supported the American myth of exceptionalism (Hodgson 2009: 11–12). *Again the Magic* provides a historically romanticised vision of migration, evoking a mythical past when America guaranteed prosperity to foreigners. Kleypas clearly minimises the problematic aspects of migration and of transatlantic relationships, even at the time in which the novel is set. This is not to say, however, that all criticism is absent. McKenna's efforts to present the US as a democracy and a meritocracy are openly questioned when he is publicly humiliated by one of his American fellow travellers, a member of the New York upper class:

> 'The reason the Shaws have prospered, Lady Aline, is because my brother decided to place his family's welfare at the mercy of *an uneducated immigrant* who happened to make a few lucky choices.' She began to laugh. 'A drunkard and a *docker* – what a distinguished pair. And my future lies completely in their hands. So very amusing, don't you think?' (138, my emphasis)

Here, the idealised image of America is shattered to pieces, revealing in this new society an elitist view of the world not unlike that of the English peerage that had first spurned McKenna. (As will be discussed below, a similar conclusion can be extracted from reading *Scandal in Spring*.) Interestingly enough, one of the first characters to realise the hypocrisy of the American aristocracy is Lord Westcliff, Lady Aline's brother. The English Earl perceives in the Americans the same despotic attitudes that define the English class system.

Throughout the series, Kleypas goes to great lengths to distinguish between these snobs and the people who represent true Americanness. Gideon Shaw would be one such character: a secondary romance hero in *Again the Magic*, Shaw technically belongs to the American aristocracy because his money is 'old, if only by New York standards' (148), but contrary to his family, he does not deny his family's humble entrepreneur roots. For him, they are almost a source of pride:

> Shaw seemed to enjoy making his New York family cringe with his cheerful references to his great grandfather, a crude and outspoken sea merchant who had amassed a staggering fortune. Subsequent generations of refined and well-mannered Shaws would have preferred to forget their vulgar ancestor . . . if only Gideon would let them. (Kleypas 2004a: 42)

Other American characters manifesting a genuine American identity would be Matthew Swift, from *Scandal in Spring*, and Rafe Bowman, the hero of *A Wallflower Christmas*. At the time that he is first introduced in the series, Matthew is the right hand man of Thomas Bowman, an American magnate, and his decisions are of great importance for the family's business. While Matthew is neither a peer nor an exceedingly wealthy man, Bowman offers a good account of his origins since he has a 'good name and good blood to go with it' (Kleypas 2006b: 10). Halfway through the novel, however, the hero's real self is uncovered. He was born as Matthew Phaelan, and in his youth he worked as a servant to a rich young man. After being wrongly accused of theft, Matthew escaped to New York, where he started a new life and prospered. In this regard, he has a lot in common with McKenna: both men create a name for themselves (in Matthew's case, literally) through single-mindedness and hard work. *Scandal in Spring* also shows the corruption of American society in relation to Matthew's situation: '"The trial was a farce" . . . Matthew smiled wryly. "Justice may be blind," he said, "but it loves the sound of money. The Warings were too powerful, and I was a penniless servant"' (243). With their triumph over material disadvantage and generalised corruption, both McKenna and Matthew represent the best of Americanness. They possess a high degree of moral stamina and a desire for self-improvement, coupled with a strong confidence in their own abilities and an entrepreneurial spirit. The characters' respective happy endings sanction their behaviour, and implicitly reaffirm the ideals they represent.

Rafe Bowman embodies the authentic American spirit as well, by acting as a role model for wealthy American entrepreneurs. Whereas Thomas Bowman cares solely for his own benefit and the improvement of his family's name, his son's economic activities have other goals. As Rafe tells the heroine, Hannah, at some point, he is not necessarily after profit but rather real happiness, one of the American inalienable rights: "'The pursuit of happiness. It's in our Declaration, as a matter of fact . . . It's not a law, it's a right'" (Kleypas 2008: 78). In a way, Rafe can also be compared to Gideon Shaw from *Again the Magic* because both men are born into wealth but keep their true origins in mind, and they are not exclusively driven by blind ambition. In light of his father's reservations concerning his marriage, Rafe reproaches him, insisting that the Bowmans cannot boast about a distinguished lineage either (Kleypas 2008: 106).

So far, we have seen how the *Wallflowers* series provides a very clear definition of what constitutes the genuine American spirit. On the one hand, 'American' applies to those characters who pursue the American Dream of material prosperity through hard work and perseverance. That is the case of McKenna, an Englishman who totally identifies himself with these principles:

> McKenna had become an American the very second his foot had touched Staten Island all those years ago . . . he had been reinvented and forged in a country where his common blood was not a hindrance. In America he had learned to stop thinking of himself as a servant. (Kleypas 2004a: 105)

The same holds true for Matthew Swift, a character who has climbed up the social ladder thanks to his natural abilities and his entrepreneurial spirit. On the other hand, true Americanness is also represented by Gideon Shaw and Rafe Bowman, two heroes who continue to abide by these basic precepts, despite the fact that they are born into the upper class and partake easily in political and economic power.

As it happens, the American heroes are not the only exponents of these American principles of self-promotion, hard work and material success. These values are also championed by the English heroes: Simon Hunt, who will be discussed presently, and Marcus, Lord Westcliff, and Sebastian St Vincent, the two business-like lords that will be analysed in the next section.

In the final pages of *Again the Magic*, McKenna and Lady Aline travel back to the US. They leave behind an England in which the aristocratic system, despite its majestic splendour, still prevents the lower classes from improving themselves. *Secrets of a Summer Night* introduces a hero who destabilises this unfair class system, and illustrates the decline of the upper classes when faced with the values of (American) entrepreneurship. This hero is Simon Hunt, a businessman whose fortune comes from financial speculation in the railway industry.[3] In spite of his flamboyant success, he is introduced succinctly as 'Mr. Hunt – the butcher's son' (Kleypas 2004b: 10). As the heroine Annabelle points out, Hunt incarnates 'the threat that industrial enterprise posed to the British aristocracy's centuries old entrenchment in estate farming' (22). His greater wealth and success, together with his overt pride in being born into the educated middle class (149), exclude Simon from participating in the society of English aristocrats. The heroine, herself from a well-to-do family, becomes progressively aware of the snobbism and conservatism inherent in the peerage system (222). While it is clear that Simon's blood is not that of a gentleman, meaning nobleman, by the end of the story the hero's beliefs are clearly preferable to those of the English nobility. Through Simon's character, the novel reinforces the view that (American) entrepreneurship is more desirable than aristocratic (English) elitism and inactivity.

Kleypas's devotion to the values that define the American identity in her work reaches its peak in the characterisation of the two business-like lords, Lord Westcliff and St Vincent. Inevitably, this results in a complex reworking of the gentleman trope, which will be detailed below.

Business-like Lords: The Best of Both National Identities

The *Wallflowers* series broaches the subject of gentlemanliness in relation to Englishness and Americanness. The critic Christine Berberich has pointed out that 'gentleman' is a vague term with multiple meanings, evoking 'images of feudal landlords or snobbish "toffs"' as well as 'issues of education, style, manners, or simply inner values' (Berberich 2007: 5). Moreover, she notes that, as a literary trope, the gentleman 'has always been considered a stock figure of Englishness', an idea 'furthered by Englishmen and foreigners alike' (25). These reflections seem very pertinent for the topic at hand, since the novels under consideration ponder whether one is born a gentleman or rather becomes one. Ultimately, this trope turns into just another way of vindicating the superiority of certain American-coded values like self-reliance, equality of opportunity and fierce competition.

Early on in the series, the label 'gentleman' applies only to those characters with aristocratic lineage, like Westcliff and St Vincent. As we have seen, neither McKenna nor Simon Hunt is considered a proper gentleman, as in a man of noble birth. Gideon Shaw is closer to gentlemanly status; as quoted earlier, his wealth is considered 'old', or respectable enough. Progressively, however, the term broadens its meaning and is applied to the *nouveaux riches* too. Matthew is a good case in point. His fiancée Daisy states in *Scandal in Spring* that this particular hero 'most certainly became a gentleman' when he prospered in New York society (Kleypas 2006b: 242). As for Rafe, the heroine, Hannah, reprimands him for acting in an ungentlemanly fashion (Kleypas 2008: 92), thus implying that gentlemanliness can be learned. Overall, the series suggests that blood is indeed important but it is not enough to make a true gentleman. The term is appropriated by those characters with lower backgrounds, who redefine it as a combination of conduct and education, but above all, different ethics: that is, American ethics. In light of this situation, the two aristocratic heroes in the series are forced to adopt this mentality if they wish to be considered authentic gentlemen. As Kamblé asserts, Kleypas's business-like lords act contradictorily: 'not only do they have ancestral land, but they have diversified their holdings to include new factories, railway lines, shipping and mining operations, and so on and are generating profits from these sources' (Kamblé 2014: 45).

The clearest example of this inconsistency is Marcus, Lord Westcliff. As a member of the English landed gentry, he matches traditional expectations about Englishness. Westcliff is a well-educated man who takes pleasure in spending time outdoors, hunting on his estate and entertaining his guests in his country house. At the same time, Westcliff emerges as a shrewd businessman in the manner of the American entrepreneurs, with fewer prejudices towards the *nouveaux riches* than they themselves have. In subsequent books, the Earl surrounds himself with peers and entrepreneurs alike, judging his acquaintances by their intrinsic value rather than by their titles or fortunes. What is more, at one point the narrator explains that Westcliff would give up his title if possible because 'he had never been able to accept the concept of one man's innate superiority over another' (Kleypas 2004a: 42). He is largely presented as an exception to the widespread corruption and stagnation of the English peerage.

Notwithstanding the emphasis that all characters put on Westcliff's liberal and democratic ideas, it must be noted that, on occasion, he does not hesitate to use the power that the inequality of the English system bestows on him due to his privileged birth. Sometimes, the character sounds almost tyrannical, as in the following passage from *Scandal in Spring*:

'This property you are standing on has been in my family's possession for five centuries, and on this land, in this house, *I am the authority*. Now, you will proceed to tell me in the most *deferential* manner you can manage, what grievance you have with [Matthew Swift].' (Kleypas 2006b: 237, my emphasis)

In this novel, Westcliff deploys his aristocratic privilege to stop Matthew's unjust prosecution (246–7). The Earl's actions are ethically praiseworthy, and clearly fall in line with the idea that the US is 'morally exceptional' (Hodgson 2009: 10). Westcliff feels morally obliged to step up and defend the powerless, even if this requires interfering with the established law.

Stony Cross Park symbolises Westcliff's dual nature. On the one hand, it stands for mythical Englishness, and the old manor in Hampshire is admired by all characters, peers and businessmen alike. In *Again the Magic*, Gideon Shaw refers to it as a 'paradise' (Kleypas 2004a: 53). Matthew Swift's words are also full of praise (as well as stereotypes):

> this was exactly what he had *imagined* England would look like, the manicured gardens and the green hills beyond, and the rustic village at the feet of the grand estate.
>
>   The house and its furniture were ancient and comfortably worn at the edges, but it seemed that in every corner there was some priceless vase or statue or painting he had seen featured in art history books. Perhaps a bit drafty in the winter, but with the plenitude of hearths and thick carpets and velvet curtains, one could hardly say that living here would be suffering. (Kleypas 2006b: 41, my emphasis)

On the other hand, Stony Cross Park owes its paradisiacal reputation to its owner, and this splendour is a consequence of Westcliff's keen interest in the financial, free-market economy. Paradoxically, his inborn capitalist ethos keeps the emblem of his aristocratic privileges intact.

St Vincent's case is similar to Westcliff's. Both heroes are heirs to important titles but they lead opposite lives. Where Westcliff has always been an entrepreneur, in *It Happened One Autumn* and in the early chapters of *Devil in Winter*, Sebastian plays the part of the perfect aristocrat, whose purpose in life is to inherit his father's duchy and live off its rents. The mere idea of working for a living is unconceivable, and literally represents 'an inconvenient distraction' from an easier and untroubled existence (Kleypas 2006a: 34). He is the only character in the series to acquire a taste for business in the novels, undergoing a remarkable transformation from peer to businessman. Upon his marriage in *Devil in Winter*, St Vincent develops a 'nagging curiosity' and finds himself inexplicably drawn to Jenner's, the gambling club he has just inherited from his father-in-law (Kleypas 2006a: 73). Against the odds, the self-indulgent peer puts on the mask of the entrepreneur and, displaying an ability with finances that very few people were aware of, rescues Jenner's from bankruptcy and even doubles the club's profits. His metamorphosis into a business-like lord distresses St Vincent, however, and initially makes him doubt his own identity. As his factotum warns him:

'Are you a nobleman? You're not living like one. You're sleeping in a gaming club, in a room recently vacated by a pair of whores. Are you a man of leisure? You've just ended the evening breaking up a fight between a pair of sodden idiots ... If you want to survive here, you'll have to change. You can't pose as an aristocratic idler who's above this sort of thing.' (139–40)

Ultimately, his dilemma is solved and the hero embraces this newfound entrepreneurial side.

The transformation of both Westcliff and St Vincent into business-like lords comes at the expense of the peerage's contempt. Their interest in the free-market economy and industrialisation contradicts the unpreoccupied behaviour displayed by the novels' aristocracy, and their conduct seemingly endangers the most mythical aspects of Englishness, represented here by the landed nobility. However, these heroes' interest in business is essential to safeguard their titles and privileges inasmuch as the survival of places like Stony Cross Park and St Vincent's future inheritance depend on their owners' wealth. The parties, soirées and hunting expeditions that Westcliff celebrates on his estate, for instance, and which clearly represent a glamorous and romanticised idea of Englishness, would not exist except for his eagerness to become an entrepreneur. As for St Vincent, his economic success at Jenner's gratifies his sybarite tastes. Therefore, the embrace of entrepreneurship and (American) individualism allows both characters to preserve the tokens of mythical Englishness: a bucolic existence in their splendorous aristocratic residences.

Conclusion

The *Wallflowers* series evokes, revises and examines conventional and essentialist views on Englishness and Americanness. The heroes in these novels are either born in the US, or are models for the famous American mantra 'hard work leads to success'. McKenna, Gideon Shaw, Simon Hunt, Matthew Swift and Rafe Bowman are all *nouveaux riches* who have defied the rigid class system that historical romance novels associate with England and, by extension, with the UK. With their defence of hard work, capitalism and industrialisation, all of which are presented as purely American values, these characters challenge aristocratic privilege and embody mythical aspects that the collective imaginary has traditionally associated with the English aristocracy and its lifestyle. However, these values coexist with a latent admiration for those same privileges that are being questioned. Hero figures like Lord Westcliff and St Vincent attest to the great appeal of mythical Englishness, even though the superiority of American principles ultimately overrides that fascination. The characters' adoption of an (American) entrepreneurial mentality allows their aristocratic lifestyle to survive the impending rise of the bourgeoisie to power and ironically confirms middle-class triumph. These business-like lords feature the best of both English and American national identities, as Kleypas imagines them, astutely combining a fascination for mythical aristocratic mores (Englishness) with the solid entrepreneurial mentality that has historically dominated the American economic system.

Throughout these pages, I have argued that the choice of an English setting in the *Wallflowers* series is far from coincidental. It allows for an exploration of Americanness, its values and its historical relationships with England and with the UK as a whole. The novels reassure readers of what the American identity is and what the country stands for, and they do so by going back to the earliest years of the republic and locating its defining characteristics: individualism, self-promotion, material success and industrial capitalism. These archetypical American traits are highlighted by contraposing both countries, and the identification with an American ethos depends, as has been demonstrated, on a rather conservative and monolithic understanding of Englishness that fosters the fantasy of American exceptionalism. In comparing these two countries, the novels achieve a twofold purpose: reinforcing the links between the US and the UK, and maintaining and perpetuating America's distinctive identity.

An interpretation of the *Wallflowers* series simply as patriotic propaganda would be problematic and reductionist. Even though the novels' version of Americanness may strike us as rather conservative and too complicit with industrial capitalism, almost akin to the one deployed mostly by Republican politicians since Ronald Reagan in the 1980s, Jayashree Kamblé has argued that this tacit acceptance of capitalism stems from the fact that romance novels are, in themselves, a product of this economic system. Kamblé further explains that the romance genre 'may not condemn the economic structure in which they function but they are not capitalist propaganda or blind affirmation either' (Kamblé 2014: 47). As we have seen throughout these pages, some degree of protest and critique is present in the texts. In addition to this, we must bear in mind that the marketplace for romance novels is highly competitive and a writer's continuing viability depends on her ability to engage the readership. Therefore, criticising the basic tenets that are collectively associated with the US could have dire consequences for authors who wish to prosper in this market, Lisa Kleypas included.

What is certain is that the popularity of the *Wallflowers* series remains strong, even though it has been well over a decade since these books were published.[4] Through these historical romance novels, Kleypas offers readers the opportunity to reaffirm their identity, and regain historical consciousness by means of reflecting on British–American relationships. Readers of the *Wallflowers* series may rejoice in certain values and principles that have not only built the American nation and shaped its identity, but also strongly influenced the modernisation of England and of the rest of the UK. For all the differences that these novels portray between both identities, the fact that the US continues to define itself in relation to the UK hints at the long-lasting romance between these two nations.

Notes

1. For the feminist critic Janice Radway, for instance, romance reading possesses a combative element inasmuch as it suspends women's everyday responsibilities during the reading time (Radway 1987: 211).
2. Veera Mäkelä raises a similar question in this volume. Whereas she discusses the suitability of the Regency setting to forward feminist ideals, I am more interested in the identity politics of historical romance.
3. Except for St Vincent, all heroes are involved in the industrial revolution. McKenna, Gideon Shaw, Simon Hunt and Rafe Bowman work collaboratively in the railway industry. Lord Westcliff, too, takes part in their business. Matthew Swift establishes new soap factories in Bristol, UK, expanding Bowman's business beyond American territory. Historically speaking, all these enterprises helped to transform the economy and society in the nineteenth century. The fact that Kleypas chose these occupations suggests that she wanted to guarantee the heroes' victory and show the importance of the (American) values they incarnate.
4. At the time of writing, St Vincent's story, *Devil in Winter*, was chosen as the number one romance novel of all time by the readers of *All About Romance* (2018), a well-known website specialising in romantic fiction.

Works Cited

All About Romance (2018), 'The AAR Top Ten Romances . . . with a New Number One!'. Available at: <https://allaboutromance.com/the-aar-top-ten-romances-with-a-new-number-one/> (last accessed 24 May 2019).

Berberich, C. (2007), *The Image of the English Gentleman in Twentieth-Century Literature: Englishness and Nostalgia*, Aldershot and Burlington: Ashgate.

Berberich, C. (2015), 'Bursting the Bubble: Mythical Englishness, Then and Now', *Journal of Postcolonial Writing*, 51:2, pp. 158–69.

De Groot, J. (2016), *Remaking History: The Past in Contemporary Historical Fictions*, London and New York: Routledge.

Edensor, T. (2002), *National Identity, Popular Culture and Everyday Life*, Oxford: Berg.

Hodgson, G. (2009), *The Myth of American Exceptionalism*, New Haven, CT: Yale University Press.

Kamblé, J. (2014), *Making Meaning in Popular Romance Fiction: An Epistemology*, New York: Palgrave Macmillan.

Kleypas, L. (2004a), *Again the Magic*, New York: HarperCollins ebooks.

Kleypas, L. (2004b), *Secrets of a Summer Night*, New York: HarperCollins ebooks.

Kleypas, L. (2005), *It Happened One Autumn*, New York: HarperCollins ebooks.

Kleypas, L. (2006a), *Devil in Winter*, New York: HarperCollins ebooks.

Kleypas, L. (2006b), *Scandal in Spring*, New York: HarperCollins ebooks.

Kleypas, L. (2008), *A Wallflower Christmas*, New York: St Martin's Press.

Radway, J. (1987), *Reading the Romance: Women, Patriarchy and Popular Literature*, London: Verso.

Ramsdell, K. (2012), *Romance Fiction: A Guide to the Genre*, Santa Barbara: Libraries Unlimited.

Regis, P. (2003), *A Natural History of the Romance Novel*, Philadelphia: University of Pennsylvania Press.

Vivanco, L. (2016), *Pursuing Happiness: Reading American Romance as Political Fiction*, Penrith: Humanities-Ebooks LLP.

CHAPTER 12

Imagine: The Beatles, John Lennon and Love Across Borders

Theodore Louis Trost

Introduction

The story of the Beatles begins in Liverpool. Situated about 200 miles to the northwest of London, Liverpool falls a significant distance from the capital and the nation's centre of power. Viewed in relation to the sea, however, Liverpool arises as a major port city. It had been a key commercial hub across the Atlantic, bringing untold wealth into Great Britain on account of the ships that left Liverpool to collect African slaves, transported them to the Americas, and returned to Liverpool with cotton from the New World (Millard 2012: 43–4). Prominent Liverpool merchant James Penny once argued before a committee of Parliament that the abolition of slavery would completely ruin the economy of northern England (Coslett 2007). For his eloquence, he was rewarded with a large silver centrepiece from the Liverpool town council in 1792 (International Slavery Museum). A suburban Liverpool street, and eventually a song by the Beatles, would bear his name: 'Penny Lane' (Beatles 1967a).

By virtue of their home town, then, the Beatles were incorporated from the beginning into a special relationship that prevailed between Britain and America. This special relationship developed over centuries. The relocation of religious dissenters to the colonies, the slave trade, a revolution and other wars, and transatlantic commercial and passenger traffic are but a few of its constituent elements. The term acquired significant resonance in the post-World War II era, when Winston Churchill suggested that the future of the whole world depended upon 'a special relationship between the British Commonwealth and Empire and the United States'. Churchill had in mind a military alliance that would provide security to a war-weary world, even as it entered a new age of nuclear destruction and the separation that ensued from the partitioning of Eastern Europe behind what Churchill called an 'iron curtain'. But there was also a romantic component to Churchill's vision as he spoke of the partnership in most intimate terms, not only as a co-mingling of traditions, convictions and 'kindred systems', but as the guarantor of a bright future for all nations 'for a century to come' (Churchill 1946).

This chapter considers themes that arise in the commerce between the UK and the US as encountered through various activities of the twentieth-century's most popular rock 'n' roll group, collectively known as The Beatles and consisting of the musicians John Lennon, Paul McCartney, George Harrison and Ringo Starr. Particular focus is placed upon guitarist John Lennon, whose declarations, songs and public performances challenged received assumptions concerning the special relationship and reimagined the relationship not only for his own time but for generations to come. The first part of the chapter sketches the Beatles' early love for America and America's reciprocation of that love. The enthusiasm associated with this romance subsided somewhat as a result of John Lennon's critical remarks concerning the Beatles' celebrity in contrast to the popularity of Jesus. Although they decided not to return to America as a touring ensemble after the Christ controversy, the Beatles managed to maintain their relationship with America through the love songs they continued to produce. The second part of the chapter, therefore, reviews the theme of love as it changed and developed in Beatles songs during the later 1960s, maintaining from across the Atlantic an enduring courtship between the band and their American fans. The third part of the chapter examines John Lennon's reappropriation of the love song, expanding it outward from his intimate relationship with Yoko Ono to social commentary and compassion for the world as he embarked upon his solo career. Lennon's attention during this period was inevitably directed back to America, whose military escapades, particularly in Vietnam, rendered insecure the promise of peace that Churchill had so hopefully articulated for both nations in 1946. Lennon's critique of US policy led to a protracted immigration trial that ultimately altered US policy toward immigrants and that illuminates contemporary debates concerning the fate of immigrants in both the US and the UK. In the end, this exploration shows how the Beatles in general, and Lennon in particular, both advanced and reshaped US and UK relations as Winston Churchill had envisioned this 'special relationship' through the recurrent trope of love, understood in terms both romantic and political, and expressed in the fantasies of desire and identity contained within popular songs.

The Special Relationship: Courtship and Disenchantment

Well into the twentieth century, Liverpool served as a major terminus for transatlantic passenger travel. The fathers of both John Lennon and George Harrison had worked as seamen (Millard 2012: 45). The oft-romanticised Cunard Steamship Company was headquartered in Liverpool from 1840 until 1967 (see also Randell and Weedon in this volume). Over the years, it transported luxury passengers, as well as dispossessed immigrants, across the waters. Among its employees were the so-called 'Cunard Yanks', stewards and other personnel who traversed the Atlantic regularly between New York and Liverpool and brought back from abroad numerous phonograph recordings made by American artists (Millard 2012: 69–71; Jonze 2015). Some of these recordings inevitably found their way on to the shelves of the NEMS record shop in Liverpool, whose proprietor, Brian Epstein, 'aimed to have everything in stock' (Davies 2002: 164). Intrigued by the latest sounds, many of them produced by African American artists, the members of the Beatles frequented the record shop and became friends with the proprietor. By the end of 1961, Brian Epstein had become the young group's manager and promoter of their brand of rock 'n' roll music.

The Beatles honed their musical skills in the small nightclubs of Liverpool. As their set lists and early recordings reveal, they were drawn primarily to music by Americans, black and white, including Chuck Berry, Buddy Holly, Little Richard and Elvis Presley (Inglis 2012: 84–6). The band released their first single, 'Love Me Do', in 1962 (Beatles 1962). Several other singles quickly followed and by early 1963 they had released their first album in the UK, *Please, Please, Me* (Beatles 1963a). Of the album's fourteen tunes, eight were written by Lennon and McCartney. As if to underscore the ongoing commerce between the UK and the US, all of the 'cover' songs on the album were composed by Americans.[1] Thus, the Beatles' embrace of American music was a key component of their early success.

On their first transatlantic tour, the Beatles ventured forth by plane from London to America along the trade routes established before them by wind, sail and steam engine. Something of a rivalry between nations had taken place in the previous decade to establish regular jet traffic across the Atlantic. Indeed, the British Overseas Air Corporation (BOAC) had 'inaugurated the modern era of passenger jet travel' on 4 October 1958, with a flight from London to New York. But BOAC used British-made Comet jet planes that carried only a limited number of passengers and, when the winds were contrary, required a stop along the way (Tweedie 2008). Three weeks later, Pan American World Airways introduced a regularly scheduled transatlantic jet service on the Boeing 707, an American-made aircraft with greater passenger capacity and longer range (Bender and Altschul 1982: 476).[2] The Beatles' arrival in New York on 7 February 1964, via Pan Am, underscored a certain proximity between nations and a lessening of the distance between cultures that flying on the quintessential American carrier implied. It also suggested an endorsement of the American ways that their music celebrated.

One dimension of this gesture is captured in an iconic Associated Press photo taken on the tarmac of the airport in New York (Figure 12.1; AP Images 1964). The four Beatles stand at the bottom of the Jet Clipper's stairway, waving to the crowd, with the Pan Am symbol hovering overhead and behind them. American corporate dominion is somewhat undercut by George Harrison, who holds a rival flight bag in his right hand. Across the front is emblazoned a stylised logo of 'The BEAtles', with the words 'British European Airways' (BEA) positioned underneath, thereby incorporating the group into that airline's commercial exploits in the European sphere. John Lennon, meanwhile, holds two bags in his left hand, as if to conjoin competing forces; however, his BEA bag is obscured by the Pan Am bag that hovers over it. This 'cover-up' suggests semioticly certain tensions in the 'special relationship': it could indicate a publicity victory for Pan Am; or perhaps it represents an underlying intimacy between the two nations, or at least, solidarity among the youth of both nations.[3]

Figure 12.1   The Beatles arrive at John F. Kennedy International Airport (formerly Idlewild), in New York, 7 February 1964. (Source: AP Photo.)

The Beatles arrived on American soil at the 'John F. Kennedy International Airport'. The airport's name had been changed only recently from 'Idlewild Airport' after the assassination of President Kennedy in November of the previous year (Benjamin 1963: 1). The nation was gripped with loss. Jacqueline Kennedy framed the matter for reporter Theodore White in *Life* magazine with a poignant reference to ancient English lore (and a recent Broadway production): 'For one brief shining moment there was Camelot . . . and it will never be that way again' (White 1963: 159). Into this void, the Beatles appeared like minstrels at the castle gate to offer their songful affirmations of life – even life after death. The Arthurian court in America had come to an end, perhaps, but the Beatles' courtship of America was just beginning. Or, as one writer ventured, 'Just as the country was coming to terms with the loss of a young leader who represented hope and idealism . . . the even younger Beatles came along and uplifted spirits . . . with their version of hope' (Turner 2006: 83). An official at Kennedy airport, who had witnessed the Beatles' arrival there, observed: 'We've never seen anything like this here before. Never. Not even for kings and queens' (Gardner 1964: 25). Over the course of the next three years, the Beatles performed in concert on over sixty occasions, instigating a frenzy – dubbed 'Beatlemania' – wherever they went. During this period of active touring, the Beatles placed thirteen number one singles and eight number one albums in the American charts (Whitburn 2001: 56; Bronson 1992). Their British invasion of America seemed unassailable.

But then, in 1966, the love affair that Americans had with the Beatles came under threat. During a brief respite from their labours, three of the Beatles, John, George and Ringo, settled into separate residences on Saint George's Hill, a private estate to the southwest of London in the town of Weybridge, Surrey. Their repair to manorial surroundings served as theme for a series of interviews in the *Evening Standard*, conducted by their friend, Maureen Cleave, under the heading 'How Does a Beatle live'? In his conversation with Cleave, twenty-five-year-old Lennon made casual observations about politics, fame and his posh surroundings (Cleave 1966a: 10–11). The reaction in Britain to Lennon's words was unremarkable. However, when the interview was reprinted in the socially progressive American teen magazine *DATEbook* alongside Cleave's interview with Paul McCartney, there was a general outcry against the Beatles. Wrath focused upon Lennon's comments concerning the fate of contemporary Christianity:

> 'Christianity will go,' [Lennon] said. 'It will vanish and shrink. I needn't argue about that; I'm right and I will be proved right. We're more popular than Jesus now; I don't know which will go first – rock 'n' roll or Christianity. Jesus was all right but his disciples were thick and ordinary. It's them twisting it that ruins it for me.' (Cleave 1966a: 10)

Among other sources, the outcry was instigated by disc jockeys Tommy Charles and Doug Layton of Radio Station WAQY in Birmingham, Alabama, the originators of a 'Ban the Beatles' campaign. For the sake of puritanical orthodoxy in a struggle against the British infidel, a modern witch hunt was undertaken to destroy Beatles records and paraphernalia just as their fourth American tour commenced (Turner 2006: 25–8). Even the Ku Klux Klan got involved, notably in the person of South Carolina Grand Dragon, Bob Scoggin, who tossed Beatles records into the flames of a burning cross, in Chester, South Carolina, on 11 August 1966 (Murrmann 2014).

While Lennon's perceived attack upon Christendom instigated a national commotion, Paul McCartney had advanced a more direct critique of American culture. Disheartened by race relations in America as he had witnessed them during an era of civil rights protest, McCartney was quoted on the cover of the September 1966 edition of *DATEbook*, saying, 'It's a lousy country where anyone black is a dirty n*gger!' (Cleave 1966b: 11). The group's own aversion to institutional racism in America, meanwhile, had been codified in their concert contracts, which prohibited performance before segregated audiences (BBC News 2011). Somehow, McCartney's words were glossed over by Beatles foes and fans alike. Still, the general possibility of lethal violence from offended religionists, the specific threat of Klan-inspired disruptions during their concert in Memphis – including the threat of assassination – and the ongoing danger of being crushed by over-enthusiastic fans (after all, the group was still loved by millions),[4] caused the Beatles to leave America after their 1966 tour, never again to perform together in a concert venue before a public audience (Doyle 2017).

Renewing the Courtship: Love Songs and the Universal Power of Love

The Beatles stopped touring the US after 1966 but they maintained their intimate, 'special relationship' between the US and the UK through the medium of song. They remained purveyors of love songs, or even 'silly love songs,' as McCartney would put it some years later (McCartney 1976). As songmakers, the Beatles stood in a long tradition that included the medieval troubadours and the composer of the biblical 'Song of Songs', and reached all the way back to the mythical precincts of Eden – where the affinity between people is recorded in the jubilant lyric attributed to Adam: 'This at last is bone of my bone and flesh of my flesh' (Genesis 2: 23). Catherine Roach has argued that the Western romance narrative is essentially 'mythic or religious' in nature. The 'healing power of love', or what Roach calls elsewhere in her writings the 'resurrection power of love', is sustained by the convention of the romance genre with its promise that 'they all live happily ever after' in the end (Roach 2016: 101–2). Since the 'paradise' of 'happily ever after' is assumed from the beginning (compare 'this at last' from Genesis), Roach concludes that 'the romance story is narrative eschatology' (Roach 2010; Roach 2016: 176); it is a story about an end time (eschaton) when all conflict is resolved and harmony prevails. While the pleasure of the written or sung text lies in the resolution it anticipates – in the hope the text sustains while it is being performed – the silly little love song and the wider romance narrative keep alive the possibility that, ultimately, the whole society will be 'transformed for the better' (see Mäkelä in this volume).

Critics have noticed significant development over time in the quality of the affection contained in the Beatles' songs and its presentation on their later albums (Regev 2012: 543–5). An indication of how far the Beatles would eventually travel in their development of the love theme can be seen in relation to the song 'Words of Love', written by their American hero, Buddy Holly – whose band 'The Crickets' influenced the Liverpool lads in their choice of an insect moniker (Meisel 2010: 144–6). The Beatles performed a cover version of the song on their fourth British LP, *The Beatles for Sale* (Beatles 1964b). In Holly's song, the serenader asks his companion to say the words 'I love you' in 'whispers soft and true'. The very act of speaking, it seems, will make the love between the two of them become real. This plea would have fit in well on any of the Beatles' earlier albums – where love is often no more complicated than just holding hands[5] and a simple 'P.S. I Love You' (Beatles 1962) sustains a relationship across distances. But Holly's phraseology undergoes transformation when it reappears in 'The Word', from the Beatles' sixth album, *Rubber Soul* (Beatles 1965b). In the later song by Lennon and McCartney, the act of vocalisation – saying the word – takes on liberating qualities. For the Beatles, Holly's 'word' has become a message to the nations; their 'Word' is directed not simply to one human being but to humanity in general. The singer concludes that his mission is to share the word 'love' with 'everybody', thereby bringing 'light' to the world.

This expansion of the love song beyond the confines of the boy-meets-girl romance narrative is one of the innovations the Beatles explored during their period of studio confinement and refinement. A particularly poignant change in orientation occurs on the album *Sergeant Pepper's Lonely Hearts Club Band* with George Harrison's song 'Within You Without You' (Beatles 1967b). Amidst sitar, tabla and an orchestra of violins and cellos, Harrison's lyrics move from a casual conversation between companions to the suggestion that with 'our love' the world itself could be saved. In this song, the inevitable 'happily ever after' of romance is incorporated and transformed to embrace the whole world in the realisation that 'we're all one'. While Harrison's song might suggest a mystical, or otherworldly, communion, it also contains an implied critique of social and political forces that maintain disunity.

A month after *Sergeant Pepper's* appeared, the Beatles released the single 'All You Need is Love' (Beatles 1967c). Written primarily by Lennon, the lyrics complimented Harrison's earlier work, albeit in a significantly more upbeat setting. The appeal to the universal power of love resonated with the Beatles' American audience for various reasons. Love, in the form of non-violent direct action, had served for at least a decade as the foundation of Martin Luther King, Jr's ongoing campaign for civil rights; it was the basis for King's position, enunciated in the spring of 1967, against the war in Vietnam (King 1963; King 2003). Meanwhile, 'hippies' in San Francisco and other American locales quickly adopted 'All You Need is Love' for their own anthem as the 'Summer of Love' vibrated across the nation. Love here has to do with 'learning to be you in time' and letting others be themselves as well. As John Lennon remarked in an interview three years after the release of 'All You Need is Love':

> I think if you get down to basics, whatever the problem is, it's usually to do with love. So I think 'All You Need is Love' is a true statement . . . I'm talking about real love, so I still believe that. Love is appreciation of other people and allowing them to be. Love is allowing somebody to be themselves and that's what we do need. (Lennon 1971)

'All You Need is Love' expands the notion of love as it had been articulated in the Beatles' earliest songs. But importantly, it does not deny the quest for intimacy. It even incorporates the earlier songs 'Yesterday' (Beatles 1965a) and 'She Loves You' (Beatles 1963b) into the extended mantra 'love is all you need' as the song fades out. Interpersonal romantic love and universal inclusive love are related; the former supports and opens up to the latter.

The universal appeal of 'All You Need is Love' was engaged for a specific ideological purpose. The song was composed for presentation on televisions around the world on the occasion of the 'Our World' satellite broadcast. Beamed out on 25 June 1967, 'Our World' was the first live, international, satellite television production. Opera singer Maria Callas, the painter Pablo Picasso and the 'global village' theorist Marshall McLuhan, among other notables, appeared in separate segments that were broadcast live to the world from their respective countries. The Beatles' performance of 'All You Need is Love' concluded the broadcast, which was seen by over 350 million people and perhaps as many as 700 million. Three-and-a-half years earlier, the Beatles left their native land and managed to reach over 70 million viewers on *The Ed Sullivan Show* (Davies 2002: 241). Now, by some estimates, they reached ten times as many people without even leaving the confines of the Abbey Road studio (Beatles Bible n.d.). While their god-like omnipresence might not have been sufficient to prove Lennon's earlier claim that the Beatles were more popular than Jesus,[6] it did suggest both a receptivity to their message of universal love and a popularity of global dimension. Over the course of a few years, the Beatles' love songs had matured from an emphasis on courtship and romantic love and widened the UK–US special relationship of love across the Atlantic to love around the world. This wider vision was at least anticipated by Churchill, who insisted that 'special associations' like the one between the US and the UK not only were of benefit to the United Nations, but were 'indispensable' for the advancement of its goals (Churchill 1946).

From Universal Love Back to the Particular: John and Yoko's 'Love Across the Atlantic' and the Politics of Romance

After 1967, the Beatles released four more albums, *The Beatles* (the 'White Album') (Beatles 1968), *Yellow Submarine* (Beatles 1969a), *Abbey Road* (Beatles 1969b) and *Let It Be* (Beatles 1970). During this period, John Lennon's relationship with American-educated, Japanese avant-garde performance artist Yoko Ono blossomed and the couple were married on 20 March 1969. Whereas the thematic range of the Beatles' songwriting had expanded from the particular to the universal – as Lennon's own late Beatles' song 'Across the Universe' suggests (Beatles 1970)[7] – during his solo career, Lennon endeavoured to access the universal through the particular. For Lennon, partnered intimacy, anchored in expressions of romantic love with Yoko, provided the basis for a universal politics of love that both imagined a transformed world and encouraged people to perform works of personal and political transformation.

Borrowing from the tactic of the 'sit-in', used in the American South to advance the cause of integration at lunch counters, John and Yoko performed 'bed-ins' in protest against the US's war in Vietnam. They invited the press into their wedding chamber and used this most intimate of domestic sites as a venue for addressing matters of international diplomacy. A month after their marriage, in a ceremony that took place on the rooftop of Abbey Road studio, John substituted the name 'Ono' for 'Winston', the middle name he had been bequeathed at birth. According to Yoko Ono, Lennon disliked the 'wartime connotation' inherent in the name Winston and 'the implication that he was somehow a subscriber to the upper-class British empire and all that' (Coleman 2000: 491–2). Ironically, Lennon could not quite undo the special relationship his Churchillian association signalled. As noted above, Churchill had called upon the US and the UK to form bonds of cooperation through military alliance and the exertion of moral force to ensure world peace in the aftermath of World War II (Churchill 1946). Lennon advocated for peace as well; his advocacy, however, led him to critique the many military actions of the US that posed a threat to world peace.

And so, the most personal matrimonial symbol of a fertile wedding bed became the site of fruitful political protest through Lennon's new romantic and artistic relationship with Ono (Kruse 2016). Using their Montreal honeymoon suite as both pressroom and recording studio, the song 'Give Peace a Chance' was recorded 'live' on 1 June 1969; many friends and members of the press contributed to the performance, which was attributed to the Plastic Ono Band (Lennon 1969). The lyrics distinguish between what 'everybody's talking about' – the gossip generated by the mass media – and what really matters: the universal cry for peace that is enunciated in the song's title and constitutes its chorus. 'Give Peace a Chance', a song composed by an Englishman, quickly became the national anthem of the American anti-Vietnam war movement (Perone 2001: 57). Under the direction of folksinger and activist Pete Seeger, for example, the chorus was sung repeatedly for over ten minutes by hundreds of thousands of people during the 15 November 1969 March on Washington to end the Vietnam War (Wiener 2010).

Lennon's most popular anthem for peace was 'Imagine' (Lennon 1971). It was released a year after the Beatles officially dissolved and at a time when Lennon was seeking residency in the US. Atop a simple bass, drums and piano arrangement, with a string section in the background, Lennon constructs his dream of a new world. It is a world without heaven or hell; a world without the discourse of established religions that had disturbed the Beatles' last tour of America; a world without borders, without countries, and without the requirement to kill other people on behalf of a particular nation. Lennon invites his listeners into this world through a bold act of imagination. As in the romance narrative that propelled so many of the Beatles' songs, the end that Lennon seeks is proleptically present from the start, in the articulation of the desire for the world to 'live as one'. Unabashedly identifying himself as a 'dreamer', Lennon insists that he is not alone; rather, he is a member of a community of dreamers intent upon 'sharing' the world. During the course of his three-minute song, Lennon transports the 'happily ever after' of the romance narrative from the personal realm to the sphere of the political, thereby transforming the conflict of his engagement with America into a new world order brokered in and through his engagement with Yoko Ono.

Conclusion: Dreaming of Love Across Borders

After a protracted struggle with US Immigration and Naturalization Services, John Lennon was granted permanent US residency on 27 July 1976 (Wiener 2000). The name that appeared on the 'green card' confirming this status was 'John Winston Ono Lennon'. The 'Winston' had been 'diplomatically added back', according to one biographer, to aid in Lennon's immigration battle despite his long-standing effort to disassociate himself from Churchill (Coleman 2000: 492). And so, just as Pan Am had asserted American commercial interests over a marker of British identification when the Beatles first arrived in New York (compare Figure 12.1 above), a marker of British identity was reinserted into Lennon's identification card to confirm his status as a permanent resident in America.

While amassing evidence on John Lennon's behalf, Leon Wildes, Lennon's lawyer, uncovered a prevailing practice within the Immigration and Naturalization Service that deferred indefinitely the deportation from the US of selected individuals on humanitarian grounds. On the basis of this unofficial policy of 'deferred action', Wildes built his case for Lennon's permanent residency in the US (Wildes 2016). Once exposed by Wildes, and publicised by him in several law journal articles, this practice was formalised and eventually became 'the inspiration for President Barack Obama's Deferred Action for Childhood Arrivals' (DACA) Act (Frey 2017: 92). Obama's executive action put in place policies that had been proposed in, but never passed through, the US Congress under the heading of the 'DREAM Act'. This name was based, ostensibly, on the acronym for 'Development, Relief, and Education for Alien Minors'. But for those familiar with Lennon's song 'Imagine', the name has other resonances. However, those resonances hit a wall, both literally and figuratively, during the period immediately following Obama's presidency. In the US, then Attorney General Jefferson Sessions characterised 'Dreamers' as 'lawbreakers' and the Trump Administration sought their deportation (Shear and Hirschfeld 2017). Meanwhile, across the Atlantic, the question of how to welcome outsiders within the borders of Europe became a source of relentless political strife. In the UK, the desire to limit immigration served as a key factor leading to the vote to leave the European Union (Carl 2018). Even as the UK negotiates its separation from Europe and the United States tightens its borders to keep others out, Lennon's song remains to keep alive the dream that someday 'the world will live as one'.

This story of the Beatles suggests both tension and intimacy in the special relationship between the UK and the US. When they left London Heathrow airport in early February 1964, John, George, Paul and Ringo repeated a pattern of transatlantic crossings that had included, at one time or another, the slave trade, the relocation of immigrants, luxury travel, and competition for pre-eminence in the field of aviation. Their wild reception in the US was tempered significantly during their fourth tour when a kind of religious fervour that had animated earlier immigrants from England was directed against the Beatles in objection to remarks made by John Lennon concerning Jesus. Their American tour also exposed them to the racial tensions that characterised American life, as well as the threat of violence that accompanied those tensions.[8] Through it all, the Beatles continued to extol the virtues of romance in their love songs, which, however, progressed from the desire to hold hands with a beloved to the desire to save the world with love.

This motive of love propelled John Lennon, in collaboration with Yoko Ono, beyond any particular 'special relationship' that might obtain between the UK and the US to focus their efforts in opposition to American policies that threatened world peace. But despite their critical engagement, Lennon and Ono ventured to the US again in 1971, in part because they felt that, as a biracial couple, they would be better able to pursue happiness in New York City (Wildes 2016: 189). Tension and intimacy, romance and politics, idealistic dreaming and performative protest, love ballad and bold critique: the story of the Beatles and John Lennon illuminates these key elements in the US–UK relationship. Surprisingly aligned with Churchill's vision of a partnership that ultimately would be sustained by the 'principle of common citizenship' (Churchill 1946), but surpassing and completing it, Lennon imagined a love that extended not merely across the Atlantic, but across all borders.

Notes

1. These include 'Chains', by Gerry Goffin and Carole King, and 'Baby It's You', by Luther Dixon, Mack David and Burt Bacharach. Their second British LP, *With the Beatles* (Beatles 1963c), also featured six cover tunes, five of which were written by African Americans (for example, 'Roll Over Beethoven', by Chuck Berry, and 'You Really Got a Hold on Me', by Smokey Robinson). The sixth, 'Till There Was You', was composed by Robert Meredith Wilson, a white American, from his musical, *The Music Man*.

2. In contrast to the fastest piston-engine planes, jet travel 'halved the flying time between cities' (Bender and Altschul 1982: 475). Travel by propeller plane also involved the inconvenience of intermittent stops in places like Gander, Newfoundland; Reykjavik, Iceland; and Shannon, Ireland.

3. The Beatles' tribute to the British aviation industry would later be memorialised in their song 'Back in the USSR' (Beatles 1968), with its reference to 'BOAC' – British Overseas Air Corporation. BOAC united with British European Airways (BEA) in 1974 to form British Airways. Pan Am, meanwhile, met its demise on 4 December 1991, a consequence of the airline's inability to adjust to the neoliberal agenda of deregulation that was advanced during the Reagan era (Trost 2014: 1023, 1034).

4. 'Paperback Writer' (Beatles 1966a) was the number one song in America in June and by August the double single 'Yellow Submarine/Eleanor Rigby' (Beatles 1966b) was atop the charts (Bronson 1992: 201, 205–8).

5. Compare, for example, 'I Want to Hold Your Hand' (Beatles 1963d) and 'If I Fell' (Beatles 1964a).

6. According to one source, there were about 1.2 billion Christians world-wide in the late 1960s (Christianity in View n.d.).

7. 'Across the Universe' praises the omnipresence of a love of which the narrator is invited to partake, perhaps through transcendental meditation and the repetition of the mantra 'Jai guru deva om'. Unlike Lennon's later songs, which seek, in one way or another, to change the world, the surmise of the chorus in this song is that nothing will (and nothing should?) change 'my world'.

8. The threat of gun violence, directed at the Beatles in Memphis (Doyle 2017), rings both tragically and ironically, as Memphis was the site of Martin Luther King's assassination on 4 April 1968, and Lennon was assassinated in New York on 8 December 1980.

Works Cited

AP Images (1964), 'The Beatles Arrive in New York'. Available at: <https://apimagesblog.com/blog/2015/02/06/the-beatles-in-1964> (last accessed 3 March 2019).

Beatles, The (1962), 'Love Me Do/PS I Love You', London: Parlophone 45-R 4949.

Beatles, The (1963a), *Please, Please, Me*, London: Parlophone PMC 1202.

Beatles, The (1963b), 'She Loves You', London: Parlophone R 5055.

Beatles, The (1963c), *With The Beatles*, London: Parlophone PMC 1206.

Beatles, The (1963d), 'I Want to Hold Your Hand', London: Parlophone R 5084.

Beatles, The (1964a), 'If I Fell', from the album *A Hard Day's Night*, London: Parlophone PMC 1206.

Beatles, The (1964b), *The Beatles for Sale*, London: Parlophone PMC 1240.

Beatles, The (1965a), 'Yesterday', from the album *Help!*, London: Parlophone PMC 1255.

Beatles, The (1965b), *Rubber Soul*, London: Parlophone PMC 7009.

Beatles, The (1966a), 'Paperback Writer', London: Parlophone R 5452.

Beatles, The (1966b), 'Yellow Submarine/Eleanor Rigby', London: Parlophone R 5493.

Beatles, The (1967a), 'Penny Lane', London: Parlophone R 5570.

Beatles, The (1967b), *Sergeant Pepper's Lonely Hearts Club Band*, London: Parlophone PMC 7027.

Beatles, The (1967c), 'All You Need is Love', London: Parlophone R 5260.

Beatles, The (1968), *The Beatles*, London: Apple PMC 7067–7068.

Beatles, The (1969a), *Yellow Submarine*, London: Apple PCS 7070.

Beatles, The (1969b), *Abbey Road*, London: Apple PCS 7088.

Beatles, The (1970), *Let It Be*, London: Apple PCS 7096.

Beatles Bible (n.d.), 'The Beatles on Our World: All You Need Is Love'. Available at: <https://www.beatlesbible.com/1967/06/25/the-beatles-on-our-world-all-you-need-is-love/> (last accessed 3 April 2019).

BBC News (2011), 'The Beatles Banned Segregated Audiences, Contract Shows', 18 September. Available at: <https://www.bbc.com/news/entertainment-arts-14963752> (last accessed 3 April 2019).

Bender, M., and S. Altschul (1982), *The Chosen Instrument: Juan Trippe, Pan Am, The Rise and Fall of an American Entrepreneur*, New York: Simon and Schuster.

Benjamin, P. (1963), 'Idlewild is Rededicated as John F. Kennedy Airport', *New York Times*, 25 December, pp. 1, 54.

Bronson, F. (1992), *The Billboard Book of Number One Hits*, 3rd edn, New York: Watson-Guptill.

Carl, N. (2018), 'Leavers Have a Better Understanding of Remainers' Motivations than Vice Versa', London School of Economics and Political Science, *Brexit*, 5 April. Available at: <https://blogs.lse.ac.uk/brexit/2018/05/04/leavers-have-a-better-understanding-of-remainers-motivations-than-vice-versa/> (last accessed 3 March 2019).

Christianity in View (n.d.), 'Statistics and Forecasts for World Religions: 1800–2025'. Available at: <http://christianityinview.com/religion-statistics.html> (last accessed 3 March 2019).

Churchill, W. (1946), 'The Sinews of Peace', International Churchill Society. Available at: <https://winstonchurchill.org/resources/speeches/1946-1963-elder-statesman/the-sinews-of-peace/> (last accessed 14 February 2019).

Cleave, M. (1966a), 'How Does a Beatle Live? John Lennon Lives Like This', *The Evening Standard* (London), 4 March, pp. 10–12.

Cleave, M. (1966b), 'How a Beatle Lives: The Scene Shifts from Weybridge to London', *The Evening Standard* (London), 25 March, p. 8.

Coleman, R. (2000), *Lennon: The Definitive Biography: 20th Anniversary Edition*, London: Sidgwick and Jackson.

Coslett, P. (2007), 'Penny Lane', BBC Liverpool, 15 February. Available at: <http://www.bbc.co.uk/liverpool/content/articles/2007/02/15/abolition_penny_lane_feature.shtml> (last accessed 3 March 2019).

Davies, H. (2002), *The Beatles: The Authorized Biography*, New York: Norton.

Dempsey, D. (1964), 'Why the Girls Scream, Weep, Flip', *New York Times Sunday Magazine*, 23 February, pp. 15, 69–71.

Doyle, J. (2017), 'Burn The Beatles, 1966: Bigger Than Jesus?', *PopHistoryDig .com*, 11 October. Available at: <https://www.pophistorydig.com/topics/burn-the-beatles-1966/> (last accessed 10 April 2019).

Frey, R. M. (2017), 'John Lennon vs. the USA' (book review), *The Federal Lawyer*, January/February, pp. 92–3.

Gardner, P. (1964), 'The Beatles Invade, Complete with Long Hair and Screaming Fans', *New York Times*, 8 February, pp. 25, 49.

Inglis, I. (2012), *The Beatles in Hamburg*, London: Reaktion.

International Slavery Museum (n.d.), 'Liverpool and the Slave Trade'. Available at: <http://www.liverpoolmuseums.org.uk/ism/slavery/europe/liverpool.aspx> (last accessed 3 March 2019).

Jonze, T. (2015), 'Cunard Yanks: The Sailors who Taught Britain How to Rock 'n' Roll', *The Guardian*, 1 July. Available at: <https://www.theguardian.com/music/2015/jul/01/liverpool-merseybeat-cunard-yanks-sailors-taught-britain-to-rocknroll> (last accessed 3 March 2019).

King, Jr, M. L. (1963), *Strength to Love*, Philadelphia: Fortress.

King, Jr, M. L. (2003), 'A Time to Break Silence', in J. Washington (ed), *A Testament of Hope: The Essential Writings and Speeches*, New York: Harper, pp. 231–44.

Kruse, R. J. (2016) 'Geographies of John and Yoko's 1969 Campaign for Peace: An Intersection of Celebrity, Space, Art, and Activism', in O. Johansson and T. L. Bell (eds), *Sound, Society and the Geography of Popular Music*, New York: Routledge, pp. 11–32.

Lennon, J. (1971), 'All You Need is Love' (interview excerpt), 'Beatles Ultimate Experience: Songwriting & Recording Database: Magical Mystery Tour'. Available at: <http://www.beatlesinterviews.org/dba13tour.html> (last accessed 3 March 2019).

Lennon, J., and the Plastic Ono Band (1969), 'Give Peace a Chance', London: Apple 13.

Lennon, J., and the Plastic Ono Band (1971), 'Imagine', London: Apple 1840.

McCartney, P., and Wings (1976), 'Silly Love Songs', Los Angeles: Capitol 4256.

Meisel, P. (2010), *The Myth of Popular Culture*, London: Wiley-Blackwell.

Millard, André (2012), *Beatlemania: Technology, Business, and Teen Culture in Cold War America*, Baltimore: Johns Hopkins University Press.

Murrmann, M. (2014), 'Burn Your Beatles Records!', *Mother Jones*, 12 August. Available at: <https://www.motherjones.com/politics/2014/08/burn-beatles-records-lennon-jesus/> (last accessed 3 March 2019).

Perone, J. E. (2001), *Songs of the Vietnam Conflict*, Westport, CT: Greenwood.

Regev, E. (2012), 'Lennon and Jesus: Secularization and the Transformation of Religion', *Studies in Religion*, 41:4, pp. 534–63.

Roach, C. M. (2010), 'Getting a Good Man to Love: Popular Romance Fiction and the Problem of Patriarchy', *Journal of Popular Romance Studies*, 1:1, 4 August.

Available at: <http://jprstudies.org/2010/08/getting-a-good-man-to-love-popular-romance-fiction-and-the-problem-of-patriarchy-by-catherine-roach/> (last accessed 3 March 2019).

Roach, C. M. (2016), *Happily Ever After: The Romance Story in Popular Culture*, Bloomington: Indiana University Press.

Shear, M. D., and J. Hirschfeld (2017), 'Trump Moves to End DACA and Calls on Congress to Act', *The New York Times*, 5 September. Available at: <https://www.nytimes.com/2017/09/05/us/politics/trump-daca-dreamers-immigration.html> (last accessed 3 March 2019).

Trost, T. L. (2014), 'The Pan Am "Quipper" as Site of Anxiety: Managing Emotion in an Era of Neoliberalism and Corporate Decline', *American Quarterly*, 66:4, pp. 1021–37.

Turner, S. (2006), *The Gospel According to the Beatles*, Louisville: Westminster-John Knox.

Tweedie, N. (2008), 'Transatlantic Jet Flight Celebrates 50 Years', *Travel*, 13 August. Available at: <https://www.telegraph.co.uk/travel/3146988/Transatlantic-jet-flight-celebrates-50-years.html> (last accessed 3 March 2019).

Whitburn, J. (2001), *Top Pop Albums 1955–2001 Billboard*, Menomonee Falls, WI: Record Research.

White, T. H. (1963), 'For President Kennedy: An Epilogue', *Life*, 55/23, 6 December, pp. 158–9.

Wiener, J. (2000), *Gimme Some Truth: The John Lennon FBI Files*, Berkeley: University of California Press.

Wiener, J. (2010), 'Nixon and the 1969 Vietnam Moratorium', *The Nation*, 12 January. Available at: <https://www.thenation.com/article/nixon-and-1969-vietnam-moratorium/> (last accessed 14 February 2019).

Wildes, L. (2016), *John Lennon vs. the USA*, Chicago: American Bar Association.

Part Four

Political Coupledom: Flirting with the Special Relationship

'Political Soulmates': The 'Special Relationship' of Reagan and Thatcher and the Powerful Chemistry of Celebrity Coupledom

Shelley Cobb

Roosevelt and Churchill sitting side by side. Reagan and Thatcher laughing together. Bush and Blair walking and talking. Trump and May holding hands. These simple images of US presidents and UK prime ministers invoke what the media calls the 'special relationship' between the United States of America and the United Kingdom of Great Britain and Northern Ireland. The supposed specialness of Anglo-American relations is the subject of ongoing critique by journalists, political theorists, military analysts and former members of government (see Aldous 2013; Coleman 2004; Langley 2014; McKercher 2017; Mumford 2018; Ratti 2018; Smith 1991; and Wheatcroft 2014). In their commentaries about the political and historical consequences of this transatlantic relationship, all of these writers devote some attention to the personal relationship between the two leaders. However, none pays significant attention to the role played by visual representations of the two leaders together in constructing the special relationship as a powerful cultural discourse. These images of the personalised relationship of the individual prime minister and president subsume the history and (inter)national politics of the transatlantic relationship under their representation of companionship and coupledom. This transmogrification is especially effective with two leaders like Thatcher and Reagan. In media images of these two together, their charismatic personas synergistically combine to confer a celebrity couple aura upon them.

This chapter argues that President Ronald Reagan, who served in office from 20 January 1981 to 20 January 1989, and Prime Minister Margaret Thatcher, who was in office from 4 May 1979 to 28 November 1990, are the most iconic representatives of the Anglo-American special relationship. This is in part because their closely aligned domestic policies to reduce the welfare state and increase the reach of laissez-faire free market capitalism during their concurrent terms in office established the neoliberal order of contemporary late capitalism. Though all subsequent presidents and prime ministers have accepted this state of affairs (with only some tweaking to the left or right), Thatcher and Reagan, together, represent its origin, as well as its entrenchment. Reinforced by their shared ideologies and political agendas, the unwavering myth that they had an intimate and happy personal relationship endowed the recurring images of their togetherness with the iconicity of a celebrity couple. Consequently, as I show below, both positive and negative representations of them deflected any substantive structural critiques of their neoliberal programmes because the political was subsumed into the personal. After a dissection of key special relationship tropes established by President Franklin D. Roosevelt and Prime Minister Winston Churchill, and a review of some of the relationships between other US and UK leaders that have been less than iconic, this chapter outlines elements of Reagan and Thatcher's celebrity in order to analyse key media images of their relationship that have two distinct but interconnected functions. First, mainstream media images of Reagan and Thatcher constructed them as political soulmates, intimate friends and a happy couple. Second, satirical visual renderings of Reagan and Thatcher engaged the image of soulmates to represent them as a romantic and/or sexual couple; this attempt at critique, however, only reinforced the power of their celebrity coupledom. I then conclude with a brief analysis of the ways in which current President Trump and Prime Minister Theresa May have been compared to Thatcher and Reagan and argue that images of the special relationship between these leaders engage long-standing racist and xenophobic tropes that first emerged in the relationship between Churchill and Roosevelt.

The Special Relationship: On Again, Off Again

In addition to the strong military alliance between the US and the UK during World War II, the importance of the relationship between Churchill and Roosevelt has been long celebrated and well documented (Kimball 1998; Cimino 2018). After the Pearl Harbor attack on 7 December and the entry of the US into the war, Churchill met with Roosevelt in Washington, DC, on Christmas Eve, 1941. Roosevelt gave a short Christmas message on the radio that ended with these words of introduction: 'And so I am asking my associate, [and] my old and good friend, to say a word to the people of America, old and young, tonight, – Winston Churchill, Prime Minister of Great Britain' (National Archives). After thanking his 'illustrious friend – The President', Churchill then encouraged the listeners to take 'delight' in the Christmas spirit even as war was consuming the world; while away from home, Churchill declared that he found comfort 'in the commanding sentiment of comradeship in the common cause of great peoples who speak the same language, kneel at the same altars, and, to a very large extent, pursue the same ideals' (International Churchill Society). Since then, relations between Britain and the US have maintained a distinctive character that is rooted in that wartime alliance and the idealised relationship between Churchill and Roosevelt. As Richard Aldous notes, 'Its tone is one of shared culture, history and struggle burnished in fighting a global war together' (Aldous 2013: 8). And it was Churchill who, in a 1943 telegram to the Foreign Office, coined the phrase used to this day: 'It is my deepest conviction . . . that unless Britain and the United States are joined in a *special relationship* another destructive war will come to pass'. He would then use it in the House of Commons in 1945 and to an American crowd in 1946, both times speaking about the necessity of the transatlantic relationship for world peace (Reynolds 1988: 94).

Beyond the term itself, Churchill's description of the special relationship has set its parameters. Beneath his appeal to 'the common cause of great peoples who speak the same language [and] kneel at the same altars' lies Churchill's conviction that 'the white race was superior', as the historian Kehinde Andrews has argued (*Good Morning Britain* 2018). It is something of an open secret that Churchill was a racist and a colonialist, who had a 'gung-ho fondness for imperial slaughter' (Seymour 2018) – a factor that has been denied in the school history curriculum (Seymour 2018) and justified or dismissed in popular histories of the war-time Prime Minister (*Good Morning Britain* 2018). The transatlantic special relationship was forged in the racist and colonialist structuring logic that constituted Churchill's worldview and that, to this day, invests the transatlantic special relationship with notions of the racialised superiority of Britain and the US. This underlying racialised ideology is, I would argue, key to two other special relationships also discussed in this volume: the Gulf War alliance of Tony Blair and George W. Bush (see Hamad in this volume) and Theresa May's attempts to secure post-Brexit trade support from Donald Trump (see Ewen in this volume). Of course, the 'success' of the special relationship (as a political project and a cultural ideal) has not been consistent since World War II, and many of the leaders' relationships have been less iconic in their imagery than Churchill–Roosevelt and Thatcher–Reagan. As such, they highlight the unique combination of historical, political and personal factors that made Thatcher and Reagan recall Churchill and Roosevelt, as well as generate their own mythology as a 'special' couple.

In *Britain, America and the Special Relationship Since 1941*, B. J. C. McKercher critically examines the on again–off again history of the special relationship. In 1945, soon after close of World War II, the special relationship ran into trouble when Churchill's Conservative Party lost to the Labour Party. The personal relationship between President Harry Truman (in office 12 April 1945 to 20 January 1953) and Prime Minister Clement Attlee (in office 26 July 1945 to 26 October 1951) was 'business-like without any special rapport' (Miscamble 2007: 204). Prime Minister Anthony Eden (6 April 1955 to 9 January 1957) and President Dwight D. Eisenhower (in office 20 January 1953 to 20 January 1961) were at odds during the Suez Canal crisis. Eisenhower wanted to distance the US from anything that looked like 'old-style imperialism' (McKercher 2017: 63). Consequently, as McKercher shows, 'Anglo-American relations weakened . . . [and] a general international view developed that Britain ceased to be a major Power [sic]' (64).

There was a brief return to a happier transatlantic relationship when Prime Minister Harold Macmillan (in office 10 January 1957 to 18 October 1963) provided 'a public face to Anglo-American amity . . . in meetings with Eisenhower' (McKercher 2017: 66). Macmillan continued to strengthen the relationship after Eisenhower's term ended by working with President John F. Kennedy to 'contain the Russians', leading some observers to portray the Kennedy–Macmillan era as '"Golden Days" for Anglo-American relations' (132). But the transatlantic relationship quickly became troubled again. The relationship between Prime Minister Harold Wilson and President Lyndon B. Johnson 'was probably the worst between any British prime minister and US president' because of the tensions over the Vietnam war' (Coleman 2004). The Wilson–Ford period and the following years under Prime Minister James Callaghan (5 April 1976 to 4 May 1979) and President Jimmy Carter (20 January 1977 to 20 January 1981) were times of turmoil: the oil crisis, combined with rising inflation, weakened both nations' econo-mies; the International Monetary Fund intervened in the British economy while labour woes were made manifest in strikes during the 1978–9 Winter of Discontent; meanwhile, America suffered a crisis of confidence after the revolution in Iran brought about the occupation of the US embassy in Tehran. All of this would set the stage for Thatcher and Reagan, who reignited the transatlantic relationship and imbued it with wartime-like discourses of defence, freedom and leadership.

Celebrity, Politics and Charisma

Reagan and Thatcher both entered office at a time of 'spiritual, physical, economic, ethical, religious or [and] political emergency', contexts that, as the philosopher Max Weber has shown, are particularly conducive for the appearance of supposedly 'natural' or 'charismatic' leaders (Weber 2007:

17). Both leaders fought election battles at heightened times of national anxiety, resulting from economic recession, political upheaval, cultural clashes, and threats to their global power and influence during the 1970s. Those political contexts created the conditions in which both Reagan's and Thatcher's charismatic styles could speak to millions of their citizens (even if millions of others reviled them), and their individual personas were a vital factor in the power of their coupledom.

One of the key ways in which the charisma of Reagan and Thatcher was expressed and maintained was through their ability to give rousing and memorable speeches. While Governor of California, Reagan spoke at the 1974 Conservative Political Action Conference, addressing the crowd with the famous phrase 'We will be as a shining city upon a hill', which evoked the founding of America as a 'Christian nation'.[1] Throughout his presidency, Reagan made several speeches lauded at the time, from his 1983 'Evil Empire' speech to his 'Morning in America' speech of 1986, and his television address to the nation after the Space Shuttle Challenger disintegrated shortly after its launch from Cape Canaveral in 1986. Reagan's own speechwriter described him thus:

> He had a voice I likened to a fine Merlot being poured gently into a crystal goblet . . . [and he held] an audience by using descriptive words and metaphors – the baseball announcer who could make listeners smell the grass, hear the peanut vendors, and see a centerfielder skid across the grass as a line drive barely stuck in the webbing of his mitt. (Khachigian 2011)

His ability to use language and his voice to hold an audience – or, in other words, his abilities as a performer – are the qualities Khachigian prizes. As Reagan himself noted with regard to his political acumen, 'Politics is just like showbusiness' (Lepore 2012).

In *The Fall of Public Man*, Richard Sennett shows how

> the modern charismatic leader destroys any distance between his own sentiments and impulses and those of his audience; and so focusing his followers on his motivations, deflects them from measuring him in terms of his acts . . . The electronic media play a crucial role in this deflection. (Sennett 2002: 265)

Reagan was very adept at using radio and television to his advantage. And, as Sennett's point suggests, the intimacy of these media created a conduit that heightened Reagan's skills in addressing and connecting with the general public in a conversational style. Very early in his political career, he became known as 'The Great Communicator'. His presidency became so entwined with this persona that it also became the evidence that he lacked the actual leadership knowledge and skills required because he appeared to be all performance and no substance. On TV, both *Spitting Image* in the UK (1984–96) and *Saturday Night Live* in the US (1975–) satirised this image of Reagan when they presented him as a bumbling fool who 'did not know anything' – a statement about the President's knowledge of the Iran–Contra scandal that Donald Regan, Reagan's Chief of Staff, testified to before Congress (Iran–Contra Hearings Testimony).[2] Arguably, these comedic representations of him only confirmed the power of his charisma. The parodic images of Thatcher and Reagan as a couple, as I show below, function similarly.

Thatcher also became known for her skills at communication and oration. Since the Victorian era, the House of Commons' weekly session, 'Prime Minister's Questions' (PMQs), has been an opportunity for MPs to ask direct questions of the Prime Minister. Thatcher was the first prime minister to allow television into the House of Commons in 1989, at which point PMQs became a weekly staple on the BBC. The conventions of parliamentary debate make it well known as a place of machismo and grandstanding that encourages boisterousness from participants. Thatcher adapted quickly to the environment and her televised sessions were known for their vociferousness and noisiness. Thatcher's adaptation to leadership in this environment included, infamously, coaching to lower the timbre of her voice, while at the same time she continued to perform proper femininity (signified in her ever-present handbag). As Jacqueline Rose has noted, Thatcher's self-presentation of her femininity was one of contradictions ranging from 'the most phallic of self-images (the iron-lady), to the insistence on her femininity as utterly banal (the housewife managing the purse-strings of the nation)' (Rose 1998: 19). Heather Nunn makes clear that these contradictions meant that Thatcher could also be masculinised as needed to shore up her persona as a strong leader, 'a woman who was "the best man"' (Nunn 2002: 13). Her identity as 'the lady' who was tougher than any man was established in 1976, when she gave the Cold War speech, 'Britain Awake', that made the case for strengthening national defence against an attack from Soviet Russia. The Soviet Army newspaper *Red Star* gave her the nickname the 'Iron Lady', which she later co-opted in her famous 'The Lady's Not for Turning' speech at the 1980 Conservative Party conference, in which, despite rising unemployment and recession, Thatcher refused to perform a 'U-turn' on her liberalisation of the economy.

The ability of both Reagan and Thatcher to communicate with the electorate through self-presentation (that is, their personas of authenticity rather than just the authority of their positions) exemplifies Sennett's argument that the highly mediated politics of contemporary society 'makes its citizens feel a leader is believable because he can dramatize his own motivations'; he adds, usefully for this chapter, 'Leadership on these terms is a form of seduction' (Sennett 2002: 265). Khachigian's description of Reagan's verbal skills exemplify the kind of performative leadership that Sennett articulates. Inevitably, though, leadership as seduction is gendered, and this imagery evokes both a sophisticated man of taste and the all-American male. Thatcher's charisma was often, if not always, sexualised. Surrounded by men in her cabinet, 'her femininity added a frisson of sexuality to their engagement with her and disturbed the public school code of conduct and decorum formerly operating within the all-male preserve of the party's higher echelons' (Nunn 2002: 15). The Prime Minister's frisson of sexuality for the men around her also would come to inform the representation of her relationship with the President.

Both Thatcher and Reagan were leaders with seductive charms who enthralled those around them, as well as their many admirers, who bought into the presentation of each as a strong leader who would restore national pride. Of course, both were also widely despised and vilified by citizens of their own countries for the damage they caused to social welfare programmes and for their imperialist foreign policies and actions (such as Reagan's support of Latin American dictators and Thatcher's invasion of the Falklands). However, when brought together as Cold War leaders by their mutual distrust of the Soviet Union and their shared concern to reinvigorate the transatlantic relationship, their qualities as charismatic leaders combined to make them into a formidable couple who would capture the media's attention.

The Synergy of the Happy Couple and the Sexualised Satirising of the Special Relationship

Of course, Thatcher and Reagan's relationship was platonic and built over years of working together as political allies, but they are often described (and satirised) as having personal affection and feelings for each other. Despite his book's title, *Reagan & Thatcher: The Difficult Relationship*, Richard Aldous describes in detail how, according to memoirs and histories of the time, they are remembered as getting along and becoming fast friends. Their first meeting in April 1975 was as governor and opposition leader. They had planned a short '"meet and greet"', but in the end they spent closer to ninety minutes talking' (Aldous 2013: 12). Reagan's campaign adviser, Peter Hannaford, said, 'They fell into conversation as if they'd been friends for years . . . They were peas in a pod. The chemistry was perfect, and on policy they saw eye to eye' (Aldous 2013: 12). Reagan himself would say of their encounter, 'I liked her immediately', and Thatcher would recall that she 'was immediately won over by his charm, sense of humour and directness' (Aldous 2013: 15).

In our edited collection, *First Comes Love: Power Couples, Celebrity Kinship and Cultural Politics*, Neil Ewen and I argue that relationships are a key ingredient in maintaining and sustaining (and sometimes reinvigorating) celebrity (Cobb and Ewen 2015: 5). Analyses that focus on individuals, as if they retain their status without any connection to or relationship with other celebrities, ignore the role that companionship and partnership have in celebrity and in creating multiple types of celebrity couples. They can range from the tumultuous relationship of Hollywood stars Elizabeth Taylor and Richard Burton to the brotherly British working friendship of television presenters Ant and Dec.[3] Whether romantic or not, and no matter if each is more famous on their own or only famous when together, the celebrity couple functions as a unit.

In her work on screen star couples, Martha Nochimson articulates the combined charisma of what she calls the 'synergistic couple':

> the synergistic couple cannot be reproduced at will . . . it emerges from an unpredictable process of combination, a multiplication process in which a third entity is created, a hyphenated entity . . . there is no comparable recombination possible. (Nochimson 2002: 22)

Though Thatcher and Reagan were never given a portmanteau like 'Brangelina',[4] they were often represented as more than just political allies or as having the rejuvenated special relationship of the wartime brotherhood of Churchill and Roosevelt. As outlined above, the contexts of their times and their individual charisma created the conditions and possibilities for achieving their radical policies. Working together multiplied that process, and by virtue of their mixed gender relationship and the synergy and chemistry they exuded, they were often represented as a happy couple. There are several memorable pictures of them laughing together that continue to circulate regularly in the media: before a NATO meeting in 1985; in a golf cart at Camp David; on a break at the 1981 Ottawa Summit; during a presidential visit to London in 1984; dancing together at a White House ball in 1988. They often look like confidant(e)s sharing inside jokes.

In the photo from Camp David, Reagan is driving the golf cart. He wears a tartan collared shirt, unbuttoned underneath a V-neck sweater, looking much more casual than Thatcher who is wearing a blazer over one of her signature high-neck pussy-bow blouses. Though her hair is, as it was usually, stiffly coiffed, there is clearly a breeze dishevelling the President's usually stiff quiff style. They are both turned to their left, Thatcher looking over Reagan's shoulder, both with wide smiles for the audience of journalists and photographers. The smiles appear genuine, as if Reagan has just made a joke. They seem to have a rapport with each other and the press (other photos caught either seconds before or seconds after have them waving) and, in that moment, carefree, though the stated agenda for the meeting included talks with the Soviet Union and nuclear arms control (Reuters 1984). As an Associated Press photo, it appears regularly in news stories about the special relationship, as do all of the others mentioned above (see Week Staff 2013 and Leger 2013).

Granted, the photo-op of the US President States driving a golf cart around Camp David with a British Prime Minister or another foreign leader as passenger is fairly common. Still, the images of George W. Bush driving with Gordon Brown, and even George H. W. Bush driving with Margaret Thatcher, do not have the friendly ease that constructs the image of Reagan and Thatcher. The other transatlantic couples do not exhibit even a friendly chemistry. The photos of Thatcher and Reagan's time together are the documentary images of their synergistic relationship, which has been continually reinforced since then: in Geoffrey Smith's joint biography *Reagan and Thatcher* (1991); in the former *Sunday Times* editor Harold Evans's comment, upon Reagan's death, that 'the relationship between Thatcher and Reagan was closer even than Churchill and Roosevelt' (Wheatcroft 2014); in comments by Bernard Ingham, Thatcher's Press Secretary, who described the two of them as 'political soulmates' (CNN 2013); and even in Richard Aldous's revisionist biography *Reagan & Thatcher: The Difficult Relationship*, which inevitably reinforces the image that it tries to deconstruct (a smiling Thatcher and Reagan at a press conference appears on the book's cover).

In fact, I argue that all attempts to critique their image as the quintessential couple of the special relationship paradoxically bolsters the power of that image. In a 2013 CNN news item on the death of Margaret Thatcher, BBC reporter Nick Robinson comments that '[i]t was easy to satirise the relationship between Margaret Thatcher and Ronald Reagan but no one doubted that it was based on deep affection and genuine respect' (CNN 2013). The parodies began early in 1981. *The Economist* mocked the Prime Minister's economic policies and expressed the magazine's anxieties that Reagan might adopt them for the States with a cartoon cover of both leaders in bathing suits at the seaside. Thatcher, positioned in the foreground, beckons to Reagan: 'Come in, it's freezing!' (It's Freezing 1980). That same year, the British Socialist Worker's Party

(SWP) printed an anti-nuclear poster to protest against the investment the two leaders had committed to the nuclear arms race during the Cold War. In a parody of the famous *Gone with the Wind* film poster, the SWP replaced the iconic image of Clark Gable carrying Vivien Leigh with Reagan and Thatcher and a tag-line that read 'She promised to follow him to the end of the earth, He promised to organise it' (National Portrait Gallery). Still the highest-grossing film of all time, *Gone with the Wind* is remembered as an epic romance of burning passion, played by two actors idolised as among the biggest stars of their generation. The SWP's Thatcher–Reagan version draws on the film's iconicity to present their relationship as volatile and dangerous, and seems meant to link their role in the nuclear arms race to the crimes and abuses of slavery.

Other political caricatures of the couple attempt to make similar critiques. The famous *Punch* magazine ran several caricatures of the two leaders together, lampooning their relationship: one has them in a war-zone with nuclear weapons above and Thatcher shooting a machine gun at a target shaped like a Soviet general, while Reagan stands behind her, saying 'Say . . . you're beautiful when you're angry' (Mahood 1982). The infamous British television show *Spitting Image* used its grotesque puppet caricatures to spoof both leaders, regularly running jokes that suggested that Reagan lusted after Thatcher. In one episode, after grabbing and kissing Thatcher, the Reagan puppet walks away and says, 'What a fine-looking woman. Too bad I'm only screwing her country' (Wikiquote n.d.). It is, of course, their synergy and close relationship that it is so easy to exaggerate, and these images satirise it by imagining that their chemistry might also be because they were having sex.

All of these spoofs of their special relationship picture them as a sexual couple to make a political critique of their conservative policies (in relation to nuclear arms, the Cold War and the economy), which had deleterious effects on millions of people. The punch line of each is that their power and ambitions are simply individualised, sexualised desires. Problematically, though, the sex joke plays on the chemistry that, whether it was genuine or not, they performed for the media. Their combined charisma imbues the images and distracts from the political critique. In fact, all of the jokes imply that Thatcher and Reagan are bad people who simply cannot control themselves in their passion for each other and for their neoliberal project. This implies that replacing them fixes all the problems they created: nuclear proliferation, the destruction of their own nations' welfare states, and the bloodshed of postcolonial military interventions around the world. However, as noted, Thatcher and Reagan's neoliberal project was so effective in its transformation of economics, the welfare

state and the increased culture of individualism that successive governments of the Labour and Democrat parties, respectively, did not significantly alter it in any structural way; at best, they temporarily mitigated
its worst destructive effects. Moreover, alongside their neoliberal agenda,
they continually relied on the conservative insistence that the family must
replace the state, even as neoliberalism's emphasis on individual entrepreneurialism and free markets, alongside the radical reduction of the welfare
state, made family stability and community identity nearly impossible.

Like all celebrity couples, Thatcher and Reagan's special relationship
'dramatise[s] companionship in a contemporary world in which neoliberal
policies have increasingly compromised the pursuit of togetherness and
community' (Cobb and Ewen 2015: 6). Their exaggerated companionship
in positive representations appealed to their supporters and reinforced
their images as charismatic leaders who connected with and cared for their
constituents; the negative images portrayed them as charismatic individuals, led by their passions to ignore the needs of ordinary people who
would be better served by better leaders. As such, Thatcher and Reagan's
celebrity coupledom functioned as a distraction for structural arguments
against their politics and continued to act as a comfort for those who supported them, while reinforcing the ideologies of the special relationship.

Conclusion

After Donald Trump won the presidency in November 2016, Iain Duncan
Smith, who had relatively recently resigned his Cabinet post in Prime
Minister David Cameron's government, wrote:

> For the last eight years President Obama made it abundantly clear that he did
> not consider the UK as any more important in his international relations than
> any other country, particularly Germany and the EU itself. The so called 'special
> relationship' wasn't very special and not much of a relationship . . . In the UK,
> we have a choice. We can, like so many others, indulge ourselves in an orgy of
> complaint about the result – we have already seen that kind of behaviour over
> the Brexit result. Or we can . . . seize this opportunity to engage the new admin-
> istration and remind them of our enduring friendship in good times and in bad.
> (Ashmore 2016)

The racist and xenophobic tropes established in the Churchill–Roosevelt
relationship discussed above are clear here: while Barack Obama was President, the transatlantic relationship was not so special. Smith's racist dog
whistling implies that Obama has more affinity with 'any other country'
than the one that shares its language and its religion (as Churchill said) and

that Obama would rather side with their common World War II enemy, Germany. Smith therefore recommends that the UK government reach out to the new President, who is clearly invested in the superiority of white Anglo-Americans. And Prime Minister May, who assumed office by virtue of the Conservative Party's leadership election after Cameron's resignation, did just that as quickly as she could.

There is an immovable myth that Thatcher was the first world leader to visit President Reagan after his inauguration. Actually, the leaders of Jamaica and South Korea got there first but the myth is central to the image of Thatcher and Reagan as the quintessential special relationship. The current British Prime Minister Theresa May has often tried to copy and invoke Thatcher, especially in her relationship with President Trump. The British papers billed their meeting in January 2017 as the first official visit of a foreign leader to see Trump in the White House, though he had already met with the Prime Minister of Japan a week after he won the election. Importantly, a Number 10 spokeswoman said: 'the President-elect talked about enjoying the same relationship that Reagan and Thatcher did' (Mason and Asthana 2016). Unsurprisingly, the 'special relationship' between May and Trump immediately became a sexual joke in the media after a photo from May's visit showed the couple holding hands as they walked down some steps together (see Ewen in this volume). Several caricatures of them as the couple from *La La Land* (2016) invoke the romantic passion of that film, which eventually goes wrong, including a work of graffiti on a wall in London that the artist, Bambi, titled 'Lie Lie Land' (Bullen 2017). Moreover, there are two recreations of the *Gone with the Wind* poster, already described above, in which May and Trump replace Thatcher and Reagan. One is an internet meme, which keeps the poster the same but with the tag line 'She promised to follow him to the end of the earth. He promised to arrange it' (MEME n.d.). The other is a drawing on a centre-right website that shows them in the iconic pose but without the film poster details. It is attached to an article about May's first American visit that ends:

> A famous left-wing poster of the 1980s portrayed Thatcher and Reagan as Scarlett O'Hara and Rhett Butler from *Gone with the Wind*. It did neither of them any harm. We thus present an updated version, courtesy of Carla Millar. For the Prime Minister, as she prepares to meet with the President, tomorrow truly is another day. (Goodman 2017)

Without irony, this passage invokes the romanticisation, not to mention the sexualisation, of the transatlantic special relationship that suffuses the images of Thatcher and Reagan. Moreover, it revels in the ability of their celebrity coupledom to deflect political critique and act as cover for destructive right-wing politics. It expresses the hope that May and Trump can create the same effect, thereby making it clear that the 'special relationship' is not about love across the Atlantic. It is about power.

Notes

1. Reagan borrowed the phrase from John Winthrop (1587–1649), Puritan and Governor of the Massachusetts Bay Colony, who referenced Matthew 5: 14–16 (Winthrop 1892: 307).
2. According to Thatcher's first Foreign Secretary, Lord Carrington, while discussing President Reagan over a drink one evening, she said to him, 'Peter, there's nothing there' as she tapped the side of her head (Wheatcroft 2014).
3. Richard Burton and Elizabeth Taylor were Hollywood stars during the classical period; they appeared together in *Cleopatra* (1963) and were famous for having an affair while filming. Ant and Dec are two male British television presenters who were the hosts of *I'm a Celebrity, Get Me Out of Here* (2002–).
4. 'Brangelina' is the portmanteau celebrity name given by *People Magazine* to Brad Pitt and Angelina Jolie when they became a public couple (see Díaz 2015).

Works Cited

Aldous, R. (2013), *Reagan & Thatcher: The Difficult Relationship*, London: Arrow.

Ashmore, J. (2016), 'Iain Duncan Smith: UK Must Not Indulge in "an Orgy of Complaint" over Donald Trump', *Politics Home*, 10 November. Available at: <https://www.politicshome.com/news/uk/foreign-affairs/news/80667/iain-duncan-smith-uk-must-not-indulge-orgy-complaint-over-donald> (last accessed 6 March 2019).

Bullen, J. (2017), 'Street Artist Reveals "Lie Lie Land" Sketch of Theresa May and Donald Trump Waltzing on Islington Wall', *The Evening Standard*, 17 February. Available at: <https://www.standard.co.uk/news/london/street-artist-unveils-lie-lie-land-sketch-of-theresa-may-and-donald-trump-waltzing-on-islington-wall-a3469211.html> (last accessed 6 March 2019).

Cimino, A. (2018), *Roosevelt and Churchill: A Friendship that Saved the World*, London: Chartwell.

Cleopatra, film, directed by J. L. Mankiewicz. US: 20th Century Fox, 1963.

CNN (2013), 'Thatcher and Reagan's Special Relationship', 8 April. Available at: <https://www.youtube.com/watch?v=akGg_WVZxpg> (last accessed 12 March 2019).

Cobb, S., and N. Ewen (eds) (2015), *First Comes Love: Power Couples, Celebrity Kinship and Cultural Politics*, New York: Bloomsbury Academic.

Coleman, J. (2004), 'Harold Wilson, Lyndon Johnson and the Vietnam War, 1964–68', *American Studies Today Online*. Available at: <http://www.americansc.org.uk/Online/Wilsonjohnson.htm> (last accessed 18 November 2018).

Díaz, V. (2015), '"Brad & Angelina and Now . . . Brangelina!": A Sociocultural Analysis of Blended Celebrity Couple Names', in S. Cobb and N. Ewen (eds), *First Comes Love: Power Couples, Celebrity Kinship and Cultural Politics*, New York: Bloomsbury Academic, pp. 275–94.

Good Morning Britain (2018), itv.com, 9 October. Available at: <https://www.itv.com/goodmorningbritain/news/churchill-was-a-racist-and-comparable-to-hitler-says-academic> (last accessed 6 March 2019).

Goodman, P. (2017), 'Trump and May. She Channels Reagan and Thatcher in the First Speech of her American Visit', *Conservative Home*, 27 November. Available at: <https://www.conservativehome.com/thetorydiary/2017/01/may-and-trump-she-channels-thatcher-and-reagan-in-the-first-speech-of-her-american-visit.html> (last accessed 6 March 2019).

I'm a Celebrity Get Me Out of Here (2002–), TV series, directed by C. Powers. UK: ITV Granada.

International Churchill Society, 'Christmas Message 1941'. Available at: <https://winstonchurchill.org/resources/speeches/1941-1945-war-leader/christmas-message-1941/> (last accessed 6 March 2019).

Iran–Contra Hearings Testimony, Iran–Contra Investigation, Archives.org. Available at: <https://archive.org/stream/Iran-ContraHearingsTestimonyTranscripts/1987-irn-0008_Regan-Weinberger_djvu.txt> (last accessed 6 March 2019).

'It's Freezing' (1980), *The Economist*, 25 November to 5 December, cover image.

Khachigian, K. (2011), 'What made Reagan the Great Communicator', *Orange County Register*, 5 February. Available at: <https://www.ocregister.com/2011/02/05/ken-khachigian-what-made-reagan-the-great-communicator/> (last accessed 13 March 2019).

Kimball, W. (1998), *Forged in War: Churchill, Roosevelt and the Second World War*, New York: HarperCollins.

La La Land, film, directed by D. Chazelle. US: Lionsgate, 2016.

Langley, A. (2014), *Blair, Bush and Iraq*, Oxford: Raintree.

Leger, D. L. (2013), 'Thatcher, Reagan Relationship Altered History', *USA Today*, 8 April. Available at: <https://eu.usatoday.com/story/news/world/2013/04/08/thatcher-reagan-political-soulmates/2063671/> (last accessed 6 March 2019).

Lepore, J. (2012), 'The Lie Factory', *The New Yorker*, 24 September. Available at: <https://www.newyorker.com/magazine/2012/09/24/the-lie-factory> (last accessed 6 March 2019).

McKercher, B. J. C. (2017), *Britain, America and the Special Relationship Since 1941*, London: Routledge.

Mahood, K. (1982), 'Say, You're Beautiful When You're Angry', *Punch*, Punch Limited. Available at: <https://punch.photoshelter.com/image/I0000fW.ZC.nEBKY> (last accessed 13 May 2019).

Mason, R., and A. Asthana (2016), 'Theresa May Plans Trump Charm Offensive After Snub to Nigel Farage', *The Guardian*, 15 November. Available at: <https://www.theguardian.com/politics/2016/nov/14/theresa-may-plans-trump-charm-offensive-after-snub-to-farage> (last accessed 12 March 2019).

MEME (n.d.), 'Gone with the Wind'. Available at: <https://me.me/i/vladimir-putin-in-avvocialian-will-cold-war-productions-gone-with-7897419> (last accessed 29 April 2019).

Miscamble, W. D. (2007), *From Roosevelt to Truman: Potsdam, Hiroshima, and the Cold War*, Cambridge: Cambridge University Press.

Mumford, A. (2018), *Counterinsurgency Wars and the Anglo-American Alliance: The Special Relationship on the Rocks*, Washington, DC: Georgetown University Press.

National Archives, 'Educator Resources – Documents Related to FDR and Churchill'. Available at: <https://www.archives.gov/education/lessons/fdr-churchill> (last accessed 6 March 2019).

National Portrait Gallery, 'Gone with the Wind' (Ronald Reagan; Margaret Thatcher). Available at: <https://www.npg.org.uk/collections/search/portrait/mw251471/Gone-with-the-Wind-Ronald-Reagan-Margaret-Thatcher> (last accessed 6 March 2019).

Nochimson, M. P. (2002), *Screen Couple Chemistry: The Power of 2*, Austin: University of Texas Press.

Nunn, H. (2002), *Thatcher, Politics and Fantasy: The Political Culture of Gender and Nation*, London: Lawrence & Wishart.

Ratti, L. (2018), *A Not-So-Special Relationship: The US, the UK and German Reunification, 1945–1990*, Edinburgh: Edinburgh University Press.

Reuters (1984), 'Reagan and Thatcher to Meet in December', *The New York Times*, 29 November. Available at: <https://www.nytimes.com/1984/11/29/world/reagan-and-thatcher-to-meet-in-december.html> (last accessed 6 March 2019).

Reynolds, D. (1988), 'Re-thinking Anglo-American Relations', *International Affairs*, 65:1, pp. 89–111.

Rose, J. (1988), 'Margaret Thatcher and Ruth Ellis', *New Formations*, 6 (Winter), pp. 3–29.

Saturday Night Live, TV series, directed by D. R. King et al. US: NBC, 1975–.

Sennett, R. (2002), *The Fall of Public Man*, London: Penguin.

Seymour, R. (2018), 'The Real Winston Churchill', *Jacobin*. Available at: <https://www.jacobinmag.com/2018/01/winston-churchill-british-empire-colonialism> (last accessed 6 March 2019).

Smith, G. (1991), *Reagan and Thatcher: The Inside Story of the Friendship, and Political Partnership, That Changed World Events from the Falklands War to Perestroika*, London: W.W. Norton.

Spitting Image (1984–96), TV series, created by P. Fluck, R. Law and M. Lambie-Nairn. UK: ITV.

Weber, M. (2007 [1922]), 'The Essence of Charisma and its Workings', in S. Redmond and S. Holmes (eds), *Stardom and Celebrity: A Reader*, London: Sage, pp. 17–24.

Week Staff, The (2013), 'Thatcher and Reagan: A Look Back at One of the World's Most Powerful Political Alliances', *The Week*, 8 April. Available at: <https://theweek.com/articles/465811/thatcher-reagan-look-back-worlds-most-powerful-political-alliances> (last accessed 6 March 2019).

Wheatcroft, G. (2014), 'The Thatcher-Reagan Love Affair Wasn't All Plain Sailing', *The Guardian*, 10 November. Available at: <https://www.theguardian.com/ commentisfree/2014/nov/10/margaret-thatcher-ronald-reagan-love-affair-churchill-roosevelt> (last accessed 12 March 2019).

Wikiquote (n.d.), *Spitting Image*, 'Ronald Reagan'. Available at: <https:// en.wikiquote.org/wiki/Spitting_Image> (last accessed 29 April 2019).

Winthrop, J. (1892 [1630]), 'A Model of Christian Charity', in E. C. Stedman and E. M. Hutchinson (eds), *A Library of American Literature: Early Colonial Literature, 1607–1675*, New York: Webster, pp. 304–7.

CHAPTER 14

'I Will Be with You, Whatever': Bush and Blair's Baghdadi Bromance

Hannah Hamad

Introduction

In August 2006, British film and television actor Riz Ahmed, performing as his rap persona Riz MC, released 'The Post 9/11 Blues'. The song arises in the context of the illegal warfare waged by powerful Western Anglophone nations on the beleaguered peoples of countries of the global South, already subjected to the tyranny of brutal dictators and regimes. In a noteworthy discursive juxtaposition of innocent childhood romance with bloody mass murder, the song features the politically charged lyrics: 'Bush and Blair in a tree, K-I-L-L-I-N-G'. In this way, it adapts the chant familiar to countless schoolchildren in playgrounds across the UK and the US that singles out for mockery pairs of children who are believed to be engaged in some manner of childhood flirtation. Here, however, the replacement by Ahmed of the double S in 'kissing' with a double L transforms the romantic connotations of this word to the bloody and murderous meaning of the newly formed replacement word 'killing'. Intimations of love are thereby substituted with suggestions of slaughter. Ahmed is, of course, referring to the deaths caused by the political and military alliance between UK Prime Minister Tony Blair and US President George W. Bush as they waged war in Afghanistan and Iraq in the years following the 11 September 2001 terrorist attacks in New York and Washington.

Through his adoption of this particular mode of irreverence, Ahmed also appositely invokes the discourse of what would very soon thereafter be dubbed a 'bromance' in popular discursive parlance. Furthermore, as indicated by the lyrics excerpted above, and as argued elsewhere by popular music scholar Amy McDowell, he does this in order to mount a popular cultural critique of millennial right-wing politics, particularly the aforementioned military interventions in the Middle East (McDowell 2017). The term 'bromance' refers to the relational dynamics that pertain to homosocial relationships between male friends in which, as film scholar

Nick Davis has argued, concerning the emergence of bromantic discourses of masculinity in popular cinema of the 2000s and 2010s, 'the intimate bond between two men, while ostensibly platonic, carries . . . emotional . . . [and] perhaps even romantic or erotic weight' (Davis 2014: 109).

As one discursively prominent formation of masculinity, 'bromance' garnered an immense level of currency in early millennial US and UK media cultures. This could be seen even before the widespread adoption in popular vernacular of this single-word epithet, as the phenomenon had already been variously termed 'man crush' (Davis and Needham 2009: 9) and 'guy love' (Becker 2009: 121); meanwhile, its antecedents in academia can be found in discussions of, for example, 'queer straight masculinity' (Becker 2009: 121) and, of course, 'homosociality' (Kosofsky Sedgwick 1992). It has also been succinctly described by Glyn Davis and Gary Needham as 'a queer form of bonding between straight men', whereby '[t]he borders of homosociality, masculinity, and acceptable physical affection are troubled and toyed with . . . thereby indicating a wider cultural awareness of sexual identity fluidity' (Davis and Needham 2009: 9). Scholarly interest in bromance as a trope and a discourse has thus far focused primarily upon the emergence of a 'bromantic turn' (DeAngelis 2014) in Hollywood production cycles (see below), but also in other areas of the entertainment media, including television drama like the BBC's *Sherlock* (2010–17), reality TV, such as MTV's *Bromance* (2008–9), and popular music (Hamad 2011, for examples).

The dynamics of relational masculinities that are referenced by the term 'bromance', and by popular cultural iterations thereof, have variously showcased some of the range of possibilities, ambivalences and limitations of the ostensibly platonic but often extremely homoerotically charged intimacies in relationships between men in mediated form across the representational landscape of millennial and postmillennial popular culture. But, as illustrated above, arguably nowhere in the sphere of Anglophone media culture has there been more at stake for the world in the uptake of bromantic discourse than in the mediation of the Blair–Bush political alliance in the 2000s and beyond, and the potential power it had to shine a topical light on their atrocities. This chapter thus interrogates the mediation of the transatlantic 'special relationship' (Dumbrell 2006; McKercher 2017) between Tony Blair and George W. Bush through the discursive lens of 'bromance'. This formation of mediated masculine intimacy attained considerable currency over the course of the 2000s. It peaked towards the end of that decade and thus coincided with both the end of the Blair–Bush era and the popular success in the UK and the US of a cluster of so-called 'bromantic comedy' films. A trio of films from 2009 typifies the genre:

Todd Phillips's *The Hangover* (2009), Lynn Shelton's *Humpday* (2009) and, epitomically, John Hamburg's *I Love You, Man* (2009), which, 'bromance' scholar Michael DeAngelis argues, 'merits distinction as the quintessential model for the cinematic bromance' (DeAngelis 2014: 11).

This high point in the cinematic depiction of bromance not only coincides temporally with popular cultural mediations of the Blair–Bush special relationship. It also lends itself to them, providing cultural commentators with an apposite and timely means by which to critique satirically much of what is at stake in mediating the political, economic and military alliance between these two Anglophone nations through the irreverence of this topical gender discourse of masculine intimacy. Viewing the facets of the Blair–Bush special relationship through its depictions in popular film and other popular media not only sheds light on the nature of their political relationship, but also illuminates real-world resistances to its hegemony, the negotiation of which resulted in war and bloodshed.

The Landscape of the Popular Mediation of Romantically Signified Relationships

The same period that saw the emergence and popularisation of 'bromance' also saw the emergence and rapid popularisation of the phenomenon of the blended celebrity couple name. In her work on this recurrent discursive motif in celebrity culture's negotiation of discourses of romantic couple-dom, scholar and celebrity journalist Vanessa Díaz has demonstrated that the mid-2000s saw a pronounced intensification of the popular discursive use of portmanteaus as a means by which to refer to the names of celebrity couples, using a convenient verbal shorthand that also had a high degree of cultural currency (Díaz 2015: 275). Díaz's study of celebrity weekly magazines shows that portmanteaus became ubiquitous as a way to refer to all manner of romantically paired celebrities across the spectrum of contemporary media, although her particular focus is on Hollywood celebrities (276–7). According to Díaz, the morphing of two celebrity names 'is a practice that promotes [imaginary intimacy] between consumers and celebrity couples, thus encouraging the personal interest and investment of individuals in those couples' (277). She continues,

> The combining of celebrity couples' names by media outlets, the social circulation of these names, and the subsequent practice of combining names of non-celebrities is indicative of the power of social circulation of media, the potential impact of current social norms on media-marketing tactics, and the public appetite for fabricated intimacy with celebrities. (2015: 277)

Highlighting some of what is potentially at stake in the popularisation of the blended celebrity couple name, Díaz further suggests that '[o]ne of the goals of the celebrity media industry is to promote something that makes people feel invested in, attached to and intimate with', and that in Anglophone media in the 2000s, the celebrity portmanteau emerged as a noteworthy means by which the celebrity media industry was achieving this goal (276).

Significantly, then, the reach of the phenomenon of the celebrity portmanteau was so wide, in some noteworthy instances, that it extended beyond mainstream and entertainment media-based celebrity culture to inflect political discourse and media communication of political culture as well. This is vividly exemplified by the former UK Labour Party Communications Director Alastair Campbell, who, when writing about the relationship between UK Prime Minister Tony Blair and US President George W. Bush in his published diaries from this period, deliberately and knowingly collapses their names into a portmanteau-cum-acronym, refer-ring to them as 'TBGB' (Campbell 2013: xx).[1] Aligning them by associa-tion in this way with their mid-2000s entertainment media contemporaries like 'Brangelina' (Brad Pitt and Angelina Jolie), 'TomKat' (Tom Cruise and Katie Holmes) and 'Bennifer' (Ben Affleck and Jennifer Lopez/ Jennifer Garner), Campbell's preferred epithet for Blair and Bush lays bare the ease with which even those closest to them were willing and able to view the ostensibly political alliance between Bush and Blair through the lens of celebrity coupledom.

However, Blair and Bush do, of course, stand out from their Hollywood contemporaries in the sense that the outcome of their 'special relationship' saw half a million Iraqi people, among many others, killed in a controversial (to say the least) war, the after-effects of which produced civil war, violent extremism and the collapse of Iraq's already precarious infrastructure.[2] More than a decade later, the long-awaited Chilcot report was finally published on 6 July 2016 (Committee of Privy Councillors 2016). Commissioned by then British Prime Minister Gordon Brown in 2009 (following the departure from government of his predecessor, Blair), the report detailed the findings of the public inquiry into the role played by the UK in the war that was waged on Iraq by coalition forces between 2003 and 2011. While this report was comprised of twelve book-length volumes containing 2.6 million words, a single small phrase of six words stood out above all the others, rising to discursive prominence in the UK news media's coverage of the outcome of the inquiry. On Thursday, 7 July 2016, those six words were reproduced in hugely enlarged font as front-page headlines on the UK's national newspapers (including, but not limited to, *The Guardian*, *The Times*, *The Daily Mirror*, *The Sun* and *The*

National (of Scotland)); they have since become notorious: 'I will be with you, whatever' (Committee of Privy Councillors 2016: 89).

These words were attributed to Tony Blair himself. They were reported to have come from a memo, which was referred to in the media reportage at the time of the report's publication as 'a secret letter' (Masri 2016) that had been sent by Blair to Bush on 28 July 2002 (Booth 2016). As detailed in the report's executive summary, 'While the note was marked "Personal" (to signal that it should have a restricted circulation), it represented an extensive statement of the UK Government's position by the Prime Minister to the President of the United States' (Committee of Privy Councillors 2016: 89). In this memo, Blair promised to back the plan that was being formulated by the US President to go to war with Iraq. The plan called for an imminent invasion of the small Middle Eastern country, which had been beleaguered by the tyranny, oppression and mania of dictator Saddam Hussein since his infamous rise to power in the late 1970s (for more on the latter, see Farouk-Sluglett and Sluglett 1990 [1987]: 205–13, and Baram and Rubin 1993: xi).

Ironically (and tragically), Saddam had retained his position of power in the ways that he did, and for as long as he did, in part because he had been enabled in the 1980s by former UK and US leaders Margaret Thatcher and Ronald Reagan/George H. W. Bush (see Cobb in this volume). Under their respective leaderships, the UK and the US supplied Saddam with the weapons that equipped him to wage war on Iran from 1980 to 1988. In addition, their assistance made it at least possible that Saddam would be able to develop 'weapons of mass destruction'. Of course, following the 'Coalition' invasion of 2003, neither the UN weapons inspectors nor any Coalition forces were subsequently able to determine that such weapons even existed. The US and the UK under Margaret Thatcher and George H. W. Bush then endeavoured to conceal the parts they played in facilitating Saddam's invasion of Kuwait in 1990. As journalist Alan Friedman wrote, in his highly detailed exposé of what was known at the time as 'Iraqgate', 'the Thatcher and Bush governments allowed lethal technology and equipment to flow to Iraq, in the face of explicit warnings that the goods could be used in Saddam's nuclear and chemical warfare projects' (Friedman 1993: frontmatter).

Blair and Bush after Chilcot

In the aftermath of the Chilcot report, the romantic connotations of the Blair–Bush letters proved themselves to be instantly irresistible to satirists, commentators, culture jammers and memesters across various social media spanning the spectrum of platforms that comprise the mainstream online mediascape. One particularly vivid response to the pledge 'I will be with you, whatever' came three days later, on Saturday, 9 July 2016, via the micro-blogging social media platform Twitter. An operator with the user handle 'Call Me Ishmael' (@fqxjv) posted a response to the publication of the Chilcot report and referred explicitly to Blair's memo to Bush as a 'valentine'. This designation cemented a connotatively romantic reading of the mainstream's media's reference to it as a 'secret letter' (Masri 2016), and offered the relationship between Bush and Blair as an example of the discourse of bromance expounded above (again, the term is used explicitly); furthermore, the partnership was described as 'a bromance which will live in infamy' (Call Me Ishmael 2016). In conjunction with this anchoring written text, Call Me Ishmael also attached an image to expose the Blair–Bush 'special relationship' as at once connotatively romantic and explicitly homoerotic. In so doing, the Twitter user depicts the power dynamic in this relationship as weighted manifestly in favour of Bush and of America. Specifically, the image is a mid-shot portrait of a naked male couple, one in the proprietary embrace (from behind) of the other. The embracing man has the face of Bush superimposed on to his naked body, while the embraced man is Blair. The two figures are portrayed in monochrome but in prominent colour is the star-spangled banner, displayed as a shawl with which Bush envelops Blair.[3]

Elsewhere in the mainstream news media, left-leaning UK newspaper *The Guardian* invoked the title, and all of the loaded connotations it carries, of the Nora Ephron-scripted 1989 film *When Harry Met Sally*, directed by Rob Reiner – one of Hollywood's best-known romantic comedies of the postclassical period. The intertextual exposé, 'When Blair Met Bush' (Hopkins 2016), offers a post-Chilcot retrospective of Blair and Bush's initial face-to-face encounters (including their infamous first meeting at Camp David on 23 February 2001), and of the subsequent alliance between the US and the UK that precipitated the invasion of Iraq by coalition forces, the ensuing war and its aftermath. This is one of many examples of such discourse in the media, whereby the producers of cultural meanings surrounding the Blair–Bush 'special relationship' draw upon intertextual references to the formal conventions, the tropes or the cultural logics of Hollywood's romantic comedy and romantic drama genre films. As developed in the following case study examples, this is done in order to make sense of the personal and political alliance of these national leaders and to provide a popular cultural frame through which audiences and users are invited to understand and mediate those alliances.

Lil' Bush

The politically satirical animated television series *Lil' Bush* (2007–8) showcases one example from noughties popular film and television of the mediation of Blair and Bush's alliance that adopts the discourse of bromance to create cultural meanings that signify in romantic terms around the nature of this relationship. In particular, the discourse of romance that had then been circulating around this political relationship first becomes the object of *Lil' Bush*'s gleeful satire in the season 1 episode 'Gay Friend/Mexican' (2007), which depicts small child avatars for Blair and Bush. The two become fast friends against the wishes of their parents (especially their mothers), who are troubled by the closeness of their relationship. Blair and Bush then become cheerleaders for their school's American football team. In his chapter on satirical television depictions and discourses of US presidents in the postnetwork era, media scholar Jeffrey P. Jones explains the premise of the series, its form and its mode of address (Jones 2009: 37–63). As Jones expounds, *Lil' Bush* is an inherently modally intertextual example of political satire; it both invokes and parodies 'the style of other animated children's programming where familiar older characters are cast as younger versions of themselves (shows like *Muppet Babies* for example)' (52). Correspondingly, in this way, '[George W.] Bush is portrayed as a moronic and hubristic First Child [at a depicted time when] his father George H. W. Bush is still in the White House' (52). Jones goes on to explain that

> Each episode presents a new situation for Lil' George as he cavorts with his pals Lil' Cheney [the avatar for the then US Vice President Dick Cheney, who was famously 'hawkish' in the US waging of war in Iraq], Lil' Condi [the avatar for the then US Secretary of State Condoleezza Rice, another key figure in the US administration's waging of war on Iraq – one who has openly admitted since that the US objective in Iraq was not to bring democracy to its beleaguered people, but to overthrow Saddam Hussein and thus effect regime change (O'Connor 2017)], and Lil' Rummy [the avatar for the then US Defence Secretary Donald Rumsfeld who, like Bush and Cheney, was famously 'hawkish' in the US waging of war in Iraq]. (Jones 2009: 52)

After Lil' George meets Lil' Tony Blair in the aforementioned third episode of *Lil' Bush*, a noteworthy sequence devotes itself and its humour to the notion that, as Jones summarises it, 'Lil' George's parents think he might be gay because of his overly close friendship with Lil' Tony Blair' (Jones 2009: 54), and the scenario unfolds via a set-piece musical number called 'Special Buddy'. The sequence commences in earnest after Lil' George and Lil' Tony go to bed distressed after having their friendship condemned by their parents. Lil' George's mother (First Lady Barbara Bush in the depicted context) puts him to bed with the words: 'I don't wanna hear *any* more about Lil' Tony. I'm putting a stop to this . . . I don't want any son of mine turning . . . *British.*' The source of the humour here lies, of course, in the double entendre that aligns Blair's Britishness with homosexuality, which is unfavourably compared to Americanness, which is thereby aligned with normative sexuality – normative masculinity in particular. In the equivalent scenario with Lil' Tony and his mother, the double entendre is made via her expressed fear that, with Lil' George's influence, her son will be 'driving on the wrong side of the road' – at once a reference to cultural differences in driving conventions between the UK and the US, and also an entrenched and well-known euphemism for homosexuality. Thereafter, the song 'Special Buddy' commences as the soundtrack to a montage sequence that depicts Blair and Bush's friendship as highly romantically and erotically charged: via a cheerleader chant ('T-O-N-Y, I ain't got no other guy'); the use of love heart motifs; the depiction of the two lads riding a pony together and holding hands; and with explicit reference to their desire to 'grow up' and 'start some wars'. In this combination of overt satire and extreme caricature, the humour somewhat oversteps the representational boundaries of straight bromance (which typically forecloses the possibility of same-sex romance after having invoked it) with the near-explicit suggestion of homosexual behaviour, thereby presenting an overtly queered relationship between Blair and Bush.

'W'

Elsewhere in entertainment media of this period, Oliver Stone's Bush biopic *W.* (2008) features a sequence that contains archive news media footage of an anti-Iraq War protest march, in which two of the protesters wear cartoon masks of Blair and Bush respectively. Advancing one step further than the episode of *Lil' Bush* discussed above, this overt queering of the Blair–Bush bromance includes footage of these masked protestors performing a full-on kiss between Blair and Bush. In the main body of the film, the relationship between the two leaders is depicted in more straightforwardly familiar bromance territory. In the words of bromance scholar Michael DeAngelis, Bush and Blair are seen to have 'an emotionally intense bond' and to 'demonstrate an openness to intimacy that they neither regard, acknowledge, avow, nor express sexually' (DeAngelis 2014: 1). A reading of their depicted relationship as adhering to the discursive characteristics of bromance is particularly cemented in one scene that depicts

Bush (Josh Brolin), Blair (Ioan Gruffudd) and Condoleezza Rice (Thandie Newton) walking at Camp David and talking about the imminent plans to invade Iraq. Framing, blocking, the body language of the performers, and the homoerotically charged regimes of looking produced by the editing here intersect to produce a reading of this scene that corresponds to a reading of Blair and Bush's relationship as a bromantic one. Blair and Bush maintain eye contact with one another throughout the scene, but rarely do they make eye contact with Rice; the shot is blocked to place Blair and Bush in close physical proximity to one another, while Rice hovers at their side at a slight physical remove, on the edge of the frame; and the conversation is staged as one taking place between Blair and Bush, with Rice little more than an onlooker, making little squeaks of affirmation as Bush lays out his plans for war. As DeAngelis argues,

> although bromance often confines female characters to secondary roles, their narrative function is actually quite central because women in bromance narratives serve as a reminder to the male protagonists that their feelings and expressions of homosocial intimacy must remain within heteronormative parameters. (23)

Thus, despite her peripheral presence and perfunctory role in the discussion of the Iraq invasion, Rice's presence serves an important function in cementing the articulation of the bromance discourse circulating around Blair and Bush in this film.

The Special Relationship

Richard Loncraine's HBO film *The Special Relationship* (2010) is another example of a film from this period that depicts the Blair–Bush relationship via the discourse of bromance, and one that does so by resorting to some of the formal and modal conventions of the Hollywood romantic comedy and romantic drama genres. In fact, the film is best understood as part of the aforementioned late 2000s to early 2010s cluster of bromantic comedies that emerged elsewhere in Hollywood during that period. For the bulk of its run time, *The Special Relationship* is actually concerned principally with the relationship between Blair (Michael Sheen) and Bush's predecessor as US President, Bill Clinton (Dennis Quaid). The pair are initially presented (via the language and representational discourse of romantic love) as having been 'political soulmates' during the early years of their acquaintance, after Blair had first been elected Prime Minister in May 1997, and for the best part of Clinton's second term as President. However, the film's final minutes depicting the transition of power between Clinton and Bush at the end of Clinton's second term is of greatest concern to this chapter. This transition is constructed and portrayed using the formal conventions and thematic and discursive tropes of Hollywood's romantic genres. These are invoked to represent the political regime change from Democrat to Republican that took place following the presidential election of November 2000, and which is correspondingly seen through, first, the changing nature of Blair's relationship with Clinton, and then the early days of Blair's relationship with Bush. In short, the film's final scene between Blair and Clinton is articulated fairly straightforwardly via the discourse of (spent) romance as a 'break-up' (Jeffers McDonald 2007; Grindon 2011). Meanwhile, the film's only scene to depict an initial encounter between Blair and Bush is articulated with irony and self-reflexivity as a 'meet-cute' (Jeffers McDonald 2007; Mortimer 2010). The tone of *The Special Relationship* correspondingly moves from romantic drama to romantic comedy, as the film modally shifts its narration of this relationship from dramatisation to documentary, but with charged and meaningfully executed manipulation of news media archive footage.

The beginning of the end of Blair and Clinton's relationship follows an awkward 'farewell' dinner at Chequers. Clinton is on his final presidential visit to the UK in the weeks following the US presidential election of 2000. As Blair and Clinton await news of the outcome, the heretofore affectionate and convivial affect between them turns manifestly frosty. As Hillary Clinton leaves the dinner table on senatorial business (having been newly elected to the Senate) and Cherie Blair bids them goodnight, the men are left alone. A conversation ensues that plays out like an unfaithful romantic partner laying bare certain misdeeds for the other's judgement. As Blair attempts to explain himself, Clinton listens with barely concealed bitterness and hurt, and with marked passive aggression. That night, both are awakened to receive news that US courts have found in favour of Bush, who has duly been announced President. Clinton refuses Blair's eye contact and sits tight-lipped in front of the kitchen television. He stands up, walks to the refrigerator and demands to know of Blair: 'What are you going to do with Bush?' Blair responds that he intends 'to be in the room where the big decisions are made'. When Clinton calls him out on his hubris, it becomes Blair's turn to play the lover with bruised feelings: 'I'm not sure how to take that, Bill.' Clinton takes the initiative in hammering the final nail into the coffin of their relationship by asking Blair, 'What business does a progressive centre-left politician from a tiny little island in Europe have making friends with folks like that [the Bush administration]?' However, he pre-empts an answer in his damning follow-up: 'But then again. I'm not sure that you *are* a progressive centre-left politician any more. Or if you ever were.' He then stands up, turns his back on Blair and exits the room with the curt announcement 'I'm going to say goodnight. I might sleep late, I hope you don't mind. I'm tired. I need the rest.' He leaves without looking back. Once Clinton is out of earshot, Blair consents to their ostensible break-up with the dismissive comeback, 'Go ahead. Sleep as long as you like.'

Next morning, and to the sound of a melancholy non-diegetic score, Clinton departs Chequers in his presidential chopper after a half-hearted goodbye from Blair, who has been caught 'cheating' already, as Clinton, outside looking in, observes him smiling on the phone to Bush, the two of them already on first-name terms. In their final exchange, Clinton tries to determine whether his entreaties against forming a relationship with Bush have made an impact but Blair gives away nothing. Clinton concedes that, in light of their 'break-up', he will have to become like everyone else, and simply watch their inevitably ensuing joint press conference to 'scrutinize the body language for tell-tale signs'.

The film follows on from this prophetic line of dialogue, modally transitioning from dramatisation to (heavily subjectively rendered and highly manipulated) documentary, as it flashes forward to Blair and Bush's notorious joint press conference at Camp David in February 2001. This is presented using archival news media footage, and the footage is manipulated to invite audiences to read Blair and Bush's body language, and to read it as romantically charged. Blair, grinning broadly, stands on the right of the frame, to the left of Bush, as he is introduced and welcomed by the new President as America's 'strongest friend' and 'closest ally' (turning to make eye contact as he utters these words, to Blair's manifest delight). As the camera slowly zooms in on Bush's face until he is in close-up, Bush explains: 'We've had a nice walk around Camp David and got to know each other. And as they told me, he's a pretty charming guy. He put the charm offensive on me!' Bush laughs. Blair laughs. The press laughs. 'And it worked!' Bush turns to look at Blair. There is a contrived eye-line match edit as the shot cuts to a close-up of Blair returning an adoring gaze to Bush.

Bush himself even goes so far as to invoke the possibility of same-sex attraction and sexual activity between the two of them when, in response to a journalist's question about their common interests, he jokes, 'Well, we both use Colgate toothpaste.' Blair then cements the queerness of this joke with his response: 'They're going to wonder how you know that, George.' The film then freeze-frames on Bush and Blair as the two of them look into each other's eyes and shake hands (Bush with his hand on Blair's shoulder). The shot fades to black and the film ends.

The pathos of the earlier scene depicting the end of the Blair–*Clinton* bromance is offset and relieved by the humour of the latter scene depicting the beginning of the Blair–*Bush* bromance. However, the use of irony in the latter is meaningful, since, with the benefit of hindsight that audiences of a straight romantic comedy would not typically be granted by the film, we know what will happen next in their relationship. Far from 'happy ever after', the growth and the development of this alliance leads to death, destruction and global divisions on an enormous scale.

Conclusion

The political alliance between Tony Blair and George W. Bush was characterised by the hawkishness of the two leaders with regard to their respective and joint military interventions in the Middle East, alongside the ease with which their political relationship lent itself to satire and parody. After all, the alliance arose contemporaneously – and in part due to its discursive harmony – with the cultural prominence of the bromance trope as a means of understanding masculine intimacy. As highlighted at the outset of this chapter by the song lyrics of Riz MC, their relationship operated due to their shared politics of destruction. Further, as this chapter has demonstrated through its discussions of the preceding case studies, mediating the Blair–Bush relationship at a discursive intersection of romance and violence shines an illuminating and irreverent light on the real life-and-death stakes resulting from the relationship, as well as the media's efforts to portray and negotiate the efficacy of the 'special relationship'. Reiterating the evaluation of Call Me Ishmael on the fallout of Blair and Bush's political partnership and personal relationship: it is a bromance that will live in infamy.

Notes

1. It should be noted here that Campbell attributes the coining of 'TBGB' to Blair's former foreign policy adviser, John Holmes (2013: xx), and that he prefaces any use of this portmanteau acronym with the explanation that it serves a dual function to refer to Blair's respective relationships with Gordon Brown (the Chancellor of the Exchequer from 1997 to 2008, the duration of Blair's time as British Prime Minister) on the one hand, and George W. Bush (who was elected to the US presidency three and a half years into Blair's premiership) on the other (xx). Campbell explains that, according to Holmes, 'TB's problems are caused by his relationships with two GBs – George Bush and Gordon Brown,' referred to thereafter as 'the TBGBs' (xx).

2. This figure refers to the number of deaths that occurred in the country (approximately 460,000) as a direct or indirect result of the war, according to the findings of a *PLOS Medicine* survey (Hagopian et al. 2013).

3. The mediation of the Blair–Bush 'special relationship' in these kinds of romantic and erotic signifying terms did, of course, long pre-date the 2016 publication of the Chilcot report. Indeed, the image in the 'Call Me Ishmael Tweet' is augmented and adapted from a previous version that had been circulating in the online mediascape long before this immediate post-Chilcot moment. A 25 October 2016 Bubbletoonz.com meme was posted by Dave Edwards and featured the caption 'Don't worry Tony, nobody will ever know the true extent of our "special" relationship.'

Works Cited

Baram, A., and B. Rubin (1993), 'Introduction', in A. Baram and B. Rubin (eds), *Iraq's Road to War*, New York: St Martin's Press, pp. ix–xv.

Becker, R. (2009), 'Guy Love: A Queer Straight Masculinity for a Post-Closet Era?', in G. Davis and G. Needham (eds), *Queer TV: Theories, Histories, Politics*, London and New York: Routledge, pp. 121–40.

Booth, R. (2016), '"With You, Whatever": Tony Blair's Letters to George W. Bush', *The Guardian*, 6 July. Available at: <https://www.theguardian.com/uk-news/2016/jul/06/with-you-whatever-tony-blair-letters-george-w-bush-chilcot> (last accessed 24 February 2019).

Bromance, TV series, created by E. Goldberg and J. C. Henry. US: MTV, 2008–9.

Call Me Ishmael, *Twitter* (9 July 2016).

Campbell, A. (2013), *The Alastair Campbell Diaries: The Burden of Power – Countdown to Iraq*, London: Arrow.

Committee of Privy Councillors (2016), *Chilcot Report: Report of the Iraq Inquiry: Executive Summary*, Kingston upon Thames: Canbury Press.

Davis, G., and G. Needham (2009), 'Introduction: The Pleasures of the Tube', in G. Davis and G. Needham (eds), *Queer TV: Theories, Histories, Politics*, London and New York: Routledge, pp. 1–12.

Davis, N. (2014), 'I Love You, *Hombre: Y tu Mamá También* as Border-Crossing Bromance', in M. DeAngelis (ed.), *Reading the Bromance: Homosocial Relationships in Film and Television*, Detroit: Wayne State University Press, pp. 109–38.

DeAngelis, M. (2014), 'Introduction', in M. DeAngelis (ed.), *Reading the Bromance: Homosocial Relationships in Film and Television*, Detroit: Wayne State University Press, pp. 1–26.

Díaz, V. (2015), '"Brad & Angelina: And Now . . . Brangelina!": A Sociocultural Analysis of Blended Celebrity Couple Names', in S. Cobb and N. Ewen (eds), *First Comes Love: Power Couples, Celebrity Kinship and Cultural Politics*, New York and London: Bloomsbury Academic, pp. 275–94.

Dumbrell, J. (2006), *A Special Relationship: Anglo-American Relations from the Cold War to Iraq*, 2nd edn, Basingstoke and New York: Palgrave Macmillan.

Farouk-Sluglett, M., and P. Sluglett (1990 [1987]), *Iraq Since 1958: From Revolution to Dictatorship*, London and New York: I. B. Tauris.

256 HANNAH HAMAD

Friedman, A. (1993), *Spider's Web: Bush, Saddam, Thatcher and the Decade of Deceit*, London: Faber and Faber.

'Gay Friend/Mexican' (2007), season 1, episode 3, 27 June, *Lil' Bush*, TV series, created by D. Cary. US: Comedy Central, 2007–8.

Grindon, L. (2011), *The Hollywood Romantic Comedy: Conventions, Histories, Controversies*, Oxford and Malden, MA: Wiley-Blackwell.

Hagopian, A., A. D. Flaxman, T. K. Takaro, S. A. E. Al Shatari, J. Rajaratnam, S. Becker, A. Levin-Rector, L. Galway, B. J. Hadi Al-Yasseri, W. M. Weiss, C. J. Murray and G. Burnham (2013), 'Mortality in Iraq Associated with the 2003–2011 War and Occupation: Findings from a National Cluster Sample by the University Collaborative Iraq Mortality Study', *PLoS Medicine* 10:10: e1001533.

Hamad, H. (2011), '"My Wife Calls Him My Boyfriend": Gary Barlow and Robbie Williams' Reconciliatory Bromance', *Flow TV*, 25 February. Available at: <http://www.flowjournal.org/2011/02/my-wife-calls-him-my-boyfriend/> (last accessed 24 February 2019).

Hopkins, N. (2016), 'When Blair Met Bush: How the UK Went to War in Iraq', *The Guardian*, 9 July. Available at: <https://www.theguardian.com/uk-news/2016/jul/09/iraq-war-after-blair-and-bush-met-the-tempo-changed> (last accessed 24 February 2019).

Humpday, film, directed by Lynn Shelton. US: Magnolia Pictures, 2009.

I Love You, Man, film, directed by John Hamburg. US: DeLine Pictures, 2009.

Jeffers McDonald, T. (2007), *Romantic Comedy: Boy Meets Girl Meets Genre*, London and New York: Wallflower.

Jones, J. P. (2009), 'With All Due Respect: Satirizing Presidents from *Saturday Night Live* to *Lil' Bush*', in J. Gray, J. P. Jones and E. Thompson (eds), *Satire TV: Politics and Comedy in the Post-Network Era*, New York and London: New York University Press, pp. 37–63.

Kosofsky Sedgwick, E. (1992), *Between Men: English Literature and Male Homosocial Desire*, New York: Columbia University Press.

Lil' Bush, TV series, created by D. Cary. US: Comedy Central, 2007–8.

McDowell, A. (2017), 'Muslim Punk in an Alt-Right Era', *Contexts*, 16:3, pp. 63–5.

McKercher, B. J. C. (2017), *Britain, America and the Special Relationship Since 1941*, London and New York: Routledge.

Masri, L. (2016), 'Tony Blair's Secret Letters to George W. Bush on Iraq War Released', *ABC News*, 16 September. Available at: <https://abcnews.go.com/International/tony-blairs-secret-letters-george-bush-iraq-war/story?id=40370046> (last accessed 24 February 2019).

Mortimer, C. (2010), *Romantic Comedy*, Abingdon and New York: Routledge.

O'Connor, T. (2017), 'U.S. Wars in the Middle East Were Not Supposed to Bring Democracy, Condoleezza Rice Says', *Newsweek*, 12 May. Available at: <https://www.newsweek.com/us-war-middle-east-bring-democracy-rice-608640> (last accessed 2 October 2018).

Riz MC (2006), 'The Post 9/11 Blues'. Available at: <https://www.youtube.com/watch?v=AKTsJpfC0IQ&list=RDAKTsJpfC0IQ&start_radio=1&t=22> (last accessed 20 May 2019).

Sherlock, TV series, created by M. Gatiss and S. Moffat. UK: BBC, 2010–17.

The Hangover, film, directed by T. Phillips. US: Legendary Pictures, 2009.

The Special Relationship, film, directed by R. Loncraine. US: Rainmark Films, 2010

W., film, directed by O. Stone. US: Global Entertainment, 2008.

When Harry Met Sally, film, directed by R. Reiner. US: Castle Rock Entertainment, 1989.

CHAPTER 15

Holding Hands as the Ship Sinks: Trump and May's Special Relationship

Neil Ewen

Introduction – A Titanic Disaster

In August 2018, while talks between the UK and the European Union (EU) to negotiate the terms of the UK's departure from the EU were dominating news cycles, a short film called *Brexit: A Titanic Disaster* (2017) went viral across social media platforms. Created by Comedy Central writer Josh Pappenheim, it mocked the prominent 'Leaver' and erstwhile British Foreign Secretary Boris Johnson's comment that 'Brexit means Brexit and we are going to make a Titanic success of it' (Johnson 2016); it also tapped into growing fears that the negotiations were going so badly that Britain was drifting towards the iceberg of a 'No Deal' Brexit in March 2019.[1] Featuring scenes from James Cameron's iconic romantic blockbuster *Titanic* (1997), with the faces of high-profile politicians doctored into the footage, the film was watched more than ten million times in a matter of days (Townsend 2018). It begins with a foghorn bellowing and former Prime Minister David Cameron warning that 'there is no going back from this'. Then, as water starts to overwhelm the ocean-liner, his successor, Theresa May, urges the people to 'come together and seize the day'. Labour Party leader Jeremy Corbyn, playing a slow lament on a violin, says 'the British people have made their decision', and an image of the pound sterling falls off the ship and crashes into the water. Cabin lights then illuminate the split vote, 48 per cent against 52 per cent, on opposite sides of the ship as it breaks down the middle and sinks into the ocean.[2]

While the film is clearly partisan and aimed at the sympathies of 'Remainers', it is also quite witty. And though its message is unsubtle, its ending intrigues. Where *Titanic*'s tragedy of the young couple being torn apart offers a terrible finality (albeit assuaged by Celine Dion's soaring, if trite, insistence that their love 'will go on'), the ending of *Brexit: A Titanic Disaster* is more ambiguous, uncertain and creepy. While May is left floating on the water, huddled, freezing and waiting to be rescued, the narrative ends by cutting to the scene in the original film where Jack

Figure 15.1   Donald Trump as Rose Dewitt Bukater from *Brexit: A Titanic Disaster* (2017). © Comedy Central UK.

(Leonardo DiCaprio) is painting the nude Rose (Kate Winslet). However, in the 'remake', Jack's head is replaced with a smiling Nigel Farage,[3] and Rose, lying naked and prone, is replaced with a wistful-looking Donald Trump (Figure 15.1). As such, *Brexit: A Titanic Disaster* ends by speaking more or less directly to the so-called US–UK 'special relationship'. There is a particular resonance here in the film drawing on the history of what was a doomed transatlantic crossing – the *Titanic*'s maiden voyage from Southampton to New York in 1912. Beyond this, the film's ending hints towards how the recent surge of authoritarian–nationalist–populist politicians – of which Trump is the nominal leader – has thrown the notion of the transatlantic union into crisis. It is this unfolding process that concerns the present chapter, which first examines media coverage of the current iteration of the special relationship between Trump and May, before suggesting that Farage has 'cuckolded' the Prime Minister. It considers all this in light of the UK's current crisis and suggests that the pseudo-romantic imagery used to mediate the special relationship is the symptom of a culture unable or unwilling to address the root causes of its decline.

The Vicar's Daughter and the Pussy-grabber

In January 2017, Prime Minister May visited Washington to meet President Trump for their first official engagement. During the trip, May addressed the Republican Party conference in Philadelphia and talked about the US–UK special relationship, which many British commentators had suggested was under threat from the unpredictable new incumbent of the White House (Observer Editorial 2017). May said that it had been 'America's destiny to bear the leadership of the free world and to carry that heavy responsibility on its shoulders' but that the UK 'had been proud to share that burden and to walk alongside you at every stage'. Rather than attempt to distance the UK from a US under a President whose 'America First' nationalist–populist philosophy advocated increasing isolationism, May's strategy was to double down and to highlight the importance of co-operation between the two countries:

> As we rediscover our confidence together – as you renew your nation just as we renew ours – we have the opportunity – indeed the responsibility – to renew the special relationship for this new age. We have the opportunity to lead, together, again. Because the world is passing through a period of change . . . we can take the opportunity once again to lead. And lead together. (May 2017)

Earlier that day, the two leaders held hands while walking to a joint news conference on the lawn of the White House. This awkward scene became the defining image of their encounter, with footage filling news bulletins and photographs adorning newspaper and website front pages (Batchelor 2017). While speculation about the reasons for the hand-holding subsequently took up inordinate column inches (Owen 2017), and notwith-standing the fact that looking comfortable in public is not exactly Theresa May's forte (Telegraph Reporters 2017), the main thrust of the coverage suggested that the awkwardness of the encounter dramatised the funda-mental differences between a Prime Minister whose persona is based on being a vicar's daughter transported straight out of the 1950s, and a popu-list, 'pussy-grabbing' President (Jacobs et al. 2016), whose self-proclaimed raison d'être is to smash the propriety of the establishment.

Soon after, and pointedly on Valentine's Day, 2017, *The Guardian* pub-lished an extended feature on the special relationship (Wheatcroft 2017). Embellished by a large photograph of the hand-holding incident, Geoffrey Wheatcroft's piece is an excoriating critique of the 'myth' of US–UK rela-tions, characterising May as the latest in a long line of British prime minis-ters debasing themselves by bending the knee to US presidents. 'Invoking the special relationship', he writes, 'is a way of evading the truth' that, since 1945, the UK's influence on the world stage has been waning inexorably, 'allowing one prime minister after another to desperately and sometimes abjectly cling to the belief that she is the best friend of the most powerful person on the planet'. Wheatcroft continues:

Dealings between American presidents and British prime ministers have been excruciatingly one-sided. Tony Blair's service to George W Bush in the invasion of Iraq was only the most extreme case of this game of give and take, in which the president is given everything and takes everything, offering nothing in return. (Wheatcroft 2017)

Wheatcroft considers May's conduct as particularly demeaning, however, since she rushed to Washington, upset that she was a long way down the list of world leaders whom Trump had called after his election. May 'had felt the humiliation of seeing Nigel Farage and Michael Gove meet the President-elect ahead of her: evidence of Trump's genuine special relationships, with rightwing nationalism and with Rupert Murdoch' (Wheatcroft 2017). Here, Wheatcroft is referring to, first, the infamous incident on election night when the President posed for photographs with members of the self-proclaimed 'Bad Boys of Brexit' (Banks 2016), including Nigel Farage and Arron Banks,[4] in the golden lift of New York's Trump Tower (Stanley 2016)[5]; and second, to *The Times*' exclusive interview with Michael Gove, a member of Theresa May's cabinet, and journalist Kai Diekmann, of the German newspaper *Bild* (Trump Interview 2017) – the first sit-down interview Trump granted to the foreign press, and one conducted with the Australian–American media mogul Rupert Murdoch in attendance (Pickard and Garrahan 2017).

I will explore the media's treatment of Trump's relationship with Farage below. For now, it is worth contemplating the ways in which the media's framing of the special relationship through pseudo-romantic imagery and innuendo fits into a pattern that, Shelley Cobb argues, began with Ronald Reagan's relationship with Margaret Thatcher (see Cobb in this volume) and, Hannah Hamad, argues continues through the Bush–Blair years (see Hamad in this volume). Indeed, the act of holding hands has become a repeated interaction between Trump and May, as well as a new obsession for media coverage of them. For it to happen once was, perhaps, a misfortune. For it to happen twice suggested a pattern. When it happened a third time, it could legitimately be surmised that it was a strategic PR decision.

Apart from some criticism that May should have rejected Trump's political advances as a statement of Britain's independence and a disavowal of an intolerant regime (Edelstein 2017), the first hand-holding incident was treated by the media as a bizarre and slightly humorous oddity, and one in a series of examples whereby Trump's physical interactions with other political figures became the focus of intense scrutiny. Public handshakes with French President Emmanuel Macron, Canadian prime minister Justin Trudeau and Japanese President Shinzo Abe, to cite just three examples, have all been the subject of curiosity, mockery and often speculation about what the body language says about Trump's masculinity (Tanner 2018). Holding hands with a female leader such as May is inevitably circumscribed by Trump's notorious reputation as a lothario, and specifically by his shameful comments to media personality Billy Bush in the 'Access Hollywood' tape, released during Trump's presidential campaign in October 2016, where he was recorded saying that 'When you a star . . . you can do anything' and that when he meets beautiful women he feels entitled to 'grab them by the pussy' (Jacobs et al. 2016).[6] As such, when Trump holds May's hand, the kind of tired insinuations of heterosexual romance between leaders (a feature of the ways in which Reagan and Thatcher's relationship was mediated) turns into something weirder and more sinister. The public and physical conjunction of two such differing personalities, representing two countries of increasingly inequitable power, leads to a rump of media coverage ripe with speculation, dark humour, and nauseating overtones about personal interactions that are inevitably read metaphorically as saying something about the state of the political union between the two countries.

In July 2018, when Trump and May held hands for a second time on the steps of Blenheim Palace during Trump's first state visit to the UK (a visit memorable for the 'Baby Trump' blimp flown by protestors in London), the media was thus enraptured (Bartlett 2018). The next day, at the Prime Minister's country house, Chequers, they held hands for a third time, after which the BBC posed the question: 'Do Trump and May hold hands every time?' (BBC News 2018). Typically described as 'painfully awkward', these moments were dissected by pundits positing possible explanations for the repeated action (Harvey-Jenner 2018).

Even if Trump does have a phobia of stairs, as speculation first suggested in January 2017 (Owen 2017) and as Theresa May seemed to confirm the following September, when she called it a 'moment of assistance' (BBC News 2017b), the particularly awkward physical interaction of holding hands while straining not to trip in front of a global audience has a peculiarly potent symbolic power, encapsulating the contemporary nature of the special relationship as performed by these two leaders: Trump reaches out and grabs for what he wants, while May is desperate to be grabbed (in the political sense). The former is born of entitlement; the latter is the result of desperation. May knows that associating with Trump risks opprobrium or ridicule and, certainly after the first time it happened, that this close physical interaction serves only to draw attention to their every move. Yet, she is working within the context of Britain's long slide from power at a point in history where the self-inflicted harm of Brexit means that the country is at risk of being cut adrift. If being grabbed by a stair-phobic vulgarian is the price to pay for recognition and a little orientation, May has done the sums and calculated that the risk is worth it.

Britain Adrift

May's need for recognition by the US President is circumscribed by the UK's slide into constitutional crisis, which came to a head with the Brexit referendum in June 2016; this, in turn, had followed the Scottish independence referendum in September 2014, when the people of Scotland had narrowly voted against seceding from the UK by 55.3 per cent to 44.7 per cent. These events highlighted the fragile nature of the UK as a viable political project and revealed a dramatic fragmentation of any sense of Britain as a coherent 'imagined community' (Anderson 1991). The interregnum that followed the Brexit referendum – and which could continue for many years into the future – was defined by political paralysis at Westminster, an absence of political leadership, acute anxiety about the socio-economic consequences of Brexit, and a media culture filled with endless, earnest musings on the condition of Britishness. The left/right political axis that once provided conceptual bearings broke apart to reveal new formations of 'Leavers' and 'Remainers', and the possibility that the UK could fragment along national lines became increasingly more real. In a political climate as fraught as at any time in living memory, and with the Prime Minister lacking political power at home, May's attempts to sustain ties with the US was an obvious strategic ploy.

The UK crisis is the culmination of a long history of gradual structural disintegration. Indeed, the idea that Britain, as an over-centralised and off-kilter multinational state, might be coming apart at the seams is not a new one. Theorists have been pondering the potential unravelling of the UK for generations. Linda Colley, in *Britons: Forging the Nation 1707–1837* (2009), argues that a coherent Britishness was created on the basis that an isolated island state shared a common enemy (France), was bound together by a shared religion (Protestantism) and participated in a shared project of disseminating capitalism around the globe (Empire). With the Empire having dissolved, the foundations for a shared sense of British identity effectively collapsed. Meanwhile, in *The Break-up of Britain* (1982), Tom Nairn posits that a British nationalism did not develop in a 'normal' fashion at the beginning of the modern era and that the UK therefore lacked ideological glue. As the world's pre-eminent power during the eighteenth and nineteenth centuries, Britain was never forced to define itself in terms of national myths in the ways that other 'peripheral' countries were compelled to do in opposition to the global hegemon, and so with the rise of Scottish nationalism in the second half of the twentieth century, the foundations of the UK started to wobble.

Echoes of Nairn's argument can be heard in contemporary theoretical work, such as Anthony Barnett's *The Lure of Greatness* (2017) and Mike Wayne's *England's Discontents* (2018), which highlight the fact that English nationalism tends to be romantic and located in visions of a past tinged with imperial nostalgia. Wayne argues that the predominant images and tropes that have been coded as English (monarchy, Church, Empire, World War II) are much more readily available imaginatively than liberal, never mind radical, ones. As such, this constructs a worldview that sees the EU as leeching sovereign power from the UK not only politically and economically, but symbolically, too. Meanwhile, Paul Gilroy's concept of 'postcolonial melancholia' suggests that the post-World War II period of history has been dominated by a longing for a return to Britain's long-lost imperial greatness, which is necessarily exclusionary, reactionary and hostile (Gilroy 2004).

We might therefore understand the Leave campaign's 'Take Back Control' narrative during the EU referendum campaign as so affectively powerful because it drew effectively on a long history of postimperial nostalgia elaborated consistently by a largely Eurosceptic British media. This is not to say that reasoned arguments for leaving the EU do not exist. However, the potential benefits of leaving the EU, from a right perspective that sees the it as overly bureaucratic (Gillingham 2018) and a left perspective that sees it as being fundamentally neoliberal and anti-democratic (Lapavitsas 2018), continue to be drowned out in mainstream discourse by loudmouth nationalist–populist voices who point to immigrants and other scapegoats to offer easy cultural answers to complex socio-economic problems. Primed by years of Thatcherism, Blairism and postfinancial crisis austerity, weary populations are drawn to charismatic public figures who propose alternatives to a tired establishment.

In the context of Britain cutting itself adrift from the EU, May has little choice but to reanimate the cultural script of the transatlantic special relationship that has been constructed as being mutually beneficial to both countries and personified as an intimate relationship between two leaders. Previous versions of this personal relationship – Thatcher/Reagan and Blair/Bush – appeared to reinvigorate the UK's position and influence in global politics, while the media obsession with the intimacy of the leaders' relationships worked to distract from the material consequences of their policies. The media's repeated publication of images of Trump and May holding hands, as well as the *Titanic* video and other satirical images of them as a couple, do the ideological work of deflecting the ineptitude of May's leadership during Britain's biggest crisis since World War II and seek to ridicule Trump further: a strategy that simply shores up his base support. Concurrently, May's relationship with Trump has not resuscitated the UK's position in global politics because it is irrelevant to the deeper problems afflicting Britain as a country.

A Rival Rather than a Friend?

Wheatcroft's article is just one notable contribution to a recent upsurge in attention on the special relationship, stimulated by Trump's singular ability to generate controversy and to draw attention to himself. In February 2017, for example, in response to Trump signing Executive Order 13769 (commonly referred to as 'the Muslim travel ban'), Members of Parliament debated whether a state visit invitation should be extended to the President. During this debate, the Speaker of the House of Commons, John Bercow, announced that he was 'strongly opposed' to Trump addressing the Houses of Parliament during a mooted state visit to the UK because the right to such addresses was 'an earned honour' and not an 'automatic right', and 'opposition to racism and sexism' were 'hugely important considerations' (BBC News 2017a). The state visit was then postponed, seemingly at Trump's request, because of fears that it would generate mass protests (Hughes 2017; Haaretz 2017). And in June 2017, Trump instigated widespread opprobrium when he tweeted criticism of London Mayor Sadiq Khan's response to the London Bridge terror attack, hours after seven people were killed and forty-eight injured (Pengelly 2017). Such events and actions have led to widespread media commentary suggesting that the special relationship is under threat of collapse. Trump's 'working visit' to the UK in July 2018 (a state visit having been deemed more trouble than it was worth) generated a rash of biting headlines such as 'Has Trump Broken the Special Relationship?' (Landale 2018); 'Trump Lays Bare Britain's "Special Relationship" Delusion' (Freedman 2018); 'Trump Visit Tests Britain's "Special Relationship" with U.S.' (Castle and Freytas-Tamura 2018); 'Special Relationship? Trump and May's Is Almost Pathological' (Crace 2018); and the memorable 'Trump and May: How the Special Relationship Devolved into a Greasy Dumpster Fire' (Thompson 2018).

Another explosion of critical attention occurred in November 2018 in response to Trump's visit to Europe, during which he caused outrage and invited ridicule for missing a ceremony to mark the centenary of the Armistice in France because it was raining (Chazan and Allen 2018; Rozsa 2018), and reportedly berated Theresa May for having the temerity to call to congratulate him on his party's performance at the US midterm elections (Cole 2018). A prominent *Guardian* columnist wrote that, increasingly adrift from the EU, the UK is now a 'vassal state' of the US, which is no longer a reliable ally and is headed by a President who is a 'rival' rather than a friend, and 'potentially something worse' (Kettle 2018). Although the majority of anxiety about the special relationship is located in Britain, some sections of the US commentariat share these concerns. For example, David Frum, a former speechwriter for George W. Bush, argues that American presidents have historically wanted the UK to be at the heart of Europe, to veto anti-American actions by other EU countries, especially France, and that Brexit was a problem for both sides of the special relationship. Frum notes that after the relationship had cooled under the Obama presidency, Trump had been expected to reinforce the US–UK union by giving preferential trade deals to the UK in the event of Brexit. But, as Frum concludes, this is an increasingly forlorn hope (Frum 2018).

As well as media commentary, Trump's rise to power has inspired academic reconsideration of the special relationship. A British Council report in July 2018 suggested that the 'relationship between the UK and the US' continues to be 'special and thriving', and that 'what really matters to people on both sides of the Atlantic' is 'culture and history – not politics'. It acknowledges that there is 'ongoing debate amongst UK commentators about just how special it is' and suggests that the report 'should dispel some of that anxiety' (Donaldson 2018). On the other hand, sociologists Oliver and Williams (2017) suggest that Trump has caused widespread anxiety in the UK, and that 'coming to terms' with him 'will not be easy', but note that cooperation in terms of intelligence gathering and sharing, special forces and nuclear weapons will ensure that the special relationship survives his presidency. Meanwhile, the political scientist Graham K. Wilson suggests that there will be three key consequences to Brexit that will frame the UK's future relationship with the US: the economy, diplomacy and sentiment. Wilson claims that it is too early to tell the economic consequences of Brexit, and although US businesses like doing business with the UK (due to common language, laws and light-touch regulation), he stresses that this relationship is far more important to the UK than the US. In terms of diplomacy, Wilson rehearses the long history of closeness between the countries, which continues to this day, writing that the UK will be desperate for this to continue: 'without friends in Europe and diminished by leaving the EU, the United Kingdom needs friends badly'

(Wilson 2017: 553). Finally, Wilson notes the importance of sentiment between the countries, in terms of exchanges, scholarships and personal ties. 'The challenge for the UK', however, 'is that it is easier to evoke sentiment about the UK's past than present' (553). Intriguingly, Wilson concludes that 'It is likely that these commonalities of sentiment will produce the sort of symbolic opportunities – visits to the White House, photographs in the Rose Garden, perhaps even an address to both houses of Congress – that British prime ministers usually crave' (554).

Conclusion – Farage Cuckolds May

Wilson's article was probably written before the inglorious spectacle of May and Trump's first hand-holding episode at the White House, and certainly before the media started revelling in painting the pattern of holding hands as a bizarre ritual. Perceptively, though, Wilson framed his article by noting the close association between the Brexit vote and Trump's election, particularly in terms of the new President's links to Nigel Farage. Farage and Trump are linked by their similar charismatic styles as populist politicians (Moffitt 2016) who campaign and sell themselves on breaking the status quo and taking down the political elite. Their genius lies in their abilities to do this convincingly whilst being part of the very elite that they proclaim to despise.

Farage has been a thorn in May's side since she assumed office. A consummate showman, he has repeatedly attacked the Prime Minister, who he says is 'betraying' Brexit, and has sought to undermine the her authority (Farage 2019a). He has achieved this most obviously by repeatedly ingratiating himself with the US President in tones that often echo the transatlantic bromance between Bush and Blair (see Hamad in this volume).

Months before May spoke at the Republican Party conference, Farage addressed the Republican National Convention in Cleveland, Ohio, and met with senior party operatives (O'Toole 2016). In August 2016, Farage addressed a Trump campaign rally in Jackson, Mississippi, having been given a rousing introduction by the candidate.[7] And, as mentioned above, on the night Trump was elected and while May was waiting patiently by the phone, Farage cuckolded May by gatecrashing Trump Tower in New York to tweet photographs of himself with the President-elect in a gaudy gold elevator (a 'buddy-photo' described by the *Guardian*'s art critic, Jonathan Jones, as being 'somewhere between a Martin Scorsese film and a scene from the heyday of the Third Reich' [Jones 2016]). The next day, Trump called on May to appoint Farage as UK ambassador to the US (Wilkinson and Alexander 2016).

Farage has been the prime mover in this mutual love affair. He is, by turns, apparently besotted with the President (his homoerotic summary of Trump's final debate with Hillary Clinton: 'He looked like a big gorilla prowling the set. He is a big alpha male' [Mahdawi 2016]) and acutely aware of the politics of the romance. In a *New Yorker* profile, Farage discussed Trump as 'the leader of the pack', but one who was vulnerable because everybody around him wanted something from him. 'I'm not threatening [to him] in any way at all,' said Farage. 'I think he sees somebody who has been through similar kinds of battles, and he is just happy to talk to me' (Knight 2016). This mischievous projection of intimacy is indubitably an attempt to construct a union shorn of the awkwardness that defines Trump and May's relationship, and something that was taken to a nauseating extreme on Trump's birthday in June 2017, when Farage channelled Marilyn Monroe's famous serenading of Jack Kennedy by tweeting a photo of himself with a bottle of Trump wine in hand under the caption 'Happy birthday Mr. President' (Farage 2019b).

This relationship is played out knowingly and with a wink to the audience. Both Trump and Farage are adept at manipulating large swathes of

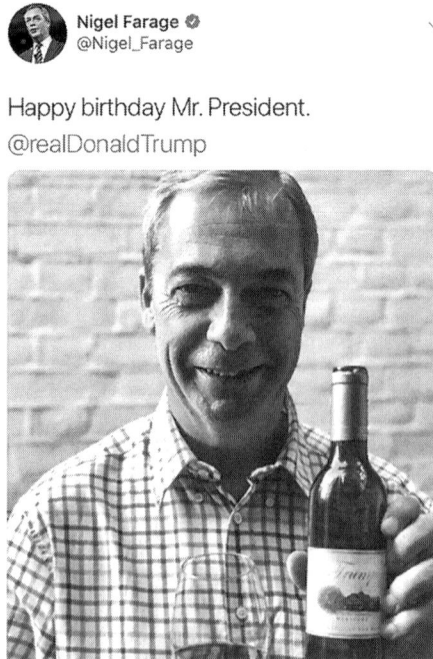

Nigel Farage ✓
@Nigel_Farage

Happy birthday Mr. President.
@realDonaldTrump

Figure 15.2   Nigel Farage toasts Donald Trump with a bottle of Trump wine. Screenshot from Farage's Twitter feed @Nigel Farage.

the media into sympathetic representation, and those parts of the media who attack them simply serve to maintain their profiles. The media is so keen to reproduce images of Trump and Farage together because they make the special relationship something of a joke while also reinforcing its cultural importance. And herein lies the rub for the special relationship as it currently stands, and as it has stood since at least Reagan and Thatcher: if so much media coverage is going to persist in the trivialising process of reducing politics to spectacle, and to gauge the health of these countries through focusing on the personal interactions of two leaders, then the so-called special relationship will continue, whether those leaders love each other, hate each other or bounce between the two. But it does not tell us anything really profound about whether the ships on which we are travelling are actually going to sink.

Notes

1. A referendum on continued UK membership of the EU took place on 23 June 2016, resulting in 51.9 per cent of voters in favour of leaving the European Union. On 29 March 2017, the UK invoked Article 50 of the Treaty on European Union, giving the European Council formal notice of the UK's withdrawal from the EU at midnight on 29 March 2019. The cleavage between those who wish to leave the EU (commonly referred to as 'Leavers') and those who wish to remain in the EU (commonly referred to as 'Remainers') threw the UK into political crisis and exposed deep cultural divisions across UK society. After Article 50 was invoked, UK and EU negotiators struggled for agreement on a deal that would provide continuity once EU law – including Single Market and Customs Union access – ceased at the time of the UK's exit. Anxiety about a 'no deal' scenario increased exponentially in the lead-up to the deadline.
2. The sinking ship is only one of myriad disaster metaphors that Brexit has inspired. Perhaps the most prominent has been the idea that a 'no-deal' Brexit is akin to the UK walking off a cliff edge. A front cover of *The New Yorker* in June 2016, featuring a character doing a Monty Python–inspired 'silly walk', is a particularly powerful example of this trope (Mouly 2016).
3. Nigel Farage is a British politician, radio talk show host and anti-EU campaigner. A Member of the European Parliament (MEP) since 1999, Farage is best known as the erstwhile leader of the UK Independence Party (UKIP) and as a figurehead for the campaign for Brexit. Farage garnered widespread media attention when Donald Trump paid him some attention in the lead-up to and aftermath of Trump's election. As of March 2019, Farage is Vice-Chair of the pro-Brexit organisation 'Leave Means Leave' and the leader of the Brexit Party.
4. Arron Banks is a British businessman and political donor, who rose to prominence after his large donations to UKIP and the Leave.EU campaign fronted

by Nigel Farage. Leave.EU funds were subject to an investigation by the National Crime Agency and MPs subsequently investigated allegations of Banks's links to Russia (Martin 2019).

5. Jo Littler (2019) brilliantly critiques these photographs, naming Trump and Farage 'normcore plutocrats'.

6. Melania Trump's refusal to hold hands with her husband on certain occasions – widely seen as a rebuke or an expression of her supposed unhappiness – also informs this discourse (see Fredericks 2018).

7. On the stump, Trump described Farage as 'the man behind Brexit and a man who brilliantly led the United Kingdom Independence Party . . . and won against all odds' (Right Side Broadcasting Network 2016).

Works Cited

Anderson, B. (1991), *Imagined Communities*, London: Verso.

Banks, A. (2016), *The Bad Boys of Brexit: Tales of Mischief, Mayhem and Guerrilla Warfare in the EU Referendum Campaign*, London: Biteback.

Barnett, A. (2017), *The Lure of Greatness: England's Brexit and America's Trump*, London: Unbound.

Bartlett, N. (2018), 'Donald Trump Holds Theresa May's Hand AGAIN as He Climbs Steps at Blenheim Palace', mirror.co.uk, 12 July. Available at: <https://www.mirror.co.uk/news/politics/donald-trump-holds-theresa-mays-12907887> (last accessed 18 February 2019).

Batchelor, T. (2017), 'Donald Trump and Theresa May Caught Holding Hands in White House Photo', independent.co.uk, 27 January. Available at: <https://www.independent.co.uk/news/world/americas/donald-trump-theresa-may-caught-holding-hands-white-house-photo-a7550386.html> (last accessed 18 February 2019).

BBC News (2017a), 'Speaker Bercow: Trump Should Not Speak in Parliament', bbc.co.uk, 6 February. Available at: <https://www.bbc.co.uk/news/uk-politics-38884604> (last accessed 18 February 2019).

BBC News (2017b), 'Trump Hand Holding Was "Moment of Assistance"', bbc.co.uk, 8 September. Available at: <https://www.bbc.co.uk/news/uk-politics-41204204> (last accessed 18 February 2019).

BBC News (2018), 'Do Trump and May Hold Hands Every Time?', bbc.co.uk, 13 July. Available at: <https://www.bbc.co.uk/news/av/uk-44828436/do-trump-and-may-hold-hands-every-time> (last accessed 17 February 2019).

Brexit: A Titanic Disaster (2017), film, directed by Josh Pappenheim. Comedy Central UK YouTube channel, 3 April. Available at: <https://www.youtube.com/watch?v=svwslRDTyzU> (last accessed 3 February 2019).

Castle, S., and K. Freytas-Tamura (2018), 'Trump Visit Tests Britain's "Special Relationship" with U.S.', nytimes.com, 11 July. Available at: <https://www.nytimes.com/2018/07/11/world/europe/trump-uk-visit.html> (last accessed 1 March 2019).

Chazan, D., and N. Allen (2018), 'Donald Trump Attacked for Skipping Armistice Commemoration "Because It Was Raining"', telegraph.co.uk, 11 November. Available at: <https://www.telegraph.co.uk/news/2018/11/10/donald-trump-brands-emmanuel-macrons-call-eu-army-insulting/> (last accessed 3 February 2019).

Cole, B. (2018), 'Trump Berated British Prime Minister Theresa May During Call to Congratulate Him on Midterms', newsweek.com, 14 November. Available at: <https://www.newsweek.com/trump-berated-british-prime-minister-theresa-may-during-call-congratulate-him-1214549> (last accessed 18 February 2019).

Colley, L. (2009), *Britons: Forging the Nation 1707–1837*, revised edn, London and New Haven, CT: Yale University Press.

Crace, J. (2018), 'Special Relationship? Trump and May's Is Almost Pathological', theguardian.com, 13 July. Available at: <https://www.theguardian.com/us-news/2018/jul/13/special-relationship-trump-and-mays-is-almost-pathological-john-crace> (last accessed 3 February 2019).

Donaldson, A. (2018), *A Special Relationship? Exploring the Future of UK–US Cultural Ties*, britishcouncil.org. Available at: <https://www.britishcouncil.org/sites/default/files/j062_thought_leadership_a_special_relationship.pdf> (last accessed 21 January 2019).

Edelstein, J. H. (2017), 'Theresa May, I Hope You Cringed at Trump's Grasp. The Alternative is Grim', theguardian.co.uk, 28 January. Available at: <https://www.theguardian.com/politics/2017/jan/27/theresa-may-donald-trump-hand-holding> (last accessed 18 February 2019).

Farage, N. (2019a), 'Leavers Must Accept That the Brexit Betrayal Is Happening Now', telegraph.co.uk, 17 January. Available at: <https://www.telegraph.co.uk/politics/2019/01/17/ready-return-battle-save-brexit/> (last accessed 5 March 2019).

Farage, N. (2019b), 'Happy Birthday, Mr President', Twitter, 14 June. Available at: <https://twitter.com/nigel_farage/status/875067723939753986?lang=en> (last accessed 5 March 2019).

Fredericks, B. (2018), 'Melania Trump Still Doesn't Want to Hold Hands with Donald', nypost.com, 24 April. Available at: <https://nypost.com/2018/04/24/melania-trump-still-doesnt-want-to-hold-hands-with-donald/> (last accessed 5 March 2019).

Freedman, L. (2018), 'Trump Lays Bare Britain's "Special Relationship" Delusion', ft.com, 13 July. Available at: <https://www.ft.com/content/714a7fa4-85ba-11e8-9199-c2a4754b5a0e> (last accessed 1 March 2019).

Frum, D. (2018), 'Mr. Brexit', *The Atlantic*, 15 November 2018. Available at: <https://www.theatlantic.com/ideas/archive/2018/11/brexit-crisis-trump-abandoning-uk-and-eu/575977/> (last accessed 7 April 2019).

Gillingham, J. (2018), *The EU: An Obituary*, revised edn, London: Verso.

Gilroy, P. (2004), *After Empire: Melancholia or Convivial Culture?* London: Routledge.

Haaretz (2017), 'Trump UK Visit Postponed After Twitter Spat with May, British Media Reports', haaretz.com, 1 December. Available at: <https://www.haaretz.com/us-news/trump-u-k-visit-postponed-after-twitter-spat-with-may-british-media-reports-1.5627466> (last accessed 18 February 2019).

Harvey-Jenner, C. (2018), 'Donald Trump Held Theresa May's Hand Again and It's Painfully Awkward to Watch', Cosmopolitan.com, 13 July. Available at: <https://www.cosmopolitan.com/uk/reports/a22136801/donald-trump-held-hands-theresa-may-again-awkward/> (last accessed 17 February 2019).

Hughes, L. (2017), 'Donald Trump's State Visit to Britain "Postponed" Until Next Year', telegraph.co.uk, 11 July. Available at: <https://www.telegraph.co.uk/news/2017/07/11/donald-trumps-state-visit-britain-postponed-next-year/> (last accessed 18 February 2019).

Jacobs, B., S. Siddiqi and S. Bixby (2016), '"You Can Do Anything": Trump Brags on Tape About Using Fame to Get Women', theguardian.com, 8 October. Available at: <https://www.theguardian.com/us-news/2016/oct/07/donald-trump-leaked-recording-women> (last accessed 4 March 2019).

Johnson, B. (2016), 'Brexit Means Brexit and We Are Going to Make a Titanic Success of It', spectator.co.uk, 3 November. Available at: <https://blogs.spectator.co.uk/2016/11/brexit-means-brexit-going-make-titanic-success/> (last accessed 4 March 2019).

Jones, J. (2016), 'The Unholy Power of that Farage-Trump Buddy Photo', guardian.com, 23 November. Available at: <https://www.theguardian.com/commentisfree/2016/nov/23/farage-trump-buddy-photo-ukip> (last accessed 5 March 2019).

Kettle, M. (2018), 'Trump Isn't Going Anywhere. It's Time for "Europe First"', theguardian.co.uk, 8 November. Available at: <https://www.theguardian.com/commentisfree/2018/nov/08/trump-europe-first-america-britain> (last accessed 18 February 2019).

Knight, S. (2016), 'Nigel Farage on the Story Behind his Friendship with Trump', newyorker.com, 30 November. Available at: <https://www.newyorker.com/culture/persons-of-interest/nigel-farage-on-the-story-behind-his-friendship-with-trump> (last accessed 5 March 2019).

Landale, J. (2018), 'Has Trump Broken the Special Relationship?', BBC.co.uk, 16 May. Available at: <https://www.bbc.co.uk/news/uk-politics-44128158> (last accessed 21 January 2019).

Lapavitsas, C. (2018). *The Left Case Against the EU*, Cambridge: Polity.

Littler, J. (2019), 'Normcore Plutocrats in Gold Elevators', *Cultural Politics*, 15:1, pp. 15–28.

Mahdawi, A. (2016), 'How to Stop Nigel Farage Being the Face of Britain in the US', guardian.com, 11 October. Available at: <https://www.theguardian.com/commentisfree/2016/oct/11/britain-nigel-farage-donald-trump-better-role-models> (last accessed 5 March 2019).

Martin, A. J. (2019), 'MPs Call for Government to Examine Russian Influence on Brexit', news.sky.com, 18 February. Available at: <https://news.sky.com/story/mps-call-for-government-to-examine-russian-influence-on-brexit-11640694> (last accessed 4 March 2019).

May, T. (2017), 'Prime Minister's Speech to the Republican Party Conference 2017', gov.uk, 26 January. Available at: <https://www.gov.uk/government/speeches/prime-ministers-speech-to-the-republican-party-conference-2017> (last accessed 17 Feb 2019).

Moffitt, B. (2016), *The Global Rise of Populism: Performance, Political Style, and Representation*, Redwood City: Stanford University Press.

Mouly, F. (2016), 'Barry Blitt's "Silly Walk off a Cliff"', *The New Yorker*, 24 June. Available at: <https://www.newyorker.com/culture/culture-desk/cover-story-2016-07-04> (last accessed 7 April 2019).

Nairn, T. (1982), *The Break-up of Britain: Crisis and Neo-Nationalism*, new edn, London: Verso.

Observer Editorial (2017), 'The Observer View on Britain's Relationship with America', theguardian.com, 29 January. Available at: <https://www.theguardian.com/commentisfree/2017/jan/29/observer-view-britain-america-theresa-may-donald-trump> (last accessed 24 April 2019).

Oliver, T., and M. Williams (2017), 'The UK–US Special Relationship: Between a Trump Rock and a Brexit Hard Place', #LSEThinks, 20 January. Available at: <http://blogs.lse.ac.uk/brexit/2017/01/20/UK–US-special-relationship-between-a-trump-rock-and-a-brexit-hard-place/> (last accessed 16 January 2019).

O'Toole, M. (2016), 'Nigel and Geert's Wild Republican Convention', foreignpolicy.com, 21 July. Available at: <https://foreignpolicy.com/2016/07/21/nigel-and-geerts-wild-republican-convention/> (last accessed 5 March 2019).

Owen, G. (2017), 'The Obscure Truth About THAT Picture: Theresa May Had to Take Hold of Donald Trump's Hand Because the US President Has BATHMO-PHOBIA – a Fear of Falling Down Steps and Slopes!', dailymail.co.uk, 28 January. Available at: <https://www.dailymail.co.uk/news/article-4167600/Theresa-held-Trump-s-hand-stairs-fear.html> (last accessed 17 February 2019).

Pengelly, M. (2017), 'Donald Trump Berates London Mayor over Response to Terror Attacks', theguardian.co.uk, 4 June. Available at: <https://www.theguardian.com/uk-news/2017/jun/04/trump-berates-london-mayor-sadiq-khan-terror-attacks> (last accessed 18 February 2019).

Pickard, J., and M. Garrahan (2017), 'Rupert Murdoch Secretly Sat in on Interview with Donald Trump', ft.com, 9 February. Available at: <https://www.ft.com/content/74408ae0-eeb3-11e6-ba01-119a44939bb6> (last accessed 17 February 2019).

Right Side Broadcasting Network (2016), '"Mr. Brexit" Nigel Farage Speaks at Donald Trump Rally in Jackson, MS'. Available at: <https://www.youtube.com/watch?v=oj4K9fr_WgY> (last accessed 24 April 2019).

Rozsa, M. (2018), 'Trump Mocked by Winston Churchill's Grandson After Taking a Rain Check on WWI Ceremony', Salon.com, 12 November. Available at: <https://www.salon.com/2018/11/12/trump-mocked-by-winston-churchills-grandson-after-taking-a-rain-check-on-wwi-ceremony/> (last accessed 3 February 2019).

Stanley, T. (2016), 'Donald Trump and Nigel Farage – the Picture that Says It All About 2016', telegraph.co.uk, 13 November. Available at: <https://www.telegraph.co.uk/news/2016/11/13/donald-trump-and-nigel-farage---the-picture-that-says-it-all-abo/> (last accessed 17 February 2019).

Tanner, C. (2018), 'From Macron to Trudeau, a Short History of President Trump's Awkward Handshakes', usatoday.com, 24 April. Available at: <https://eu.usatoday.com/story/news/politics/onpolitics/2018/04/24/macron-trudeau-short-history-president-trumps-awkward-handshakes/547103002/> (last accessed 5 March 2019).

Telegraph Reporters (2017), 'Theresa May's 9 Most Awkward Moments', telegraph.co.uk, 5 October. Available at: <https://www.telegraph.co.uk/women/politics/theresa-mays-8-awkward-moments/> (last accessed 19 February 2019).

Titanic (1997), film, directed by J. Cameron. US: Paramount Pictures.

Thompson, I. (2018), 'Trump and May: How the Special Relationship Devolved into a Greasy Dumpster Fire', vanityfair.com, 13 July. Available at: <https://www.vanityfair.com/news/2018/07/trump-and-may-special-relationship-dumpster-fire> (last accessed 1 March 2019).

Townsend, M. (2018), 'A Titanic Success: How Boris Johnson Inspired my Viral Brexit Satire', theguardian.com, 18 Aug. Available at: <https://www.theguardian.com/culture/2018/aug/18/titanic-success-viral-video-satirising-brexit-10m-views> (last accessed 18 Nov 2018).

Trump Interview (2017), 'Full Transcript of Interview with Donald Trump', thetimes.co.uk, 16 January. Available at: <https://www.thetimes.co.uk/article/full-transcript-of-interview-with-donald-trump-5d39sr09d> (last accessed 26 April 2019).

Wayne, M. (2018), *England's Discontents: Political Cultures and National Identities*, London: Pluto.

Wheatcroft, G. (2017), 'Will Trump's Presidency Finally Kill the Myth of the Special Relationship?', theguardian.com, 14 February. Available at: <https://www.theguardian.com/politics/2017/feb/14/will-trump-presidency-finally-kill-myth-of-special-relationship> (last accessed 21 January 2019).

Wilkinson, M., and H. Alexander (2016), 'Nigel Farage Hits Out at "Cesspit" of Politics as Downing Street Rejects Donald Trump's Call to Make Him British Ambassador to the United States', telegraph.co.uk, 24 November. Available at: <https://www.telegraph.co.uk/news/2016/11/22/donald-trump-recommends-nigel-farage-british-ambassador-united/> (last accessed 5 March 2019).

Wilson, G. (2017), 'Brexit, Trump and the Special Relationship', *The British Journal of Politics and International Relations*, 19:3, pp. 543–57.

CHAPTER 16

'Prince Harry Has Gone Over to the Dark Side': Race, Royalty and US–UK Romance in Brexit Britain

Nathalie Weidhase

In an unprecedented move in November 2016, the Communications Secretary of Prince Harry released a statement condemning 'the racial undertones of comment pieces' and the 'outright sexism and racism' of social media comments regarding the Prince's relationship with self-identified biracial American Meghan Markle (Knauf 2017). Headlines like the one above, drawn from *The Telegraph* (Watson 2016), are indicative of these evidently 'racial undertones'. Once the engagement was officially announced in November 2017, coverage continued in a similar vein: the bride's former life as an actor on the legal drama *Suits* (2011–) became widely entangled with discussions of race and racism, and the state of the monarchy in the UK.

Markle is not the first divorced American to marry into the British royal family, of course. In 1936, Edward VIII abdicated to marry socialite and divorcée Wallis Simpson, who received a markedly cold reception (Pigeon 2015). Eighty years on, divorce does not hold the same scandalous import. However, the British royal family still carries significance as a point of cultural affirmation regarding the connections between family, marriage and the nation (Turner 2012), as my analysis of the media coverage of Markle and Prince Harry's relationship in what follows evidences. Furthermore, I posit, this royal romance becomes a 'special relationship' that has to carry the weight of even more consequence, emerging as it does in a period marked by the rise of nationalist politics in both the US and the UK. The British monarchy still captivates the British public, especially around occasions such as weddings and funerals. Indeed, events such as the death of Princess Diana in 1997 and the public mourning that followed can be considered 'as a performance of the nation and a vehicle for the production of a national public sphere' (Shome 2001: 324). I argue that Prince Harry's engagement to Meghan Markle was of similar significance, if not magnitude. Markle and Prince Harry are 'arguably the most high-profile interracial relationship of the West' (Asava 2017: 1). The

British monarchy, however, has long been thought of as inherently white, and is connected to how 'we', the public (as this notion is predominantly constructed by the media), imagine the nation. The racial politics of the royal family, and their relation to public life, have always been complex and are increasingly a site of contestation. As Michael Billig argued in his 2004 study of nationalism in the UK, the British public still thinks that 'the nation should be represented by the image of a British, white family' (2004: 68), but this whiteness cannot be addressed, for fear of making visible the racism within the royal family. Race and racism have become renewed topics for debate after the 'Brexit vote'. After a hard-fought campaign, on 23 June 2016 the UK voted to leave the European Union (EU). The vote was largely motivated by anti-immigration sentiments (Virdee and McGeever 2017), while the aftermath saw an increase in racist hate crimes (Dearden 2017) and the release of a UN report that identified a 'Brexit-related' growth in racism in the UK (Gayle 2018).

A mixed-race thirty-six-year-old American actor from an 'ordinary' background marrying into the most traditional and privileged of British institutions at this particular moment in British history can thus be mobilised to create an alternative, more progressive picture of Britain, and Markle has been examined extensively in this vein by the UK (and international) media. For this chapter, coverage from UK broadsheets (*The Times*, *The Guardian*, *The Daily Telegraph*, *The Independent*), tabloids (the *Daily Mail*, *The Sun*, the *Daily Express*) and political commentary magazines (*The Spectator* and *The New Statesman*) from the time of the royal statement in November 2016 until April 2018 was collected and analysed. This coverage reveals that Markle's entry into the royal family is used as a catalyst to work through a range of national fantasies, hopes and anxieties related to Brexit and the kind of country the UK is and might want to become. The British monarchy experiences a revival due to its assumed modernisation through the inclusion of a woman of colour, but my analysis reveals how deeply attached to discourses of imperial nostalgia the UK media landscape is.

Race and Racism in Brexit Britain

Before delving into the Brexit politics of the media coverage here, it is worth returning to the 'racial undertones' of the media coverage and its exoticising nature. Sometimes this takes on almost subtle tones, such as this *Sun* article, which claims that Markle brings 'a freshness, diversity and warmth to the chilly corridors of Buckingham Palace' (Morton 2018: 10). More explicitly, the *Daily Mail* celebrates how 'the Royal Family's perhaps rather sluggish gene pool was enriched by a talented and imaginative adventuress' (Glover 2017). And Rachel Johnson in the *Scottish Mail on Sunday* explains, 'Genetically, she is blessed. If there is issue from her alleged union with Prince Harry, the Windsors will thicken their watery, thin blue blood and Spencer pale skin and ginger hair with some rich and exotic DNA' (Johnson 2016). These comments allude to the purity of royal blood and lineage, a concept used to justify their elevated position (Billig 1992), even while they are also alluding to anxieties about the royal family's limited genetic heredity. Johnson's comments present a telling mix of sexist and racist undertones. Described as 'extremely easy on the eye', Markle's contribution to the royal family is seen in biological terms, where her mixed-race 'DNA' serves to liven up the royal bloodline. Mixed-race women are regularly thought of as 'essentially transgressive and destabilizing to the hegemony', which is both 'disorienting but also exciting, hence her seductive power over white men' (Asava 2017: 19). Simultaneously, descriptions like 'adventuress' and references to her 'exotic DNA' conjure images of Western imaginations of the (sexualised) African wilderness (Collins 2005), ready to be conquered by a representative of British colonial history, and Johnson's article is an example of the construction of the mixed-race woman as seductress. What these comments also reveal is an anxiety about the purity not merely of Markle's motives, where her character becomes a stand-in for her racial make-up. It is the purity of the royal family that is under threat, and by extension Britishness, as 'racial mixing erodes whiteness' and thus 'disproves the imagined homogeneity of the nation' (Asava 2017: 15).

Similar coding is evident in coverage of her upbringing, which is framed as a constant struggle, even though, as the daughter of a social worker and a Hollywood lighting director, she lived a solidly middle-class life. Her life trajectory, *The Sun* suggests, is emblematic of the American Dream 'of having it all, achieving her success by dint of hard work and ability' (Morton 2018). Further, the *Daily Mirror* sees a 'perceptive young schoolgirl from a broken home' who 'knew she would have to fight for what she believed in' (Alridge 2017), and Sarah Vine commends her work ethic, even though she was 'brought up in less-than-ideal circumstances in a tough environment' (Vine 2017). The *Daily Mail* is even less subtle in the construction of Markle as a product of a broken black home with their headline 'Harry's Girl Is (Almost) Straight Outta Compton' (Styles 2016), an area of Los Angeles associated with hip hop artists and gang crime. Place is important here: both America in general (and implicitly its racial politics) and LA in particular locate Markle as the black 'Other'. Not only do these descriptions mark her as from a background that is the opposite of the privileged upbringing of her future husband. In contrast to the overwhelming white-ness of the royal family, they also mark her as black, partly through utilis-ing the stereotype of the strong black woman. Furthermore, the history constructed here tells a postracial (Springer 2007) narrative of overcoming obstacles in the face of discrimination – in fact, this overcoming is proof that racial inequality no longer exists, a narrative that is then imposed on the UK.

Indeed, the new royal was instrumentalised to prove that the UK had left racism behind, contrary to numerous studies that argue just the oppo-site (for example, Gayle 2018). Even an incident that was often criticised explicitly in some quarters as racist and as indicative of a problematic royal history and colonialism was elsewhere understood to demonstrate progressive politics – as, for example, when Princess Michael wore a blackamoor brooch to the Queen's Christmas lunch, which Markle also attended. The blackamoor, a European art style, portrays usually African men in an often exoticised and/or subservient manner. The *Express*, however, wrote:

> What gave Princess Michael's choice of Christmas decoration particular piquancy this year of course was the fact that one of the fellow guests was Meghan Markle, Prince Harry's betrothed who, as we are constantly reminded, is mixed-race, as if that's what defines her. (Kelly 2017)

The author criticises the discussion of Markle's heritage and hints that the constant return to her racial make-up is what is actually racist, not the brooch depicting a figure that embodies 'a political history grounded in two millennia of travel and conquest, enslavement and exile' (Bosman 2006: 124). Others suggest that 'there has been barely a ripple of dissent about Meghan Markle's engagement to Prince Harry' (Bailey 2018). Britain's monarchy, from these accounts, has left racist structures and personalities firmly in the past.

Markle's arrival, indeed, is celebrated as a sign not only of a changed British monarchy, but of a changed nation. *The Sun* argues that the char-acteristics that previously would have excluded her from joining the royal family are now 'seen as positives, demonstrating how much our royals and our country has [sic] changed for the better' (Parsons 2017). Similarly, the *Evening Standard* understands the monarchy as 'playing its part in effecting social change' (d'Ancona 2017), and *The Telegraph* argues that the engagement is 'emblematic of a nation that has changed utterly, no longer hidebound by stuffy traditions and populated by Establishment courtiers seeking to probe Shakespeare's observation that the course of true love never did run smooth' ('Modern Romance' 2017). Here, evoking Shakespeare, the quintessential British author, serves both to reject a 'stuffy past' and simultaneously to embrace British cultural achievement. This complex relationship with British institutions is further explored in *The Independent*:

> They have given contemporary faces to an ancient institution and made it seem more relevant [. . .] Paradoxically, some of the forces which have taken us down the road of EU withdrawal – anxieties about globalisation and fear of modernity – are threatening to drive a reversion among many in British society to the insular attitudes of a bygone age [. . .] Is it too mad to wonder, once the Brexit dust settles, whether the younger royals may – against all the odds – represent a Britain looking forward to the future rather than an imagined past? (Gore 2017)

The article identifies nostalgia as an important factor in the vote for leaving the EU and acknowledges that the royal family is symbolic of that version of Britain. Indeed, an 'imperial longing to restore Britain's place in the world' (Virdee and McGeever 2017: 1) has often been credited as one of the driving narratives behind the Brexit vote. However, this discourse of change serves only to reaffirm a sense of imperial Britain: the monarchy 'returns' to public life as a signifier of Britishness, albeit slightly (perhaps cosmetically) modernised.

Cheering Up the Nation, Uniting the Nation

Not only were the impending nuptials received by some as a sign of progress in general, but news of the wedding also seemingly lifted the mood of the nation when the country was downtrodden by its recent political climate. *The Guardian* suggests it is 'no doubt a bright spark' when Britain was 'blighted by rotten politics and on the path to be broken by Brexit' (Edelstein 2017). Now, an institution that, in many ways, is symbolic of Britain's imperial history is meant to provide a relief from a political development that is equally symbolic of the nation's imperial nostalgia (Virdee and McGeever 2017) and brings momentary relief and respite from politics. The *Daily Mail* is excited by 'a glamorous Anglo-American wedding at a time when some in Britain feel down in the dumps over Brexit, and a bit unloved by the world' (Glover 2017). Similarly, *The Sun* compares the difference in reception between Wallis Simpson and Meghan Markle: unlike the 'full-scale constitutional crisis' caused by Simpson, this 'American divorcee is arriving just in time to unite us when we need it most' (Rinder 2017). It seems that it is not just the royal family that is cheering up the nation, but Markle's particular brand of international,

American glamour. An attractive, successful American willing to marry a British Prince, to become part of a British institution, and part of the British nation by extension, is seen as a sign that perhaps Britain is not completely undesirable.

Celebrating the romantic spectacle as a welcome distraction from everyday politics, indeed, serves to unite the country. *The Telegraph* refers to the wedding as 'a great national occasion' and encourages us 'to celebrate as a nation' ('Modern Romance' 2017). Very little room is left for rejection of, or indifference to, the events, and when rejection (for example, from republicans) is anticipated, this is framed in decidedly negative terms. Constructing dissenting voices as outsiders, the *Scottish Daily Mail* writes: 'The rest of us, of course, see things very differently – those of us who do not take ourselves too seriously' (MacLeod 2017). Similarly, the publication's national edition elaborates: 'Most sane, patriotic people, though, will simply get on with enjoying the party' (Sandbrook 2017). Uniting behind the monarchy is equated with love for one's country, which is portrayed as 'sane', ergo the 'normal' way of feeling about these events. The British monarchy here functions as an integral part of British identity, and not joining in the celebrations signifies a lack of identification with the nation, as well as a generally objectionable dourness.

What this kind of coverage creates is an imagined community (Anderson 1983) that unites in celebrating the happy couple. Royal events like weddings 'revivify our own memory of marriage, of our connection to our parents and grandparents [. . .] and they form a connection, however fragile and unclear, between family and nation' (Turner 2012: 88). This unity is the very purpose of the royal family in twenty-first-century democracies. Further, Turner suggests that 'the real value of constitutional monarchy is that in times of great crisis it can provide the illusion of stability' (Turner 2012: 86), in contrast to impermanent parliamentary politics. The ritualistic nature of royal weddings provides the illusion of stability and reminds the country of its history during the uncertainty of parliamentary Brexit politics and a currently unpredictable future.

More significantly, in the context of the political divisions emanating from Brexit, is the royal wedding's perceived ability to reaffirm the UK's unity as a union of four nations. The *Daily Mail* suggests that the wedding 'will be a chance for the United Kingdom's four nations to remember the ties of history and culture that still bind us' (Sandbrook 2017). However, this also highlights how the use of the unifying term 'Britain', in the context of both the monarchy and Brexit, can be misleading. While England and Wales voted to leave the EU, Scotland and Northern Ireland voted to remain, and this has since posed constitutional challenges throughout the withdrawal process. A similar divide emerges in the media and public attention to the royal wedding. *The Sunday Herald* describes the reaction north of Hadrian's Wall as 'a massive yawn, if pollster YouGov is to be believed', with 62 per cent of Scots 'indifferent to the upcoming royal wedding, the highest percentage among any group polled' (Didcock 2017). Indeed, *The Scotsman* suggests that increased royal coverage in the British media is part of the glorification of a past Britain, arguing that 'in these Brexit times, this recharged royalism seems to come as part of a package of retro-nationalist nostalgia, a whole narrative of Britain's return to a more red-and-white and blue, pre-European Union identity' (McMillan 2017). The intense fascination with the royal family is identified as a distinctively English phenomenon, not a generally British one, and one that shows a regressive fondness for past imperial 'greatness' rather than the progressive politics championed in the coverage of Markle. Remarkably, this article names the current English political and cultural climate 'retro-nationalist nostalgia' – current developments are not called patriotism, as with the *Daily Mail* above, but *nationalism*, which has much more sharply negative connotations (Viroli 1995) as an ideology that often incorporates feelings of superiority over and exclusion of other nations. Coverage of the royal wedding then serves to present a unified image of the UK, and at the same time make visible the divisions operating in the country.

The Transatlantic Politics of Wedding Invitations

It is not only on the national stage that the wedding reveals ongoing political tensions and issues of contestation – the role of the royals has also increased in the realm of international relations. While royals like Prince William have already been sent on European Brexit tours to, for example, Denmark to raise the UK's profile abroad (Grippler 2018), the coverage of Meghan Markle has mainly focused on the American connection (and, as explored further below, the Commonwealth). UK and US politics often develop in similar ways, but few developments in recent history have seemed as similar as the Brexit vote and the election of Donald Trump, both in 2016 (Wilson 2017) – and both are developments that have a longing for the past and anti-immigration sentiments at their hearts. Although the UK and the US seem to be united by this political trend, it, so far, has not resulted in a visibly successful reaffirmation of the 'special relationship' (Wilson 2017).

Instead, *The Sunday Telegraph* hopes that Meghan Markle 'may even be able to improve the "special relationship"' (Walter 2017). This signifies a personalisation of politics and is further developed in discussions around the royal wedding, and the wedding dress in particular. Markle's entry into the royal family is considered part of a wider effort to modernise the British monarchy. As such, the *Evening Standard* acknowledged the wedding's marketing potential in 'the rebranding of the royal family', as, in 'post-Brexit Britain, how we sell the country abroad becomes all the more important. Might [Markle] opt for an American designer to strengthen relations?' (Weir 2017). Here, the royal family is a brand that is used to advertise and promote the UK nationally and internationally (Balmer 2011), and the wedding dress becomes politicised and analysed for its potential to 'strengthen relations' with the US.

Speculation around the wedding invitations are motivated by similar concerns and rumours of the guest list were examined in relation to their diplomatic impact. Particular attention was paid to which US President would be invited: former President Barack Obama, on friendly terms with Prince Harry (Stewart 2017), or current President Donald Trump, who Markle has called 'misogynistic' and 'divisive' (Oppenheim 2018). A good relationship with Trump is considered key to a fast establishment of a trade barrier-reducing Free Trade Agreement (FTA) between the US and the UK. At the time of writing, FTAs have been a key focus of Brexit media coverage, as they are one of the main reasons for leaving the EU, the Single Market and the Customs Union (Trommer 2017), and failure to secure FTAs quickly may be detrimental to the Brexit process. Thus Donald Trump's unpredictable and divisive approach to politics, combined with an urgent need to negotiate a post-Brexit free trade agreement with the US as quickly as possible, made for anxious coverage.

For example, the *Daily Mail* announced: 'REVEALED: HARRY WON'T INVITE OBAMA TO WEDDING', followed by concerns that the wedding 'was branded a "diplomatic time bomb" if Barack Obama was invited, but not Donald Trump' (Shakespeare 2018). The *Express* refers to the potential lack of invitation for Trump as an 'embarrassing snub' (Parfitt 2018) that could 'offend Donald Trump and damage the British national interest as we try to get a new trade deal with the Americans after Brexit' (Thalassites 2018). What these articles reveal is that the UK cannot rely on the power of the 'special relationship' alone. While the UK and the US are somewhat united in their drift towards populist and nationalist politics, these same issues have now complicated their relationship. The difficulties and management of these international relationships are then imposed on the personal relationship of an American actor and a British Prince, and their wedding becomes responsible for bringing two nations together. Markle's relations with the Commonwealth are explored in similar ways. Having lived for several years in Toronto while filming *Suits*,

Markle has spent significant time in the Commonwealth, and this connection is exploited in media coverage of the royals and the UK's future position in the world.

The Commonwealth and the Royal Family in a Post-Brexit UK

While parts of the Leave campaign mobilised the postimperial hope that 'Britons would venture forth across the globe in the spirit of the buccaneers of the time of Elizabeth I' (Wilson 2017: 545) in their quest for votes, again at the time of writing (autumn 2018) the UK government is still undecided about the direction of future relations with the EU and beyond, which makes for uncertain trade relation talks. However, one possible future avenue for increased economic and political links is the Commonwealth. As the then UK Foreign Secretary Boris Johnson wrote of the Commonwealth Heads of Government Meeting in London in April 2018, 'Brexit will give us the ability to open a new era of friendship with countries across the world. A key theme of the London summit will be how to boost trade within the Commonwealth' (Johnson 2018). Indeed, it is part of the 'Global Britain' government strategy to foster stronger relationships with the countries of the Commonwealth. That this strategy has internally been called 'Empire 2.0' (Virdee and McGeever 2017) perhaps gives away the ideological underpinning of the project, and the ways in which Markle's relationship with the Commonwealth is covered reflect this imperial nostalgia.

The Commonwealth consists of fifty-three nations, many of them former colonies of the UK. In sixteen of these, the Queen is head of state. Holly Randell-Moon suggests that the continuing significance of a monarchy 'is often justified by the idea that a democratic state benefits from an enduring and transcendent symbol of British parliamentary and Commonwealth traditions' (Randell-Moon 2017: 397) as a unifying force. In a post-Brexit future, the UK in return hopes to benefit from the already existing ties with the Commonwealth through political alliances and increased trade, and the royal family seems to assume a key role in harvesting this goodwill. Markle herself has expressed interest in the Commonwealth: for example, in the engagement interview in November 2017, during which she stated her interest in working with and travelling to the Commonwealth (BBC 2017). This interest was further cemented on the day of her wedding, when she wore a veil embroidered with flowers from all fifty-three Commonwealth nations. Markle's first royal engagement connected to the Commonwealth was the Commonwealth Day service, followed by attendance at events at the Commonwealth summit in April 2018. Speculation around the significance of the Commonwealth to Markle's work as a royal began long before this event. On the day of the engagement announcement, the *Evening Standard* reported the Queen's plans to use the couple as 'Commonwealth super envoys', whose popularity 'will help boost post-Brexit trade and ties with nations' (Jobson 2017). The *Express* calls Markle 'The Royal Family's secret weapon', who is 'launching a Commonwealth charm offensive' (Stinson 2018). Their royal expert explains the racial politics of the new recruit:

> The fact she is biracial will have enormous appeal to many in the Commonwealth who have previously viewed the Royal Family as remote. The royals are used for 'soft power' very effectively in visits abroad, this would certainly apply to the Commonwealth as it does to Europe, to promote goodwill during and after Brexit. (Stinson 2018)

Markle's racial and international background works to legitimise the increased role of the royal family in political life, in which her race is an asset to be instrumentalised in the quest for positive post-Brexit relations. Highlighting her race in this way is remarkable because 'the Brexit campaign and the subsequent Global Britain project are made more alluring precisely through the erasure of the racist underside of the actual Empire project of yesteryear' (Virdee and McGeever 2017: 4). Meghan Markle's presence is integral to the construction of this illusion. Markle can fill this role precisely because she, as a mixed-race woman, is seen to have the 'capacity to move between and among several racial identities that are interchangeable' and can utilise 'whichever identity may be situationally appropriate for a specific interactional context' (Rockquemore 2004: 129).

Part of what enables Markle to 'switch' between identities is the American Hollywood glamour she is seen to embody. Glamour is often associated with (classical) Hollywood (Wilson 2007) and takes different forms in national contexts. In the UK, for example, Princess Diana became '(almost) reigning beauty and ultimate icon of conventional "glamour"' (Wilson 2007: 104) in a time when the UK was famous for parodies of glamour in the form of, for example, the 1980s 'New Romantics' like Boy George and Adam Ant. Markle contributes a penchant for fashion to the royal family, which had been absent for over twenty years. And because the genesis of this sparkle is distinctively un-British, it helps to rebrand the monarchy as modern and as having international, cosmopolitan flair.

Even more explicit markers of difference are considered charming. When, at the Commonwealth Summit, Prince Harry introduced her to

the British word 'plaster' for the American 'band-aid', newspaper coverage focused on the hilarity of the situation. *The Evening Standard* reported
Prince Harry's jokes 'about their "language barrier"' (Coulter 2018), which
prompted 'much laughter from his audience' (Blott 2018). Markle's Americanness is part of her allure and is perhaps a 'safe' type of foreignness. This
is markedly different from much (tabloid) press coverage of immigration,
which recurrently paints immigrants as a foreign, invasive threat to Britain (Khosravinik 2010; Moore et al. 2018). Indeed, *The Telegraph* points
out that, due to the political and cultural similarities between the US and
the UK, 'an American marrying into Britain hardly counts as foreign at
all' (Hannan 2017). This marks a significant change of tone from the last
time an American married into the British royal family. Wallis Simpson's
otherness and 'unsuitability' to the British monarchy, 'American, childless,
thrice-married and sexually deviant', positioned her as 'the antithesis of
her sister-in-law – Queen Elizabeth, loving wife and dedicated mother' –
and therefore 'by extension, as the antithesis of Britain' (Pigeon 2015: 13).
Markle is allowed some proximity to Britain and Britishness, as long as
she remains charming, and any signs of difference can be rendered non-
threatening. Indeed, her assimilation into Britain and Britishness is closely
scrutinised. At the Commonwealth Day service, Markle was seen singing
the British national anthem for the first time, where 'The camera focused
on the former *Suits* star singing the words "happy and glorious" during the
televised event' (Collier 2018). The camera here works as an instrument to
surveil Markle's entry into the royal family and Britishness, and implicitly
judges how well she performs markers of national identity – the positive
coverage then serves as a preliminary blessing.

It remains to be seen how the current enthusiasm holds up once the
wedding sparkle wears off, and Markle will be under more scrutiny as a
working royal. However, what the engagement has already demonstrated
is the degree to which the UK still has a problematic and unresolved relationship with race, racism, and an imperial past that casts its shadow over
current Brexit politics. With the UK struggling with its image and position in the world, the royal family and its newest member are rediscovered
as a symbol of the nation and national unity. While Markle's engagement
to Prince Harry in the middle of the Brexit negotiations is incidental, the
marketing of this occasion is not: Markle, as a woman of colour, offers the
possibility of a progressive image of both the monarchy and the country at
a time when it is in the spotlight for its reactionary political developments.
Ultimately, however, a conservative institution cannot cover up the ideological underpinnings of a deeply regressive politics, and instead works
only to make visible the imperial nostalgia at the heart of Brexit.

Works Cited

Alridge, G. (2017), 'A Princess in Waiting: MEGHAN IS A PERFECT FIT FOR PRINCE HARRY', *Daily Mirror*, 3 December, pp. 6–7.

Anderson, B. (1983), *Imagined Communities: Reflections on the Origin and Spread of Nationalism*, New York: Verso.

Asava, Z. (2017), *Mixed Race Cinemas: Multiracial Dynamics in America and France*, London: Bloomsbury.

Bailey, S. (2018), 'We Must Put the Windrush Outrage in Perspective', *Scottish Mail on Sunday*, 22 April, p. 25.

Balmer, J. M. T. (2011), 'Corporate Heritage Brands and the Precepts of Corporate Heritage Brand Management: Insights from the British Monarchy on the Eve of the Royal Wedding of Prince William (April 2011) and Queen Elizabeth II's Diamond Jubilee (1952–2012)', *Journal of Brand Management*, 18:8, pp. 517–44.

BBC (2017), 'Prince Harry and Meghan Markle: Engagement Interview in Full', *bbc.co.uk*, 27 November. Available at: <http://www.bbc.com/news/av/uk-42139382/prince-harry-and-meghan-markle-engagement-interview-in-full> (last accessed 24 May 2018).

Billig, M. (1992), *Talking of the Royal Family*, London: Routledge.

Billig, M. (2004), 'Keeping the White Queen in Play', in M. Fine, L. Weis, L. P. Pruitt and A. Burns (eds), *Off White: Readings on Power, Privilege, and Resistance*, 2nd edn, London: Routledge, pp. 65–73.

Blott, U. (2018), 'Ladies First!', *Mail Online*, 18 April. Available at: <http://www.dailymail.co.uk/femail/article-5630235/Harry-lets-Meghan-meet-delegates-him.html> (last accessed 16 July 2018).

Bosman, A. (2006), '"Best Play with Mardian": Eunuch and Blackamoore as Imperial Culturegram', *Shakespeare Studies*, 34, pp. 123–57.

Collier, H. (2018), 'Meghan Markle Arrives for First Official Royal Engagement with the Queen to Mark Commonwealth Day', *The Evening Standard*, 12 March. Available at: <https://www.standard.co.uk/news/uk/meghan-markle-arrives-for-first-official-royal-engagement-with-the-queen-to-mark-commonwealth-day-a3787901.html> (last accessed 12 October 2018).

Collins, P. H. (2005), *Black Sexual Politics: African Americans, Gender, and the New Racism*, London: Routledge.

Coulter, M. (2018), 'Meghan Markle and Prince Harry Joke About Their "Language Barrier" at Commonwealth Summit', *The Evening Standard*, 18 April. Available at: <https://www.standard.co.uk/news/uk/meghan-markle-and-prince-harry-joke-about-their-language-barrier-at-commonwealth-summit-a3817331.html> (last accessed 18 May 2018).

D'Ancona, M. (2017), 'Now the Monarchy Is Playing Its Part in Effecting Social Change; The Fact that Meghan Markle's Mixed-race Background Is Seen as No Big Deal is a Big Step Forward for Britain', *Evening Standard*, 29 November, p. 16.

Dearden, L. (2017), 'Hate-crime Reports Rise by Almost a Third in Year as Home Office Figures Illustrate EU-referendum Spike', *The Independent*, 17 October. Available at: <https://www.independent.co.uk/news/uk/crime/hate-crimes-eu-referendum-spike-brexit-terror-attacks-police-home-office-europeans-xenophobia-a8004716.html> (last accessed 19 July 2018).

Didcock, B. (2017), 'Unhappily Ever; After?', *The Sunday Herald*, 2 December, p. 25.

Edelstein, J. H. (2017), 'Don't Get Too Excited for Meghan Markle. The British Monarchy is Oppressive', *The Guardian*, 27 November. Available at: <https://www.theguardian.com/commentisfree/2017/nov/27/meghan-markle-british-monarchy-oppressive> (last accessed 18 May 2018).

Gayle, D. (2018), 'UK has Seen "Brexit-related" Growth in Racism, says UN Representative', *The Guardian*, 11 May. Available at: <https://www.theguardian.com/politics/2018/may/11/uk-has-seen-brexit-related-growth-in-racism-says-un-representative> (last accessed 19 July 2018).

Glover, S. (2017), 'My Heart Cheers the New Royal Fairy Tale. My Head's Full of Foreboding . . .', *Mail Online*, 29 November. Available at: <http://www.dailymail.co.uk/debate/article-5130651/STEPHEN-GLOVER-heart-cheers-new-royal-fairy-tale.html> (last accessed 13 May 2018).

Gore, W. (2017), 'Could a Mixed-race, Trump-bashing Actress Be Just What the Royals Need?', *The Independent*, 28 November, p. 4.

Grippler, A. (2018), 'Pod Save the Queen: How Political is a Royal Tour?', *mirror. co.uk*, 1 February. Available at: <https://www.mirror.co.uk/news/uk-news/pod-save-queen-how-political-11949839> (last accessed 20 May 2018).

Hannan, D. (2017), 'Is the Irish Border Row a Ploy to Pry Northern Ireland from the UK?', *The Telegraph*, 3 December. Available at: <https://www.telegraph.co.uk/news/2017/12/03/irish-border-row-ploy-pry-northern-ireland-uk/> (last accessed 12 October 2018).

Jobson, R. (2017), 'Queen to Use Harry and Meghan as Commonwealth Super Envoys; Couple's Popularity Will Help Boost Post-Brexit Trade and Ties with Nations', *Evening Standard*, 29 November, pp. 4–5.

Johnson, B. (2018), 'Commonwealth Has Key Role to Play in the Bright Future for Britain', *Express Online*, 11 March. Available at: <https://www.express.co.uk/news/politics/929977/Boris-Johnson-Commonwealth-key-role-bright-future-Brexit-Britain> (last accessed 13 May 2018).

Johnson, R. (2016), 'Sorry Harry, but Your Beautiful Bolter Has Failed My Mum Test', *Scottish Mail on Sunday*, 6 November, p. 33.

Kelly, F. (2017), 'Remainers Criticising the Blue Passport are Showing Their True Colours', *Express Online*, 27 December. Available at: <https://www.express.co.uk/comment/columnists/fergus-kelly/896974/Traditional-blue-passport-Remainers-Brexit-Princess-Michael-brooch-Christmas-cheese> (last accessed 14 May 2018).

Khosravinik, M. (2010), 'The Representation of Refugees, Asylum Seekers and Immigrants in British Newspapers: A Critical Discourse Analysis', *Journal of Language and Politics*, 9:1, pp. 1–28.

288   NATHALIE WEIDHASE

Knauf, J. (2017), *A Statement by the Communications Secretary to Prince Harry*. Available at: <https://www.royal.uk/statement-communications-secretary-prince-harry> (last accessed on 3 January 2018).

MacLeod, J. (2017), 'The Left's Sneering Contempt for Those of Us Happy for Harry', *Scottish Daily Mail*, 30 November, p. 20.

McMillan, J. (2017), 'How will Scots React to This Nostalgic Vision of Merry Old England?', *The Scotsman*, 29 November. Available at: <https://www.scotsman.com/news/opinion/joyce-mcmillan-how-will-scots-react-to-this-nostalgic-vision-of-merry-old-england-1-4649411> (last accessed 14 May 2018).

'Modern Romance' (2017), 'A Modern Romance to Celebrate as a Nation', *The Daily Telegraph*, 27 November 2017, p. 23.

Moore, K., M. Berry and I. Garcia-Blanco (2018), 'Saving Refugees or Policing the Sea? How the National Press of Five EU Member States Framed News Coverage of the Migration Crisis', *Justice, Power and Resistance*, 2:1, pp. 66–95.

Morton, A. (2018), 'Making a Markle on History', *The Sun*, 3 April, p. 10.

Oppenheim, M. (2018), 'Meghan Markle: How the Chomsky-reading Trump Critic Will Have to Bite her Tongue when she Enters the Palace', *The Independent*, 17 May. Available at: <https://www.independent.co.uk/news/uk/home-news/meghan-markle-trump-royal-wedding-politics-feminism-prince-harry-a8356001.html> (last accessed 22 May 2018).

Parfitt, T. (2018), 'Brexit SHOCK: Donald Trump "to Visit Irish Border" as Row Threatens to Derail EU Talks', *Express Online*, 25 March. Available at: <https://www.express.co.uk/news/politics/936678/Brexit-latest-news-Donald-Trump-Irish-border-Theresa-May-European-Union-Northern-Ireland> (last accessed 13 May 2018).

Parsons, T. (2017), 'Meghan and Harry Prove Royal Family Has a Proud Future', *The Sun*, 3 December 2017, p. 15.

Pigeon, R. (2015), 'Royal Renunciation: Edward VIII and the Problems of Representation', *Film & History*, 45:2, pp. 13–23.

Randell-Moon, H. (2017), 'Thieves Like Us: The British Monarchy, Celebrity, and Settler Colonialism', *Celebrity Studies*, 8:3, pp. 393–408.

Rinder, R. (2017), 'Meghan Markle Has Arrived at Just the Right Time for a Country that Feels Like It Is Sinking into Permanent Division', *The Sun*, 2 December, p. 52.

Rockquemore, K. A. (2004), 'Deconstructing Tiger Woods: The Promise and the Pitfalls of Multiracial Identity', in H. M. Dalmage (ed.), *The Politics of Multiracialism: Challenging Racial Thinking*, Albany, NY: SUNY Press, pp. 125–42.

Sandbrook, D. (2017), 'A Bride Descending from Slaves and Why the Royal Family Keep Proving the Sneering Snobs Wrong . . .', *Mail Online*, 28 November. Available at: <http://www.dailymail.co.uk/news/article-5123183/Why-Royal-Family-proving-sneering-snobs-wrong.html> (last accessed 11 May 2018).

Shakespeare, S. (2018), 'Prince Harry and Meghan Markle WON'T Invite "Good Friend" Obama to the Royal Wedding in a Bid to Avoid a "Diplomatic Row" over Snub to Donald Trump', *Mail Online*, 22 January. Available at:

<http://www.dailymail.co.uk/news/article-5295379/Obama-isnt-going-Harry-Meghans-wedding.html> (last accessed 15 May 2018).

Shome, Raka (2001), 'White Femininity and the Discourse of the Nation: Re/membering Princess Diana', *Feminist Media Studies*, 1:3, pp. 323–42.

Springer, K. (2007), 'Divas, Evil Black Bitches, and Bitter Black Women: African American Women in Postfeminist and Post-Civil-Rights Popular Culture', in Y. Tasker and D. Negra (eds), *Interrogating Postfeminism: Gender and the Politics of Popular Culture*, Durham, NC: Duke University Press, pp. 249–76.

Stewart, N. (2017), 'When Harry Met Barry: Welcome to the Real Special Relationship', *The Telegraph*, 18 December. Available at: <https://www.telegraph.co.uk/men/relationships/harry-met-barry-welcome-real-special-relationship/> (last accessed 22 May 2018).

Stinson, N. (2018), 'The Royal Family's Secret Weapon: How Meghan Is Launching a Commonwealth Charm Offensive', *Express Online*. Available at: <https://www.express.co.uk/news/royal/948119/Meghan-Markle-royal-family-Commonwealth-Prince-Harry> (last accessed 19 May 2018).

Styles, R. (2016), 'Harry's Girl Is (Almost) Straight Outta Compton', *Daily Mail*, 2 November. Available at: <http://www.dailymail.co.uk/news/article-3896180/Prince-Harry-s-girlfriend-actress-Meghan-Markles.html> (last accessed 20 May 2018).

Suits, TV series, created by A. Korsh. US: USA Network, 2011–.

Thalassites, J. (2018), 'What Will Prince Harry Say? Meghan Markle WEDS Without Royal Fiancée [sic]: but Who's the Groom?', *Express Online*, 19 April. Available at: <https://www.express.co.uk/news/royal/948266/royal-wedding-royal-news-meghan-Markle-prince-harry-suits-tv> (last accessed 16 May 2018).

Trommer, S. (2017), 'Post-Brexit Trade Policy Autonomy as Pyrrhic Victory: Being a Middle Power in a Contested Trade Regime', *Globalizations*, 14:6, pp. 810–19.

Turner, B. S. (2012), 'In Defence of Monarchy', *Society*, 49, pp. 84–9.

Vine, S. (2017), 'Motherly Meghan's Just What Her Little Boy Lost Really Needs', *Mail Online*, 29 November 2017. Available at: <http://www.dailymail.co.uk/debate/article-5127197/Meghans-just-Harry-really-needs-writes-SARAH-VINE.html> (last accessed 14 May 2018).

Virdee, S., and B. McGeever (2017), 'Racism, Crisis, Brexit', *Ethnic and Racial Studies* online first. Available at: <https://www.tandfonline.com/doi/full/10.1080/01419870.2017.1361544> (last accessed 22 May 2018).

Viroli, M. (1995), *For Love of Country: An Essay on Patriotism and Nationalism*, Oxford: Oxford University Press.

Walter, S. (2017), 'Couple Could Put "Special Relationship" Back on Track', *The Sunday Telegraph*, 3 December, p. 7.

Watson, S. (2016), 'Prince Harry Has Gone Over to the Dark Side', *The Telegraph*, 4 November. Available at: <https://www.telegraph.co.uk/women/life/shane-watson-prince-harry-has-gone-over-to-the-dark-side/> (last accessed 26 September 2018).

Weir, L. (2017), 'Let Meghan Mania Begin – and that Means the Right 'Big Day' for this Very Modern Bride', *Evening Standard*, 28 November, p. 15.

Wilson, E. (2007), 'A Note on Glamour', *Fashion Theory: The Journal of Dress, Body and Culture*, 11:1, pp. 95–108.

Wilson, G. K. (2017), 'Brexit, Trump and the Special Relationship', *The British Journal of Politics and International Relations*, 19:3, pp. 543–57.

Index